ALL THE AGENTS
AND SAINTS

Stephanie Elizondo Griest

ALL THE AGENTS
AND SAINTS

Dispatches from the U.S. Borderlands

THE UNIVERSITY OF NORTH CAROLINA PRESS

Chapel Hill

This book was published with the assistance of the
Anniversary Fund of the University of North Carolina Press.

Manufactured in the United States of America

The University of North Carolina Press has been a member
of the Green Press Initiative since 2003.

Cover illustration: Ana Teresa Fernández, *Erasing the Border
(Performance Documentation)* (2016), oil on canvas, 68 × 42 in.
Courtesy of the artist and Gallery Wendi Norris.

LIBRARY OF CONGRESS CATALOGING-IN-PUBLICATION DATA
Names: Elizondo Griest, Stephanie, 1974– author.
Title: All the agents and saints : dispatches from the
U.S. borderlands / Stephanie Elizondo Griest.
Description: Chapel Hill : The University of North Carolina Press, [2017]
Identifiers: LCCN 2016047328 | ISBN 9781469631592 (cloth : alk. paper) |
ISBN 9781469631608 (ebook)
Subjects: LCSH: Mexican Americans—Texas. |
Mohawk Indians—New York (State) | Mexican-American
Border Region. | Canadian-American Border Region.
Classification: LCC F395.M5 E45 2017 | DDC 972/.1—dc23
LC record available at https://lccn.loc.gov/2016047328

Portions of chapters 1, 2, 4, 7, 8, and 18 were originally published, respectively,
in *Sangam House Reader*, vol. 3 (New York: Sangam House, 2015); the *Dallas
Morning News*, September 12, 2010; *Earth Island Journal*, Spring 2012, 38–43;
Oxford American, Spring 2015, 62–75; *Oxford American*, Fall 2013, 35–37; and
The Best Travel Writing, Volume 10 (Palo Alto, Calif.: Travelers' Tales, 2015),
120–28; and *Witness*, Winter 2014, http://witness.blackmountaininstitute.
org/issues/volume-27-number-3-winter-2014/three-nations-crossing/.

FOR MY HOMELAND, CORPITOS

CONTENTS

MAPS

INTRODUCTION

The Descendants

WE ALL KNOW THE RULES. CROSS AN INTERNATIONAL BORDERLINE without the proper papers and—unless luck or privilege protects you—get arrested, imprisoned, and expelled. But what happens when an international borderline crosses over *you*, slicing your ancestral land in two? Division-by-force has been the confusing fate of peoples the world over. This book explores its living legacy among two: the Akwesasne Mohawks, whose territory was split between Canada and the United States by a series of treaties signed between 1783 and 1850, and the Tejanos of South Texas, who were severed from their native Mexico by the Treaty of Guadalupe-Hidalgo in 1848.

Were I not myself a Tejana who had recently spent a year near Akwesasne, I would find this pairing odd. More than 2,000 miles stand between our communities, and—with the exception of Catholicism—our cultures hold little of that ground in common. Mohawks traditionally subsisted on hunting, farming, and fishing in one of the coldest regions of the United States, whereas my forefathers tended cattle in one of the hottest. They are matriarchal; we tend toward machismo. We are fanatical about football; Mohawks don't just revere lacrosse, they invented it.

We also experience our respective borders quite differently. Many Mohawks refuse to acknowledge the lines at all. They are a sovereign people who employ their own police force and operate their own library, museum, media, school, and court. They look not to Washington or Ottawa for governance but to the Haudenosaunee (Iroquois) Confederacy, of which they have been members for centuries. Many vote in tribal elections but not federal, state, or provincial ones because they view those systems as foreign (and even hostile) to their own. I know one Mohawk who regularly switches residency from one side of the border to the other whenever one government happens to offer better benefits, but most live near the homesteads their families have held for generations.

Yet because Akwesasne's (recognized) territory spans just 26,350 acres along land also governed by New York, Ontario, and Quebec, its citizens are profoundly affected by the borderlines in their midst. Many must contend with Customs and Border Patrol agents multiple times a day: to get to work, to take their children to school, to grab a Dunkaccino, to attend a Longhouse ceremony or Mass. I have yet to meet the Mohawk whom this does not enrage. Protests are frequent at Akwesasne, as are bridge closures and other acts of civil disobedience.

Most Tejanos I know resent the obstructions in our roadways, too. However, the only time I've seen us demonstrate was when Congress decided to build a border wall that carved up our neighborhoods. Many of us view the wall not as a safeguard to homeland security but as yet another threat to our once-thriving binational community. Not so long ago, we crossed the borderline all the time. Our in-laws lived in Matamoros; our clients were in Reynosa; our dentist was in Progreso. Our *tías* could get their hair *and* nails done for the price of a blow-out in McAllen. And who could resist a salt-rimmed margarita at the Cadillac Bar?

Then in 2006, Mexican president Felipe Calderón declared war on the drug cartels, sparking retaliations that claimed upward of 10,000 lives a year. As reports of beheadings began to top the local news hour, many Tejanos who could shift their activities northward did so. Besides a few journalists and activists, no one I know ventures south to the border towns anymore—my family included. Fear has constructed a wall far taller than what Congress envisioned.

This raises another key difference between Akwesasne Mohawks and the Tejanos of South Texas. Akwesasne is largely self-contained. There is no better place for Mohawks to learn their robust language, traditions, and ceremonies than right inside their nation. Indeed, Akwesasne is one of the only places where such is even possible. Tejanos also boast a vibrant culture that includes a world-famous cuisine (Tex-Mex) and a pop goddess (Selena). Yet the nostalgic among us feel that the only place to truly grasp our heritage is in Mexico, even if we no longer have family there. Having historically been treated as outsiders by whites and as traitors (or worse: strangers) by Mexican nationals, we have a visceral desire to know what inside us is Mexican, what is gringo, and by what alchemy our ancestors fused the two.

For Mohawks, then, the borderline is mostly a physical obstruction that insults their sovereignty. For Tejanos, it is more of a psychic block that stifles our connectivity.

But the purpose of this book is not to spotlight the differences in our communities. Those are readily apparent. No, what startled me about Akwesasne was how often I experienced déjà vu there. Practically every major story I'd heard in half a lifetime in South Texas was echoed at some point that year at Akwesasne. Whether the issue was environmental degradation, language loss, drug trafficking, the diabetes epidemic, or confrontations with the Border Patrol, our communities not only had endured the same struggles but had shared similar methods of transcendence as well. Activists heeded the cries unheard by federal or social services, while artists elevated the spirits. Mexican patron saint La Virgen de Guadalupe and Mohawk saint Kateri Tekakwitha appeared right when her respective believers needed her most.

Much too often we hear about the U.S. borderlands only from the politicians who dictate their policies from afar. Rarely do we learn from the descendants of the regions' early inhabitants. Starting first with the Tejanos of South Texas and then moving on to the Mohawks of Akwesasne, I align their stories side by side as a *testimonio*, or a document of witness, of what life there is truly like.

LET'S START WITH A FEW DEFINITIONS. Identity is everything when you live in the periphery, but are you born a Chicana, or do you become one? Is being Mohawk solely a matter of blood quantum, or do cultural values play a role, too? Where does "American" fit into either equation? In these pages, I honor the identities my sources have selected for themselves. Here are some you'll encounter:

A Tejana/o is a person of Mexican descent who grew up in Texas and is a U.S. citizen. Many Tejano families have been around for centuries and are thus fond of the saying "We didn't cross the border; the border crossed us." A Chicana/o, meanwhile, can be any U.S. citizen of Mexican descent. Back in the fifties, it was a derogatory designation, but nowadays it usually refers to a Mexican American who is self-actualized and politicized.[1] Latina/o is a catchall term for any U.S. citizen of Latin American descent, be they Mexican American, Peruvian American, or Cuban American. So is Hispanic, but I

---

1. My favorite definition of Chicana/o comes courtesy of Michele Serros: "A pissed-off Mexican." She should know: in 2014, this best-selling author of *How to Be a Chicana Role Model* launched a social media campaign against the Mexican fast-food chain Chipotle for its "Cultivating Thought" series that printed short stories on its cups and take-out bags (*¡órale!*) yet failed to include any Mexican, Chicana/o, or even Latina/o writers on its inaugural roster (*¡híjole!*).

am not particularly fond of that word (*hisss*-panic) so have mostly avoided it. While some scholars and activists have started decolonizing these terms by omitting their (cis-)gendered endings in favor of the more inclusive "Chican@" and "Latinx," I declined to do so here because they weren't being used by the communities I write about during the time of my research. When referring to someone who is a citizen of Mexico, I use the term "Mexican national." Unless quoting someone else, I try to avoid "American" because it could apply to anyone from *las Américas*—North, Central, and South.

After much hand-wringing, I've decided to use the terms "Native American," "indigenous," and "Indian" interchangeably. Although the first two terms are thought to be more respectful by outsiders, I've found that most community members themselves prefer "Indian." Canadians use the term "Aboriginal peoples" when referencing First Nations, Inuits, and Métis as a collective, so I do here as well.

Haudenosaunee (or "People of the Longhouse") is the indigenous name of the Iroquois Confederacy,[2] which unites six nations: the Onondaga, Oneida, Cayuga, Seneca, Tuscarora, and Mohawk. While all Mohawks are Haudenosaunee, not all Haudenosaunee are Mohawks, in other words. Because the Mohawk Nation of Akwesasne straddles the U.S./Canadian borderline, it is tempting to refer to its regions as being on "the U.S. side" or "the Canadian side." Having preceded those governments by millennia, Mohawks tend to say "south of the river" and "north of the river" instead. For outsiders attempting to abide by international law, this designation can be confusing, since one section of their nation is south of the river but also technically in Quebec, Canada. More on this later, but be forewarned: it's a mind-warp. The river in question is the mighty St. Lawrence.

Though I self-identify as Tejana, Chicana, and Latina, people usually take me for a gringa when they meet me. Protesting assumptions is futile in the borderlands. Appearance alone determines whether your citizenry is questioned and allegiances tested on a back road far from earshot. For much of my life, I wallowed in guilt over the privilege my light skin and blue eyes have granted me, but I've come to recognize the vanity of this emotion. Guilt does not free anyone from a detention center or equip a home with a septic

---

2. Some scholars trace "Iroquois" to a French word derived from a Basque/Algonquian pidgin term meaning "killer people." I'll be using "Haudenosaunee" throughout the book unless quoting someone else.

tank. The only proper response to privilege is to grip it like a baseball bat and shatter injustice with all of your might.

Many of the people you are about to meet strive to do just that, in realms ranging from the quelling of narco-violence and environmental racism to the preservation of Native sovereignty. I have modified several of their identities to protect their privacy as well as to ward off possible reprisals. Some were interviewed multiple times during the writing of this book (2007 to 2015). In certain instances, it made sense to collapse the time frame for narrative's sake, so a number of stories that developed over the course of months or years have been relayed as having occurred in a day or week.

While I fact-checked the "verifiable truths" that appear in these pages—stats, dates, and so on—I took the personal stories at face value, however whimsical they may have seemed. Spirituality is a powerful force in borderlands north and south, and rather than interrogate anyone's belief systems, I respected them. At no point did I feel anyone was being emotionally untrue to me, and even if they were—lies shape our reality, too.

Now that the disclaimers have ended, may the stories begin!

ALL THE AGENTS
AND SAINTS

PROLOGUE

Nepantla

FEW DETAILS REMAIN ABOUT HOW MY GREAT-GREAT-GREAT-grandfather Juan de Dios Silva crossed into southern Texas (or what he likely still considered northern Mexico). Family legend has him on horseback. A distant relative claims the year 1879. All we know for certain is that after abandoning his hometown Cruillas—a tiny village in Tamaulipas—he somehow wound up at the biggest cattle empire the world has ever known, the King Ranch.[1] There, he worked as a vaquero until the end of his days. His sons and daughters proudly carried on the tradition, trading hard labor for the ranch's cradle-to-grave protection. So did the next generation, and the next. My mom spent every summer there, helping her cousins finish up their chores and then primping for the dance that Saturday. I, in turn, celebrated holidays there, whacking piñatas and fetching another beer for my *tíos*. Our vaquero days ended in the late 1980s, however, when the ranch modernized and corporatized. Family members lost not only their jobs and homes but also their traditional way of living as they retreated from the ranch and headed into the city. Today, whenever we wish to visit our *abuelos'* graves, we must first obtain a permit.

I grew up in Corpus Christi, which is about 150 miles north of the border, along the coast. My childhood consisted of tamales at Christmas, sand castles on Sundays, and sunshine nearly every day of the year. I seem to have inherited Juan de Dios's wanderlust, though, because in college I studied the language of the farthest country I could fathom—Russia—and then jetted off to Moscow to become a foreign correspondent. Throughout my twenties, I chased stories around the globe, never staying anywhere longer than a year, and often for just a few days or months. Cairo. Beijing. Tashkent. Havana.

---

1. How big? About 825,000 acres. That's bigger than Rhode Island, or Luxembourg. Welcome to Tejas.

1

Every state but Hawaii. Quelimane. I reveled in rootlessness. Took pride in not owning a fork.

Now that I've reached my early thirties, however, my nomadic lifestyle seems to be existentially untethering me. Anything that could have diverted attention from my writing—a house, a partner, a community, a legitimately paying job, children, pets, plants—has been avoided for so long, it has slipped into the realm of the unobtainable. The bulk of my books and clothes, meanwhile, are scattered in attics around the world. With so few attachments, I am starting to feel like I could blow away and no one would notice.

Normally when I meet a crossroads, I buy a plane ticket. Nothing ties me down, so I keep moving. Yet it is becoming apparent that if I never stand still, nothing ever will.

In 2007, I follow the magnetic pull of home. Part of the draw is journalistic. If the latest headlines are to be believed, the southern borderlands have transformed into a death valley in my absence, poisoned by petrochemical industries, ravaged by the drug war, and soon to be barricaded by a seventy-mile-long steel wall. It's become the nation's chief crossing ground for undocumented workers as well, unknown hundreds of whom perish in the scrub brush while evading the Border Patrol. My beloved hometown, meanwhile, is on the verge of being named "America's fattest city," with an obesity epidemic under way. Other national distinctions too insulting to discuss (Dumbest? *¿Qué?* Least literate? *No me digas.* Worst credit scores? *Did they go to Robstown or what?*) bring out the defense mechanism in us all.[2]

My inner reporter wants to know how all of this came to be. And so I walk the streets of my earlier self, past the grounds of Yeager Elementary School, past the slides and the swing sets, through the patches of sun-bleached grass. Past the houses where the Garcias and the Escamillas and the Bledsoes and the Moraleses used to live, where the neighborhood pool stood before someone filled it in, where the stationery store stood before it became a discount mattress outlet, where the nightclub stood before it became a gentleman's club and then another nightclub and then a building with boarded-up windows,

---

2. On behalf of my fellow Corpus denizens, who have taken an unfair share of media beatings, I'd like to spotlight our city's charms: democratic beaches that let you park where you please; a bayfront memorial to our superstar, Selena; piers that sell the freshest fish and chips imaginable; constant mariachi accompaniment; and the least pretentious people around. We also take pride in being the birthplace of the League of United Latin American Citizens, the American GI Forum, and the famed burger chain Whataburger. Not for nothing have we been deemed the seventh "happiest" city in the United States.

where the Indian restaurant stood before it became a Japanese steak house and where Granny's Fried Chicken stood before it became Sang's Imperial Cafe.

I fast conclude that my South Texas is my childhood South Texas. I know only the places I have always known, the places I have never *not* known. Everywhere else I have traveled, I have been an explorer, always seeking the least-known roads. But here, when I want an Italian meal, I go to Luciano's because that's where my family has always gone for Italian and I order eggplant parmesan because that's what I have always ordered when I want Italian and go to Luciano's.

It seems time to chart my own South Texas—not only to forge a new way of being here but also to better understand my inherited one. I have long suspected that growing up in a biracial family in the liminal space between nations created an inner fissure in me as well. All my life, I have waffled between extremes: gringa/Chicana; cosmopolite/cowgirl; agnostic/Catholic; journalist/activist; Type A/free spirit. The Aztecs coined a term for living in the state of in-between-ness: *nepantla*. That is how they described their struggle to reconcile their indigenous ways with the one Spanish colonizers forced upon them in the sixteenth century. More recently, the Tejana writer Gloria Anzaldúa turned nepantla into a metaphor for a "birthing stage where you feel like you're reconfiguring your identity and don't know where you are."

Maybe that is why I find myself in the borderlands now. Stories will always be my major motivating force, but out here, there is an additional one as well. After so many years of feeling split in two, I seek to finally fuse.

PART I

The Texas-Mexico Borderlands

*The U.S.-Mexican border es una herida abierta where the
Third World grates against the first and bleeds. And before a
scab forms it hemorrhages again, the lifeblood of two worlds
merging to form a third country—a border culture.*

GLORIA ANZALDÚA

1

The Miracle Tree

A CURIOUS THING HAPPENS WHEN MY TEJANO FRIENDS GATHER around a table. We might start off griping about work or family or the *pinche* traffic, but sooner or later our conversation takes a turn. Someone will mention a dream from the night before, about a lost little girl in a long white dress who kept running away, and how he's had that same dream every few months for years now, and what could it mean? Then someone will say that, a few weeks ago, she heard someone creaking up the stairwell and thought it was her husband, *pero* no: he was away on a business trip; she was home all alone. And then someone will confess that she removed the antique mirror hanging in her hallway last week because her six-year-old kept seeing a strange lady in it. Suggestions are made for cleansings ("Sage is supposed to be good for that") and curings ("If my abuelita was still around, she'd slide a bowl of water beneath your bed") and purifications ("Have you tried that egg thing yet?"), each preceded with an earnest, "Not that I *believe* in this, but . . ." When we finally take our leave, shuffling en masse out the door, someone notices that the moon is waxing, which means one thing, or that it's waning, which means something else, and we half-walk, half-run to our cars and quickly lock the doors.

Greg and I haven't been here five minutes when I sense it will be another one of those nights. For starters, we're visiting the ranch of the acclaimed painter Santa Barraza, whose very name means "saint" in Spanish. Growing up, one of her tías was a *curandera* who brought her along to Mexico for trainings and eventually opened a healing chapel in South Texas.[1] Post-college, Santa started traveling to Mexico herself, studying Aztec, Mixtec, and Mayan art, pictographs,

---

1. Throughout the seventies, people traveled to Tía Eva's chapel from all around, Santa says. Eventually, however, she started getting ill from handling so many spirits and had to stand in a pan of water while conducting her healings to avert the negative energy. Then the Catholic church accused her of witchcraft, so she closed the chapel altogether. Though Tía Eva has since passed, she lives on in the mystical elements of Santa's work.

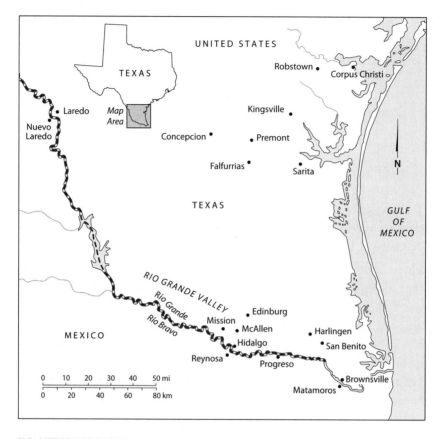

U.S.-MEXICAN BORDER

and philosophy. She then taught at places like the School of the Art Institute of Chicago and exhibited around the world before deciding she missed the desert landscape that inspired her work. In 2006, she bought nineteen acres near Kingsville and created a homestead with a studio. Decking its walls are life-size portraits of the icons of this region: La Virgen de Guadalupe pulsing a blue-veined heart inside her chest; La Malinche in a field of maguey with a fetus curled at her breast; La Llorona rising from a pool of water; Selena emerging from a house. Each woman shimmers beneath a spotlight in an explosion of red, yellow, purple, and blue, a monument to heritage and to dignity.

In high school, I bought postcards of Santa's work at an art museum and have hung them on the walls of every residence I have lived in since. Entering her studio, then, feels like stepping into a memory palace, a labyrinthine space that is both fantastical and familiar. This sensation intensifies when, in the midst of an otherwise ordinary conversation, Santa asks if we've visited the miracle tree.

Shaking my head, I ask what makes it miraculous.

"It talks," she says with the same nonchalance she might have said, "It sways."

"With—words?"

Santa stares at me with her large dark eyes. "Yes, words."

"What . . . does it sound like?"

"Real ugly. Like a demon. But it cured my sister Frances."

Years ago, Frances suffered a stroke in Austin. Santa and their ninety-year-old father hurried to her bedside, carrying a Bible, a crucifix, a bottle of olive oil,[2] and a leaf shed by the miracle tree. For hours he massaged the oil while Santa rubbed the leaf across Frances's body, murmuring prayers. Then one of Frances's toes began to wiggle.

"Suddenly, her leg lifted straight up in the air," Santa says, flinging up an arm for emphasis. "The nurses couldn't believe it. One ran into the room and said that shouldn't have happened for a year."

I was weaned on stories like this. Legions of tías and tíos told me about little girls flying from rooftops; about *brujas* wielding horsehair whips; about lady ghosts wailing down by the river. As a child, I so feared the power of *el mal de ojo*, I could not admire a newborn without touching her, lest she fall ill. Spirits inhabited even inanimate objects. I talked to our cars and wept when they were sold. Refused to part with old toys or clothing. Splashed water on all that was tainted. This half of me, the part steeped in culture and memory, believes in miracles. Shivers at their mention.

An inner skeptic, however, was born in journalism school and nurtured in a succession of newsrooms. Editors trained me to hunt for veracity rooted in certifiable fact. The only way they'd believe in a talking tree is if I chopped one down, dragged it into their office, and interrogated it in front of them. While I appreciated the reasons for this rigidity, it eventually grew limiting, so I gravitated toward the more freewheeling form of creative nonfiction, where verifiable facts are spun into truths (and, if you're really lucky, Truth). In this genre, the question is not whether a tree can talk but why someone would wish it so.

---

2. An evangelical Christian, Santa's father believed the olive oil was holy because it had been perched atop the radio when it broadcast a service by the Galvan Revival Church. He deemed the miracle tree sacrilegious, though, so Santa had to use its leaf discreetly.

I glance over at Greg, clad in his trademark black. We met in junior high, when we used to spend our weekends roaming the halls of Sunrise Mall. He couldn't escape Corpus fast enough either, and a decade of travels had whisked him across Spain, Argentina, Japan, and Mexico before crash-landing him back here. Over the years, we have traveled many miles together for his art and my prose, and in the process, he's become my barometer for possibility. When his eyes meet mine, we grin. Time for a road trip.

ACCORDING TO SANTA, the miracle tree belongs to an elderly woman who lives near Premont, a town of 2,700 about seventy miles southwest of Corpus. The farm road out there passes through land unfathomably vast and lined with cotton fields and oil wells. There are neither forests nor hills out here, no water beyond the pools that appear up ahead and then vanish. Predatory birds soar overhead. Cactus bloom from rooftops. Hand-painted crosses rise from the ditches.

Eventually we reach Broadway, Premont's main thoroughfare—a string of boarded storefronts and an abandoned elementary school tangled in weeds. The electronic sign at Amanda's BBQ flashes "Viva Mexico!" while a gas station advertises "Tacos, Gas, Beer." The local bank is called Cowboy Country Federal Credit Union.

We polish off a leaden meal at Oasis, one of the town's last standing restaurants. The food is cheap—hamburgers for $3.99—and artery-blocking. Chicken-fried steak. Chicken-fried chicken.[3] Battered green beans. Gizzards and gravy. Menudo and tortillas. Chalupas and quesadillas. The hybrid menu matches the hybrid clientele, a blend of Tejano families and sunbaked white men in work boots and jeans, all dining in booths patched with duct tape so the springs don't spill out. Our waitress asks where we are from.

When traveling, I field this question regularly, but no one is ever satisfied with my response. "You don't *seem* Texan," they say, as if expecting me to whistle for my horse or spit a wad of chew. When Tejanos question my origins, however, I feel like I've been gone so long, I've become unrecognizable—an outsider to the community I consider my own.

---

3. Nope, not fried chicken, but chicken-fried chicken. Similar to its cousin, chicken-fried steak, it is a chicken breast pounded thin, heavily battered and deep-fried, then drowned in white or brown gravy and served with a heap of mashed potatoes and a slice of Texas toast (that is, one that's bigger than your plate).

"We're from here."

"Here?" she asks, brow crinkled.

"South Texas," I say, a bit defensively.

"Corpitos," Greg clarifies, which makes us all laugh. Corpitos is a nickname for Corpus Christi that denotes both affection and deprecation.

"Oh, *Corpitos*." She smiles as if to say, You're still not one of us—but you're close.

After cruising Broadway a couple more times, we pull into Lopez Tire Co. to ask for directions. It is a bitter-cold day, so cold the weatherman instructed everyone to haul in their pets and plants last night. South Texans can endure triple digits with aplomb, but when the thermometer dips below fifty, we panic. The last time Corpitos experienced an icy rain, police responded to more than 200 vehicular accidents within a seventeen-hour period. Every school, mall, and bridge shuttered for miles.

A Tejano with a handlebar moustache trots out to greet us, rubbing his shoulders and shivering.

"We're, uh . . . we're looking for the tree," I say.

No need to clarify: he promptly gives directions. When I ask how we'll recognize it, his eyes donut: "Es gigantisimo!"

We follow 716 until it ends, past farmland and *ranchitos*, past jackrabbits and nopalitos, then turn left. In the distance soars a solitary tree, perhaps ten feet higher than the nearest telephone pole. With its sea-green mane undulating in the wind, it resembles an arboreal mermaid presiding over miles of scrub brush. A chain-link fence surrounds the tree, and as we draw near, we see that it has been interwoven with rosaries, maybe a hundred or more. Plastic and beaded, they clatter against the steel.

We pull into the driveway, a pile of packed sand. Vacant cabins are scattered about in varying states of disrepair, but the main house has recently been painted lemon. Its window hosts a nativity scene: Mary, baby Jesus, and an assorted cast of winged or bearded crew. As we tramp through the sand toward its front door, a woman steps out. She is wearing a long red cardigan over a leopard-patterned blouse and a rosary of heart-shaped beads. Her hair is poodled and her cheeks are Pepto-pink. This must be the tree's keeper, Estella Palacios Garcia. She appears to be eighty years old.

"Did you listen to my tree?" she demands, hand on hip. "Go on. Listen. I wait inside my chapel."

We retreat. Fake floral bouquets sprout from the dirt, their petals bleached by the sun. A slip of blue construction paper is nailed to a nearby

post: PLEASE NO WRITE ON MIRACLE TREE. I WILL FILE CHARGES FOR
DAMAGES.

Though toweringly high, the tree is no thicker than me. Its bark is smooth
as parchment and the color of ochre save for the chest-level region, where
years of adoring fingers have oiled it orange. Its branches don't begin until
eight feet up, rendering it strangely huggable. I press my ear against the trunk
and—to my great surprise—hear the sound of trickling water. It's no louder
than a meditative fountain at a yoga studio, but still. Trickling water. I gasp
and pull away.

"Do you hear that?"

"There's a little river in it!" Greg exclaims.

We circle round and round the tree, listening at different levels. The
volume fluctuates, but the sound is unmistakable. Trickling water. I rap the
trunk with my knuckles. It feels hollow inside. Do all trees sound like this?
Greg and I confer, but neither of us has listened to any lately.

We step inside the chapel, a small trailer adjacent to the house. Sunlight
streams through the windows, the only light except for the glowing grill of an electric heater. Estella sits in a chair like an oracle, her hands neatly folded in her lap.

"We heard water," I announce.

"The tree wants to tell you something but needs more time. Come back
when is not so cold."

Like all South Texans, the tree refuses to function in inclement weather.

"What do other people hear?" Greg asks.

"Oh, many thing. Sometime you hear a heartbeat. Sometime you hear a
door close and then a-knocking, and you know what it is? It is Jesus knocking
on the door."

As many Tejanos do, I grew up Catholic, and—despite my wildly divergent views on everything from abortion to the Vatican—I still claim to be
one. It's practically cultural heritage. Yet I shy away from conversations about
religion, as they haunt me about all the internal work I must do before I
can develop a spiritual *mestizaje* of my own.[4] So instead of engaging Estella
directly about her faith, I study it upon the walls, where colored pushpins
impale hundreds of photographs. Graduates wearing caps and gowns, brides

---

4. Like many illuminating ideas in border studies, "spiritual mestizaje" was first theorized by
the writer Gloria Anzaldúa. The scholar Theresa Delgadillo defines it as the "transformative
renewal of one's relationship to the sacred" as a way of defying oppression via "alternative
visions of spirituality." Through this lens, Estella's shrine can be viewed as an act of resistance.

kissing grooms, mothers kissing babies, elderly couples cumbia-dancing across a ballroom floor. Half a dozen driver's licenses align in a row.

"Miracles!" she interjects, catching my glimpse. "A man's wife, she have cancer in California and I send her oil and a picture of my tree and five month later she is healed. The cancer, it go away. Thanks be Jes—"

Some photographs are accompanied by handwritten *testimonios*, either tucked beneath the photographs or displayed inside the picture frames propped on the floor. In English, Spanish, and Spanglish, these letters either entreat the tree for mercy or express gratitude for granting it. One is accompanied by a newspaper clipping: *I am seeking justice for my son that was massacred at this prison. They send him home in pieces. May They Close All This Private Prisons! Thank you Lord, Santos Cardenas.*

"—and this woman from Mexico, she is sick, *very*-very sick of her lung, and she comes to me and asks what do I do so it go away and I say you stand against my tree for thirty minute and you pray-pray-pray to God . . ."

One wall features photos of men in military uniform, young men, barely twenty, speckled with medals and acne. Their gazes are unsettling, emitting a blend of macho pride and fear.

"—and she did and she is healed. A *specialista* of the lung, he say the cancer is gone! Erase."

She stares at us in wonder.

Estella's isn't the first miracle tree to spring up in the borderlands. In 1966, *Time* wrote about a thirty-foot acacia tree in La Feria that mysteriously began secreting a tea-colored liquid from its knothole. Neighbors started dropping by to touch the water, rub it on their bodies, and drink it. Miracles quickly followed. A blind woman's vision returned after the water was poured in her eyes; open sores disappeared from a child's face. Pilgrims descended upon the tree by the hundreds. Never mind that a string of experts said the water was sap: the believers deemed it holy.

Thirty years later, La Virgen de Guadalupe appeared in the bark of a cottonwood tree on a median in downtown Brownsville. Crowds lined up for blocks to kiss it. Next came the "crying tree" of Rio Grande City. A matriarch named Leonisia Garcia used to spend her afternoons beneath her acacia tree painting cascarones[5] to sell at Easter. She collapsed there from a heart attack

---

5. Cascarones are colorfully painted eggshells filled with confetti that get hidden in the backyard and then cracked on unsuspecting heads on Easter Sunday sometime after the *barbacoa* is served but before the poker games start.

in her ninety-second year, and the day after her funeral her family noticed foamy froth dripping from the tree branches. "We feel like that tree is now missing her," her daughter, Mary Lou Sanders, told the *Dallas Morning News*. "It is something I cannot explain." Scientists could: it was a spittlebug nest. But to the hundreds of onlookers who gathered each morning clutching Styrofoam cups, it was "miracle ice." One mother from Roma brought in her son in a wheelchair, collected a few drops, dipped in a reverent finger, and drew crosses upon his forehead. "God made a miracle to save his life," she told the newspaper. "I know he is going to make another miracle and he's going to lift my son out of that wheelchair."

When I ask Estella about these other trees, she waves a hand in dismissal. Shams, all of them. She predicted her tree's power before she even planted it. One night six years ago, she read a passage in the Bible about Jesus healing the sick with the leaves of an olive tree. When she awoke the next morning, she decided: "God, I go to the Valley to find this tree."

At a nursery near Brownsville, she told a gardener that she wished to buy a Monte de los Olivos tree from the Holy Land. What luck, he said: they had one in stock, "all the way from Jerusalem," for three dollars.

"When I buy, it is this high," she says, holding her hand a foot off the ground. "And I pray to God, 'Send me miracles, send me people to heal their cancer, to heal their tumors,' and I tell the tree and I plant it. It grow and grow and grow and then when is like this," she raises her hand another foot, "I listen and it sound like running water."

She waited until the tree was two years old ("so is not so skinny") before she spread word of its powers. Her first two visitors were a man and a woman who prayed around the tree until God appeared. The man ran away in fright, but the woman continued praying. "She stay and pray and is healed."

Soon, people were traveling across Texas to visit her tree. After a Mexican television station aired a special about it, pilgrims even crossed the border in tour buses. I ask how many had visited in all. One thousand? Two thousand?

"Fifty," she says.

"Fifty *thousand*?"

Blinking sassily, she continues on for the better part of an hour. A miracle lurks behind every handwritten letter propped upon her floor, behind every photograph pinned upon her wall, behind every rosary woven through the chain links of her fence, and she wants to share them all. And at that moment, I want to believe them. I want to be that six-year-old upon Tío Valentín's knee again, the girl who lit candles before Mass each Sunday and prayed to someone she thought could hear. For a moment, my ability to rebuild a life in South Texas after a fifteen-year absence seems contingent upon such belief.

I glance over at Greg. If he believes in talking trees, I can believe in talking trees.

His posture spells rapture. He sits perfectly erect in his hard metal chair, his hands folded inside his lap, a smile upon his lips. But his eyes have gone glazy. His head leans forward, then pitches back.

Metaphorically rising from my tío's knee, I thank Estella for her time. Greg stirs awake and follows suit. As we approach the truck, a caravan of eighteen-wheelers hurdle past, each one hauling an unmarked tank. Dust clouds swirl behind them.

"Where are they going?" I ask. We are miles from the nearest highway.

"Aye," Estella says and shudders. "They dump their tank."

"*Dump?* Where?"

"Across my street."

There doesn't appear to be anything across her street but a grove of mesquite, yet Estella says a waste pit lurks behind the trees where trailers dump their tanks late at night.

"How do you know they are dumping?"

"I hear them!" she says. "The city come to test my water and they say is no good. All these ranches, the water is no good."

Who came? When? What did they determine? My inner reporter demands three-ring binders bulging with certifiable facts. But Estella cannot supply them. She knows only that her well has been contaminated for fourteen years by something so strong, not even her miracle tree can cure it. She must buy bottled water from Premont. And since "the city" has been no help, she built a shrine to beseech the spirits instead.

We exit her property, my thoughts ablaze. Even if no one is outright dumping here, the area is littered with natural gas wells. Their reputation for tarnishing water is memorialized in the documentary *Gasland*, which shows families lighting their drinking water on fire as it pours out of the tap. We continue down the road and, after a time, come upon a clearing. An open gate reveals a slender dirt path. Beyond it, a herd of bulldozers paw the earth. As we idle on the side of the road, wondering what to do, an eighteen-wheeler with an unmarked tank pulls up behind us. We watch it enter the gate and vanish inside the brush.

2

The Rebel

DEPENDING ON WHOM YOU ASK, LIONEL LOPEZ IS EITHER JIMINY Cricket—the "conscience of South Texas"—or else the region's most unrelenting pest. A sienna-skinned man with broad-rimmed glasses, he gels his hair back and razors his moustache straight. Sixty-six years of sun lines burrow into his face. When I climb into his Ford F-150, he flicks off the norteño music jangling on the radio before grinning. "Are you ready to go to Mexico, *mija*?"

We won't be traveling within 145 miles of the border today, but Lionel is being metaphorical here. He means that in less than twenty minutes we'll be witnessing poverty so desperate, it will seem we departed the United States long ago. We glide past the million-dollar mansions and palm trees lining Corpus Christi's ritziest street—Ocean Drive—and then ride Cesar Chavez Memorial Highway out of town.

Estella's poisoned well has curled my fingers into a note-taking position. Miracle trees are a matter of faith, but contaminated water can be proven by science. When I started asking around for resources, people directed me to Lionel. He is said to know this swath of Texas better than anyone.

"Back when I was a firefighter, we used to ride around in the ambulances a lot, and I saw the conditions people were living in out here," he says. "I saw their shacks. I saw their dirt roads. I saw their suffering."

Upon investigation, he learned that many were residents of *colonias*, the unincorporated communities that began cropping up in the borderlands in the 1950s, when developers foisted off cheap plots of land lacking running water, sewage systems, electricity hookups, fire hydrants, and paved roads to low-income (and largely Tejano) families. Such communities have not only proliferated in the sixty years since but also migrated north to areas surrounding Corpus, Austin, Houston, even Dallas. The secretary of state's office has counted nearly 2,300 colonias housing more than 400,000 Texans, though Lionel thinks there are several times as many.

About thirty years ago, Lionel asked his wife, Juanita, if he could take a bag of groceries to some residents he met on an ambulance run. Although they were squeezing nickels to support their own five children, she agreed. That bag evolved into turkeys at Thanksgiving. Toys at Christmas. Ice during heat waves. Soon, the two were organizing clothing drives for the colonias and teaching classes about nutrition and other life skills. Gradually, they noticed how unhealthy the residents were, compared with their neighbors back in Corpus. Diabetes was rife, as was asthma. Scores of babies had birth defects. Many people were dying of cancer. And when the colonias flooded each year during the rainy season, outhouses and septic tanks did too, causing outbreaks of infections and diarrhea. Children had to trudge through raw sewage to catch their school bus each morning. Housewives lost their toenails.

That's when the Lopezes got political. They started ringing the state's chief environmental agency, the Texas Commission on Environmental Quality (TCEQ), demanding that area creeks and water wells be tested for toxicity. They petitioned the Texas Water Development Board and South Texas Water Authority for the installation of fire hydrants or at least cisterns. They lobbied lawmakers for sanitary sewage systems. They even founded a nonprofit called the South Texas Colonia Initiative to make their requests more official.

Yet time and again, they clashed with the same foe: the odometer. Many federal and state programs finance projects only for colonias closer to the border, as geography is a key component of the government's definition of a colonia.

"We are in no man's land out here," Lionel says, shaking his head. "Our people are the forgotten ones."

On the outskirts of Robstown, Lionel hangs a left at the Exxon gas station and rumbles down a county road. The land here is so level you could shoot marbles across it, but in time some flat-topped hills crest the horizon.

"The little kids call this their mountain," he says as we draw near.

In fact, it's a hazardous waste dump with an Orwellian name: U.S. Ecology Texas. In 2010, it was processing some 78,000 containers of waste a year—including petrochemicals, agricultural chemicals, pharmaceuticals, and certain radioactive materials—and injecting the remains deep inside a multilayer landfill liner system. It is owned by U.S. Ecology, Inc., the same company that under a different name shuttered a similar plant in Winona, Texas, in 1997, after more than 600 area residents filed personal-injury lawsuits against it. Among their grievances: scores of two-headed or stillborn barn animals as well as a host of human illnesses ranging from Hodgkin's disease to lupus to albinism. Lionel has tried to rally opposition here in Robstown as well, but too many people applaud the jobs the facility brings to the cash-starved region (around 100).

We bump along a chain-link fence crowned with razor wire, then turn onto a swampy road bisecting two of the "mountains." Houses cluster just a quarter mile away. Lionel parks by the nearest one, a yellow brick ranch house. Its front door and windows open to a panoramic view of the dump—a jumble of trucks, tanks, and towers rising from otherwise flush fields. Judging by the rusted security gate and drawn curtains, the owners don't peek out much. We walk instead to the back of the house, which faces farmland, and are greeted by the Ahlriches, one of the few non-colonia families around. Virginia is a Nordic-looking woman who speaks with the precision of an attorney; Kenneth is a thin but spry seventy-six. They are eager to share the dossier they've been compiling on their neighbor. Kenneth's family has lived on this land for nearly a century, so he has had a front-row seat to the facility's forty-year reign.

"At first, we couldn't find out what it was moving in here. They said it was going to be waste incineration, but as soon as they got here, they started burying the stuff. They said there'd be no odor, no runoff, no water contamination, but they've had all that and more. In the seventies, they were so careless with their odor, my daddy would get sick and have to step off his tractor to vomit," Kenneth says, doffing his Texas Farm Bureau cap for emphasis.

The odor, he says, has "a petroleum smell," and they still catch wind of it every few days or so. Like Estella, they had to abandon their water well years ago and worry about the way their milo and grain sorghum fields extend right up to the dump's fence line—crops that will someday become someone's syrup and flour. "There's a constant flow of foul air coming over our fields. There has to be some poison in there," Kenneth says.

And so, the Ahlriches have become self-appointed industrial watchdogs. They estimate they have filed more than thirty complaints with the TCEQ over the years, including after a gas leak in March 2008. Virginia was cooking dinner when a sheriff pulled up the driveway to warn her of "a situation" over at the facility. Once outside, she caught a dizzying whiff of what she guessed to be chlorine gas.[1] She sought refuge at a church, where her throat started burning.

1. In 2010, I called U.S. Ecology Texas to inquire about the 2008 leak. A spokesperson said, "It was not chlorine gas. We don't even have it in our facility. It was bleach." While it is true that beach is not chlorine, it does contain sodium hypochlorite. When mixed with acidic chemicals, bleach can release chlorine as a gas.

"Two people went to the hospital because of it, including my piano student," she says, her ice-blue eyes never blinking. "I am uninsured, so I didn't go, but I had four weeks of throat difficulty after that."

Despite its occasional explosions and spills, U.S. Ecology Texas does make an effort to be neighborly. The company has extended multiple invitations to the Ahlriches to tour the facility and enjoy a company barbecue over the years. (They always refuse.) And each Christmas, a company representative knocks on their door to offer a twenty-five-dollar gift certificate to H-E-B[2] and an apple pie.

"We throw it back in their faces!" Kenneth says, clenching a sun-speckled fist. "Well, not literally, but we never accept it. They go into poor communities full of minority people who are too scared to do anything, and they sweet talk them and say everything is all right."

With a harrumph, he escorts us outside to his barn. The door flings open to a veritable museum of the farming industry, from the mule-drawn plows and planters his daddy used to his own John Deere monster-tractor outfitted with the newest GPS satellite system. Standing in the middle of a century of equipment, Kenneth flings out his arms, as if to embrace it. "This land means something to me. Our heart is here. That is why this hurts me so. I used to be a happy-go-lucky person, but that dump has turned me into a grumpy old man."

LIONEL AND I CONTINUE DOWN THE ROAD. We're in colonia territory now. Most houses are constructed of aluminum siding and wood, and several seem on the verge of collapse. Single- and double-wides abound, as do campers and trailers. Bedsheets flap in the wind. Auto carcasses rust in the sun.

"That one there used to belong to an old man named Mr. Vera," Lionel says, pointing to an abandoned camper enclosed by a fence. "He used a bucket for a toilet and cooked his meals outside. All he had inside was a mattress. One day I brought him some ice and found him sitting in his underwear. I said, 'Mr. Vera, why are you naked?' and he said, '*Pues*, today is wash day.'" Lionel laughs at the memory.

Evidence of such survivalist pragmatism is everywhere. Clusters of wires strung along poles reveal as many as six different homes sharing a single

---

2. H-E-B is a mega-grocery store chain named after its proprietor, Howard Edward Butt. In the state of Texas, if you need anything from aluminum foil to pears to lawn chairs, this is where you'll find it—and, in many towns, the only place.

electrical source. With wells costing anywhere from $4,000 to $7,000 to install, running water is also a communal commodity. Everyone complains about the groundwater's salty taste, though. Mixing in packets of Kool-Aid is a common solution, as is sticking to Coke.

After a time, we come upon a mobile home in especially bad condition. The siding looks as if it has been chomped on by something large and hungry. A tarp covers the more ravaged sections. We park in a mud pit and walk toward the door, dodging children's bicycles and auto parts as we do. A Mexican national in her early thirties opens the door and greets us warmly in Spanish. We enter her home, which is entirely dark save for the glow of a flat-screen TV playing a cartoon dubbed in Spanish. As my eyes adjust to the lack of light, I realize we are surrounded by pot-bellied garbage bags stacked several feet high and covering much of the floor. The kitchen doubles as a closet, with clothes and shoes strewn among stacks of tortillas and pots of beans. Cheerios speckle the carpet. With an old T-shirt, she wipes off a space for us at the table and we all sit down. I try to follow the conversation that ensues—something about how her husband has just gotten his papers after fourteen years of working here—but am too mesmerized by the condition of the house to focus. Lionel will later explain that colonia families have to pay for garbage collection. Since most can't afford it, they do without, allowing it to pile to sometimes hazardous heights and then burning it or bribing someone to take it away.

Lionel talks to the woman with the tenderness of a tío. How are the kids doing? *Pues, bien.* How have they handled this cold spell? *Yesterday morning it was twenty degrees inside.* Have they thought any more about selling the house and moving to Annaville? *Si, pero who would buy this? It would cost a fortune just to haul the trash away.* What about a septic tank? *Pues, we can't afford that either.*

Promising to look for a septic tank, Lionel rises from the table. We exchange another round of pleasantries and return to the truck. I glance over at Lionel, and he shrugs his shoulders sadly. "Ni modo," he says.

This is an expression I first learned in Mexico but have been noticing a lot here, too. No funding for your colonia because it's five miles too far from Mexico? Ni modo, that's a law; can't do much about that. A hazardous waste dump opens in your backyard? Ni modo, that's a corporation; there's no changing that either. Risk your life crossing a 2,000-mile border to wash dishes in Texas, only to dwell in squalor because you can't pay the garbage man? Ni modo, that's what you get for chasing your dreams.

SEVERAL MILES DOWN THE COUNTY ROAD, we come upon a private prison that recently opened to confine undocumented workers rounded up by the U.S. Border Patrol and Immigration and Customs Enforcement. I ask Lionel if it incarcerates its own neighbors, but he says that the majority of colonia residents are Tejanos who have lived here for generations. Undocumented workers usually stick to urban areas, where they can find work. The family we just met is an anomaly.

Residential houses stand a couple hundred yards away from the prison. The owner of the closest one is erecting an eight-foot fence around his property. "Every time he gets a paycheck, he adds a few feet more," Lionel says.

Lionel's chief concern about the prison is its pollution. When he learned that it had applied for a permit to release up to 150,000 gallons of treated wastewater a day into nearby Petronila Creek, he organized an outcry. As a concession, the prison cleaned the waterway beforehand, hauling out decades of debris. We drive out to see it. Swollen from the recent rain, the creek smacks of fermented soup, and its consistency is just as thick.

"A month or so ago, this was all doo-doo water from septic tanks," Lionel says, snapping photos with a disposable camera. "Kids swim here in the summertime, and they get sores all over their bodies. Livestock drink it and get sick. Some people even fish here." He shudders.

At Lionel's urging, scientists at Texas A&M University–Corpus Christi tested Petronila Creek for bacterial contamination and discovered its levels to be between seven and eleven times the regulatory limit. They started working with the TCEQ to determine the cause. As we walk along the bank, a crop duster flies overhead. Lionel grimaces. "They spray pesticides right down on the colonias. We've been fighting that forever."

As we head back to the truck, I realize that myriad culprits could have poisoned the wells of Estella and her neighbors. The range of possibility is staggering, as is the bureaucracy they'd need to navigate for help. No wonder she turned to a talking tree for solace. It might be the only one who listens.

Inside the truck, I search for something explaining Lionel's devotion to this mission: a political button, say, or a rosary. A bundle of sage. Anything. But the sole adornment is a lanyard dangling from the rearview mirror that reads "South Texas Colonia Initiative" beneath his grinning photo.

"I go to church," he concedes, "but that's not it. When you see something like this, you just have to do something about it. If we don't help each other out, who will?"

LIONEL WAS BORN the third of six children on a ranch twenty miles outside Corpus. His moral compass aligned early. "All of us Mexicans went to school at the ranch while the Anglos went to another school. We didn't question it until we got older, when we realized we had to go to the bathroom outside and they didn't."

He met Juanita at a dance at the local Catholic Youth Organization. (They liked each other's glasses.) They married a week after she graduated from Carroll High School, and Lionel soon found a job at a door company. "All the Mexican workers there were treated badly, and they went to Lionel for help," Juanita later tells me. "He was able to speak up for himself, whereas other people were afraid they'd lose their job, and they needed their job. Lionel has always been pro-union; he has always been like a rebel."

Lionel joined the Corpus Christi Fire Department in the early seventies and worked there for twenty-three years, until the night a meatpacking plant caught fire. The chief needed two men to combat the flames from inside, and Lionel volunteered. "Everything was okay until the bell on my air pack started ringing, which meant I was running out of oxygen, so I turned to tell my partner we needed to go, and there was this huge orange ball rolling toward us. I had never seen nothing like it before. It moved like in slow motion, until all of a sudden—*blam!*"

He awoke to find himself pinned beneath a metal door. His buddies were standing on top of it, searching for him. By the time they dragged him to safety, he had sustained injuries to his head, spine, shoulders, and knees, and many of his teeth had crumbled. The pain was so great, he retired soon after, but rather than relax with his family—which includes five children, thirteen grandchildren, and a great-grandbaby on the way—he ramped up his work with the colonias.

I am surprised to learn from Juanita that Lionel's mother used to live in a colonia. (He never mentioned it.) Juanita thinks this is what seeded his involvement. After successfully petitioning for a new drainage system to be installed on his mother's property, he helped her neighbors do the same.

"And after that, he started getting the streets fixed. He wanted to have it all done before she passed away, but . . . he didn't."

Nowadays, she says, her husband rises early each morning and drives either to a colonia to knock on doors or to city hall to pound on doors. Juanita stays home to field phone calls and e-mails and line up his appointments. He hands out "a million" business cards each week, she says, so keeping track of everyone is a full-time job. She prepares a hot meal every night, but he rarely savors it: the phone rings throughout the evening, and he insists on answering. "I always say, 'Wait, Lionel, finish eating first,' but he says no because it could be important. People know they can call about whatever thing at whatever hour and he'll be there."

THE LANDSCAPE IS TURNING FERAL NOW. Nopales crest the rooftops. Mesquite trees fuse into the brush, forming impenetrable walls. Oak trees canopy overhead. A skilled hunter could live off game alone out here: deer, turkeys, javelinas, and nilgais roam wild.[3] But while the view is scenic, colonia residents seem keen on obstructing it. They seal their windows with aluminum foil, with blankets, with planks of wood. They fortify their yards with fences.

"It's like everyone is hiding," Lionel observes.

Up ahead is a colonia called Country Estates West. Its road has all but disintegrated. Lionel slows to fifteen miles per hour to navigate its cavernous potholes. We pass by families living in aluminum shacks, in barns, in campers, in anything offering walls and a ceiling. A disturbing number of homes appear to have been torched. There are no fire hydrants out here; if something ignites, it vanishes. Nearly everyone has a guard dog chained on a very short leash. Upsettingly skinny, they howl as we ride past.

After a time, we come upon some white men standing in a clearing. One charges our truck with his fist in the air. He is twenty-something years old, sun-cooked and curly-haired. In a gruff Texan brogue, he demands why we're on his property. His party surrounds us. One man has a gun in his front pocket. All my instincts say to throw the Ford in reverse and split. Lionel opts to hop out and proffer a business card instead. "We came to ask about your water services."

The eldest man reads the card aloud. Perhaps fifty years old, he has white and blonde hair and a belly protruding over dirt-encrusted jeans. Something appears to have clawed the left side of his face repeatedly.

"Colonia? I ain't ever heard of no colonia," he says.

---

3. A little lesson on the flora and fauna of South Texas: Nopal is the Spanish term for the prickly pear cactus, whose pads make a fine breakfast when sautéed with eggs. Javelinas are wild tusked boars who emit such a foul odor, they are sometimes called skunk pigs. Nilgais are five-hundred-pound antelopes that were imported to South Texas from India more than a century ago. Skittish creatures, they are more commonly seen in menus than out in the brush.

Lionel summarizes his work, then introduces me as a writer. All four men stare at me with eyes glossy pink. Hands trembling, I reach for my notebook and click on my pen. The forest grows quiet.

"Well, welcome to the bayou!" the older man breaks the silence. "What can I tell you?"

The younger men retreat into the woods to "shoot a hundred rounds" as the man shows us his homestead. He owns 2.3 acres here and 3.1 on another lot. His son sleeps in a nearby camper featuring a Confederate flag in its window; he sleeps in an 8- by 10-foot wood hut. "This whole area floods once or twice a year and turns into a great big lake. We have to climb up top our truck and wait till the water goes down. Last time I got sick with worms and had to chew tobacco till they went away. Once, the floodwater came and it was full of diesel fuel. I was sick for three years."

He and his son used to work at the prison, but he got injured and his son got fired. They live off his disability now, which averages $12,000 a year—enough for auto expenses, property taxes, and a diet of canned soup and sandwiches, but not enough for heat. Those scratches on his face are from trying to shave this morning, when temperatures dipped into the thirties.

I ask if he's married, and his lower lip quivers. She's "right at death's door," he says, because she's "real obese" and has diabetes. He himself has had colon problems and three ruptured hernias. His chief concern is for his son, though. "If I die, he'll die. He's got attention deficit disorder and hyperactive disorder. He went to college but it didn't work out but one semester. He had to write a thesis on how evil the white man was, and the teacher gave him a zero because he wrote the white man was good. If you can't think like a liberal in college they just throw you out. If you want to know the real world, you best listen to talk radio."

We clearly should be going now, but Lionel keeps asking questions. Do you have a septic tank? Do you have access to clean water? Is your wife receiving appropriate medical care? Only after Lionel has surveyed the lot and tested the water pump does he seem satisfied. We all shake hands, and the homesteader accompanies us back to the truck. "I wouldn't go talking to my neighbor if I was you," he warns. "He's a loner and he don't like nobody on his property. He can be sort of mean."

Once we are safely locked inside his truck, Lionel chuckles. "So that was the Country Estates," he says as we hightail it back to the main road. "And I've seen worse than that."

I ask Lionel if he ever gets scared out here, and he does, but not of surly residents. No, it takes more than a loaded man to unsettle him. He worries about the "big guns," the local and state officials who disapprove of his work and the henchmen he believes are sent out to stop him.

"They have broken into my truck many, many times and stolen cameras and recording equipment. They call my phone and say I had better stop. Sometimes the sheriff will follow me all the way from the colonias back to my house in Corpus. I keep braking so that if they hit me, it's their fault. That is why I always go alone," he says, then casts a sideway glance at me. "I don't want nobody to get hurt."

IT'S 3 P.M. AND LIONEL has yet to break for lunch or even coffee. At my insistence, he pulls into a Robstown restaurant called Rolando's. As soon as we are seated, waitresses swarm our table—not to take our order but to issue their own, in a flurry of English and Spanish. One suffers from blood circulation so poor, her leg has turned purple; another has a mother on kidney dialysis. Can he help? Lionel bounds back to his truck and returns with pamphlets about a free prescription drug program. After offering to enroll them, he promises to arrange for transportation next time they visit a clinic.

Over heaping plates of *carne guisada*, rice, and beans, Lionel rattles off his goals for the upcoming year. He wants a septic tank for every family and a fire hydrant in every colonia. He wants more creeks tested for toxicity. Above all, he wants a community center from which to better organize his constituency. To accomplish all that, however, he'll need a squadron.

"We'll need grant writers. We'll need carpenters. Electricians. Plumbers. Toxicologists," he sighs, then rolls up a corn tortilla. "But who is going to do all that work for free?"

This is the key difference between writing about a far-flung community and your own. The decision to wield a pen rather than, say, a hammer gets increasingly hard to justify. At various points over the years, I have vowed to stop trying to describe things and start trying to change them, but each time, I've concluded that words are the only tools I know how to use. So rather than meet Lionel's gaze, I (shamefully) sneak a sip of *horchata* instead. Who besides him, indeed?

3

The Venerable

THE SUN IS JUST BEGINNING ITS EVENING MELT ACROSS THE HORIZON.
The sky turns lavender; the sorghum fields glow crimson. A maguey[1] undulates its aquamarine leaves like a desert octopus. Somewhere along Chapman
Ranch road, not far from Bishop, Greg pulls over. "I want to show you something," he says.

The land before us is overgrown with weeds as high as our knees. We
wade toward a cinder block house abandoned long ago. Spiderwebs mend
the shot-out windows. Braids of vine slither up one wall; black and green
mold creeps down another. Greg points out a paint-splattered pattern and
grins—and, just like that, what was previously an eyesore becomes an aesthetic. We circle around the house, marveling at the plant life burgeoning
from the rooftop and the wooden door, distressed just so.

Out back is an old warehouse, equal parts rust and tin. We slip in through
a door cracked open. Inside is an arsenal of tractor tires. Some are as tall as
me. Greg emits a low whistle, then throws a rock at a tire suspended from
the rafters above. Suddenly, there is movement—a chaos of buff and white.
Owls! Two—no, three. Five. Eight! The kind that look like they're wearing opera masks, swiftly exiting their balcony nests. Soundlessly, they circle
above our heads. Their wingspan is immense, upward of three feet in length.

---

1. Volumes could be written about the maguey's significance in the Texas-Mexico
borderlands. Historically, the plant provided food, drink, medicine, and fiber for clothing.
Today, Tejanos seed them in their front yards for good luck. The best story I've heard
about the maguey comes courtesy of Santa Barraza's mother, who contended that lonely
soldiers copulated with the plant during the Mexican Revolution, leaving fetuses on the
leaves. When Santa recreated that image in a painting, however, her mother protested,
calling it witchcraft. Unperturbed, Santa continues using magueys in her work today,
posing the plants directly behind her central figures so that they appear to have wings.

They render the rafters almost invisible. For a thrilling moment, I see only black eyes and white feathers. Then they swoop out the door behind us.

My paternal grandmother collected owls. Every summer, when Dad and I drove to Kansas for a visit, I would rush to her bedroom to admire her latest acquisitions. Conditioned, perhaps, by years of Winnie-the-Pooh cartoons, I thought her porcelain figurines signified a fine intelligence. Once I learned to put pencil to paper, we started a written correspondence that lasted until her death my senior year in high school. After the funeral, when Mom, Aunt Jolene, and I sorted through her jewelry boxes, the piece I claimed was a silver owl with green glass eyes that dangled from a chain. It hangs now above my writing desk, a tribute to the woman who first encouraged my efforts there.

The sight of owls swirling overhead, then, engulfs me in her reassuring presence—something I haven't felt in years.

I am eager to share this story when Greg and I gather in Santa's living room a few nights later. Many of her paintings feature the women in her family, so I know she'll appreciate it. At the first mention of owls, however, Santa gasps. "*Lechuzas*?! That's a bad omen." She goes on to explain how, in Mexican folklore, witches turn into owls in the dark of night to cast their spells more discreetly.

This, in essence, is why I moved to Mexico when I turned thirty a few years ago. As a "Chicana writer," I felt obligated to know such cultural markers as whether owls should be feared or revered. For months I roamed the countryside, talking to everyone whose path I crossed, aspiring not only to learn the language of my maternal family but also to absorb some of their mindset as well. I came to realize that internal culture-clashes are actually an intrinsic part of the Mexican experience—a legacy of blending colonial and indigenous bloods (or, in my case, Pennsylvania Dutch and Tejano). One grandmother's spirit animal is almost by definition another's demon.

So while Santa's revelation doesn't launch me into identity crisis mode—as it would have, pre-Mexico—my existential divide widens a bit. And since I've already reached a vulnerable place, I might as well venture further.

"We went to see the talking tree," I announce.

"And?" Santa asks.

"It didn't say a thing."

"It was too cold," Greg jokes.

Nobody laughs.

Santa looks me over thoughtfully. Clad in one of her trademark huipiles, or hand-embroidered Mexican blouses, she is nestled in the cushions of her couch, her wire-rimmed glasses perched professorially on her nose, her thick black hair rippling down her back. Because her art has traveled with me to so many places—because her Virgen de Guadalupe has been one of the first images I have seen upon waking and the last I have glimpsed before resting— Santa has become a tether of sorts. Though she is constantly suggesting books to read and people to meet to deepen my knowledge of the borderlands, she is herself my most definitive resource.

"What are you looking for, Stephanie?" she asks.

Stories? Faith? Fusion? I take so long to respond, Greg does it for me. "She's looking for a miracle."

Santa smiles. She knows just where I should go.

A BLOND BRICK ROAD leads to Mother Julia's Solemn Place of Prayer in Kingsville, Texas. Following it through a yard freshly trimmed, I recognize Santa's contribution here. Upon the building's facade is a giant mural of a nun shrouded in indigo yet outlined in white, so that she appears illumined. One hand rests on a Bible; the other curls on her lap. She is surrounded by red and purple pansies. Bereft of laugh lines or wrinkles, her face seems timeless. She could be thirty, forty, sixty. Mother Julia, I presume.

I peek in the chapel's doorway. Strands of Christmas lights and rows of poinsettias deck the altar, as do mechanized Barbie angels who move their arms and turn their heads in unison. The surrounding pews could seat dozens but don't. Only one spot is occupied, by an elderly nun who is praying. Seeing me, she crosses herself, rises from the kneeling bench, and strides over to greet me. Even in padded black Reeboks, she stands only five feet tall. A mole hovers above her lips; white wisps peek beneath her habit.

"When you enter a shrine for the first time, mija, you must kneel down and pray," Sister Maximina says, guiding me to a pew. "Don't ask for wishes but for graces. God doesn't count, so you can ask for as many as you want. Pray first, mija, then we can talk."

Despite my struggles with faith, rattling off Hail Marys and Our Fathers moments before sleep was a ritual for much of my life. Once I started traveling, though, I realized my prayers had not developed since the pattern set at age seven. In the context of the new cultures I was exploring, my old recitations seemed vapid. Rather than reconfigure my practice—or, better yet, value it as a cultural rite of its own—I gave it up altogether. Now that I'm back in the borderlands, however, prayer seems to be an important link in reestablishing my connection here. There's just something about South

Texas's epic heat, its desert dust, its diametrically opposing forces that sends you seeking intervention. Recitation feels like a natural soundtrack to this landscape, as if you are singing along to its repetitions. *Hail Mary full of grace*: sorghum, sorghum, tractor, oil well. *Our Father who art in heaven*: cotton, cotton, cactus, oil well.

And so, I maneuver into position—knees on bench, hands clasped, head bowed, eyes shut, body still—and dip into memory. I have just recovered an old desert song when Sister Maximina walks over with a photo album. She knows I'm here to ask about Mother Julia, and she can hardly wait to begin.

JULIA NAVARRETE GUERRERO was lured by the Lord when she was fifteen years old. Growing up the only daughter among six brothers in Oaxaca, Mexico, at the end of the nineteenth century, she'd already been schooled in submission, but a Jesuit priest taught her the importance of being penitent, too. "I prayed with a profound quiet of spirit and abundant tears and immense desires to suffer," she explains in her autobiography, *My Journey*. To deepen her practice, she began slipping bitter aloes into her food, depriving herself of sweets, and—while praying three creeds—suspending herself from nails so that she hung in the form of a cross. "Coming down," she writes, "I would feel a general swoon that I believed was pleasing to Our Lord."

Eventually a band was slipped on her fourth finger, a golden ring that declared in fine script on its inner lip *Amo a mi solo Cristo*. And she did. Enough to decline a flesh-and-blood man who asked her to be his bride. Enough to leave her family behind and join a nunnery. Enough to take a vow of poverty, chastity, and obedience so she could wholly live for him. For Julia was enraptured with Christ, not only beseeching his grace throughout the day but also rising multiple times in the night, her rosary wound between her fingers. Her devotion caught the attention of a priest looking to establish a new congregation of women, and at age twenty-two, Julia was asked to lead it. This unleashed a torrent of jealousy from the other nuns, but no matter: She was now Mother Julia, Superior General, Julia de las Espinas del Sagrado Corazón. She marked the transition by carving a monogram of Jesus upon her breast and burning it with a hot piece of iron. "In this way I was marked forever as belonging totally to Jesus," she writes. "The ardor of the spirit exceeded the pain of the flesh."

At the height of the Mexican Revolution, Mother Julia hustled her nuns across the international borderline and settled into a one-room house in Kingsville. She had no money for a mission, not a penny cut in half, yet within weeks she transformed the house into a school and enrolled a flock of students. She taught the neighborhood children in the afternoon and ministered to the neighborhood adults in the evening and embroidered handkerchiefs throughout the night to sell to the neighborhood ladies the following morning. Mother Julia purportedly worked so hard she forgot to eat and even to drink, but she never failed to pray. No, she prayed until she felt invaded, until "He took full possession" of her, whereupon she fainted in bliss.

After establishing her mission in South Texas, Mother Julia continued on, ultimately opening forty-five congregations of the Missionary Daughters of the Most Pure Virgin Mary in Mexico and the United States. And ever since dying in 1974, at the age of ninety-three, she has apparently worked even harder than before. People say she resuscitated a little girl who drowned. Woke a stuntman who split open his head in a moto crash. She mended marriages and healed the ailing and otherwise sent the celestial equivalent of smoke signals from above.

This is why southern Texans and northern Mexicans pray to Mother Julia to this day, why they sink to their knees and plead for intercessions, why mothers tuck her prayer card into the billfolds inside their purses, why truckers paste her photograph inside their big rigs. And it is why Sister Maximina has dedicated her life to spreading word of this woman's virtue. She wants the Vatican to canonize Mother Julia so that she'll officially be deified as a saint.

JOINING ME IN THE PEW, Sister Maximina opens the photo album. Its images are shot in color film but capture a black-and-white world of habits and bedsheets. Mother Julia is the golden raisin in the middle. Flipping the pages, Sister Maximina narrates a bit of her own story. How she was the youngest of fourteen children and studied at school under the same order of sisters she serves today. How she "fought the call" to become a nun herself because she couldn't bear to leave her family. How finally, at age twenty-five, while working at a drugstore in Taft, she surrendered to God's lure.

A decade into her own life of poverty, chastity, and obedience, Sister Maximina learned that Mother Julia had taken to her bed and was unlikely to rise again. A clutch of nuns was caring for her in Mexico but needed younger hands. Whenever anyone asked why she hadn't volunteered her services, she blamed her studies. The truth, though, was she didn't want to witness Mother Julia's suffering.

"But then a sister said, 'Wouldn't it be wonderful to say I was there when Mother Julia needed me?' And wow, mija, that was a dagger to my heart."

Late one night, two of Sister Maximina's seven older brothers drove her to Toluca, Mexico, for her new assignment. She prayed the entire way. By the time she arrived, Mother Julia was five months from death. Among her ailments was poor circulation. A massive sore had formed at the base of her spine. Wounds rippled across her back and legs. When she moved, she oozed, yet her smile remained beatific.

The sisters used only traditional medicines on Mother Julia, herbs brought over in paper bags by the indigenous people of Huasteca. They picked flowers from the garden, soaked them in a basin, and bathed her with fragrant water each day. Sister Maximina's duty was to dip gauze in medicinal extract and wrap Mother Julia's wounds. She smiles as she recounts this for me, then thrusts up her palms. "These hands have held a saint, okay?"

But one terrible morning, hours before dawn, the end seemed near. The sisters panicked. Forgoing traditional treatment, they summoned a white-coat doctor. After a brief examination, he started assembling an IV.

"He made an incision in her arm and, excuse the word, but he was such a *brute*, as he was trying to get in the IV, a little piece of her flesh came out *and he didn't even notice*!" Sister Maximina stamps the floor with her Reebok. "Fortunately I was there, and I kept it. That man just didn't know who he was treating."

Flesh wasn't all she saved that morning. She also fished Mother Julia's catheter out of the trash.

"*Mira*," she says, removing the crucifix tucked inside her blouse. Taped to the back of the black lacquered wood is a sliver of plastic. "Do you see what's there, mija, inside that catheter?"

Staring closely, I make out a tiny stain within.

"Blood!" she crows. "Mother Julia's blood."

She unzips a Pyrex Portables bag and removes a wooden jewelry box. This belonged to Mother Julia too, she says, turning its lock with a tiny silver key. Two pairs of surgical scissors are taped beneath its lid; bundles of soiled gauze cover its contents. She removes a golden locket from a gift box and opens it. Inside are a miniature photograph of Mother Julia and a slice of her flesh. I clasp it in my hands as Sister Maximina rummages through the Pyrex Portables bag.

"Where are you where are you where are you," she murmurs. "Here, here. *Mi-ra*."

She opens a piece of paper that has been folded many times, then allows me to peek at its contents. It looks like expired spice. Paprika, perhaps. Cayenne pepper.

"Saint's blood!" she cries.

However dizzying this collection might seem, it is actually upholding a Roman Catholic tradition that dates back to at least the second century. Because many of the earliest saints were martyred for their faith, they were viewed as having suffered as Christ did, thus achieving a sublime perfection. Taking the symbolic body of Christ (the Eucharist) at an altar surrounded by the physical bodies of saints, then, became a prized spiritual experience—especially during the Middle Ages, when some relics were believed capable of producing miracles. Churches grew competitive with their reliquary collections and, as demand increased, developed a ranking system. First-class relics are pieces of a saint's actual body: bones, blood, teeth, hair, fingernails, bits of flesh, and, in the case of Jesus, foreskin.[2] Second-class relics consist of a saint's earthly possessions, not only religious accoutrements like robes and rosaries but also more pedestrian items like eyeglasses and combs. Weapons involved in the martyring of saints also fall into this category: spikes, knives, stones, and, in the case of Jesus, thorns from his crown and nails from his cross. Third-class relics, meanwhile, are objects that came into physical contact with first-class relics, while fourth-class relics touched second-class relics. This explains Sister Maximina's ire with the doctor who assembled Mother Julia's IV: he was mishandling primo relics.

We have now reached the final pages of Sister Maximina's photo album. Just a few more images of bedsheets; just a final blur of veils. In a low voice, she remembers how, early the morning of November 21, 1974, she was sent to buy saline. As she rushed about from one *farmacia* to the next, a sister ran up, wide-eyed and urgent. They hurried home together.

First, Mother Julia asked all of the sisters gathered around to pray the rosary. Next, she asked them to sing. Then she didn't ask for anything. Her eyes had been closed for much of the morning, but suddenly they glittered open as they had in her youth, when she prayed to the point of ecstasy, to the point of collapse. She smiled as she greeted her love of seventy-four years. Then she closed her eyes and was gone.

---

2. That's right. Someone saved Jesus's foreskin—or, apparently, foreskins (as, depending on the source, there were anywhere from eight to eighteen enshrined in various European churches throughout the Middle Ages). A friend of mine, David Farley, once spent a year in the Italian hill town of Calcata investigating the mysterious 1983 disappearance of a Holy Foreskin from a church there. Read all about it in his book *An Irreverent Curiosity*.

IT CAN TAKE DECADES—CENTURIES, EVEN—to be deemed a Catholic saint. First comes the obligatory five-year waiting period[3] to allow mourners time to grieve you as well as to improve your odds of an objective evaluation. Then the church dispatches a postulator who scrutinizes your writings, teachings, and other "acts of holiness" and presents the evidence to the Congregation for the Causes of Saints. If deemed worthy of the pope's consideration, you are declared a "Servant of God." To advance on to subsequent stages of sainthood, you must then bring about a miracle (or two).[4]

Mother Julia started performing miracles within a year of dying, says Sister Maximina. The first was for her gardener, who lived with his family in a rural farm community near Toluca. One day, his wife asked their son to mind the little sister while she did the wash. The boy promptly ran off to play. When the mother went searching, she found her three-year-old floating in a ditch, face down, dress bubbled up. The gardener ran to their neighbor's house for a truck, and they sped off to the nearest clinic. But the doctor found no vital signs. He said their child was dead. The parents rushed their daughter to a second clinic, praying all the way. Again, the doctor said she showed no vital signs. The gardener fell upon his knees as his baby girl was laid upon a stretcher. Remembering Mother Julia, he begged for her intercession. He prayed and he prayed and he prayed to her. A hospital aide came to wheel his daughter away. Then one of her toes started twitching.

Such holy acts have earned Mother Julia the title of "Venerable," which is the second of four stages to sainthood. Before she can advance to the next one—"Beatified"—she needs to perform a miracle the church can verify.

The miracle part—that's no problem, says Sister Maximina. She just did another one last week. A Kingsville woman gave birth to a two-pound baby. The doctor predicted she wouldn't last the night, but the mother bowed her head and pleaded for Mother Julia's grace. Now her girl is growing *gorda* and strong.

"But for the church, a miracle has to happen like *that*," Sister Maximina snaps her fingers. "No medicines or hospitals or anything. They need medical records, documentation by doctors and witnesses. And we don't have that yet."

She leans in close. "To tell you the truth," she whispers, "sometimes I think they're picky."

3. This waiting period can be waived by the pope for cases considered urgent, such as those of John Paul II and Mother Teresa (who were canonized nine and nineteen years after their deaths, respectively).
4. Martyrs—or people who die for their faith—are cut a little slack in this requirement. They must generate only one miracle.

FOR FORTY YEARS NOW, Sister Maximina and the other nuns in her convent have been memorializing the legacy of Mother Julia. An infinity of bake sales, clothing drives, bingos, raffles, and casino nights enabled them to buy back the property her old schoolhouse was originally built upon and transform the former tenant's house into a chapel. ("And it wasn't cheap," Sister Maximina says. It wasn't: $50,000.) Now they are raising another $50,000 to open a museum on the site. They plan to hang Mother Julia's photographs there, her pamphlets, her robes, her prayer cards. The saucer she ate her toast upon. The pillow she laid her head upon. The wheelchair in which she took her final spins. They won't display any of Mother Julia's relics there, though—neither her catheter nor her blood. "I don't want to risk losing them," Sister Maximina says.

Not long ago, Sister Maximina marked her seventy-first birthday. The other nuns are even older. It is doubtful any will live to see their Mother Superior canonized. I personally find this crushing, the Catholic equivalent of Kafka publishing only a few stories or Van Gogh selling just one painting before their deaths. Yet the mystically minded are our nimblest border crossers. They traverse both space and time. If these nuns cannot alchemize Mother Julia from a mortal into a divine in this lifetime, they have faith that younger hands will spring up in the next. Which is maybe why—no matter what question I ask—Sister Maximina keeps lifting her palms in memory of that final morning she and her sisters gathered around the bed of their Mother Superior. They didn't just witness the death of that living saint. They served as her aerial midwives.

"And that, mija," she says, rising from the pew to indicate our interview is through, "that is a grace from God I will never repay."

4

The Activist and the Ordinance

SUZIE CANALES WAS CRUISING THE BACK ROADS OF CORPUS CHRISTI with her sister Cindy when something sinister caught their eye off the side of the road. They pulled over and retraced their route, walking against traffic. Though still within the city limits, they were far from any residential neighborhood. Down the knoll and beyond some trees, they could make out a pond-size body of darkness. Cindy ran back to lock the car. *Don't go down there without me!* Naturally, Suzie did.

The water was thick as sludge and the color of scorched coal. It exuded an odor Suzie couldn't place. Like tar, but danker. Cautiously, Suzie stuck a foot upon the mud bank surrounding it. Her shoe sank a few inches, but it seemed firm enough to hold her. What could it be? Given all the oil refineries in the area—Citgo, Flint Hills, Valero—the possibilities were endless. It could be crude oil. Hydraulic fracturing fluid. Drill cuttings. Petroleum waste. She took another step. It could be a benzene bath. A carcinogenic stew. A toxic—

Suddenly, she was submerged in it. Chest-high. A scream escaped. Sludge filled her open mouth and, in her panic, she swallowed. The darkness slithered down her throat. She flailed her limbs until they found something solid beneath. A pipeline of sorts. She clenched it between her feet.

Seeing her sister struggle, Cindy half-ran, half-tumbled down the knoll toward the bank. Finding a grassy spot, she extended her hand. Little sister to big sister. Growing up, these women weren't especially close. Suzie had been the baby for seven years, until Cindy wailed along. Suzie had resented her ever since. Only now, in their forties, were they starting to connect. Now that they had lost their older sister, Diana. Now that they had formed a coalition to fight what might have killed her.

The sisters locked eyes and gripped hands. *On the count of three. One. Two.* But Suzie's hands were too slick. She slipped deeper into the sludge. Cindy screamed with frustration before reaching out once more. Again, she lost her grip. Suzie sank further into the murk. The third try. *This is it.* They stared hard into each other's eyes. *This is too much!* They burst out laughing. That's when Cindy's adrenaline surged. Clutching her sister by both wrists, she yanked her from the swamp. The two stumbled backward onto the mud bank where Suzie lay in a heap. *I swallowed some. I swallowed some.*

As baptisms go, Suzie's was gruesome but fitting. Here was a woman who had dedicated her life to fighting oil companies—and she nearly drowned in one of their pits.

OIL REFINERIES ARE THE FIRST SIGHT to greet you upon entering my hometown. They line both sides of the interstate, a city onto themselves, sprawling across hundreds of acres of land as they rise in towering mazes of pipe and steel, looking both antiquated and futuristic as they emit plumes of smoke into the sky. Their storage tanks are mostly painted hospital green or tenement cream, though some sport murals of dolphins and sea turtles and say things like "Sharing the Earth with Responsibility: CITGO." Powdery black hills of the petroleum byproduct known as "petcoke" abound.

Because they are the backbone of our economy, criticizing these refineries makes you a polarizing figure. If someone doesn't work for a refinery themselves, their tío surely does. So city officials tend to wince when Suzie Canales comes knocking at the door. They dispatch their secretaries to stonewall her. Industry reps are even less diplomatic: they reach for the phone and dial security. The media love her, since she's a reliable source of opinion. She appears on the evening news so often, though, she can seem like a zealot. When I mention my plans to have breakfast with her one morning, a friend asks, "You mean, the crazy one?" But that's why I want to meet Suzie. Like the other Tejanos I've been admiring lately—Santa Barraza, Lionel Lopez, Sister Maximina—she appears to have transcended the typical preoccupations of family, career, and self and channeled her fervor into something greater.

In her early fifties, Suzie has cropped black hair, a prominent nose, olive skin, and melancholic eyes. Her earrings are shaped like bunches of grapes; beaded bracelets adorn her wrists. She has the air of a guidance counselor from an at-risk high school: deeply empathetic, yet a little wary, too. At the Town & Country Diner, she orders the bacon-and-egg special before saying, more to herself than to me, "Where should I begin?"

Suzie grew up on the west side of Corpus Christi—the part of town where multiple generations gather each Sunday for backyard *barbacoa*, where sons tinker beneath their trucks while their fathers shout encouragement from the front step, where young moms put on lipstick before pushing strollers down the street, where every taqueria with a hand-painted sign should be frequented. Suzie's father mostly worked as a construction supervisor, but he also picked up shifts as a security guard at the refineries. When the girls were little, their mom would pack an ice chest full of chicken, rice, and beans, and the family would spread out on a knoll overlooking the industrial park for dinner al fresco. At dusk, the refineries lit up like Christmas—a soft glow of golden lights, the red ones occasionally blinking. Rounding out their neighborhood was a municipal garbage landfill called Greenwood. Though unsightly, it bothered them only when it rained and made the air reek of spoiled eggs. The family would dart about the house sealing windows whenever the sky turned slate, despite the soothing winds.

Suzie fostered two dreams as a child: becoming a nurse and moving to New England (because it sounded regal). She ditched the first plan during her second semester of nursing school when she glimpsed a patient in a hospital bed with a tube stuck up one nostril and bile spilling out the other. That left New England. She married a navy man who promised to take her there. Together, they lived in places like San Diego, Hawaii, and Washington, raising two children along the way. By early 1999, her husband was primed for retirement. They planned to move to Pennsylvania for the millennium.

It happened one morning in February. The kids were late for school. Suzie was watching her son, Jason, tie his shoes when a vision took his place.

"A vision?" I interrupt.

"I don't know if you believe in this kind of thing," she says, then hesitates.

"I do," I say, more forcefully than intended.

She studies me for a moment, then describes how her sister Diana appeared before her, face up and frighteningly still, "as if she were in a casket, but there was no casket." The image lasted just a second before vanishing. For two weeks, Suzie wondered what to do about it. Then her mother called to say that Diana's breast cancer had returned. It was now stage 4 and had metastasized to her brain. Diana was forty-two years old.

Suzie had to make a decision. Should she move her family back to Corpus to help her sister through this? Or should they continue on to New England as planned? Her husband was game for either, but Suzie couldn't shake the feeling that returning to Texas would wreck their marriage. *If I move back home, we'll be over within a year.* This haunted her to the core. Twenty years they'd spent together. Twenty years of seizing each new duty station by storm—camping in the Olympic Mountains, visiting Amish markets in Ohio, and, on quiet nights, playing board games with the kids.

Yet home has a gravitational pull like no other. They returned to Corpus in September. Diana died that December, two days before the millennium. Friends descended upon them, rosaries wrapped around their wrists. *Aye, so young. You know, my niece has breast cancer too.* Neighbors she hadn't seen in years. *My sister died of breast cancer last year. She was even younger than Diana, only thirty-five.* Former classmates from Cunningham Middle School. *I heard three of your sisters got hysterectomies. Me too, and I'm just thirty-eight.* The services blurred into a fog of grief. *Remember my little brother? He's passed. My big brother too. Pues, they had cancer, both of them.*

Before departing the funeral home, the family gathered in a huddle. *Did anybody notice all that talk of cancer?* They had. Someone started compiling a list of the dead. The names quickly filled two pieces of paper. By the time they grabbed a third, they vowed to investigate. First, they ran an ad in the *Thrifty Nickel* and *Adsack*, asking Greenwood residents to contact them if anyone in their family had cancer. Within days, they were fielding calls about teenage girls undergoing hysterectomies. The local CBS affiliate noticed their ad as well and rang them for details. Though nervous about public speaking, Suzie agreed to a slot on the evening news. Soon, her telephone was ringing incessantly. Suzie typed up a health survey she found on the Internet, ran off hundreds of copies, and distributed them to her brothers and sisters.[1] They fanned out in their old neighborhood, knocking on every door, and returned with stories not only of cancer but of birth defects and immunodeficiency diseases as well. People complained of migraine headaches, asthma attacks, nosebleeds.

Meanwhile, Suzie started researching the history of the area and learned that it used to be littered with oil and gas production companies.[2] Pipelines ran right beneath their old neighborhood. She combed through property records. She searched through city planning archives. She flipped through

1. Activism runs strong in this family. One of Suzie's sisters, Juanita, is married to Lionel Lopez, who directs the South Texas Colonia Initiative. "Must have been in the water," Juanita jokes.

2. According to the Port of Corpus Christi's website (http://www.portofcc.com), back in the thirties, Nueces County was home to "3,760 wells in 89 oil fields, within a radius of 125 miles of the port."

volume upon volume of minutes from meetings of the railroad commission, the city council, and the school board, not even knowing what she was looking for until one afternoon at the Office of Planning Commission when she found the minutes from a 1942 meeting devoted to the topic "What to Do with the Negroes?"

I suck in my breath; Suzie closes her eyes and nods.

Their solution: race-zoning ordinances that placed the city's African American population in neighborhoods adjacent to the ship channel, right where the refineries were being built. Tejanos, meanwhile, were zoned by some oil waste dumps that had been repurposed as landfills, including the one bordering Suzie's old neighborhood. Greenwood, it turned out, had been built atop a forty-seven-acre hazardous waste dump. When Suzie and her classmates marched around during band practice after school, they were hovering over covered oil pits.

Although those ordinances have long since been outlawed, many of the families remain. Heavy industry, meanwhile, has proliferated. By the millennium, Corpus Christi was home to six oil refineries plus a slew of chemical manufacturing plants and gas processing units, all located along a fifteen-mile strip called Refinery Row that is surrounded by impoverished neighborhoods of color. These are the borderlines that lurk in every community: class and race.

After city officials dismissed Suzie's health surveys as "anecdotal evidence," she plunged into activism full-time. In 2000, the family founded a grassroots organization called Citizens for Environmental Justice (CFEJ), with Suzie as director. Though she'd never received formal training in college, she learned basic toxicology and epidemiology as well as bureaucratic legalese. She typed up reports. Sent out press releases. Conducted community meetings. Organized press conferences. Appeared on television and radio shows.

Meanwhile, her husband struggled to readjust to civilian life. The kids—now grown—were making their own friends and leading their own lives. Nobody needed him anymore. His days stretched like putty. He sulked in the doorway while Suzie pounded on the keyboard.

You're ignoring me.

What do you mean? I followed you around for twenty years—kept your house, raised your kids. It's my turn now.

Eventually another woman caught his gaze: twenty-eight years old, with two little ones of her own.

You want another baby? All right. I'll give you one.
You can't. You're all messed up.

Contaminated, he meant, from living so long atop a toxic waste dump. They'd always wanted a third child, but after their son, Suzie had a miscarriage. Then another. Then a third. Then a fourth.

Suzie's marriage dissolved nearly a year to the day after returning to Corpus. Stirring her cup of diner coffee, she softens her voice. "People often ask if I could do it all over again, would I have moved back? But I already had that choice. And I decided to do it anyway."

Suzie maintains certain military privileges such as health insurance, but she is on her own financially. CFEJ has received a few grants and she's won some major awards[3] over the years, but nothing to subsist on. Office jobs sap too much time; she needs a flexible schedule so she can attend meetings and press functions and rallies and parent-teacher conferences.

"Parent-teacher conferences?" I ask.

"Oh yes. I'm raising one of my daughter's sons too, so I'm a single mom on top of everything else," she says, shaking her head. "What can I say? It takes a village."

Lately, she's been working at Luby's, a family-style cafeteria. For $7.25 an hour, she dons a blue uniform, tucks her hair inside a net, and scoops salads and gelatins into a tower of bowls that she proffers one by one to an unceasing line of customers. It can be humbling at times, particularly when she gets yelled at for dropping the occasional bowl, but it allows her time to think.

Suzie feels certain that industrial contamination poisoned her sister. The problem is how to prove it. There are plenty of reports about the high rates of birth defects, cancer, and respiratory illnesses in fence-line communities (that is, neighborhoods bordering heavy industries). The refineries themselves admit to releasing millions of pounds of hazardous air pollutants each year. But there has yet to be a widely accepted scientific study that establishes a direct correlation between the two—and attempts to do so have proven contentious. In 2008, for example, CFEJ helped secure funding for a

---

3. Some of Suzie's accolades include the Congressional Hispanic Caucus Institute's Award for Outstanding Achievement in Environmental Justice, the HERO award from the University of Texas Medical Branch National Institute for Environmental Health and Sciences, and the *Texas Observer*'s 2012 People's Friend Award. The honor she finds most gratifying, however, is a 2015 "trailblazer" award from the Corpus Christi League of Women Voters. "Locally, I am considered a pain in the ass, so to be recognized here, well, I just can't believe it. I'm supposed to be the troublemaker!" she told me.

pilot study by the Texas A&M School of Rural Public Health that discovered blood and urine samples collected from residents living along Refinery Row contained 280 times as much benzene[4] as samples from other U.S. residents and 14 times as much benzene as a sample taken from gas station attendees in Mexico. A toxicologist hired by the refinery Flint Hills quickly discounted the study, however, concluding from state data that there was not enough benzene in the air circulating around the refineries to produce such results. After months of getting bombarded by industry personnel questioning the legitimacy of his research, the lead Texas A&M scientist, Dr. KC Donnelly, died of esophageal cancer before he could complete it.[5] His colleagues eventually released a new study revising his figures downward (although a quarter of the people tested still recorded elevated benzene levels). A 2011 federal study then showed "normal" levels of benzene in the community.

But while the correlation between refineries and ill health is considered "ambiguous" in Corpus Christi, the connection between refineries and power is not. Citgo alone has a $345 million annual impact on our local economy. Its spokesman recently completed two terms on our city council, and Valero's senior manager of public affairs got elected in 2014. Flint Hills, meanwhile, is owned by Koch Industries, whose majority stakeholders— Charles and David Koch—have a collective net worth of more than $100 billion and whose political action committee bankrolls scores of ultraconservative campaigns and causes. Koch Industries contributed hundreds of thousands of dollars to Rick Perry during his fourteen-year reign as Texas governor, as did Valero Energy and other oil and gas companies. Perry in turn repeatedly challenged and even sued federal regulators for trying to enforce the Clean Air Act in Texas and appointed a climate change skeptic to run our state's chief environmental agency, the Texas Commission on Environmental Quality.

True, these industries have been fined over the years for violations of various sorts. In 2007, Citgo became the first refinery ever tried and convicted on criminal charges for illegally allowing two huge tanks full of toxic chemicals to vent in the open air for almost a decade. Members of CFEJ and other fence-line residents testified at the hearings, during which prosecutors

4. Benzene, a natural part of crude oil and gasoline found in petroleum products and cigarette smoke, is a known carcinogen. Short-term exposure can cause drowsiness, dizziness, and unconsciousness; long-term effects include leukemia and shrunken ovaries.
5. In an e-mail to Suzie dated December 9, 2008, Dr. Donnelly wrote, "I am having to dodge a number of consultants to CITGO & other refineries who want to shred our study."

demanded $2 billion in fines. But when the federal judge finally handed down Citgo's sentence in 2014—before a crowd of eagerly awaiting fence-line residents, most of whom were minority and many of whom were elderly—he slashed three zeros off that request, fining the multinational corporation only $2 million. And Citgo promptly announced it would appeal.

It didn't take Suzie long to decide she was better off conducting her own studies. After learning how to monitor air quality herself from a non-profit group, she loaded up some buckets, air pumps, and collection bags and started driving around Refinery Row at night and on weekends with her sister Cindy, collecting air samples. Every refinery operates a fleet of security guards with whom the sisters quickly got acquainted: practically every other weekend, one pulled them over for interrogation. Reminding themselves that their father once did this work, the sisters answered their questions respectfully. After all, the guards probably lived in the neighborhood, too.

No, sir, we're not terrorists. We're activists. We're here to monitor air quality.

No, sir, we're not with the TCEQ, *but you can give them a call. They know who we are.*

In March 2006, Suzie and Cindy piled into their Jeep and spent the afternoon monitoring Citgo, which refines upward of 165,000 barrels of crude oil a day. Suzie hoped to photograph Citgo's coker unit, which she says releases a cloud of heavy particulates every eleven hours. CFEJ was on the verge of publishing a new report, and she thought a belching coker would make a good cover. Cindy drove slowly down the public road, snapping photos, while Suzie filmed the facility with her camcorder. A few miles into their venture, a security guard from Valero pulled them over. They explained their project, and he permitted passage. Assuming he would notify other guards in the area, they sped on.

Suddenly, the coker unit erupted. A cloud burst into the sky like a demonic firecracker, maybe four stories high. Within seconds, blackness coated the Jeep, reeking of hydrocarbons. Grit swept into the sisters' eyes, their ears, their noses, their throats, their mouths. Cindy frantically flashed photos while Suzie rolled the camcorder.

Are you getting it, are you getting it?

I got it, I got it.

Lights flashed behind them. Another security guard, this time from Citgo.

Hello, officer. We just got stopped by Valero five min—

Driver's license?

The port police arrived as the security guard called in the sisters' information and detained them. While waiting at the station, Cindy started feeling queasy. She wiped particulate matter off her face. Ten minutes passed. She blew particulate matter from her nose. Another ten minutes passed. She coughed particulate matter from her lungs. Ten more minutes passed. Particulate matter churned in her belly. Twenty minutes passed.

At last, Citgo security returned.

Look, you know who I am. We've got to go. My sister is sick.

Oh no, you're not. You ladies are waiting right here.

Detaining us is illegal and you know it. We're going.

This isn't over.

Days later, the U.S. Coast Guard gave Suzie a call. Apparently, she had been reported to the National Resource Center for conducting "suspicious activity." The FBI wished to interview her: when could she come in?

Suzie stares at me, still incredulous years later. "And I said, bullshit. I'm not going anywhere. They need to come to my apartment full of doilies and see I'm just a little old grandma."

The Coast Guard and FBI arrived on her doorstep, a two-bedroom apartment in a 700-unit complex on the south side of Corpus. She welcomed them in, turned on her tape recorder, and started pulling down the plaques from the walls that recognize her community work. She told them about babies born with holes in their hearts and little girls dying of leukemia. An hour later, they thanked her and left. It seemed prudent to share her side of the story before Citgo beat her to it, so Suzie made a few calls. The front page of the *Corpus Christi Caller-Times* soon featured her headshot beneath the headline ACTIVIST NO TERROR THREAT, FBI SAYS. Once again, her telephone started ringing. She tried to laugh off the "terrorist" charge, but the headline truly haunted her.

"And those readers' comments," Suzie says.

And those readers' comments. They were vicious: "Suzie is an environmental wacko"; "Suzie Canales has done nothing but bring attention to herself for years. She is using these people for her own cause. . . . I wonder how Suzie changes the color of her hair without chemicals"; "If I had to choose between hydrofluoric acid and Suzie Canales, I'd have to go with the acid because it's much less corrosive than she is."

Activism has invigorated Suzie's life, giving it focus and meaning. Yet she thinks this work might be shortening it, too. She has high blood pressure. Tension ripples through her limbs. Like her brother-in-law Lionel, she sometimes looks in her rearview mirror and swears she is being followed. Infamy might be a blessing in this regard: "I've been in the media so much, it would be obvious if something happened to me."

When I ask how she maintains her fervor, she reflects for a moment before citing her spiritual practice. Prayer has become especially rejuvenating for her. She prays for courage. She prays for endurance. She prays for words. "I don't see myself as a smart person. I have no degrees, and so often I am arguing with people who have Ph.D.s."

What Suzie does have is rage. Not just at the refineries but at the government: "They are supposed to be there to protect everybody, and they're not."

So when she received an invitation to attend the first-ever White House Forum on Environmental Justice in November 2010, she rejoiced. At last, a chance to hold the truly powerful accountable. Then she read the fine print: no travel assistance provided. She dialed the White House Council on Environmental Quality to explain that, by definition, environmental justice activists are low-income people of color. How did they expect her to fund the trip? *If you can't afford it, you can always watch it on your home computer, via live stream.* Suzie resigned to do that—until word leaked out in the local activist community. Someone offered her frequent flyer miles; another pledged to cover her hotel. That December, Suzie took a few days off from Luby's, arranged childcare for her grandson, and jetted off to Washington.

The forum was set to begin at 9 A.M., but Suzie was so excited she arrived at 8. Denied early entrance, she was shown to a café across the street where a coffee cost half her hourly wage. Once inside the White House, she was directed to a water fountain in another building when she asked for something to drink. For lunch, she was dispatched to a cafeteria, where she had to buy her own ham sandwich.

"There is no way they do that to all those movie stars and celebrities always visiting!" she mutters.

One hundred activists had gathered that day from across the nation. The sessions, however, featured only cabinet secretaries and other top Obama officials. The first batch devoted ninety minutes to reprimanding the Bush administration for failing to prioritize environmental justice. Not the Obama administration, they crowed: their Plan EJ 2014 would apply cutting-edge technology to study fence-line communities around the country.[6]

---

6. Indeed, the EPA soon awarded $7 million in grants to researchers to study how low-income communities are impacted by pollutants.

This revelation made Suzie squirm. "I kept thinking, that's how they're going to help us? Another study? They're already studying us to death!"

At last, a question-and-answer session began. Many of the activists' hands shot in the air, but only two were permitted to speak before coordinators announced the arrival of the attorney general. Suzie checked the agenda. Only five minutes of discussion had been allotted for dialogue. She looked around the room. The other activists were shaking their heads, clearly upset, but no one was speaking out. Rising to her feet, Suzie maneuvered to the front of the auditorium and stared into the crowd.

"Hi there. My name is Suzie Canales. I traveled here all the way from Corpus Christi, Texas, but I didn't come to be talked to."

The activists turned to her. The White House aides turned to her. The reporters turned to her. The cameras turned to her.

"I came here because I thought I was going to be able to voice concerns. Plans like EJ 2014 are just bureaucratic words on paper. They do nothing for our communities."

The activists nodded in agreement while the aides scrambled about. Suzie concluded her remarks and sat down, trembling. A reporter darted over and crouched beside her. "Ma'am, can we interview you?" Suzie scribbled her phone number as an aide asked to escort her outside. "I hope you're not kicking me out," she said, loud enough for everyone to hear.

People craned their neck as she was shown to the door. The first person she encountered outside was Attorney General Eric Holder. Extending his hand, he asked Suzie how she was doing. "Not very well, sir. I didn't come here to be talked to."

The aide hurried her along to the Eisenhower Executive Office Building next door, where Environmental Protection Agency chief Lisa Jackson awaited on a love seat. Patting the space beside her, she asked Suzie what the EPA could do to help. Suzie handed her CFEJ's newest report: "Why EPA's Attempts to Achieve Environmental Justice Have Failed and What They Can Do about It."

"Instead of giving us more documents that have no value to us, you need to roll up your sleeves."

She asked Jackson to prioritize the needs of communities who live in the shadow of industry, relocating them if necessary. And if the federal government was unwilling to shut down polluting factories, at the very least it should stop protecting them by conducting endless risk assessments and studies. When Jackson rose from the love seat, Suzie asked if she would hear from her again. Jackson promised so.[7] An aide escorted Suzie back to the auditorium. For the rest of the day, conference attendees stopped to thank her, even in the bathroom. Soon after, Suzie generated yet another headline: ENVIRONMENTAL JUSTICE ACTIVIST URGES EPA CHIEF "TO ROLL UP YOUR SLEEVES" AT TENSE W. H. FORUM. Only it wasn't the *Corpus Christi Caller-Times*. It was the *New York Times*.

"I know, I know," Suzie says, laughing for the first time this morning. "I can't believe me sometimes."

BEFORE PARTING WITH SUZIE, I ask about visiting a fence-line community. Of the many to choose from—Hillcrest, Oak Park Triangle, Academy Heights—she suggests Dona Park. Sandwiched between a ship channel, a Valero refinery, and an interstate, its residents suffer a long list of indignities. Gas explosions shatter their windows. Oil slicks their children's wading pools. Their yards (and their urine) have been tested repeatedly for arsenic, cadmium, and lead. They've been instructed by the Texas Department of Health and Human Services to abandon their tomato plants and to let their tangerines rot off their trees. But their biggest concern lately has been the demolition of a nearby ASARCO/Encycle plant, she says.

A multinational corporation with a 120-year history, ASARCO (American Smelting and Refining Company) started smelting zinc in Corpus in 1941. In its heyday, it employed nearly 800 workers who oversaw the production of some 100,000 tons of zinc a year. The national zinc market price plummeted in the seventies, though, around the time the company got sued for violating the Texas Clean Air Act. The plant shut twice in the eighties before getting bought by a subsidiary called Encycle, which turned it into an industrial waste recycling plant. Due in part to a disastrous whistleblower report, it finally shuttered in 2002.

Communities across the nation had similar experiences with ASARCO, which racked up billions of dollars in environmental damages. When the company finally filed Chapter 11 bankruptcy in 2005, it was declared the largest environmental bankruptcy in U.S. history. Some ninety communities in

---

7. Although Suzie has, as of July 2015, never heard directly from Jackson again, she did receive follow-up from the EPA chief via Al Armendariz, a scientist who briefly held the position of EPA regional administrator in Texas. Beloved by activists and scorned by industry personnel for publicly supporting the idea of relocating fence-line communities (among other things), Armendariz took a job with the Sierra Club after causing a scandal for comparing his enforcement strategies to Roman crucifixions.

twenty-one states won a $1.79 billion settlement to clean up their neighborhoods and compensate former workers. But while that sum might sound impressive, it represented less than 1 percent of what claimants requested. It has also grown exceedingly difficult for communities to request remediation because Mexican steel giant Grupo México bought ASARCO in 1999.

A U.S. bankruptcy court and the TCEQ ordered the Corpus plant razed in December 2010, and demolition crews rolled in the following spring. Yet, 600 feet from the facility sits Dona Park, which houses nearly 300 families. Dismantling a polluting plant might seem like a green victory, but according to Suzie, residents worry about the harm the demolition might bring. The EPA has documented asbestos throughout the site, and the whistleblower report that helped sink ASARCO/Encycle accuses it of a host of dirty deeds, including dumping unrecycled hazardous waste into tanks certified as recycled to customers and environmental agencies; keeping 3,000 or more hazardous storage units over the permitted number (500) and then hiding them during inspections (where they sometimes leaked); and accepting waste from the former army chemical warfare depot at the Rocky Mountain Arsenal, which is included on the government's Superfund list of the most hazardous sites in the United States.

As a protection measure, demolition crews agreed to erect ten-foot tarps around the site and to cease working whenever northerly winds—that is, downwind from the plant to the neighborhood—exceed fifteen miles per hour. An engineer, meanwhile, got charged with overseeing an air monitoring system that screens for heavy metals. What Suzie and everyone at Dona Park want to know is, will these precautions be enough?

AS IT HAPPENS, one of my tíos used to work for ASARCO, for fourteen years in fact. Growing up, my cousins and I thought Tío Valentin was a dashing man, always clad in cowboy boots, a cowboy hat, and a silver belt buckle shaped like an *E* for Elizondo. Though he has since shaved off his handlebar moustache and traded in his ropers for Hawaiian shirts, he still drives a mighty big truck. He picks me up one morning in the summer of 2011, and we drive out to his former workplace for a tour.

The last time I visited ASARCO/Encycle, it resembled a cross between Willy Wonka's Chocolate Factory and Chernobyl. It had pea-green cooling towers with enormous fans in their bellies, old casting buildings, rusty water towers, drum shredders, metal silos, orange-brick warehouses whose windows had been shot out, neutralizer tanks, decontamination feed tanks, and colossal caustic tanks that looked like geriatric Tin Men.

A few months into the demolition, many of those structures have now been obliterated to shards and scree. Steel rods protrude from the rubble as if waving in surrender. From Upriver Road, there are no tarps in sight, although we can see mist rising from the snowblowers used to stifle dust flow.

"You see that, mija?" Tío Valentin points out the trademark smokestack, 315 feet of brick and mortar striped red and white like a barber pole. Back in the seventies, he and a buddy used to scale its narrow stairwell to change the lightbulbs on the aircraft warning device. "We'd climb straight up, no safety equipment or nothing. I would be saying Hail Marys and Our Fathers the whole time."

"Why did you do it?"

He blinks in surprise. "We got two and a half times our salary! We had families to feed."

Dismantling the smokestack will be the demolition's toughest operation. Crews plan to first remove its asbestos skin using a "wet-scraping" method. Then they will cut down the tower foot by foot with hydraulic shears, starting from the top so that pieces fall inward to the base of the stack. They plan to build an enclosed scaffold to ensure no asbestos flies away, but as Tío Valentin says, "Good luck with that. It was already falling apart back when I used to work there."

One of his first jobs at ASARCO was feeding sheets of zinc into the furnace for smelting. "It reminded me of hell, all that molten zinc at the bottom of that chute. If the sheets grabbed hold of your shirt on the way down, you'd fall down that chute and die a horrible death. And the foreman down there would be honking his horn because we weren't going fast enough. The zinc was really hot, so we'd use pieces of asbestos as potholders to pick up and stack the bars."

They couldn't use respirators because they kept getting clogged with all the smoke and debris billowing out of the chute. Instead, they tied rags around their faces and tried to duck. "We'd get red rags from the filling station . . . and [by the end of the day] they would be blue."

Tío Valentin was also instructed to dump truckloads of waste into the fields outside the plant, near the ship channel. We drive around to the back of the plant so he can show me where. Overgrown with grass and weeds, the fields are level but raised like an artificial mesa, within a baseball whack of the channel.

"I saw what we were doing and thought, this is not a good idea. There was a slope going right down into the water. I asked the foreman, 'What if it rains?' He looked at me and said, 'Yeah. I wouldn't go fishing down there if I were you.'"

DAYS LATER, I return to Dona Park to meet with a lifelong resident named Billy Placker. A muscleman with a full black beard and a mound of curly hair, he works in construction. Though he is one of the most vocal critics of the demolition, he self-identifies not as an activist but as a "radically saved Christian." His ball cap is emblazoned with GOD IS IN CONTROL across the front and I ♥ JESUS along the bill. When I recount my tío's story about dumping waste by the ship channel, Billy says he not only used to fish out there when he was a boy but swam down there, too.

"We used to go to the end of the plant, where they had a reservoir pumped full of mud that looked like liquid peanut butter, and we would take that and chunk it at each other," he says. "My daddy worked there twenty-three years, and he once took a bunch of pipes from the waste pile and made us a swing set with it. We would go by the grain elevator and shoot rats with BB guns. We could have blown the whole place up!"

He invites me inside his home to continue our conversation. A sign planted in his front yard reads "Save the Dona Park Children from Toxic Soil Contamination Lead, Cadmium, Arsenic, Zinc. Hair and Soil Samples Proved It." As we walk through his front gate, a German shepherd hobbles over, lifting its haunches.

"What's wrong with your dog?" I ask.

"We don't know. It started about five months ago."

As if on cue, the dog turns around, revealing a massive growth covering its entire backside, before limping toward a shade tree. Feeling queasy, I follow Billy inside. Modest on the outside, his house has high vaulted ceilings, black granite countertops, and a Jacuzzi inside plus a swimming pool out back. Billy remodeled it himself and beams when I compliment his handiwork.

I join him and his wife, Pat, in their living room and ask if they've noticed any unusual illnesses in their neighborhood. Billy's son has William's syndrome, a rare neurodevelopmental disorder that includes mental disability, heart defects, and elfin facial features. Two of his grandchildren who live next door have asthma and attention deficit disorder; another has a foot deformity. Turning around on the couch, Pat points at nearby houses through the window. In that house, a lady has cancer. Next door, same thing. Across the street lives a little boy with no ears.

Like many of their neighbors, the Plackers are conflicted about what to do. They have built their dream house here for a fraction of what it would cost in the city. Billy's parents, children, and grandchildren all live within a three-block radius, as do his childhood friends. There is almost no traffic here, so the kids can ride their bikes in the middle of the street. Dona Park is a community that hosts reunions every May, that throws block parties where the whole neighborhood is invited. Families have history here. Roots. How can they give that up to live in some anonymous apartment complex in Corpus?

Yet every time the Plackers step outside their door, they see dust clouds rising from the demolition. They hear bulldozers gnashing their teeth. The last time a northerly wind whirled through, Billy fell into a panic.

"I called the county commissioner, I called the news teams, and then I went over to the front gate where there was a security guard. I said, 'I'm from the neighborhood and that wind is blowing at thirty miles per hour so you have to stop this.' And he said, 'Let me tell you, I don't care what you or TCEQ says about this, this is now the property of federal bankruptcy court, and they say we can demolish it and we will.'"

Billy's black eyes grow round and serious. "Well let me tell you, the Good Lord held me back from jumping that fence and killing him then and there. And the Good Lord didn't allow me to remember what he looked like either, because if I had seen him at a 7-Eleven later that day, I might have killed him there, too."

AT FORTY YEARS, the Gonzalez family has lived in Dona Park longer than almost anybody. Their house is one of the nicest in the neighborhood, with a pine tree in the front yard and an American flag swaying from a pole. The afternoon I visit, Chihuahuas prance about the hardwood floors while Consuelo and Hipolito rest in twin leather chairs. They are visibly fatigued. Two days prior, Hipolito went into cardiac arrest for the third time and has just returned home from the hospital.

They moved to Dona Park as newlyweds in 1970, a few months after Hurricane Celia blew the roof off their first apartment and soaked all their belongings. Hipolito, a Vietnam veteran, repeatedly applied for jobs at ASARCO but always got turned down. He found work at other refineries, though, including a job loading benzene on and off trailers. While grateful to their industrial neighbors for providing them a lifetime of financial security, they too wonder about the personal cost. Their children were plagued with allergies growing up and often had bloody noses. Consuelo has had cysts in her breast, a tumor in her pituitary gland, and liver problems; Hipolito has suffered from prostate cancer and congestive heart failure. They have tried to be as cooperative with the TCEQ as possible, submitting to numerous studies over the years. "We have given them blood. We have given them pee. We have given them soil. And then they come back and want to do it all over again," says Consuelo.

They have already resolved to leave Dona Park. The question is how. Selling their home is no longer an option: its value has slipped from $89,000 to $55,000 in recent years, Consuelo says, showing me documents. Moreover, they don't want to perpetuate the cycle. "You come here because this is what you can afford, and when you leave, your homes are sold to people who don't know what is happening here. Now people are selling their property to illegal immigrants who don't know what their children are facing."

What the Gonzalezes want is a buyout. Such is not without precedence. In 2013, the former mining boomtown of Pincher, Oklahoma, dissolved its charter after nearly all of its residents accepted federal buyouts of their homes and evacuated. But the government usually funds buyouts only of homes built directly over hazardous waste sites, such as New York's Love Canal near Niagara Falls. An industry buyout is much more likely. Closer to downtown, the bulk of the residential neighborhood Oak Park Triangle was bought out in the late nineties, due to its proximity to Citgo. There are rumors about Dona Park neighbors getting bought out over the years, too. One woman is said to have received $200,000 for packing her things and bolting in the middle of the night.

"She has cancer. She won't talk about it, though, per the contract," Consuelo says. "We haven't got to that knowledge to where they would move us out yet."

And so the Gonzalezes wait. As do the Plackers. As do the other holdouts of Dona Park. After bidding Consuelo and Hipolito well, I head back to my car, passing a long line of tiny signs. Warning: Naptha Pipeline. Warning: Hydrogen Pipeline. Warning: Gas-Oil Pipeline. Warning: Benzene Pipeline. Warning: Isobutane Pipeline. Warning: Nitrogen Gas Pipeline.

It is difficult to imagine Corpus Christi without heavy industries. They contribute thousands of badly needed, well-paying jobs to our economy. Four members of my family spent their entire careers at the refineries. So did many of my neighbors. They bought homes with this income. They took vacations with this income. They put children through college with this income. They retired in comfort with this income. It is merely coincidence that I do not rely on this income myself, though I of course depend on other services these refineries provide. They fuel our cars, cool our homes, cook our meals, and enable countless other tasks I'd rather not live without. But why must these privileges come at such a painful human cost? Refineries donate hundreds of thousands of dollars a year to our local nonprofits. Why can't they extend that compassion toward cleaning up their sites or conjuring greener alternatives to help out their neighbors? And why don't more of our citizens demand so?

I STAY IN TOUCH WITH SUZIE CANALES, and in 2015 she shares excellent news. By challenging the companies' permits, CFEJ has negotiated some settlements with refineries that have enabled her spin-off group—the Environmental Justice Housing Fund—to relocate certain residents of the city's fence-line communities. I visit Consuelo and Hipolito Gonzalez that September, about six months after they left Dona Park for a 2,250-square-foot ranch-style home in a manicured neighborhood in Corpus. They proudly show me the walk-in closet of their master bedroom and the marble floors of their kitchen. "I feel like I belong here, like I should have had this since I was married," Consuelo says. "I feel like I deserved it since I was a young girl."

Even so, she maintains ties to her old neighborhood, most recently by helping Suzie review applications of other Dona Park homeowners wishing to relocate. There seems to be enough settlement money to move about a dozen families, yet they have received 126 applications. How, she wonders, will they make such tough decisions?

I return to Dona Park to find the old ASARCO/Encycle site obstructed by a thirty-foot screen that is nearly half a mile long. Through its mesh, I can make out tractors toiling in the dirt, an American flag rippling in the breeze, and, beyond that, the port. The site's new owner, a subsidiary of Plains All American Pipeline, plans to store massive tanks of Eagle Ford crude here—a prospect that so upset Consuelo, she was on the verge of applying for a loan to leave Dona Park on her own when Suzie called with news about the settlement.

Across the street, a taqueria has opened that advertises Jalisco-style seafood in its windows. Hoping its shrimp is caught far from our port, I turn down Vernon Street and drive by the Gonzalezes' former homestead. Soon after they vacated it, the Environmental Justice Housing Fund razed the property so that no new family could take up residence there. Only the lawn remains. A few properties away is another green gap—evidence of a second buyout from the settlement. Yet the neighborhood remains active. Elders relax on front porches. Kids' bikes clutter the yards.

Merging onto the interstate, I feel compelled to stop at Our Lady of Corpus Christi, a nearby Catholic chapel and college. With its Spanish colonial architecture and stained glass windows, it has made a noble attempt at beauty. Its polar blue dome is flecked with golden stars. Yet there is no direction you can turn from which you do not see a refinery. They encircle the chapel like an encroaching army of iron and steel. Rivulets of smoke snake above the sanctuary's grounds. Petcoke clogs the bird feeders. Eighteen-wheelers drown out the wind chimes.

As I pace along the sidewalk between the chapel and the college, wondering if there could ever be a prayer capable of ameliorating any of this, I remember an encounter I once had with a monk here. Brother Michael was his name. In his early twenties, he wore a cowboy hat and a long dark robe. Though he hadn't lived here long, his father worked for a refinery in Beaumont. I asked what he thought of being in such proximity to industry.

"There is this thing called Corpus Christi crud, and it stays in your lungs. I think it is because of the refineries," he said, stroking his considerable moustache. "The ground has been tainted by whatever was here before. We have all these fruit trees, but we've been told we can't eat from them. We've been forbidden to do a garden. We can't grow any food here at all."

I must have looked saddened by this, because he tried to cheer me up.

"But hey," he said with a grin, "flowers are okay!"

With that, he continued on toward the chapel. I retreated to my car, grateful at least one of us would then pray.

5

The Bonder and the Dealer

FALFURRIAS IS A MOSTLY TEJANO TOWN OF 5,000 AN HOUR AND A HALF north of the border. If you've heard of it, it's probably for one of two reasons: its U.S. Border Patrol checkpoint, which boasts one of the highest drug seizure rates in the borderlands, or its shrine to Don Pedrito Jaramillo,[1] a legendary *curandero* who died a century ago. Not for its fine dining. Yet that is why I have come. Though I could happily eat tacos six nights a week, additional options are sought on the seventh. When I complained to a friend about the region's lack of culinary diversity, he told me about a French restaurant that recently opened here. "It's real good," he said proudly. "The chef is from France."

I convince Greg to join me for the drive. Now mid-June, the sorghum has turned rust-red. Sunflowers slump, heavy with seed. Caracaras dot the sky, their necks white, their feathers black, their beaks mango-orange. It is ninety-seven degrees with almost no breeze. Downtown Falfurrias smells like hamburger patties, courtesy of a twenty-four-hour Whataburger. The window of EZ Pawn says WANT CASH? WE'LL WORK WITH YOU! The marquee of the Star of Texas restaurant says EAT HERE OR WE BOTH STARVE.

Eventually we pull into the gravel lot of a mobile home turned bistro with a banner that says ANDRE'S in red block letters. From the outside, it looks as humble as any other local eatery, but as I draw closer, I see the doormat

---

1. For a quarter of a century, Don Pedrito Jaramillo of Los Olmos Creek traveled between the Nueces River and the Rio Grande, faith-healing Mexican families who otherwise had no access to health care. A typical prescription consisted of rubbing onions or mescal across one's belly or drinking a certain amount of water for a nine-day period. According to Santa Barraza, Don Pedrito also helped alleviate hunger by requesting his patients bring in glass jars with lids. Into each, he plunked a blessed grain of rice that replenished the entire jar each morning. His shrine attracts thousands of visitors a year who say a prayer at his tomb and leave behind testimonios, photographs, crutches, and braids of hair as offerings.

is emblazoned with the Eiffel Tower. Inside, black and white photographs of France deck the salmon-colored walls alongside American flags and a Pepsi clock. An elevator version of the theme song to *Titanic* croons from the speakers. I grab a menu from the stack at the counter and, sure enough, between the requisite enchiladas and steaks, find listings for escargot, coq au vin, and boeuf bourguignon.

I glance up to see a woman in a zebra-patterned silk blouse and capris emerge from the kitchen. Her sandals glitter with rhinestones; her wrists sparkle with silver. She could be forty or she could be sixty: her auburn hair, swept into a twist and streaked with blond highlights, betrays no secrets. She strides over to greet us, beaming through dark lipstick, somehow showy and refined all at once.

"Welcome to Andre's," she purrs. Her smoky voice is heavily accented, as if she spent her youth chain-smoking in Parisian cafés. "Will you join us for lunch?"

We take our seats amid ranchers with dolled-up wives and construction workers relaxing with their buddies. Most are downing the $6.99 King Ranch Casserole Special, but I order the bourguignon and Greg opts for the chicken-fried chicken. Both are served on white china plates dusted with parsley flakes. "Enjoy!" she sings out, clasping her hands together.

My bouef has been marinated tangy-tender in wine, but Greg's chicken is the winner: fried as delicately as tempura, then drizzled in a light butter cream sauce instead of gravy. That's sacrilege in this state, but I wind up stealing half of it. When the chef returns to check on us, I barrage her with questions. Sophie Boykin is her name and she is indeed from France—Bordeaux, to be exact—but her father was an ambassador, so they traveled. She worked for the French embassy herself a few years, with stations in Dakar and Rio de Janeiro before she met the Texan who lured her here.

"I absolutely fell in love with Texas. You have the mountains, you have the cactus, you have the cowboy," Sophie says, then pauses. "Once in a while, I have an urge for civilization. I want to be stuck in traffic. So once a year I travel to France for fifteen days, and after fifteen days I am ready to come back."

"What do the locals think of your menu?" I ask.

"They say, 'Escargot, oh my God,' and I say, 'Excuse me, you have to take the slimy creature out of your mind.' I say, 'You eat meat,' and they say yes. I say, 'You eat pork,' and they say yes. I say, 'So don't bother my snails.' It's not like I go to the garden to find them. From Florida I get my shells."

We chat about the restaurant business in between her rotations around the room, where she refills iced teas and settles bills with a calculator and a pen. After the lunch crowd simmers, she joins us at our table with a mug of hot tea and daintily steeps the bag. She is the kind of woman who is so put-together, you can feel a little shabby—until she lavishes you with attention, and then you feel fabulous. At one point she leans in close, as if to reveal something juicy. Greg and I lean in too, despite being the only other people in the room.

"This," she announces, waggling her fingers at the walls, "is just for fun. Our real business is bail bonds."

"Bail bonds?"

"Oh yes, honey," she says, sitting back with a smile.

"Who do you bond?"

"Everybody," she says, taking a sip of Earl Grey. "I get the dumbasses who get paid $250 to drive $1.5 million worth of merchandise to Houston. That is 50 percent of my business. I also get the Avon Cartel. There are six of them. You see them and you think grandmother, but they take a bus from the Valley and hide drugs beneath their clothes."

"But isn't bail-bonding . . ." I search for a nonjudgmental word. "Risky?"

"When I start this business, I was nervous getting a criminal out of prison. But as you go, you see how they cry, these big grown men. I arrest people and they say, 'If I knew you were coming, there would have been a shoot-out.' And I say, 'Too bad, I am here and you are in your underwear and I will tie you up like a pig.'"

She tells us about the time she bailed out a smuggler on a $20,000 bond. Soon after his release, he kidnapped his children from their mother's house and fled. Fortunately, Sophie had given him her 1–800 number for his weekly check-in phone call, so she traced the number to an apartment complex in San Antonio. She drove there one morning, parked her car, and waited. After a time, a curtain rustled, as if someone was peeking behind it. Clad in high heels and a business suit, she tucked her Taser into her purse and knocked on the door. A little girl with big green eyes answered. Her daddy was doing the wash, she said. Sophie instructed her to go into the bedroom with her brothers and sisters and shut the door. Then she turned to see a man walk in, holding a scoop of laundry detergent and wearing only underwear.

"And he says, 'Who are you?' and I say, 'Your worst nightmare, honey. Get on your knees or I shoot you.' I don't have a gun on me—just handcuffs—but he doesn't know that. And he says, 'I need to dress,' and I say, 'No. Where you're going, you'll get a nice new suit. I think it is bright orange.'"

Usually her clients are so surprised to find her on their doorstep, she can handcuff them before they react. But occasionally they bolt, and then Sophie must chase them.

"Once, one jumps out the window and I chase him and leap and he kicks me and I kick him. He almost broke my rib. The judge adds to his bond, and guess who he calls to bail him out? Me. I say, 'Okay, honey, I come get you, and I bring you a stick,' and he says why, and I say, 'So you can beat me with it, because I would be so stupid to get you out of jail again, I would deserve it.'"

When regulations were more lenient, Sophie even used to cross into Mexico to haul back clients who broke for the border. U.S. citizens were easy to deal with: she simply paid off any *federales* she met along the way. Mexican nationals required more finesse. Once, she had a twenty-seven-year-old flee on a $250,000 bond for cocaine. She spent weeks tracking him down and finally found him sitting alone at a bar in a Mexican border town.

"I make him drink two bottles of tequila so he is drunk, then I put him in the backseat and tell the border guards, 'My boyfriend, he's drunk.' And I drive him off to jail."

While she enjoys a good chase now and then, Sophie says the trick to bail-bonding is to eliminate the possibility of flight.

"In court, the judge will say, 'I give you thirty days to take care of your affairs and then you come back for a five-year sentence,' and I say, 'Your honor, in one month my client will be drinking a tequila in Mexico City. I am not paying his $400,000.' So they go to jail immediately instead of in thirty days. That is why I always go to court with my clients."

At that, her cell phone rings. It's Sylvia, her bail bond assistant, calling to ask for her signature. "Want to see my office?" she asks, pulling away from the table.

We pile in to her sleek black Dodge. As she fires up the engine, Rush Limbaugh resounds through the speakers. "He's my favorite," she says, lighting up a Winston cigarette.

We zip along a partially constructed stretch of U.S. 281,[2] dodging bulldozers and bright orange cones as we do, and turn onto County Road 201. Sophie parks by a trailer decked with a wooden sign reading SELINA'S BAIL BOND in a feminine script.

"Who's Selina?" I ask.

---

2. After two and a half years of business, Andre's shuttered in the summer of 2010 because it became nearly impossible for customers to reach the restaurant due to the highway's expansion and its dearth of exits. Sophie predicted the new expressway would ultimately "kill this town, and the only economy will be drugs and illegals." Her husband, Larry, added, "Might as well put a cross at both ends and be done with it."

"The singer," she says, as if it were obvious. "I call it that because the people in this area like her.[3] But I spell it differently."

She swings open the office door. Sylvia, a middle-aged Tejana, is puffing on a Virginia Slims as she interrogates a client over the phone. A framed portrait of Jesus hangs on her wall, a sixteen-ounce Big Gulp sits by her side, and a cheetah-print handbag rests at her feet. Leaning over her desk, Sylvia waves an unsigned check at Sophie, who signs it with a flourish.

Van Gogh prints round out the office decor, along with a manual typewriter and a trashcan heaped with shredded documents. We follow Sophie into her own office, which features family photos and September 11 memorabilia of the Twin Towers. Propped on her long wooden desk are what she calls "my Bibles": the King James Version, covered with a needlepoint reading "When you saw only one set of footsteps, it was then I carried you," and a dog-eared volume of *Texas Criminal Laws*.

"Look at that," Sophie says, pointing at two duffle bags and three pairs of enormous Nike sneakers parked in a corner. "I hold these for my clients. They are black men from North Carolina caught hauling marijuana, forty pounds."

Opening a file folder, she hands over a copy of her bond application. Nine pages long, it is riddled with typos but remarkably thorough, with fill-in-the-blanks demanding everything from credit card and social security numbers to detailed descriptions of tattoos and piercings.

"We see who is married, who has children, and where does Grandma live, because the grandson always run to Grandma," Sophie says. "If it is a girl, Grandma don't care, but if it is a son, she will hide him. She will use her social security check to get him out of jail."

She typically charges clients 10 percent of their bond plus a $500 service fee, or $1,500 for a $10,000 bond. If she has even the slightest doubt about someone, however, she jacks up the rate.

"I charge 30 to 40 percent on the $500,000 bond. I don't go cheap. I charge those assholes the full amount because they'll wind up either in prison or dead. That's their profession."

---

3. Sophie wasn't the first to name something in honor of the Tejana superstar. In the first five months after the singer was shot and killed by the president of her fan club in Corpus in 1995, more than six hundred baby girls were christened Selena. A Corpus mother of twins even altered one daughter's spelling like Sophie did so she could have a Selena and a Selina.

And if they haven't got the money, Sophie charges collateral: mortgages, cars, land. "You know what collateral is best?" she asks, a smile spreading across her lips. "The wife's wedding band."

That's when I notice hers: a shimmering rock colossal even by Texas standards. "So, this is a pretty profitable business?"

"You aren't rich, but you live well," she concedes, noting that at one time, there were sixteen bail bond agencies in Falfurrias, roughly the same number as restaurants. "Ninety percent want to be in this business because of the money. They get money, they spend it spend it spend it, then guess what? Two years later, you get called in court, the client doesn't show up, and you must have that money to pay the state of Texas."

The most Sophie has ever lost on a bond is $40,000, but she says that represents less than 1 percent of her client history. When I ask how she stays so successful, she motions me near.

"When they first call us up, we say, 'Oh honey, no problem, we come get you out of jail right away,'" she says, her voice maple-sweet. "We wait until the deal is done, and then when they come out after forty-eight hours in jail and they are submissive, we get in their face and we tell them the rules." Her voice turns venomous. "I say, 'Do not worry about the cops, worry about me. Like you say in your language, I am *cabrona*.'"

Which is a hard word to translate, but "bitch supreme" is a start. As if to prove it, Sophie slides open the bottom drawer of her desk and removes a Stun Master 100-C, capable of delivering 100,000 volts of energy. "It is like hitting them between the legs," she says, waving it in the air. "They are paralyzed for a while, and you have time to handcuff them. My pistol is in my car."

"What do you *say* when you Taser someone?" Greg asks.

Sophie flashes another catlike grin. "I say, 'I am not here to play game. I get you your freedom. I just ask you to call me once a week and show up for your court date.' If they don't call on Friday, they have Saturday and Sunday for their drinking and relaxing, but by Monday, if they aren't calling, I am a-hunting."

Stun guns aren't the only way Sophie retains her clients. Also on her desk is a package of birthday cards, the kind you buy in bulk at the Dollar Store.

"For your clients?" I ask, sorting through them.

"Oh yes. Some people I have bailed out twenty times. Thirty times. You know when you find a hairdresser you like, and you follow them around? It's like that. Some clients, they won't call anyone but me. Once I was in downtown and this guy with jeans down to his ankles and tattoos everywhere, he comes up and he hugs me and he says, 'This is my bail bond lady!' to all his friends."

The hairdresser analogy is an apt one, as Sophie spends the bulk of her day listening to her clients dish. "They want to tell us all about their life, about how they were abused. Often they are young people who live in a broken home, and Mom or Dad is nonexistent. In this business, you are a social worker. You are a psychiatrist."

And while it's probably not in her business interest to do so, she counsels her clients, encouraging them to go back to school or at least get their GED. More than one parent has called to thank her for straightening out a prodigal son over the years. But for the most part, Sophie says, "When you walk in the door, you must take out your heart and put it in the drawer. If you don't, you can't make it in this business."

Sophie's cell phone rings again. Her husband, Larry—a watermelon grower turned bail bond agent turned French restaurateur—needs her back at Andre's. Sophie gives us a lift there, but after we say our good-byes, I ask Greg to return so we can poke around. As we coast down County Road 201, I see that Sophie has chosen a prime piece of real estate. Several other bail bond agencies dot the road—Cristellas Bail Bonds, Apex Bail Bonds, Arnoldo Mireles Bail Bonds—with billboards advertising many more. A quarter mile later, the reason comes into view: Brooks County Detention Center. Through its double perimeter security fence, I can make out men in bright orange suits exercising. At one point in our conversation, Sophie declared that 90 percent of South Texans live with drug money. "You take a drug dog and go to any bank in South Texas and it will go crazy. There is drug on every dollar."

None of this is news, of course. This is practically the only story we ever hear about our southern borderlands. But confronting it so viscerally makes me realize I have a decision to make. Is it more ethically responsible to report our region's most notorious story—or to refuse to perpetuate its stereotypes and instead portray the artists, activists, and faith keepers who salve our many wounds? I don't know the answer to this. But staring out at the inmates, whose tattoos are visible even from the road, I decide I should at least try to talk to one—to complicate the stereotypical narrative, if nothing else.

ONE BALMY NIGHT IN SEPTEMBER 2006, the Mexican drug cartel known as La Familia dispatched twenty masked men to a discotheque in the Mexican state of Michoacan. After summoning everyone's attention by turning off the music, they ripped open a sack and rolled five human heads[4] onto the dance floor. Then they escaped into the night, leaving behind a note that read, "La Familia does not kill for money. It does not kill for women. It does not kill the innocent. Only those who deserve to die. Know that this is divine justice."

Although Mexico's *narcos* had long been stealing headlines for their brazen acts, this was the event that catapulted them into international infamy. When President Felipe Calderón got sworn into office three months later, he declared war on the cartels, dispatching tens of thousands of soldiers[5] to key regions of the country to hunt them down. The narcos responded with unthinkable cruelty, dismembering victims appendage by appendage on videotapes they mailed home to families. One cartel sewed a man's face onto a soccer ball; another paid an underling[6] $600 a week to dissolve victims' corpses in barrels of lye. In time, it was no longer salacious enough to torture a victim to death. Cartels had to eradicate the entire family. Thugs started showing up at weddings and funerals and blasting everyone in sight. Then they took on entire communities. In August 2010, a cartel executed seventy-two undocumented immigrants on a ranch 100 miles from Texas. Their crime: refusing to enlist as hired assassins. Two years later, forty-nine mutilated bodies were found on the side of a highway near Monterrey. Two years after that, forty-three college students in Guerrero vanished and are widely believed to have been killed, burned, and dumped in a river by a criminal gang with the assistance of local police and by orders of the mayor and his wife.

At least 60,000 people have died of drug-related violence since Calderón took office in 2006.[7] Tens of thousands more have been carjacked, kidnapped, or beaten or have "disappeared." The cartels spare no one, slaying policemen,

4. Whose heads? Some drug dealers who dared cross the capos of La Familia, it seems. Kidnapped the day before from an auto mechanic's shop, the dealers' heads got sawed off with bowie knives while they were still alive.

5. At first, the Mexican Army was considered less corruptible than local or federal police, but stories soon emerged of soldiers demanding bribes at checkpoints, tormenting neighborhood teenagers, raping village women, fighting officials for a share of drug profits, and murdering innocent civilians. See Cecilia Ballí's January 2012 coverage in *Harper's* for more about the terror the army incited in Juarez (and beyond).

6. He has since made narco history as El Pozolero, or "The Stew Maker." Authorities believe he dissolved some 300 bodies over a ten-year period for drug lord Teodoro Garcia Simental.

7. That, at least, is the number most commonly cited by U.S. media and groups like Human Rights Watch. Statistics vary from 47,000 to more than 100,000. Given some cartels' predilection for burying their victims in secret graves while bribing officials to look the other way, we will likely never know the true death toll.

soldiers, judges, gubernatorial candidates, and state legislators alike, often in daylight in the public's view, as with the mayor from Michoacan who got stoned to death in the middle of the street. Journalists who dare cover these crimes are targeted, too. According to the *Dallas Morning News*, one gets assaulted every twenty-six hours, either by a criminal gang or by the government,[8] making Mexico one of the world's most dangerous places to be a journalist.

When I moved to Mexico in January 2005, I also found it to be a land of superlatives: it had the warmest people, the tastiest food, the most exhilarating landscapes, and the greatest stories of any place I had ever visited. I returned to the United States that August but vowed to move back soon—until gory headlines started filling my inbox. With each passing month of Calderón's presidency, the country seemed to descend further into chaos. In April 2010 I briefly visited Cuernavaca, a colonial city that had recently lost its capo-in-residence, Arturo Beltrán Leyva,[9] and was thus a ticking bomb. Two mornings after my arrival, I opened the newspaper to learn that the bullet-riddled bodies of two young men had been strung from an overpass just a few miles from my hotel the night before. Their photographs splayed across the front page: one man hooded and bare-chested, the other with his jeans puddled around his ankles. The week after I left, police evacuated the city's main plaza because of a bomb threat. By summer, the whole city was on lockdown after dark.

In his authoritative book *El Narco: Inside Mexico's Criminal Insurgency*, Ioan Grillo traces the origins of this drug war turned civil war to enterprising Chinese immigrants in the late nineteenth century. Before boarding steamships for Sinaloa to work on the railroads, Chinese laborers slipped poppy seeds into their satchels. Though most smoked the opium

8. Depending on which organization you consult and the criteria it uses, the number of Mexican journalists who have been murdered because of their work ranges from 50 to more than 100. According to Mexico's National Human Rights Commission, 90 percent of these crimes go unpunished. The situation has grown so dire, Freedom House now designates Mexico a "Not Free" nation in its annual "Freedom of the Press" reports, along with countries like Russia, China, Cuba, and Saudi Arabia.

9. Arturo ran the Beltrán-Leyva Cartel along with his brothers until December 2009, when his luxury apartment in Cuernavaca got surrounded by hundreds of special forces from the Mexican Navy. After a ninety-minute siege, Arturo, six of his aides, and a navy sailor lay dead. Hours after the sailor's funeral, gunmen burst into his family's home and revenge-killed several of his mourners, including his mother.

themselves, a few recognized its market potential. Documents show Chinese-Mexican syndicates trafficking opium into California through Tijuana as early as 1916. Jealous of their surging profits, native Sinaloans soon ran the Chinese out of town and seized their trade, growing poppies in isolated mountain ranges and smuggling the gum across the border. The trade grew briskly: Grillo cites a popular theory that even the U.S. government purchased Sinaloan opium to make morphine for shell-shocked soldiers during World War II. Mexico's marijuana production, meanwhile, skyrocketed in the sixties when hippies started driving their VW vans to border towns to load up on reefer. Nixon finally declared global war on the national habit in 1973 with the creation of the Drug Enforcement Administration, which employs more than 5,000 special agents in sixty-plus countries today. Despite those efforts, drug users in the United States currently blow about $100 billion a year on cocaine, heroin, marijuana, and meth. Analysts say as much as 40 percent of that profit goes straight back into the cartels' coffers.

So who are these narcos? Even the most famous capos started out as barely literate campesinos whose farms could hardly feed their families. Either that, or urbanites whose major employment option was slaving on a production line at a sweaty maquiladora for twelve hours a day. Narcos are typically offered a cell phone, a pair of sunglasses, and an Uzi on their first day on the job. Not only that, they are exalted in virtually every aspect of Mexican culture, from TV, magazines, and movies to a musical genre known as the *narco-corrido*, which lyricizes their triumphs in catchy ballads. Narcos even have their own pantheon, including a terrifying female spirit known as Santa Muerte (Holy Death) who resembles a fanged grim reaper wielding a scythe.[10] With nearly half of all Mexicans dwelling in poverty, it's not hard to see narcos' allure—especially for the youth population known as "ni-nis," short for *ni estudian, ni trabajan*, those who neither study nor work. Mexico has roughly eight million of those. Tack on the fact that criminal groups often operate with the complete complicity of

10. The champion of the dispossessed, Santa Muerte is revered not for her holiness but for her ruthlessness. While some scholars trace her prominence to the 1994 devaluation of the peso, others date her back to the Aztec goddesses Coatlicue and Micetecacihuatl. Santa Muerte demands total devotion from her followers and frequent offerings of candy, liquor, and cigars. When the Mexican government started destroying her public altars in 2009, due to her link to the cartels, her adherents took to the street in protest. Read more about her cult in Desirée Martín's *Borderlands Saints*.

some of Mexico's government officials,[11] law enforcement, the military, and the occasional corrupted U.S. official, and the question becomes who is *not* a narco?[12]

Though in-fighting has led to a number of splinter groups in recent years, Mexico watchers generally recognize six major drug cartels, each with its own geographical turf: La Familia Michoacana/Knights Templar,[13] the Juarez Cartel, the Beltrán-Leyva Organization, the Sinaloa Cartel, the Gulf Cartel, and the Zetas. All are fearsome, but the Zetas constitute a category all their own. Cofounded by a special forces commander of the Mexican Army to serve as a paramilitary arm of the Gulf Cartel, the Zetas syndicate built its ranks by seducing highly trained soldiers away from their platoons with the promise of glory. It is the cartel that introduced terror tactics like mass kidnappings into the war. That brags about having developed forty-three ways to kill a man in under three minutes. That counts among its leaders Miguel Ángel Treviño Morales[14] (aka "Cuarenta," or Forty), who purportedly likes to remove victims' still-beating hearts and take a bite.

According to the DEA, the Zetas Cartel is also one of the syndicates operating in Corpitos.

---

11. One of the more outrageous cases of government corruption: in 2008, Calderón's own drug czar was charged with accepting $450,000 in bribes from cartels. Per *month*.

12. Corruption, of course, doesn't halt at the borderline. In the past two decades, five sheriffs from the Texas Rio Grande Valley have been caught doing something nefarious, and there have been at least 140 convictions in corruption investigations involving U.S. Customs and Border Protection since 2004. In December 2012, an anti-narcotics police squad from the Valley got busted for reselling the dope they confiscated. People have grown so shameless, the Justice Department recently created an FBI task force to further investigate practices of police units as well as hospitals, courthouses, and school boards in the Valley, according to National Public Radio.

13. Under the reign of Nazario Moreno González (aka "El Más Loco"), La Familia obtained formidable power and cast a quasi-religious influence. After kicking out all but his most loyal henchmen, González rebranded the cartel the Knights Templar—which journalist Ioan Grillo once described as a bunch of "flesh-eating meth traffickers"—and wrote his own bible for his followers. He so brutalized his home state of Michoacan that citizens banded together in *autodefensas*, or self-defense squads, and fought back. Their saga is chronicled in Grillo's 2016 book, *Gangster Warlords*.

14. Along with two aides, eight guns, and $2 million cash, Morales finally got captured in his pickup truck after visiting his newborn child in July 2013, with nary a bullet fired. As of August 2015, he was still in prison, but given the vanishing acts of other capos via laundry baskets and under-the-shower tunnels, he might not be there for long.

ONE OF THE GREAT GEOPOLITICAL mysteries of the twenty-first century is how the United States—the chief consumer of Mexico's drugs—has avoided the bloodbath across its border. Juarez, a city that tallied more than 3,000 murders in 2010,[15] is only a slender river away from El Paso, which registered 5 homicides that year (its lowest since 1965). Four of the biggest U.S. cities with the lowest rates of violent crime are all in border states: San Diego, Phoenix, El Paso, and Austin. But this low death toll doesn't mean we're not affected by the violence. A friend of mine from Pharr, Texas, has a tío who loves to fish. Early one morning, he was wading through the river with his nets and poles when some beefy Mexicans wielding automatic weapons called him over. They were Zetas, they informed him, and this was their new port. They suggested he go home and not return. He hasn't. My Mexico-born friends, meanwhile, are literally begged not to come home for Christmas. *It's too dangerous,* their mothers say. *Stay in El Norte, where we know you are safe.* Hear enough stories like these, and eventually they take a psychic toll.

When I was a child, piling in the Chevy and driving to Mexican border towns like Progreso and Nuevo Laredo was my family's favorite way to spend a Sunday. We'd cross the border for no-prescription-necessary penicillin when one of us fell sick. We'd cross the border for *cajeta,* a goat-milk spread that tastes like caramel, when one of us craved something sweet. We'd cross the border before birthdays to buy piñatas shaped like Wonder Woman. We'd cross the border for salt-rimmed margaritas and bottles of tequila with little worms floating inside. We'd cross the border to feel Mexican. We'd cross the border to feel American. Now, we never cross. Neither does anyone else we know. The writer Chimamanda Ngozi Adichie has spoken passionately about "the danger of a single story," and how it can reduce an entire people into a stereotypical caricature. Even worse is when a community internalizes a single story about itself. In this sense, the drug war has erected a border wall that surpasses anything Congress has constructed, only in reverse. Far too many of us have stopped crossing the border to find stories of our own.

I DON'T USE DRUGS MYSELF. I was too straight to try them in high school, and by the time I moved into a co-op in college where housemates displayed their bongs on their windowsills, I suffered delusions of running

---

15. That was the last year Juarez earned the dubious distinction of "murder capital of the world." In 2011, its homicide rate dropped by more than 1,000 deaths. The Honduran city of San Pedro Sula then assumed the title.

for political office someday. (That's the Clinton administration for you.) A cousin had also succumbed to addiction, and I'd seen the toll it had taken on her family. What truly turned me off drugs, however, was dating a Colombian whose parents paid hefty bribes to dissuade cartels from turning their coffee plantation into a coca farm. After traveling to southern Colombia with him and witnessing the destruction that U.S. drug use had wreaked on a more global scale, I became one of those vitriolic Chicanas who, if offered a joint, will snap, "Sorry, I don't smoke the ashes of my people."

So after resolving to talk with a drug dealer, I'm at a loss where to begin. Judging from their (juiced up) cars and (gangster) tattoos, they don't seem to be in short supply in Corpitos. I'm pretty sure one lives down my parents' street. But journalists like Alfredo Corchado[16] have already written eloquently about the serious narcos out there—and received death threats in the process. I'd much prefer a small-town dealer who'd be willing to share his story over chai lattes in a well-lit café and then never contact me again.

I start asking around.

"Anybody know a good dealer?"

"Pot or coke?"

"Uh, I'd like to talk to them, actually."

"_____"

I do hear some wild stories this way. At one dinner party in Corpus, a middle-aged Tejana surprises us all by revealing that her father, three of her cousins, and two of her tíos have all dealt drugs at one time or another. They stopped when one tío left to pick up a load in Mexico five years ago and never returned. "I think he's dead," she says flatly, "but I don't care, because he sent someone to my house who held a gun to my son's head."

Six men invaded her home one night and ordered her entire family down on the floor. They held one gun to her head and another to her son's while they searched the house for nearly an hour, overturning every drawer. Then they warned them never to tell the police. "We're from Roma," they said—the same town where her tío once worked.

Yet she has no contacts to offer either.

Around this time, a story breaks in a nearby town that generates headlines across the state. The owner of a popular taco stand has been arrested

---

16. For a soulful memoir about the tragedy of covering Mexico's drug war as the son of migrant workers, read Alfredo Corchado's 2013 book, *Midnight in Mexico*.

for selling cocaine by rolling baggies of it into his customer's taquitos.[17] This intrigues me for a couple of reasons. First, what a clever front! Drive-thru taco stands have lines twelve trucks deep in South Texas. You could pass all matter of paper-bagged goodies through those windows, and no one would suspect a thing. Second: the dealer is exactly my age and has a family to boot. That doesn't de facto put him in the latte category, but, well, there's hope.

Deciding I could use some protection, I convince Greg to join me. Six days after the dealer's arrest, we arrive at his town at high noon. Yard signs either praise Jesus or forbid trespassing. Houses tilt, as if drowsy. About a third of the residents here live below the poverty line, which probably explains the appeal of dealing. Just a month ago, a sixty-six-year-old man got busted selling heroin and cocaine out of a home health care agency right on Main Street. Driving by, I notice the business's motto: BECAUSE THERE'S NO PLACE LIKE HOME.

To my surprise, the taco stand is open for business. Housed in a white cinder block building, its name is painted across the front in large letters. Security grills cover its windows, and a white Blazer is parked out in front. We walk inside to find five empty tables and a mural of a taco wearing a sombrero engulfed in flames. A handmade sign says RESTROOM FOR CUSTOMERS ONLY. A computerized one reads SHOES & SHIRTS REQUIRED; BRAS & PANTIES OPTIONAL.

The man working the counter—or rather, the service window that obstructs the register and the kitchen from view—is a stocky Tejano with a moon-shaped face. He looks vaguely familiar, but I don't contemplate how. I haven't eaten breakfast yet, so I can think only of food. Though the menu is printed on the Pepsi marquee above, I initiate conversation by asking what kind of taquito fillings he's offering today. In a voice that's bored but polite, he rattles off the options: bacon, chorizo, sausage, chicharrón, Spam . . .

"How about a fifty?" I ask brightly. Until last week, that's how customers requested a side of cocaine along with their guacamole here, according to the *Corpus Christi Caller-Times*.

He looks at me in surprise, his mouth a perfect O. "We don't got anymore of that," he sputters. "The health inspector came and cleared it out."

17. Boringly called "breakfast tacos" outside South Texas, taquitos are hot, fluffy tortillas stuffed with all manner of morning goodness (eggs, meats, potatoes, nopales, refried beans, cheese), slathered in salsa, rolled in aluminum foil, and rarely sold for more than $2.50. In high school, "taquito runs" were our teachers' most effective form of bribery.

"I'm surprised you reopened so fast."

"We were able to open on Friday," he says, craning his neck to look back at his kitchen. "What kind of taquito did you want?"

"Potato, egg, and cheese, please. So, how long have you been here?"

"A long time," he says, then ducks out of sight.

I return to our table to find Greg scribbling in my notebook, "I think that guy is the owner!!!"

Clearly I am not cut out for interviewing *narco-trafficantes*. It hadn't even occurred to me that he could have gotten out of jail so quick. Never mind that I had just learned from Sophie that, if you've got a $35,000 bail (as he did), you'd only need to post $3,500 plus a $500 deposit to walk free, and surely any respectable dealer is capable of that. Now I've pissed him off. He'll never agree to chai lattes with me.

When my taquito is ready, I send Greg to retrieve it and unwrap it with caution. Supersized and piping hot, there is a square of bright yellow cheese in the middle. Greg laughs as I douse the eggs with salsa for courage. After a few bites, I return to the service window and call out the dealer's name. A Tejana appears. Thirtyish with long black hair, she has his name tattooed in Gothic script across her chest.

"He's busy right now," she says, her eyes narrowing.

"I can wait."

She says it's not a good idea for him to talk to anyone "on account of what happened," so I write my phone number on the back of my receipt and depart for the nearest taqueria to debrief with Greg. Our new waitress is so bubbly, I ask what she thinks of her town's latest bust.

"People try to make life easy, but it goes to trash fast," she says. "They could have made it, real slow, but they could have made it, *pero* no, they wanted to do it the fast way."

I ask if she knows him personally, and she says of course. "They're our customers! We have all the drug dealers in here."

From there, we move on to the police station, an orange brick building without a single window. I press the intercom and ask to speak with someone. A sergeant with a goatee retrieves us. He escorts us down some hallways and up some stairwells and delivers us to the chief of police. Seated behind a wood desk, he so meets your expectations of a small-town Texas sheriff—cowboy hat, caterpillar moustache, prominently displayed gun and badge—you half-expect him to laugh and say, "Gotcha!" His office features two computers, a flat-screen TV, a new iPhone just out of the box, and a hanging cross. Elevator jazz echoes through the speakers. A detective joins us for the interview.

"They were good tacos," the sheriff attests. "I've eaten there quite a bit. I liked the *barbacoa*. But you can't run a business and do that off to the side."

They tell me how they launched a six-month investigation and, on the day of the sting, dressed a dozen officers in SWAT gear and equipped them with machine guns.

"We sent in two officers to have some tacos, and they acted as the eyeballs for the team before they showed up," the sergeant says. "We were able to get to him before he destroyed the evidence. We'd been told by an informant that he'd try to throw the coke in the grease."

"If they throw it anywhere else, we'll go on after it, like the toilet, but we can't go after it in the grease 'cause we'll get burned," the detective explains.

They found eleven baggies of coke inside a Folger's coffee can, along with some Altoids. Then they went to the dealer's house and found an additional 11.2 grams. I ask if cocaine is the drug of choice out here.

"What we have here is coke, heroin, and marijuana," the sergeant says. "It's unusual to find crack. We've only had two cases in the last three years."

"What about meth?" I ask. A *Breaking Bad* devotee, I thought I had recognized some telltale signs of meth labs while driving around.

"Meth is a white man and white lady's drug," the detective says. "Over 90 percent of this town is Hispanic, so we deal with what Mexico brings in. If you drive four miles north, you'll see meth, but Hispanics just won't take it."

"Why do so many people here sell in the first place?" I ask. "What started all of this?"

A steak knife has surfaced on the sheriff's desk. Fiddling with its blade, he muses, "We used to never lock our house here. You could hang your guns on the gun rack in the back of your truck and no one would touch them. Then things started going downhill. People started breaking in, dealing drugs. If you don't have a job, you got to do whatever it takes to get drugs. Men will steal; women will do prostitution. It is an ongoing battle, and I see nothing in the world changing to stop that. I have friends who got hooked on drugs. Even a police officer did. One used to work at our department, got out, and started selling. They lost their job, their career, their family."

After a sober moment, the sheriff perks up. "But Chinese investors are coming down!" Cracking open a DVD case, he pops a disk into the player to show us a promotional video. Smiling Chinese men in business suits emerge on the flat-screen TV. He presses every button, yet he cannot get the DVD to play. Sighing, he turns around and asks if there is anything else I need to know.

FOUR DAYS LATER, a text pops up on my phone: "Wondering if journalizing my life from a humble straight arrow life to the complex life it became has strong footing for publishing? Text me back."

I do, and he agrees to an online chat a few nights later. Nervous about his upcoming court date, he consents to some background questions but nothing that could compromise his case. I learn that he was raised in a "close to 100% Mexican" neighborhood called La Casa Blanca, or The White House. When I ask if that irony was intended, he writes that the name probably derived from the fact that white was the cheapest house paint available, so that's what everyone used. His parents were migrant workers who followed the seasons to Colorado and New Mexico, picking cotton, cucumbers, and onions. Though he escaped this grueling work himself, most of his six siblings did not. He graduated high school with honors and completed sixty hours of community college, then took some leftover financial aid and opened his taco stand in 1994. He awoke each morning at four to warm up the grill and sold about 200 a day.

"Have had up and downs but proud to say I pay for my kids doctor visits and never food stamps, etc.," he writes.

I ask for a proper sit-down interview, but he says we must wait. So I do. A few months later, I return to his taco stand to check in. He still can't talk, he says, and with reason: I soon learn from the newspaper that he has pled guilty to drug possession and gotten sentenced to eight years' deferred probation and a $2,000 fine. I allow half a year to pass, then return. His taco stand has been replaced by another. I walk inside and introduce myself. The new owners want nothing to do with me.

Next door is a barber shop. A client wearing tight black jeans and cowboy boots is on his way out, so I allow the barber a moment's rest before entering. A duct-taped barber chair stands in the middle of the room, surrounded by couches, end tables, television sets, barbells, and posters of Bruce Lee and Selena. Emerging from the storage room that doubles as his bedroom, the barber stops in his tracks. In his forties, he has a neatly trimmed moustache, pretty blue eyes, and deeply engrained laugh lines. Every curl on his head appears to have been individually coifed.

"What, are you going to hold me up?" he jokes, seeing me cowering in the doorway. "Do you want all my money? I'll get it right here."

When I mention my research, he grows even more animated. "I don't know much about him, but you could write about me! I'm full of stories. I once chopped off a guy's head and hung it right here." He points at a long, thin stain streaming down the cinder block wall beneath an old sickle. Then he pulls out a machete from behind a cabinet and waves it above his head. For a half second, there is a quarter-chance he could be serious. Then he bursts out laughing.

"I been in four movies already!" he says, pointing to a promotional poster for a flick called *Honor Sin Patria*.

Once, he was driving through the desert with a producer and a few other actors in Nuevo Leon, he says, scouting for backdrops, when two trucks pulled them over. Four Zetas stepped out holding automatic rifles. They made them lie in the dirt and asked what the hell they were doing.

"I started to think, man, I would rather go down fighting than just get shot in the back of the head, so I was about to jump one of 'em, but then the producer started talking about how we were just making a film."

After helping themselves to a camera and a handful of DVDs, the Zetas sent the crew on their way.

"They are like gremlins," the barber says. "You do away with one and another pops up. Now what they are doing, they aren't getting their own hands dirty, they are hiring people to do it for them. They don't actually live around here, though. They are just passing through."

I ask about his former neighbor, and he says he wasn't surprised to learn about his side business.

"A lot of people have asked me if I want to deal right here too. I wouldn't even have to buy it myself. They would front me the drugs and I would just keep the profit. But I always say no. I don't even *do* that stuff, and that's the truth. I have got a lot of future ahead of me. I've got a new girlfriend."

He proceeds to tell me all about her—how in high school he walked her home one day, and how she moved to Fort Worth the next. How they never said good-bye. How twenty years passed, during which they married other lovers and raised families of their own, but how a few weeks ago, she returned to town for a funeral and they ran into each other at the cash register at Taqueria Guadalajara and learned they had both recently gotten divorced.

"She said, 'Let's start saving a quarter a day so we can be together,' and I said, 'Baby no, I'm going to save a dollar a day. No, I'm going to save five dollars a day!' Then I thought about it and said, 'No, I'm going to save *twenty* dollars a day.'"

"Doesn't that make dealing kinda tempting?"

He shakes his curls. "I've saved a thousand dollars already. I bought her a promise ring, too. Real pretty, with a heart on it."

AFTER MUCH INDECISION, I take a deep breath and drive to the dealer's house. (His address was published in the newspaper.) It is a modest neighborhood of feral cats and dented cars. A man's black belt is lying in the dealer's yard. Trying to conjure Sophie's chutzpa, I walk up to his door and ring the bell. The curtain rustles. I wait an unnervingly long time before ringing again. His partner opens the door. No need for introductions. She remembers me.

"He's asleep," she says.

"It's 12:15."

"He works nights now."

Our eyes clasp in a staring contest. Just when I start thinking she's not the kind of woman who'd take lightly to her man chai-latte-ing with another, she blinks and blurts some details. "He got locked up for ninety days, so I had to shut down the business. It was too much to take care of with our son. I couldn't keep up with everything."

At that, an eight-year-old appears, cuddling a small dog.

Feeling like a bully, I blink too. Handing her my business card, I ask her man to call me.

He doesn't.

This is when I should have found myself a new dealer. I mean, really. If there are drugs on every dollar, how hard could it be? But, well, you know how when you find a bail bonder you like, you follow her around? Stories are like that, too. And so I continue checking in whenever I'm in town, every six months or so. He keeps promising he'll meet me, even pinpointing a particular week, but when the date rolls around, he falls silent. After three years of back-and-forth, he stops responding to my e-mails and phone calls altogether, though he occasionally still "likes" my Facebook posts. Judging by the photos he uploads on social media,[18] he appears to be working for an oil refinery now. That would be the first question I'd ask, should he ever grant me an interview: is there any intended irony in *that*? But I already know the answer. It was the next best-paying job in town.

---

18. Speaking of social media, according to Sophie, it's a bail bonder's best friend. Here's her strategy for finding an errant client: "Say I look for John Shmuck. I see on Facebook he tells Susan, 'We go to party at 7 P.M.' So we go pick them up. We say, 'You have a free taxi!' It is better than GPS."

6

The Agents

THE CANOPY HOVERS ABOVE THE CHECKPOINT LIKE A MAMMOTH prehistoric bird, blocking the brutish sun but trapping in everything else. Like exhaust fumes. Like noise. Like pigeons. Every day, 13,000 vehicles barrel through this station on the outskirts of Falfurrias. That's 13,000 injections of carbon monoxide, 13,000 growling engines, and 13,000 interrogations followed by 13,000 responses. And lethal amounts of pigeon shit.

U.S. Customs and Border Protection (CBP) operates more than a dozen permanent checkpoints in the Texas borderlands, but this particular one located seventy miles north of Mexico is known as the "chokepoint." When I visit one sweaty summer morning, agents had already seized 177,657 pounds of illegal drugs there that year.

"We get more cocaine than any other checkpoint in the nation, and the second most marijuana," Cabrera says. He is my handler today, a policeman turned Border Patrol agent turned public affairs officer. Flat-topped and mustachioed, he is wearing the trademark patrol uniform of sunglasses and jalapeño greens. "It might seem like we're in the middle of nowhere out here, but we're in the middle of everything."[1]

We're parking his Chevy Tahoe stamped CUSTOMS AND BORDER PROTECTION at the checkpoint station. "We've gotten a little rain," he says as he points at the nearby brush climbing nine feet high. "Thank God for GPS. All that brush looks the same. If anybody says they've never gotten lost, they're lying."

Three lanes of eighteen-wheelers, buses, trucks, campers, SUVs, minivans, sedans, Jeeps, hatchbacks, and motorcycles line up twenty-deep

---

1. Smuggling doesn't traverse a one-way street. Approximately 250,000 U.S. guns are covertly shuttled across the border into Mexico each year, meaning we are essentially arming the drug cartels ourselves.

at the checkpoint, their engines reverberating beneath the canopy. Between the honking of horns and the barking of the K-9 patrol, a migraine seems imminent. We duck inside the station, which has a barebones military feel. Front and center is a cell capable of holding seventy-five people inside its transparent walls. It's empty at the moment, but a dozen computer terminals surround it as if a scientific experiment were under way.

"Not too busy, are you?" Cabrera asks an agent with a deep set of dimples.

"¡Híjole!" he replies. "What are you trying to do, jinx us?"

More agents file in, the epitome of virility. None are especially tall, but they all seem capable of dropping to the floor and giving fifty. They greet one another in the Mexican fashion (a half-hug with a slap on the back) and smile more than you'd think a Border Patrol agent would. Thirty agents work this station at any given moment, half manning the checkpoint while the rest patrol the highway or the brush. Cabrera introduces me to Yip, the station's K-9 coordinator, who offers to show me around. We step outside again. The temperature leaps thirty degrees while the noise escalates a thousandfold. Yip laughs at my reaction. "Yeah, it's pretty chaotic out here," he says. "Sometimes we wear earplugs."

We walk down a lane of traffic, the drivers looking either bored or ticked as they start, idle, stop; start, idle, stop. Neurotically switch lanes. Start, idle, stop. Occasionally, Cabrera says, a driver will "bail" by pulling off to the side of the road so his cargo can bolt. Agents chase after them, radioing their colleagues in the brush to get ready. Over the years, they have apprehended citizens of seventy-two different nations out here, with Mexicans, Guatemalans, Hondurans, and Salvadorans being the most common. Lately, they have been catching quite a few Chinese, too. It's always a surprise, as they pay so much for the journey—anywhere from $40,000 to $80,000 apiece.

"We once found a truckload of twenty Chinese people," Cabrera says. "We got ten out of the trailer, and then we found another ten right in front. They were pretty sluggish."

Smugglers have devised infinitely many (and often deadly) ways of maximizing loads. Human cargo has been found curled inside engine compartments, wrapped around gas tanks, clinging to the undercarriage of vehicles, and cramped inside all manner of containers stacked inside trailers. Once, a man even tried slipping through a checkpoint by being upholstered into the backseat of a van.

Nodding at a nearby agent poking his head in someone's window, Yip says, "We have to ask everyone what country they're from. If they hesitate, we know something's up."[2]

"And the American public is pretty rough," Cabrera says. "They always ask, 'Are *you* a U.S. citizen? What are *you* doing here?'"

I turn to Yip for comment, but he's taking in the traffic like a farmer surveying crops. Then he whips out a walkie-talkie. "Red Arrow, lane one," he clips.

Cabrera raises an eyebrow. "Scout," he mouths.

Which means spy, or someone coasting up and down the highway, waiting for a load to get seized so that he can radio his buddies to charge forth with their own cargo while the agents are distracted. No one knows how many traffickers make it through the checkpoint undetected. Some of the agents I've met say 5 percent; others shake their head and murmur 50 percent.

Yip strides back to the station with purpose. Trailing behind, I nearly get sideswiped by a van switching lanes.

"You have to be alert out here," Cabrera warns. "Agents have gotten run over before."

Back inside the station, Cabrera introduces me to a thirty-something agent named Kooiman. Tall, bald, and competent, he looks brawny but elegant in his combat boots. Sipping from his Big Gulp, he escorts me to a back room so we can talk.

My goal here is to grasp the motivation behind becoming a Border Patrol agent, a profession that, to me at least, seems ethically questionable, heartbreaking, and dangerous. Considering that an agent's starting salary can scrape the upper forties and elevate to nearly six figures during a successful career, money is an obvious draw, especially given the dearth of alternatives in the region. But as Todd Miller documents in his book *Border Patrol Nation*, the CBP has found other ways of ingratiating itself into the public psyche

---

2. While the 1976 Supreme Court case *U.S. vs. Martinez-Fuerte* grants Border Patrol agents the right to ask such questions as you're traveling through their checkpoints, you're not legally required to answer (though an agent will surely request you pull over for secondary inspection if given the silent treatment). Unless the agent finds probable cause to detain you, you'll likely be waved on afterward, without ever revealing a thing. For some spirited displays of civil disobedience, search for "Top DHS checkpoint refusals" on YouTube.

since its formation in 1924.[3] It boasts everything from a national museum in El Paso, where the gift shop sells sterling silver Border Patrol badges soldered into crosses, to countrywide youth "Explorer" programs, where recruits as young as fourteen are trained how to track down, handcuff, interrogate, and apprehend simulated "aliens." Since 9/11, Congress has become an especially big fan of the agency, granting it a nearly $13 billion budget in 2014—more than every other federal law enforcement agency combined. This money has swollen ranks to more than 21,000 Border Patrol agents today (up from 8,500 agents in 2001 and 4,000 in 1994).

I ask Kooiman why he chose this work. He says he gave college a try but didn't last more than two semesters because of all the parties. He joined the army instead and served five and a half years, including a tour in Iraq. When he returned home to Texas, he started working at his family's business but found it couldn't quench his adrenaline.

"In the army, you've got a lot of camaraderie, and I missed that," he says. Though he isn't a fan of Falfurrias—"there are some unsavory characters here, and I'll leave it at that"—he likes the pace of its checkpoint. "It's not as fun as chasing people, but you can catch mountains of dope."

His personal record is 8,451 pounds, which he found concealed inside a tanker. He had to call the fire department to retrieve it. "It was a suicide load. I talked to the guy and he was real nervous and didn't make sense. He had $6 million worth of drugs on him, and he was going to get paid $6,000 for it. He didn't have a criminal history either. He was a black guy, a little slow."

When I remark how skilled he must be at reading people, he shrugs. "You stand out there long enough, talking to six people a minute for four hours at a time, and you'll start to notice when things are off. They might as well be wearing a sign that says 'I have something in my car.'"

Like the time he saw a kid who had tattoos all over his face and was dripping in gold jewelry yet wearing a pair of cowboy work boots. "Those boots didn't make sense," he says, "it was like he couldn't bend his toes. So I asked him to take the boots off, and there was two and a half pounds of dope inside them."

Leaning back in his swivel chair, he props his own boots on the table. "When you catch a load, you feel awesome, but you also know that guy is just

3. The Border Patrol's inaugural stations were evenly split between borders north and south, with one in El Paso and the other in Detroit.

done. I said to that kid, 'Do you understand how serious this is? Do you know what you've done? I hope for your family's sake they live nearby.'"

"Do you ever worry about the cartels coming after you?"

"I've never received a death threat, but . . . you basically steal people's drugs for a living. It's not like they're saying, 'Oh, it's okay for you to take my $6 million worth of coke.' Drug dealers have reconnaissance. They know where a lot of us live."

He doesn't seem terribly concerned about it, though, and I understand why when he mentions that a book was written about his platoon in Iraq called *The Long Road Home,* by Martha Raddatz. Turns out, he was once caught in a ten-hour attack in Sadr City that killed eight U.S. soldiers—including the son of antiwar activist Cindy Sheehan—and wounded seventy more in 2004.

But while "danger" is a relative term for Kooiman, he has seen unspeakable violence out here, too. Barely a month into the job, he fielded a call at one in the morning that a woman had been found on the highway, naked and bleeding. She had been crossing the brush with fifteen others when their coyotes—or human smugglers—attacked her, raping her, beating her, and leaving her to die in the middle of a ranch. She somehow made it to the highway, where she was spotted. When Kooiman arrived, she said her five-year-old daughter was still out there. He led a nine-hour search party, but they never found her. Days later, the coyotes called her family demanding $5,000 "or else."

"What could they do?" Kooiman says. "They didn't have that kind of money; they were poor. So they lost her. God knows what that coyote did with that child. Those coyotes are worse than drug smugglers."

Other missions have been more successful, like the little Salvadoran girl they once tracked in the brush, "the cutest little thing but completely dehydrated." For three weeks, they took turns keeping watch on her at a hospital in Corpus while doctors revived her kidneys. She survived and got reunited with her family. Stories like these are why many agents consider themselves lifeguards, out protecting their fellow citizens from criminals and saving the "aliens" from horrible deaths.

"This is an awesome place and it's a terrible place," Kooiman concedes. "I have seen kids throw their life away for a quick buck. Like that guy with two and a half pounds of coke in his boots. He was eighteen years old, going to jail for twenty years, and would serve every day of it."

He becomes silent a moment, then perks up. His lunch break is over. There's dope to find. We shake hands, and Cabrera asks if I'm ready to go.

As we walk past the cell at the front of the station, I am startled to see that six people now occupy it: five men and a woman, all dark, slight of height, and thin. An agent questions them through the speaker holes cut in the wall. Cabrera explains that they are Salvadorans who were found in the brush. On the basis of their nationality, he guesses they paid their coyote about $10,000 apiece for their travels here—every centavo lost the moment they were found.

I ask if I can speak to them. He checks with someone, but no: they could have tuberculosis or hepatitis, and the CBP can't assume that risk. There is indeed something about seeing humans caged in a cell that makes you wonder such things yourself—until you remember, wait a minute, this is exactly how immigrants have been dehumanized in the public eye for centuries. Notions of being "diseased" caused Jews to be lynched in fourteenth-century Europe and Irish immigrants to be denied so much humanity in nineteenth-century New York that many crossed into Canada nearly naked. Similarly, when an influx of unaccompanied minors starts arriving in Texas from Central America in 2013, Fox News commentators like Dr. Marc Siegel will deem it a "public health crisis," citing scabies, leprosy, and drug-resistant tuberculosis as points of concern. Fortunately, media like the *Texas Observer* will quickly point out that—thanks to high immunization rates in their home countries and, in the case of Guatemala, universal health care—these children are probably more likely to have been vaccinated against infectious diseases than Texas kids (16 percent of whom are uninsured).

On our way past the cell, I try making eye contact with the woman inside. Roughly my age, she has curly hair and is wearing a tattered shirt and pants. She had been pacing the length of the bench, but now she stops to sit on it. Dropping her head into her hands, she rocks back and forth. A man hovers close, but he doesn't seem of comfort. The others blink with exhaustion as an agent snaps their photos and records their thumbprints.

Out in the searing sun, an Americanos bus has been pulled over for inspection. Cabrera climbs aboard and I follow. The passengers appear to be Mexican nationals, their belongings stuffed in oversize plastic bags and cardboard boxes tied with string. Anxiety seems to be emanating from their seats, and glancing out the window, I see why. A passenger has been pulled off the bus for questioning. She is middle-aged with dyed red hair, wearing a hopeful blazer. Two agents are interrogating her near a pile of squashed tomatoes. She's shrinking into the juice.

One by one, the passengers stare up at me as if I too wielded authority—a sensation my body rejects. After flashing the most compassionate smile I can muster, I hurry down the bus steps, away from this invasion of privacy, away from this obstruction of journey, away from this snooping on fate.

ACCORDING TO A 2011 *FRONTLINE* DOCUMENTARY, Immigration and Customs Enforcement (ICE) set a target of 400,000 deportations *per year* in the early Obama administration—and achieved it. With ambitions like that, it's hard not to view these agencies as pseudo-gestapos prone to pounding on doors in the middle of the night and dragging noncitizens from their beds and their children. But because so many agents I meet are Tejanos (like me) whose families have lived in this region for centuries (like mine), I try to empathize with their plight. Besides oil refineries, "homeland security" is one of the few lucrative (yet legal) employment options in South Texas, especially for folks without advanced degrees. If suicide rates are any indication—at least fifteen Border Patrol agents between 2008 and 2010, or nearly twice the national average—the profession extracts an emotional toll. Judging agents solely on the basis of their profession might be as problematic as berating undocumented workers because of theirs.

These, at least, are the conclusions I draw upon meeting the visual artist Celeste De Luna. A second-generation Tejana who mostly spoke English growing up in Illinois but then got plunked in a Spanish-speaking class because of her skin color upon her family's return to South Texas, she understands the border's complexities as well as anyone. She greets me at the front door of her ranch-style home on the outskirts of Harlingen wearing a cardigan over a gray cheetah-patterned tank top and black stretch pants. Maybe forty years old, she has painted her toenails a glittery purple that matches her sequined flip-flops.

As I follow her into the kitchen, where she prepares two mugs of green tea, I notice her painting *Border Saints Fail*. In it, La Virgen de Guadalupe hovers behind a local patron saint whose dress has been collaged with a signed-and-stamped WARNING TO ALIEN ORDERED REMOVED OR DEPORTED issued by the U.S. Department of Homeland Security. Down the hallway hangs a woodcut print titled *Breach Baby* that features a fetus inside a belly wedged between a wall and a coil of barbed wire. In a sunlit studio decorated with images of Frida Kahlo and quotes by Sandra Cisneros, Celeste shows me her best-known series: four 2- by 6-foot paintings called *Compass*. In the one titled *South*, a Tejana poses by the international bridge arcing above the tree-lined Rio Grande. A Border Patrol agent guards a highway dotted with crosses in *North*, while *East* features an ICE agent in the foreground of a sprawling detention center. With a skeletal finger, Santa Muerte beckons viewers toward a parting in the border wall marked *West*. I immediately fantasize about hanging one in my office.

As we settle down with our tea, Celeste further complicates her images by sharing how, in early 2000, she encouraged her husband to work for the Border Patrol—despite the fact he entered this country illegally himself, as a young boy fleeing war-torn El Salvador with his family.

"It didn't seem that serious back then," she explains, curling a strand of silky black hair beneath her bandanna. "The Border Patrol would catch people, but they always came back, pre-9/11. It was like a game. But after 9/11, people got psychotic. They became racist in a way I hadn't experienced before, especially now with Donald Trump."

The changing political climate soon seeped onto her canvases, especially when Congress announced plans to build a wall just a few miles from their home. The palm trees and hummingbirds of her early paintings morphed into today's agents and saints. In fact, the ICE agent depicted in *East* is her husband. After deciding he couldn't "catch people and then throw them back" for a living as a Border Patrol agent, he took a job with Immigration and Naturalization Service instead. But in 2003, INS reconfigured into ICE, and he spent four harrowing years working at "Tent City," a privately run federal prison in Raymondville that used to house 2,800 undocumented immigrants awaiting deportation.[4] Celeste shows me the yellow star she painted behind his ICE badge to symbolize his "survivor guilt."

When I ask about the irony of their relationship, Celeste folds her arms across her chest. "I didn't marry an ICE agent. I married my husband. This happened to us, too. What, so he became an ICE agent, and then I was supposed to divorce him? I used to be caught up in the embarrassment of it, but this isn't my fault, and it isn't my husband's fault either. He sees it as a

---

4. Known as "Tent City" for its Kevlar tent dormitories, Willacy County Correctional Center got destroyed in a major riot in February 2015. Frustrated by its wretched conditions—including rodent infestations, tent leaks, clogged toilets, and lack of access to lawyers and medical care—prisoners used pipes and knives to seize control of the facility and held it for nearly two days as they torched the tents and damaged the plumbing and electricity. The federal Bureau of Prisons has since declared the $60 million site "uninhabitable," though county officials hope to someday resurrect their major employer.

job, and he wants to do it right and be fair. And it is good to have good people do that work."

She pauses a moment, allowing this to sink in, before reminding me that migrants aren't the only ones trapped in nepantla, the state of in-between-ness that transpires from straddling worlds. Such is the fate of every member of the borderland, no matter what documents we carry.

"Everybody is caught up in the system together," she says in a low voice. "You may not be doing law enforcement, but you are still a part of it, too."

7

The Wall

THE FIRST OBJECT REVEALS ITSELF ALMOST IMMEDIATELY: A MAN'S black Reebok, size nine. Something about its positioning inches from the steel bars suggests urgency. The fact there is only one implies struggle. And its absence of dust—which coats everything in this swath of Texas—means it hasn't been here long.

"It wasn't when I took my walk this morning, anyway," Mark Clark, a painter who lives half a mile away, confirms as he squats down for a better look.

As I lower beside him, I notice a second object lying in the dirt: a water bottle. Like the sneaker, it is also stranded in the no-man's-land between the eighteen-foot bars and the Rio Grande. Our friend the artist Susan Harbage Page sees the bottle too. After making a photo with her Canon 5D, she slips her fingers through the three-inch gap between the bars and unscrews its cap. Carbonated water fizzes out, drenching her sleeves. She drains and then tugs the bottle through the wall so that it's unquestionably on U.S. soil. Mark threatens to report her to the Border Patrol for smuggling, and we all laugh.

Because it's either that, or scream.

When I moved to China in the late nineties, the Great Wall was the first site I wished to see and the one I visited most frequently: nine times in one year. Ditto with the Berlin Wall when I later traveled to Germany: three visits in one week. I was fascinated that a government could so disregard human motivation that it fathomed hunks of stone or concrete could halt a determined citizen. When my own government started raising bars of steel en masse—after gleefully imploring others to "Tear down this wall!"[1]—I felt

---

1. President Ronald Reagan delivered this famous line at the Brandenburg Gate near the Berlin Wall during a celebration of the 750th anniversary of the city on June 12, 1987. As an idealistic junior high student, I cheered at this challenge to Mikhail Gorbachev—completely unaware that the United States had been barricading border cities like San Ysidro, California, and El Paso, Texas, since the seventies.

so disgusted, I couldn't bear to see it.[2] I'm here now only because of Susan, who is visiting from North Carolina. She has inspired me to try to view this obstruction through an aesthetic lens rather than through a political one, to explore its influence on art rather than on homeland security, to see how the wall has affected the cultural life of those sealed inside its bars rather than the social and economic life of those left outside of it.

Despite constituting 63 percent of the border, Texas was the last state to install its portion of the 670-mile wall mandated by the 2006 Secure Border Fence[3] Act. Here in Brownsville—our southernmost city—local residents and public officials launched an all-out offensive against the plan to erect thirty-four miles of concrete and steel across their county. Students marched; lawmakers lobbied; activists picketed the courthouse. Landowners dug up titles granted by the Spanish crown in the eighteenth century and started suing. Environmentalists brandished studies showing how the wall would disrupt migratory patterns of endangered species like the ocelot. Tejanos decried the disturbance to their own migratory patterns between their porches and their favorite taco stands, beauty parlors, and great-aunts' houses in Matamoros. Yet when they aired these concerns at a public hearing at the University of Texas at Brownsville (UTB) in 2008, then-Republican representative Tom Tancredo of Colorado quipped, "Why don't we just build the fence north of Brownsville then?"

Whether the wall has made this city or state or nation "safer" in the years since its inception is debatable. The following ramifications, however, are not. The wall has sliced through UTB's campus, partially destroyed a wildlife refuge, shrunk private property, and obstructed downtown's riverfront view.

---

2. Other U.S. presidents who condemned the world's walls: Franklin Delano Roosevelt ("What I seek to convey is the historic truth that the United States as a nation has at all times maintained opposition—clear, definite opposition—to any attempt to lock us in behind an ancient Chinese wall while the procession of civilization went past") and Richard Nixon, referencing China's Great Wall ("What is most important is that we have an open world. As we look at this wall, we do not want walls of any kind between peoples"). Donald Trump, meanwhile, claimed, "I would build a great wall, and nobody builds walls better than me, believe me, and I'll build them very inexpensively, I will build a great, great wall on our southern border. And I will have Mexico pay for that wall," during his announcement for a presidential bid in June 2015.

3. Let's contemplate word choice for a moment. "Fence" has a white-picket connotation: a neighborly gesture that preserves everyone's privacy and keeps cocker spaniels from running away. A "wall" implies militarization: something that incites paranoia and quashes freedoms. The U.S. government hasn't built a fence across its southern border but a wall.

It has barricaded some of the city's poorest neighborhoods while steering clear of its golf courses. It has incited dozens of landowners to file hundreds of lawsuits. It has inspired an offshore drilling rig designer to donate $3,000 worth of jasmine vines so that UTB students could make their campus portion a little less bleak. And it has become a muse to artists like Celeste, Susan, and Mark, who engage with the wall through their work.

Objects are cropping up every fifteen to twenty feet now. A belt. A shoelace. A toothbrush snapped in two. Susan photographs each one, then slips them inside the oversize shopping bag she brought along for this very purpose: one emblazoned with La Virgen de Guadalupe.

"I always buy one with the Virgin on it. That is my little offering," she explains.

Susan has been making annual trips to the Rio Grande Valley for a decade. One of her many projects entails walking along the river in search of the objects people leave behind during their crossing. After photographing them in situ, she brings the items back to her studio to re-photograph, tag, and number them, then adds them to her "anti-archive," which will eventually become an online searchable database. The last time she counted, there were nearly 800 objects inside, ranging from Bibles to pill bottles, combs, wallets, passports, clothing, and slips of paper bearing scribbled telephone numbers.

"The first one I found was a toothbrush. When I saw it, I just felt it in my whole body. I didn't even know whether I should pick it up," Susan remembers. "It was a powerful remnant of that person's life, and I felt it needed to be seen. That's what the anti-archive is: the unofficial history of immigration. The one nobody wants to look at or deal with."

Many of the archive's contents were found right here in Hope Park, a leafy strip of green that slopes down to the Rio Grande. Standing on its bank, you are either a seven-minute walk to downtown Brownsville or a seven-minute wade to Matamoros. The city founded Hope Park to commemorate its close ties with Mexico long ago. Tree-lined and bike-trailed, it would be gorgeous—were it not for the eighteen-foot steel wall cleaving through it.

"They have painted it black to make it look better, because it's rusting like a motherfucker. It has two or three coats of paint on it, and it's only three years old," Mark says, gripping a stake in his fist. In his early sixties, he has a beard straight out of *Don Quixote*.

He shows me an imprint of a hand about halfway up a steel bar—perhaps the owner of the lost Reebok. As Susan focuses her camera lens, I gaze around at the adjacent bars. When reflected off a certain angle, the sun reveals dozens of other handprints—shoeprints too. Mark says that after a good rain, immigrants leave a trail of mud all the way up one side of the wall and halfway down the other.

"I once saw some guy get thrown out of a four-door sedan, run across the street, scale the fence, and hop over the other side in fifteen seconds flat," he says.

I don't know if I could do *that*, but—grasping a bar in each hand and standing on my tiptoes—I could probably haul myself up and over if I really needed to.

Farther down the path, we come upon a storage facility surrounded by a chain-link fence topped with concertina wire. A man's gray jacket is trapped high inside the coils. Susan rises upon her toes and starts pulling. In her mid-fifties, she has a blonde pixie haircut and is wearing turquoise glasses and a bright red vest. After a cringe-inducing struggle, she frees the shirt from the razor blades and stuffs it inside La Virgen. Mark, meanwhile, has started unearthing a shirt half-buried beneath the trail. "Sometimes you come out here and it's like a *ropa usada*," he says, using the Spanish term for a used-clothing store.

The border wall ends a few feet farther at the offices of Immigration and Customs Enforcement, where a chain-link fence begins. Mark shows me the section where some chain links have been snipped, creating a gaping hole. Half of it has been mended with plastic links, but the breach is still big enough to slide a package through. Mark picks up one of the broken links lying in the dirt and drops it into my palm.

"Take it," he says. "It'll be your souvenir of Mexican ingenuity."

BORDER WALLS HAVE A HISTORY of serving as public art spaces— sometimes even before their political functions have ceased. The west side of the Berlin Wall was long a canvas for artists like Keith Haring, who deemed it "an attempt to psychologically destroy the wall by painting it." After toppling in 1989, the east side became a gallery too when some of the biggest names in the art world descended upon it to paint vibrant murals about freedom and democracy, a few of which remain to this day (albeit, crumbling). Over in the West Bank, Palestinians and Israelis have both adorned their respective sides of the twenty-six-foot concrete slabs that split their territories. Palestinian artists tend to draw flags or giant house keys, signifying their desire to return home, while international graffiti artists like Banksy[4] paint utopic murals of solidarity. Security guards at the border gate between Pakistan and India at Wagah have elevated their daily "lowering of the flags" ceremony to a dance performance, complete with jubilant goose-stepping, rifle-whirling, and moustache-twirling as bleachers full of spectators cheer. And while the rulers of the Great Wall would probably have imprisoned anyone who tried to tag it for much of its 2,300-year history, in recent years they have permitted a portion near Beijing to host an annual music festival that draws in top techno acts like Parisian DJ David Guetta and German live act Paul Kalkbrenner as well as thousands of revelers.

Certain sections of the U.S. wall have also become binational art spaces, most notably Friendship Park, which straddles the Tijuana/San Diego borderline. The park was founded in 1971 by First Lady Pat Nixon, who declared, "I hope there won't be a fence here too much longer" after ordering her security team to snip the barbed wire that marked the line then. Families have traveled to the park from across Mexico and the United States to kiss, clasp hands, and picnic through the ever-evolving barricade ever since. But in 2007, the government began a series of renovations that resulted in the current double wall that swallows the park and is open for just a few hours on weekends. It is also covered with a steel mesh that allows only families' fingertips to touch. Local artists and activists have worked hard to preserve the park's humanity by turning the eighteen-foot obstruction into a stage for poetry readings, symphonies, dance performances, yoga classes, volleyball games, and ecumenical communions enjoyed by visitors on either side of it. They have also planted a Binational Friendship Garden that flourishes in each nation.

But for the most part, if you want to see art on the U.S. border wall, you must walk along its southern side, where Mexicans have been embellishing it as fast as the U.S. government has been constructing it. Politicians plaster campaign posters; border crossers inscribe their names, home villages, and the date. Muralists and graffiti artists layer image upon image. For years, a group called the Border Art Workshop/Taller de Arte Fronterizo nailed

---

4. In December 2007, Banksy and the London-based group Pictures on Walls invited fourteen international street artists to Bethlehem to work with Palestinian artists. Anyone wishing to buy their work was informed they needed to travel there and witness Israel's occupation firsthand before placing a bid. The project—called "Santa's Ghetto"—raised more than $1 million for local charities and cast a critical eye on the West Bank Wall, which is expected to be upward of 400 miles long upon its completion.

full-size coffins upon the Tijuana wall in honor of Dia de los Muertos (the Day of the Dead) that displayed the number of immigrants who had died that year while trying to cross the borderline. The one from 1995 read 61. The one from 2000 said 499.

In 2004, Arizona artist Alfred Quiroz started making giant metal *milagros*—or religious amulets—to hang along the wall at Nogales and Agua Prieto. Some were shaped in the traditional forms of hearts, eyes, and legs, but others specifically addressed the border-crossing experience, such as the one of a coyote with a serpentine tongue. In 2011, Tijuana artist Ana Teresa Fernández tried to erase the wall altogether by painting a stretch of it pale powder blue so that it blended into the sky.[5] And since 2012, Arizona artists who call themselves the "Border Bedazzlers" have been driving to Naco, Mexico, recruiting neighborhood children, and painting landscapes decked with hearts and rainbows along their community's backdrop of corrugated metal.

The U.S. side of the wall, meanwhile, mostly remains blank. Granted, much of it consists of mesh or pylons instead of a continuous surface and is therefore tough to paint, but then—the Mexican side is too. Artists' chief deterrent here seems to be the Department of Homeland Security, which has fortified the U.S. portion with infrared cameras, heat sensors, stadium lighting, Predator drones, and the bulk of its Border Patrol force.[6] Anyone wishing to jazz up the northern side must do so covertly, as street artist Ron English once did. Renowned for "culture jamming," or slapping subversive messages atop corporate advertisements, English is a veteran of border adornment, having painted both the Berlin Wall and the West Bank Wall. When his buddies started hassling him about his own nation's wall, he bought a plane ticket to Texas. On April Fool's Day in 2011, English drove along the border wall with a few mates, found a lonely patch between La Joya and Penitas, leaped

5. That is indeed Ana Teresa Fernández on the cover of this book, performing "Borrando la Frontera," *Erasing the Border*. She painted this image from a photograph by her mother, Maria Teresa Fernández, who has been documenting the border wall between San Diego and Tijuana since the late 1990s. Learn more at http://anateresafernandez.com.
6. When someone does mount an exhibition on the northern wall, the Border Patrol quickly tears it down. In his book *Border Odyssey*, Charles Thompson documents a 2011 visit to a shrine near Douglas, Arizona, for Carlos La Madrid, a nineteen-year-old U.S. citizen killed by a Border Patrol agent, purportedly for throwing rocks. After photographing the posters and letters hanging on the wall—one of which read TO THE BORDER PATROL WHO KILLED MY BROTHER—Thompson drove on to another segment of the wall. By the time he returned half an hour later, all of the messages had been removed.

out of the car, and wheat-pasted a two-headed donkey across it. One donkey was painted like the U.S. flag; the other, the Mexican flag. Both pulled in opposite directions. They snapped a fast photo before bailing, and good thing: they passed a Border Patrol vehicle minutes later. Then English crossed the bridge into Reynosa, where—at the port of entry—he propped up a sign of Uncle Sam pointing to a peach-toned bar on a color chart that read: YOU MUST BE THIS COLOR TO ENTER THIS COUNTRY.

Another artist who has braved the northern wall is the musician Glenn Weyant. He was shocked by its existence when he first moved to Tucson from New Jersey, viewing it as "a symbol of fear and loathing. I wanted to transform it into something else . . . an instrument so that people on both sides can have open dialogue and communication," he told me during a phone interview.

He started by rapping on its iron bars with chopsticks and recording the rhythmic beats, but as the wall grew longer and taller, he swapped them out for drumsticks. Over the years, he has stroked the wall with cello bows, pummeled it with broomsticks, and made it hum with milk frothers and vibrators. "Every time I do it, it keeps the wall from being a militarized zone," he said. "Sometimes I play it with the people I meet out there, be it a Border Patrol agent or a rancher or a guy picking lemons in his backyard. It is like pressing a restart button. It's an opportunity for a narrative for something other than capitalism gone amok."

And then there are the Texans. Soon after moving to Brownsville from Washington, D.C., ten years ago, Mark opened Galeria 409, which showcases artists from the Rio Grande Valley. When the government announced it would install a wall less than a hundred feet from his business (which doubles as his home and studio), he joined the local protests. Twice he has staged flash-mob exhibits called "Art against the Wall," where artists gather in Hope Park and hang their work directly on the wall, sans permit. Among the pieces: piñatas shaped like Border Patrol agents, complete with sunglasses, walkie-talkies, and binoculars. Thirty-foot ladders made of bamboo and twine. Deflated black inner tubes fished out of the Rio Grande. A colossal funeral wreath, fastened to the steel bars.

In 2011, the exhibit was up for four hours, Mark says. "Then the viewers thinned out and it was just three artists and a Boston terrier until four Border Patrol agents surrounded us with bulletproof vests and Glocks. They said, 'We know you don't have a permit,' and I said okay and they were shocked. They had expected a confrontation, but we had made our point and so we took it down."

We are back inside his gallery now, in the heart of downtown. It is a massive space with exposed brick walls, a high wood-beam ceiling, and plenty of sunlight. I start flipping through a stack of his canvases. In a series called *Moonlit Mojada* (Moonlit Wetback), bikini-clad Latinas distract Border Patrol agents by inner-tubing down the Rio Grande while immigrants scale the wall behind them. Another project entails Aztec codices reinterpreted through the latest headlines out of Matamoros: cockfights, gunfights, kidnappings, beheadings. Mark used to walk to Brownsville's sister city to eat or stock up on art supplies a couple times a week, but he's grown wary lately.

"I try to be back on the bridge by noon on the notion that the *sicarios* [hired assassins] sleep in. I was on the bridge once when a gun battle broke out. My framer lives a block and a half away and was pinned down in his bathroom with his family for four and a half hours," he says. "Once they get going, it's totally deafening. It's worse than the Fourth of July."

Without skipping a beat, he then invites Susan and me to join him there for dinner tonight.

My hesitation is hypocritical. In the past, I've thought nothing of trekking into Burma at the height of its military rule or visiting Tajikistan or Venezuela when the State Department explicitly advised otherwise. I barely flinched hitchhiking across Moscow after the Metro closed at midnight. But even though—or, more likely, because—I grew up two hours away, the thought of walking three blocks into Matamoros for a platter of enchiladas and a round of *micheladas* unnerves me. Though I am fully cognizant that my paranoia is overblown and media-fed, it paralyzes me just the same. And I am not alone in this fear: tourism to border towns has plummeted in recent years, shuttering many of the region's beloved bars,[7] restaurants, and shops. While I refuse to consider whether the border wall has kept any noncitizens out, it is certainly reinforcing my decision to stay in.

So rather than replenish my veins with salsa and tequila, I walk with Susan to the plaza on the northern side of the international bridge and sulk atop a table. A steady stream of Mexicans flow past, some lugging shopping bags, others wheeling carts as they make their way home to Matamoros.

7. Among the losses: the Cadillac Bar. It first opened in New Orleans in the early twenties but relocated to Nuevo Laredo to take advantage of Prohibition in 1926. Thousands of U.S. citizens streamed across the border to legally chug its tequila and behold curios like Pancho Villa's saddle. My family dined there throughout the eighties and nineties. In 2010, however, the Cadillac "temporarily closed" because narco-violence had drained its clientele. It recently reopened back across the border in San Antonio.

A father carries a giant star-shaped piñata festooned with multicolored streamers. His young daughter trails behind him, bearing the stick she'll later use to whack it open and eat its candies.

Just then, a merry burst of norteño music blasts out of a nearby store. Within an instant, the middle-aged man sitting a few tables over rises to his feet. He is wearing a black shirt featuring dollar bills cascading over a rooster outlined in glitter. EL DINERO NO HACE AL GALLO, it says: Money doesn't make the cock. Keeping time to the syncopated beats, he swivels his hips and claps his hands. Three teenage girls holding fistfuls of balloons stop to watch. Smiling to himself, the man lifts his face and pumps his arms as he struts about in circles. More passersby pause to watch in amusement. Across the street, a young man wearing a red leather jacket and sneakers joins the dance too. The music puts pep into everybody's step as they cross the bridge into what used to be the same nation.

EARLY THE NEXT MORNING, Susan and I ride the aptly named Military Highway out of Brownsville, searching for more wall. It is not a contiguous structure: throughout the 1,954-mile border, the wall starts and stops without any perceivable pattern. Its height varies from place to place too, as does its price tag. The 18-foot wall that soars above the 3,500-foot peak of Otay Mountain in San Diego cost approximately $16 million a mile, while the 9-foot wall at the Tecate port of entry ran about $4 million. The "floating fence" that cuts across the dunes of Yuma, Arizona, can be mechanically lifted and repositioned whenever the sand starts to bury it. Some parts of the wall have been fashioned out of landing plates left over from the Vietnam War; others consist of 6-foot Normandy-style "X"-crosses that deter only vehicles. One wall resembles a gate from a nineteenth-century insane asylum, complete with terrifyingly large bolts and locks.

Those, at least, are the images captured in French photographer Maurice Sherif's 2012 book, *The American Wall*. He started stalking the wall from the Pacific Ocean to the Gulf of Mexico in 2006, shooting sections at midday with a large-format camera. Yet the ninety-six black-and-white images that appear in his double-volume art book are already obsolete, he told me over the phone. Many stretches of the wall are being torn down and replaced by a construction that is taller and more uniform in structure. "Psychologically, when you have one wall that is all the same, it has a real personality. It is much more intimidating," he explained.

Intimidating isn't how I would describe what I've seen thus far, but then—this journey has just begun. I am about to ask Susan's thoughts on the matter when she thrusts out her forefinger. "There it is!" she calls out.

I pull into a gravel thoroughfare across the street from a Valley Fireworks stand boasting BUY 1 GET 5 FREE! We climb up the hill where a sweep of wall begins, and I try to view it through a solely aesthetic lens. Granted, I am neither a visual artist nor an architect, but using the other walls this world has erected as points of comparison, it seems we got a boring one here in Texas. It is not austere, like the Berlin Wall, or imposing, like the Great Wall, or frightening, like the West Bank Wall. It isn't even big (like everything else in this state). It is just a row of scalable pylons, rusting stupidly in the sun.

"So, uh, where is Mexico?" I ask Susan.

We gaze into the vibrant green valley that stretches out before us, but the Rio Grande is nowhere in sight. According to the Treaty of Guadalupe-Hidalgo—the 1848 treatise that ended the Mexican War and let the United States buy large portions of present-day California, New Mexico, Arizona, Nevada, Colorado, Utah, and Wyoming for $15 million—the Rio Grande is the official borderline between Texas and Mexico. But because the river wends and floods, construction crews had to build the wall up to several miles away from it, cutting off scores of ranchers and farmers from their property and creating the seemingly nationless land before us. Not three minutes have passed when a Border Patrol vehicle rolls up and an agent sticks his head out. We ask which way to Mexico.

"The river is up ahead, but you shouldn't go down there," he warns. "It's dangerous. Anything can happen."

"Oh, but you'll protect us," Susan says with a smile.

He half-grins back. About thirty years old, he is your classic buzz-cut, boots-shined, yes-sir, no-ma'am agent. I ask if he'll give us a lift to the river. He shakes his head no and moves on.

Maybe five miles down the road, we see another section near a cornfield and park. As we approach on foot, Susan notices a box perched on a steel post. Assuming it is a camera, we wave. Sixty seconds later, a Border Patrol vehicle appears in the distance, dragging half a dozen tires behind it. Susan explains they are combing the dirt road so they can better see footprints. Thick dust billows behind the vehicle—so much that, once the driver determines we are gringas with notebooks rather than smugglers with backpacks, he turns around and retreats in the opposite direction. A second vehicle arrives minutes later.

"Just don't go south of the levee," the agent says after hearing our spiel. "It's quiet during the day, but at night, there's a lot of activity."

"Does the wall help?" I ask.

"It's a good filter, so we know where they go through," he says. "But if there's a will, there's a way. Nothing is ever going to stop them from coming. The wall just filters them through."

On our walk back to the car, Susan notices shriveled corncobs on the side of the dirt road. Upon closer inspection, we see they have been neatly eaten and discarded. A noticeable trail has been pressed through the cornfield, and when we step into it, we see a flip-flop. As Susan focuses her lens, I realize we are surrounded by iron and green. The mesquite that borders the cornfield is so tall and thick, it has fused a barricade of its own. Now that the Border Patrol has departed, we are all alone. For the second time in two days, I feel ill at ease, and the only reason I can fathom is that I am standing in the shadows of walls.

I think back to my phone conversation with Sherif. Not one of *The American Wall*'s pictures has a human being inside its frame. When I asked why, he replied, "When I was on the Mexican side, I heard people living. When I was on the American side, I heard only silence. Not the silence of contemplation, but the silence of alienation, the silence of division, the silence of isolationism."

I look again around the lonesome field before continuing on to the car. Susan exposes a final image before following.

AMONG THE MANY ARTISTS who have answered the wall's siren call is photographer Stefan Falke, who grew up fewer than 250 miles away from the Berlin Wall (and partied atop it soon after its fall). He was astonished when the United States started expanding its own wall. In 2008, he flew to Tijuana to see it, right when the city was besieged by narco-violence. Though he couldn't have asked for a flashier news story, he ultimately decided to turn his camera lens elsewhere. "When we only read and see the violent side of places for ten years, we lose the value of the people who live there," he told me during a Skype interview. "Crime stories, those represent the problem. I wanted to work on the solution."

He wound up making portraits of the artists of the borderlands: painters, sculptors, musicians, writers, performance artists, and even a few curators. Then he built a website, www.borderartists.com, to feature them all—180 at last count—in an attempt to connect the border with itself. "People need a way to express themselves when life gets difficult, and art expresses hope. It takes us out of the current situation, even if it's just for a second," he said.

Yet only a small percentage of the artists Falke has met—maybe one-third, he guessed—overtly engage with the border in their work. "The younger ones in particular refuse to buy into it," he said.

Mark has noticed this at his gallery in Brownsville, too. "I try to find artists who are political, but it is as rare as hen's teeth," he told me the night before we parted.

He could name only a handful of Texas artists who infuse border politics into their work. There's Angel Cabrales, an El Pasoan sculptor who satirizes the border's militarization by building arsenals of personal drones and Patriot missile launchers and staging performances at the wall. The Edinburg artist Paul Valadez designed certificates of achievement for border crossers for one of Mark's "Art against the Wall" exhibitions. David Freeman of McAllen has a piñata series that includes not only Border Patrol agents but immigrants in inner tubes, drones, a stretch of wall, and La Virgen de Guadalupe as well. San Antonian Bill FitzGibbons's recent opening at the International Museum of Art and Science starred modern dancers from McAllen and Reynosa performing together at a replica of the border wall decorated with flashing LED lights and ladders.

Mark ticked off a few more examples before sighing. "But everyone else might as well be painting in Denton. They just take it for granted, the stories."

Hardly any of the artists he mentioned were women. When I pointed this out, Susan called the border a gendered space. "Who inhabits it?" she asks. "The Border Patrol, and they are largely male. The people who cross, and they are largely male. In my work here, I have been chased by helicopters. I have had guns pointed at me. It's an intimidating place to be. A woman's body is a form of protest out here."

Since the most celebrated artist of the borderlands is my good friend Santa Barraza, I arrange a meeting in Kingsville to ask her opinion. She arrives at our favorite diner, El Tepatio, wearing a huipile over jeans. We order tacos and, after toasting tall glasses of *horchata*, I ask what recurring themes she notices in her students' work. As a professor at Texas A&M Kingsville (TAMUK), she has taught an entire generation of artists.

"A lot of their art is very personal," she says, sketching designs in her refried beans with a tortilla chip. "It's about sex, or it's about the men in their lives. Art now is very process-based and not very idea-based. We have been trained to produce art that negates our own culture."

"How so?"

"We're taught to use complementary colors to subdue colors so they are not too bright. But in Mexican culture, we love color."

Color is certainly her own signature. Her pallet includes peacock greens, flamboyant purples, and electric yellows swirled into life-size portraits, landscapes, legends, dreams, and codices. But while she is internationally acclaimed for memorializing the icons of the borderlands, she has steered clear of its newest one.

"I don't even agree with the wall," she says. "It shouldn't even *be* there, which is maybe why I don't deal with it in my work."

As someone who has been chronicling the borderlands for years but has only now dragged herself over to see the 670-mile wall barreling through it, I can relate to this sentiment. For many a Chicana/o artist, to include the wall in our work is to acknowledge that our government has spent upward of $3 billion dividing our community. Some of us haven't mustered the heart to do that yet.

MARK ESPECIALLY RECOMMENDED MEETING the oil painter Rigoberto A. Gonzalez, so I catch his exhibit at TAMUK before leaving Kingsville. Walking inside the spotlit space, my eyes fall first on a human head the dimensions of my own, hung at eye level. It appears to belong to a monk wearing a cloak, though the rest of his body is hidden. His large, bulging eyes cast skyward, as if beseeching grace. As I draw closer, however, I see the thin trickle of red oozing from his neckline. A news story springs to mind of the night La Familia bowled heads onto the dance floor of a discotheque. This head hanging before me is not of a monk at all but of a narco-victim freshly rolled out of a gunnysack.

Backing away from the image, I confront *On the 17th of February of 2009 in Reynosa, Tamaulipas, Mexico*—a three-paneled tableau that occupies the bulk of one wall. A crowd of life-size Mexicans gather around a mother who has collapsed to her knees in grief as her son sprawls across a street corner, a semiautomatic assault rifle at his feet. Two people hold up the mother's arms so that she forms a Pietà-like cross above him. An apostolic dozen federales mill about in riot gear as the terrorized crowd gazes on. Every face tilts in a different direction except for those of a federale and a matronly woman, both of whom stare at a fixed spot in the distance with such wide-eyed horror that I can't help but glance over my own shoulder—where more paintings of severed heads await.

Just then, the door swings open and Jesus de la Rosa, the curator of the exhibit and a friend of Rigoberto's, blazes in.

"That's me," he says, nodding at a massive painting of six thugs caught in the limb-strewn act of kidnapping a man and woman on a dark city street. A car is approaching with its high beams on, but I sense it isn't coming to help.

"You see how he's covering my mouth?" he asks, pointing at the man forcing his burly replica into submission. "That's how it has felt all of these years, like I've had to keep my mouth shut."

Jesus grew up in Nuevo Progreso and for many years ran an art gallery there—until the drug war scared away the tourists. Now he teaches studio art with Santa Barraza at TAMUK. Jesus rarely visits his family in Mexico and refuses to let his children go. "It's all about being at the wrong place at the wrong time," he says, stroking his beard. "My father's cousin was taken about two years ago. He was in the drug business. He said, 'Mom, they are going to come for me,' and that was it."

He shows me more of Rigoberto's work, each canvas increasingly daunting. A federale in combat boots brandishes the decapitated head of a naked woman, à la Cellini's *Perseus with the Head of Medusa*. La Llorona, the wailing ghost-woman of Mexican folklore, navigates a river with her children. A tattooed punk clenches a knife and grins as he crouches beneath a man whose pants puddle about his ankles. Rigoberto works in the style of seventeenth-century Baroque painters like Caravaggio, casting gruesome realism into an almost celestial light. Many paintings include at least one figure who stares directly at the viewer. When I point this out, Jesus nods. "That is Rigo's way of saying you are a part of what is happening, as much as you think you are not involved. You smoke one joint a week thinking you're not hurting anything, but you don't think about how it got into your hands. There are people who are enslaved to grow it, people who transport it, people who sell it."

His voice trails off as we stare at the images surrounding us. "It is all connected."

THE RIO GRANDE VALLEY used to seem like such a pastoral place—cowboys and snowbirds; citrus groves and taquito stands. Tíos hovering over barbecue pits, drinking Corona, while little *primos* ran around barefoot and tías gossiped in the kitchen. But as I drive the 100-plus miles back to the border, the windswept roads feel almost haunted.

Before rejoining Susan at the wall, I cut through the town of Harlingen, passing cinder block buildings adorned with signs reading GARZA

TORTILLAS, SALINAS PHARMACY, and ROBLES LAW FIRM. A side street leads me through a labyrinth of pawnshops to the office of the local psychic. HELP WITH ALL PROBLEMS THROUGH THE POWER OF PRAYER says the sign above the barred window. CARD READING/REUNITE LOVERS: 956–264–8402. Though it's tempting, I knock instead on the door labeled K&S POOLS & SUPPLY.

The door cracks open and Rigoberto A. Gonzalez peeks out. Given the macabre content of his artwork, I was half-expecting a tormented poet-type, turtlenecked and bedraggled. But no. His top half is professorial. He wears an Ivy cap, rimless glasses, and a neatly trimmed goatee. His bottom half is pure lounge: basketball shorts and slip-ons. He steps to the side to allow my passage, then bolts the door behind me.

"This place used to be a liquor store," he explains, "so I have to keep it locked. People are always dropping by asking for some."

The walls of his studio are white, the bookcases royal blue. Fat volumes of Rembrandt and El Greco crest the highest shelves, while cattle skulls occupy the lower ones. Images of the Baroque masters plaster the back wall. A jar of biscotti decks the counter. My eyes are drawn to an especially large canvas of a man hanging upside-down in the crucifix position—feet tied, arms at ninety degrees—wearing only red briefs against a black backdrop. Another news story flashes across my mind, of narcos throwing their victims off an overpass.

Rigoberto and I are the same age and grew up just 150 miles apart, he in the city of Reynosa. But while he also remembers this region being "peaceful and boring" when we were kids, he absorbed narco culture early on.

"As a child I would play with little Hot Wheels cars, and I'd put grass in the wheels because I heard that's how drugs were smuggled," he says with a chuckle. "I don't think I ever wanted to *do* it, but you dream about it, about the aura of power. I did not go into it directly, but if you look at my paintings, in a way I am involved."

He walks over to a shelf and pulls down a rifle I somehow overlooked. "This is part of my background, the culture I grew up in. Reynosa always had that aura of the Wild West, the guys with the entourage and their weapons. What is happening now is a natural evolution of that cultural mentality. The border always had that darkness to it."

"Then why does so little art reflect it?" I ask.

"The One Percent some years back, during the Cold War, realized art was a tool to be used against the people in power, so they started funding art that was nonpolitical," he says, adjusting his glasses. "That's why, if you put an agenda in your work, it is seen as not-art. There is no one addressing social themes today because they don't want us to. People usually paint figures of themselves or of a nude, not really about this greater tragedy we are seeing right now."

Rigoberto is so resolute in his contemplation of tragedy, his work has met with some local resistance. One museum director told him he'd need to create an entirely new body of work in order to be shown there, lest they "get in trouble." He has had an easier time exhibiting work in South Dakota than here in South Texas.

"There has been reluctance because of the negativity of my stories, not to mention the proximity," he says. "Yet you can't suppress it. My work is about starting a dialogue and maybe about starting the healing process. Because it's a holocaust out there."

Recently Rigoberto has begun a new series of landscapes featuring the border wall and the people who dare cross it. He hands me a pencil sketch of the river known as the Rio Grande by its northern inhabitants and as the Río Bravo by its southern, snaking through a bend. While not as grisly as his earlier work, this series won't necessarily be less violent. "I want to show a storm over the border," he says.

Rigoberto has one more thing to share before I part: a book on the drug war by Mexican documentary photographers. My entire body shudders when he flips to an image of men grinning over the row of corpses at their feet. Something about their triumph transports me to the War Remnants Museum in Ho Chi Minh City, where years ago I burst into tears over a photo of U.S. soldiers posing by slaughtered Viet Cong. Rigoberto's response is much more intimate.

"When I see the men they capture, the men responsible, the heads of the cartels, the hit men," he says softly, "when I look at them, I see that they could be my cousin or my brother. That similarity really scares me."

He removes his glasses and stares at me without blinking. "It could even be me."

OVER HOTEL BISCUITS SMOTHERED IN POWDERED GRAVY, Susan and I decide to spend the day in Hidalgo County, which has a "hopping" border, according to Mark. On the drive out from Brownsville, we traverse roads that have flatlined into silence. The sky, meanwhile, is an ocean inverted—an all-encompassing blue. One yard showcases a row of tiny American flags flapping above the chain-link fence, along with a larger flag impaled into the stump of a tree.

We park at the Old Hidalgo Pumphouse, where—according to the brochure—"steam-driven irrigation pumps transformed Hidalgo County into a year-round farming phenomenon." A garden thick with huisache and anacua surrounds the complex. A World Birding Center extends beyond it, home to tropical kingfishers, Altamira orioles, and clay-colored robins, all out of reach behind the eighteen-foot border wall.

The town of Hidalgo stretches along the banks of the Rio Grande. Earthen levees have long held its floodwaters at bay, but a few years ago some were replaced by walls that serve the dual purpose of flood control and border security. These walls are the ugliest I've seen: miles of concrete slabs teethed in tall steel posts that preside over the green like a cubist sentry. We find the hiking trail leading to the wall, but what should be a five-minute walk takes us nearly thirty. The trail is practically paved with objects.

"Here's one," Susan says, stopping midstride and reaching for her camera. I peek over her shoulder to find a toothbrush at her feet, whole and blue. A red one missing its bristles lies a few inches away, along with a broken hair clip. "This is what the border used to be like at Brownsville. It means it's really active." She slides the objects into La Virgen.

Next is a purple shirt, tangled in weeds. As she grabs one end and pulls, a Border Patrol vehicle drives by. Its back end is outfitted with a holding cell, something a dogcatcher might use. Before I can mention it, Susan says, "Whoa, look at that!" and bounds over to a Macy's bag half hidden in a clump of grass. A pair of Wrangler Originals tumbles out, then a long-sleeved shirt, and finally a handsome belt with a buckle shaped like a Longhorn. She examines the jeans. "Size 32x30. Made in China. And . . . they're still wet."

That's probably why they are here, she speculates. Over the years, she has learned that the Border Patrol does not allow immigrants to bring anything wet aboard their vehicles because there is no way to dry clothes at the station (plus they can't risk the spread of mold). Belts are also not permitted, lest they be used as weapons. Same with shoelaces. Same with hairbrushes. Same with toothbrushes.

"Bras are often a sign of rape," she says. "Coyotes will hang them on a tree afterward, like a trophy. Homemade flotation devices usually mean a baby has been brought across. Sometimes you find religious cards on the banks of the river and know someone left them there in thanks for a safe passage. You see caffeine pills, and it is so they can stay awake during the journey."

We continue down the trail. Toothbrush, toothbrush. Shoelace, shoe-lace. A water bottle, squished. A tennis shoe. Half of a comb. Most of a shirt. Nail clippers. Another shirt. A lacy black bra. Susan and I halt midstep. Yes: a lacy black bra. It isn't dangling from a tree, but still. A lacy black bra.

When this expedition began at Hope Park a few days ago, it felt like a most peculiar egg hunt. But as La Virgen began to fill, I started to see as Susan does: the objects as reliquaries, the journey as pilgrimage. But the vulnerability of this bra curled in the dirt renders the trail into a crime scene. No woman abandons her lacy black bra unless she is forced to. Unless she has surrendered the entirety of her attention.

Scattered nearby are two pairs of panties, a wallet, a travel-size Speed Stick, a pocket-size Bible (Nuevo Testamento), two pairs of socks rolled into balls, a three-ounce tube of Colgate, a pack of Trident chewing gum, five packages of pills in various colors and sizes, and a light blue handkerchief. The relief I feel from this additional discovery—maybe a Border Patrol agent made her drop everything, as opposed to a coyote ripping off that one thing?—gives way to the dread of imagining a woman walking around without these items. Nothing here is irreplaceable, of course, but the woman who packed these items did so with care. Her bra looks almost new. Her panties are still folded. So often in our culture we are the sum of our posses-sions. Indeed, at times they seem the only markers of our passage through this world. What does it mean to pare them down to the essentials—and then to lose even those?

Just ahead, a Border Patrol suv is parked by the gate of the wall. Long slabs of wood are piled against the steel. As I draw closer, I see they are ladders. Missing half their rungs, yes, and with nails protruding all over the place—but ladders nonetheless. As I try to lift one up, the door opens and an agent steps out. I think he's going to tell us to leave the ladders alone, but no. He has been sitting by himself for hours and wants some company.

"They scale the wall with these?" I ask.

"Yeah," he says. "They bring them from Mexico and store them in the brush and then we find them and bring them over here. The city picks them up and destroys them once a week or so."

He chatters on while Susan documents the ladders and I study them, only half-listening until he mentions detaining a three-year-old and a one-and-a-half-year-old the other day, both traveling alone.

"Alone?" we ask.

He nods. "There was a twelve-year-old boy who was told to help them get across. He was carrying the one-and-a-half-year-old. There are a lot of kids coming without their parents now. It is just insane."

If I were thinking more like a reporter, I would ask the set of questions that would lead me to the not-yet-broken news story about the unprecedented numbers of unaccompanied minors[8] who have just started streaming across the border from Guatemala, Honduras, and El Salvador. Alas, I receive this information as a (solipsistic) memoirist and thus file it away as further evidence of a motherland forever changed.

We bid the agent farewell and start walking along the wall. Its southern side is a mass of tangled green, beyond which runs the river. The northern side is hedged with the backyards of family homes. We pass by trampolines and wading pools, conked-out appliances and junked-out cars. We pass by an RV park crowded with campers. We pass by a generator-run, Border Patrol–operated skybox that is Soviet chic. We pass by every iteration of fence Home Depot has in stock. And we pass by so many abandoned objects, not even La Virgen can hold them all.

A siren goes off. Commotion ensues in the near distance. We quicken our pace as a Border Patrol vehicle pulls up from behind. A Tejano agent sticks out his head and informs us that sixty bodies have been found up ahead.

"*Bodies?*" I ask, envisioning a pile of corpses.

"We got two of them. The rest went back to Mexico. Where you ladies heading?"

Susan tells our story, then asks if we can walk down by the river.

"Si, pero . . ." He looks at me.

"Pero peligroso?" I ask. But it's dangerous?

"Pues, si." He rolls up the window. Sure is.

We hurry on until we see three Border Patrol vehicles idling by the wall. One is outfitted with the container cell I noticed earlier. A female

---

8. More than 68,000 unaccompanied children were caught crossing the border between October 2013 and October 2014—so many, they overwhelmed federal facilities. That July, I visited one of the makeshift shelters that had sprung up in the Rio Grande Valley: Sacred Heart Catholic Church in McAllen. In its first month of operation, volunteers offered showers, clothing, phone calls, a hot meal, and a place to rest to more than 3,000 families who had just been processed out of a detention center and were awaiting their court date. Whenever a new group arrived, volunteers formed a receiving line and cheered. "How do you deport a child to nowhere?" asked Ofelia de los Santos of Catholic Charities. "If Lebanon can handle hundreds of thousands of refugees, why can't we handle 50,000 kids?"

agent steps out, walks around back, and opens the door of the cell. Susan and I freeze in place as a middle-aged woman pops out. Maybe five feet tall with sienna skin and curly hair, she is dressed more for a day at the office—nice slacks, a jacket, pumps—than for fording an international riverbed. Susan puts her camera down as the woman climbs aboard the adjacent vehicle. Although the windows are darkly tinted, I see her head turn sharply away from us.

Next out is a fortyish man with an Olmec nose, wearing a white shirt and jeans. He pauses to look at Susan and me before stepping inside the awaiting vehicle. My hand instinctively rises and waves. What I mean by this is hard to articulate, but something like: You are here and I am here the way our ancestors have always been here but now you are being taken away from here while I still get to stand here and I am bearing witness to the injustice of that and I am sorry.

I watch the man get swallowed inside the dark of the windows and search for a place to rest his gaze. At one point, he seems to be looking at me. For half a second, I wonder whether or not to wave again. He beats me to it.

8

The Chokepoint

THE FIRST THING LEAD INVESTIGATOR DANNY DAVILA WANTS TO know is whether I have a weak stomach. We are sitting in his cramped office at the Brooks County sheriff's department on a sweltering afternoon. Before I can respond, he slides a three-ring binder that he calls "the Dead Book" my way. Inside are dozens of laminated photographs of the remains of the thirty-four undocumented immigrants who have died in this county's scrub brush this year, presumably while sidestepping Falfurrias's nearby chokepoint.

"This is the American Dream," Davila says, spreading his arms wide, as if to signal beyond the cedar-paneled room, "and this is where it stops, right here." He thumps the binder with his forefinger.

Grasping the Dead Book with both hands, I open to a random page. A dark-skinned man wearing only yellow briefs is curled into the fetal position atop a blanket.

"We find them naked sometimes, but it's not because they were abused or anything. It's just their last-ditch effort to try to cool off. They don't know that makes it worse," Davila explains.

At first glance, the man seems to have been caught in a moment of quiet contemplation: his muscles are relaxed and his gaze is soft. But as I look more closely, I see that ants are swarming his eyeballs. Turning the page before the image fully registers, I scan some typewritten reports before finding the next photograph: an engorged hand roasted purple and protruding from the dirt, its fingers extending skyward. Then a face that is half skull, half meat, and a full set of teeth. Then a belly so swollen it has split like a chorizo on a grill. Every image traumatizes me further, yet I keep flipping the pages as calmly as possible to prove I can handle it. Twenty minutes ago, a rancher called in a Code 500. The thirty-fifth body of the year has been discovered. If my stomach is up to it, I can accompany Davila on the retrieval.

BY YEAR'S END, there will be three Dead Books perched atop Davila's desk, along with a "Missing Persons" binder full of photos and e-mails sent in by anxious families in Mexico and Central America. The year 2012 will break all records for Brooks County, with 129 bodies found somewhere along 942 square miles of ranches and roads. Not only is that body count a 200 percent increase from 2011, but it comes at a time when migration across the U.S. border is at a historic low—nearly half the rate of even four years ago. In 2012, the entire state of Arizona recovered just twenty-eight more bodies than this tiny Texas county claimed.

So how did Brooks become a killing field for immigrants? First, there's U.S. policy to consider. Until the early nineties, many hopeful immigrants traveled to major ports of entry like San Diego, waited until dark, and then bolted across the international line[1] with the Border Patrol at their heels. In response, Customs and Border Protection began launching programs like El Paso's "Operation Hold-the-Line" in 1993, which mobilized so many agents at traditional crossing routes that immigrants started trekking into the desert to avoid them. After 9/11, Congress sought to "secure" the Mexico border by more than doubling the number of agents there, deploying Predator drones, and erecting the wall—all of which pushed immigrants into the most isolated (and therefore dangerous) regions of the desert for their crossings. Sparsely populated southern Arizona used to be a common transit area, but according to Davila, its recent spate of anti-immigrant legislation seems to be curbing the tide to Texas now. He's been noticing a lot of Arizona state-issued identification cards on the bodies he's helped recover lately, meaning that even established immigrants could be deciding to test their fate in Texas instead.

Then there's the weather. Texas suffered its worst-ever drought in 2011, and temperatures routinely hit triple digits here. Coyotes tend to tell their clients that they'll need to walk only a couple of hours to avoid the chokepoint (as opposed to a couple of days) and that the trail cuts through a nice ranch (instead of foot-deep sand speckled with horse crippler cactus). Unprepared for the harsh conditions, many immigrants succumb to heat exhaustion and die when the other travelers continue on without them.

---

1. So many would-be immigrants got struck and killed while darting across San Diego's freeways, Caltrans started posting yellow caution signs in 1990 that depicted a silhouette of a father, mother, and child in flight. This image has since been adopted by activists on both sides of the immigration debate and emblazoned on everything from T-shirts to book jackets to artwork that hangs in the Smithsonian.

The rise of organized crime has brought even more deaths. Ten years ago, immigrants could hire local coyotes in Mexico to walk them across the border for $1,000 apiece. Today, they usually wind up with minions of transnational networks who charge exorbitant rates to navigate the routes that offer the best chances of avoiding the Border Patrol. Their preferred terrain is often so desolate, the coyotes feel at liberty to do whatever they want with their charges. Crimes are rarely punished because border crossers are reluctant to report their coyotes' misdeeds. Retribution is too grave. In Brooks County, the bodies of the dead are often silenced too, since so few undergo autopsies. Technically, that's breaking Texas law, but—at $1,500 each—Brooks simply can't afford to determine whether a border crosser died of exposure or as a result of violence. Although taxpayers spent upward of $90 billion securing the U.S.-Mexico border in the decade following 9/11, very little funneled down to local law enforcement agencies. Brooks County's entire operating budget is just $585,000 a year, barely enough to pay its employees. Davila, after eighteen years on the job, makes only $27,000. Moreover, wild pigs and vultures usually find the bodies long before the authorities do, ravaging potential evidence.

But while there are countless possible culprits behind the surge of immigrant deaths in South Texas—overzealous "security" policies, climate change, sadistic coyotes, silence—I find only one listed in the three-ring binder on Davila's desk. In report after report, the cause of death is listed as "hiking through ranch illegally."

"I DON'T KNOW IF THIS BODY is a stinker or a bloater or what," Davila says as we climb into a black Ford F-150. He never knows what awaits him on these runs: scattered bones, a freshly vacated corpse, or something in between. I'm not sure what to hope for myself. My heart is already thumping in my throat.

Glancing around the cab of the truck, I see that we're bringing along a camera tripod, a camouflage jacket, a flashlight, gloves, a body bag, and a M4 carbine semiautomatic assault rifle, all coated in dirt. Davila explains that he does a lot of four-wheeling and off-roading on the job—hence, the grime. This Ford doesn't actually belong to him. It got impounded by the county after the owner was arrested for drug smuggling. A couple hundred such vehicles line the field adjacent to the sheriff's department, each with a date scrawled across the windshield with shoe polish, waiting to be repossessed or auctioned. Some are spanking new, while others have had their hoods rolled back like sardine cans to reveal whatever stash they held within. Many wear Houston plates, which practically scream "Search me" to Davila.

"It seems like any group, no matter who they are, is always going to Houston. From there, they get shipped all over the place," he says.

Whenever he spies a Houston plate coasting down the highway, he calls it in to see if it's been reported stolen. Other warning signs include a lack of backseats (yanked out to make more room for cargo) and reinforced springs (which give the appearance of a lighter load). Smugglers also tend to congregate in certain parts of town, such as the convenience stores off U.S. 281. "You see someone walking out with thirty chicken legs and thirty Gatorades, you know what they're up to."

We are zipping along County Road 201 now, past the detention center and Selina's Bail Bonds toward downtown Falfurrias. Davila points out landmarks like the old dairy, which used to sell sweet cream butter out of yellow and blue boxes. Now the Whataburger stands where the creamery once did, and the main strip is lined with a deserted movie theater, dollar stores, loan offices, and pawnshops. Of Brooks County's 7,200 residents, nearly 40 percent live below the poverty line.

"You find someone lost in the woods and you take them home, call their loved ones, and say, 'Hey, for five hundred bucks, I'll take them to Houston.' Then you wait for the money to be wired over, and you put them on a bus," Davila says. "I'd say 40 percent of the population here is involved like that."

Indeed, I'll turn on the news the next day to learn that the wife of the justice of the peace in nearby Kenedy County has been busted for transporting nine undocumented immigrants in her Hummer. She charged $500 a head.

As someone born and raised in Falfurrias, Davila finds it all disheartening. "That's the hardest part of this job, policing your own, the people you grew up with," he says, shaking his head and stroking his moustache. He's a handsome man, late thirties with thick black hair and dark olive skin. Though he routinely sees hideous things, he seems inherently upbeat, always joking and grinning. His name is stitched across his shirt and his rubber bracelet reads PEACE. Leaning over the steering wheel, he flicks on the radio:

This heat has got
Right out of hand.

It's Bananarama, the eighties British pop band. The song is "Cruel Summer."

A RANCH HAND WEARING a rosary as a necklace ushers us in at the gate of a sprawling Brooks County ranch, one Davila asks me not to name. We're among the last to arrive—the Border Patrol, the justice of the peace, and the sheriff are already here, and the undertaker is on the way. The body is located in the far recesses of the property, so we must travel in a caravan so no one gets lost. As we amble down the caliche road, Davila points out where gaping holes have been cut into the barbed-wire fence. Some ranchers leave out ladders in the hopes their fences might be spared, but the hikers don't seem to use them. It's the same with the water. Afraid, perhaps, of being poisoned by the big tanks painted blue especially for them, the immigrants opt to break the valves off windmills and drink that water instead.

At 3.3 miles, we switch to four-wheel drive, take a right, and begin off-roading through the brush. I am trembling now—and Davila doesn't help when he notes that this seemingly deserted ranch is actually teeming with smugglers. "There ain't *someone* looking at us. There's a whole *lotta* people looking at us."

He is constantly reminded that the smugglers monitor his actions. Not long before our meeting, a stranger approached him at the store and said, "I noticed your antenna is bent, what happened?"

Davila laughed it off—"I hit a butterfly," he told the man—but the point was clear. People know what kind of car he drives, and where and when, which is especially disconcerting given that he has a young daughter. I ask how he deals with the stress, and he quips, "I take a lot of blood pressure pills."

In time, we see a navy hoodie dangling from a fence. The truck ahead of us parks and so do we. The brush has grown too thick for driving. It's time to start hiking.

I SMELL THE BODY BEFORE I SEE IT. The scent wraps around my face like a hot towel, burning my eyes and singeing my throat. It is violent and rancid and frightening. I start breathing through my mouth instead of my nose, but that transfers the sensation to my tongue. Now I am eating death instead of smelling it.

Trailing behind Davila, I enter the woods. The brush is so dense, I must clear it with my arms before each step, half-swimming across the loamy soil. Brambles crack beneath my boots. It is ninety-five degrees.

Maybe forty feet away, a pair of black jeans becomes visible. An occupied pair of jeans, stretched out in the dirt. One foot remains inside a sneaker, but before I can spot the other, I see the arm. What's left of the arm. Not long ago, that arm must have hugged and danced, carried firewood and groceries and children, but now it has been eaten to the bone, with just a few pulpy morsels remaining. The hand, meanwhile, has been ravaged not by animals but by sun, baked so black it almost looks blue.

My eyes drift toward the midsection of the body. At first, I think it is wearing a child-size T-shirt, but then I see the belly has bloated to colossal proportions, so engorged it has exploded along the jean line. Slick black beetles crawl in and out of its crater.

It's the face, though, that unravels me. From the nose down, its remaining skin is black and leathered, but the top half is strangely untouched, the color of a bruised peach. There are deep holes instead of eyes, and the mouth is open as if silently wailing. The hair is streaming all the way down to what used to be elbows, thick and black and damp. *It's a woman*, I think, and with that realization comes the overpowering urge to scream, to continue the sound her own mouth was making before "hiking through ranch illegally" forever quieted her, to continue the collective wail they all must have been making before winding up inside the three-ring binders of Brooks County, Texas. I bite my lips until they bleed.

WE GATHER AROUND THE WOMAN—Davila, the sheriff, the Border Patrol, the justice of the peace, the ranch hand, and me—yet we stand a good fifteen to twenty feet away. We lean forward, as if over an imaginary railing, but no one steps any closer. It could be that we are respecting the privacy of this tragedy, or taking care not to trample any evidence. I've been told that these bodies harbor all matter of wildlife, including snakes and spiders. Perhaps no one wants to get bitten. Santa Barraza will later inform me that spirits hover long beyond a body's death, waiting for someone to find them and then affixing to their shoulder. Perhaps no one wants to get cursed. Or maybe we're just sparing ourselves further revulsion. Whatever the case, I too stand close-but-far, despite a pressing impulse to run up and hold what's left of the woman's hand.

The justice of the peace asks for the time. We all scramble for our watches and cell phones, grateful for the distraction. After much discussion we decide it is 12:35 on July 3, 2012, which the justice of the peace jots in her notebook. Although this woman has clearly been gone for days—three, by Davila's estimation—this will be her official time of death. And because there is no obvious sign of foul play—no hatchet sticking out of her skull, say—her death will be attributed to "hiking through ranch illegally."

Just then the undertaker arrives on the scene. He is an older man with a slender build, and he carries a white bedsheet and a large cardboard box. Breaking through our imaginary railing, he walks right up to the woman's feet, sets down his parcels, and slides on a pair of blue rubber gloves. He briskly searches her pockets, inches from the beetle pit. First he finds some dollar bills: a twenty, a five, three ones. He piles these atop the woman's thigh. Next he pulls out an LG cell phone and wipes it clean. Running his fingers along her bra line, he checks to see if anything is tucked inside, an ID maybe, or a list of phone numbers. There is nothing.

Now comes the task of slipping the woman into the bag. He unfurls the sheet and lays it out beside her, though ultimately it must go beneath her. Carefully, he rolls the woman onto her side—but that makes her scalp fall off, hair and all, with a strangely soupy sound. She has become liquid. All of her is leaking and dripping, colored fluids as well as beetles. The undertaker catches her scalp and swiftly slides it back into place, as though assisting a lady with an errant wig. While the rest of us simply stand and stare, Davila bounds over to help. They push the sheet beneath her, then roll her back on top.

"She's small," Davila announces. "Probably Guatemalan. Or Honduran."

The two men swaddle her in the sheet, half bones, half stew, and then stuff her into a black body bag with golden zippers, taken from the cardboard box. Davila, the sheriff, and the Border Patrol agent fan out thirty feet and scan the brush for approximately half a minute before heading back to their respective trucks. There is no obvious evidence in sight. We leave behind only an empty water bottle and a host of beetles. No words are spoken. No rites are given.

OVER BY THE FORD, Davila wipes his shoes on a patch of huisache. "Gotta make sure there's no bodily fluid on me, 'cause it will stink," he explains.

We notice the undertaker struggling with a gurney, and Davila hurries over. Together they prop it open, lay the body bag on top, strap it down, lift it up, and roll it into the back of the van. Davila introduces me to the undertaker, whose name is Ángel, pronounced *An-hell* in the Tejano way. I want to say "how fitting" and applaud his professional graces, but before I can speak, Davila tells him I am a writer.

Ángel shakes his head. "A lot of people write stories," he says softly, "and nothing ever gets done."

I hear this a lot, and though it never fails to shatter me, I usually brush it off with a self-deprecating remark and a smile. But there's just something about standing in the woods with a three-days-dead woman in ninety-five-degree heat that gives me the audacity to hope that maybe, just maybe, something will change this time: Congress will change and minds will change and policy will change and a humane immigration law will finally be enacted; and although that hope vaporizes into idealistic mist before I can even articulate it, there remains a spark of optimism that, by virtue of being written about, this Code 500 might be remembered—that, even if we never learn her name or whether she's Guatemalan or Honduran or for all we know Chinese, this one member of the thirty-four who died before her and the ninety-four who will die after her this single year in this solitary county of this one state could be memorialized inside of a story. And at the very least, *I* will remember her—this woman who hiked illegally through this ranch and got annihilated for it—*I* will remember what remained of her feet and of her face when I try to fall asleep at night. Is it wrong, Ángel, to pray this counts as something getting done?

I wish to say this—all of this, and a great deal more—but there is time only to feebly smile before Ángel retreats to his driver's seat, where he removes a pair of badly soiled gloves. He already knows that he'll be back tomorrow, and that I will not.

9

The Woman in the Woods

I SEE HER EVERYWHERE NOW.

Santa Barraza had warned me her spirit could latch onto my shoulder, but the woman in the woods seems to have emblazoned my corneas instead. For months afterward, she is the prism through which I view almost everything. I see her in dark spaces, like the corners of closets, but also in white spaces, like unadorned walls. I see her between the pages of books and flickering across computer screens. I see her at night, when she wards off sleep. Though I heard scores of traumatic border-crossing stories while researching my last book, hers is the one I cannot release, despite knowing only its end.

Maybe she was escaping war, or the ghosts of war, such as the ones that ravaged Guatemala and El Salvador. Maybe she was fleeing natural disaster, like the hurricane that obliterated much of Honduras, or social disaster, like the Mara Salvatrucha, which has infiltrated most of las Américas. The murderous gang could have been pressuring her husband or son to traffic drugs across the border. They could even have been cajoling her.

Or maybe she came for love. Her sister was in the United States, her cousin was in the United States, her absolutely favorite tío. Her husband was here, her child was here, her *life*, she was convinced, was here.

Whatever the push/pull—war, disaster, violence, family, hope—it must have been fierce, tremendously fierce, if it propelled her to gather all of the money she could raise or borrow and relinquish it to a stranger. Whatever her thought process, whatever her reasoning, her conclusion must have been that possibly dying in El Norte was better than living on at home.

And so she said good-bye to her mother and father, her siblings and cousins, all the tías and abuelas who helped raise her. She said goodbye to the friends whom she grew up with, her classmates and coworkers, the neighbors who lived down the road. She said good-bye to her lover and possibly even her children, then summoned all of the courage within and boarded a bus heading north. Traveling across her homeland, she must have paused to take in one last sunset across her ancestral sky. Eaten one last *pupusa* that her mother had made, one last mango picked from her backyard tree.

No matter where she came from, traveling across Mexico probably seemed worse. First there was jungle followed by mountains and rivers and desert, all infested with terrifying men trafficking drugs and guns and people. Mexican immigration officials patrolled the highways, street gangs traversed the trains, and swindlers prowled the bus stations, yet somehow she avoided them. Chances are, she had a coyote to guide her, but if she didn't—or if she did and he'd already abandoned her—she probably hired one at the border. He wouldn't have been hard to find. He saw her shuffling around the bus terminal with her flowing black hair and her skinny black jeans, and he raised an eyebrow with interest. He convinced her that he knew the way; he ensured her that he could be trusted. *Houston, no problem, I got a group of forty there last night. Los Angeles, that's easy, I was there a week ago.* Something in his cocksure voice reminded her of her long-lost tío. Something said he was safe.

Maybe she crossed into the United States by raft in the dark of night, current racing, cold water slapping her face. Maybe she crossed by folding herself into the trunk of a car or by squeezing between shipping containers in an eighteen-wheeler. Maybe she crossed by wading through sandy desert. However she did it, the odds were formidable. About a thousand people are caught each day along the 2,000-mile border and either detained or sent back home. Yet every day, unknown hundreds or thousands more slip through. One day or night, one of those lucky border crossers was her.

The triumph she felt must have been extraordinary. *¡El Otro Lado!* The Other Side. Whatever she came for, she must have imagined it would be waiting there, right across *la línea.* Her mother or brother or lover would be standing there, arms outstretched, ready to receive her. Or else, that cleaning or sewing or child-sitting job she'd heard about—the one that would finally allow her family to buy that house, pay off those debts, finance that car, and splurge on her daughter's *quinceañera* while she was at it. Her new boss would be there, ready to stuff her pockets with gringo dollars.

What she probably did not realize—what she couldn't begin to fathom— was that however far she had traveled, she was still only halfway to her destination. The border is wide; the border is vicious. Her crossing had just begun.

UNDOCUMENTED IMMIGRANTS GENERALLY SPEND THEIR first nights in the United States at a stash house. Often located on the fringes of border towns, these rental homes or apartments have traditionally served as motels for illicit travelers—a place to shower and rest while coyotes plot the next stage of the journey. But in the Texas Rio Grande Valley, these houses have degenerated into something else entirely. Ten years ago, coyotes seemed to assign no more than a dozen immigrants to each house, but police these days are finding upward of forty and fifty per house, so many they sleep in shifts (if at all). Food and water are rationed, and when immigrants complain, they often get beaten. Some groups must endure these conditions for weeks while coyotes secretly call their families and extort money for their release. In fiscal year 2012, law enforcement busted 237 stash houses in the Rio Grande Valley and apprehended 4,752 immigrants—nearly two and a half times as many people as the year before.

An especially grisly discovery occurred in Edinburg in May 2012 when a Spanish-speaking man called 911 and, in a hushed voice, pleaded for help. He was being held prisoner, he said, and feared for his life. When police arrived, scores of immigrants fled from a house and trailer at the end of a caliche road. During their search, police found even more people locked inside of a cinder block building with security bars on the windows. All told, 115 immigrants had been stowed inside the three-building property, and they claimed not to have eaten in days. They also said that their ringleader, a twenty-three-year-old Mexican national named Marcial Salas Gardunio, had greeted them upon their arrival with an ominous "Welcome to hell."

After Salas gets sentenced to a hell of his own, I persuade Greg to join me in paying the former stash house a visit. ("Only if I can wait in the car," he says.) Traveling south on U.S. 281, we pass ranch after ranch until a delta of taquerias and RV parks opens up. This is the Rio Grande Valley: one million Tejanos, Mexican nationals, and snowbirds coexisting on the northern banks of the famous river, minutes from Mexico. It's a 100-mile strip where Spanish is offered before English, where churches are either grand and Catholic or plain and Pentecostal, where the grapefruit is ruby red and the sky is denim blue, where a side of beans comes with every meal, where a Border Patrol vehicle is never far from view.

Exiting University Avenue and turning east, the fast food franchises gradually give way to mom-and-pop restaurants with hand-painted signs. Vera's King-O-Meats. Esner's Playa Azul. The local newspaper gave only an approximation of the stash house's address, so we drive up and down the avenue a few times before selecting a side street at random. The neighborhood is exceedingly humble with boarded-up windows and rotting cars, but in time a cinder block house appears behind a chain-link fence. Looking closely, we see a gaping hole has been cut through it. Is that it? Greg waits in the car with the engine running while I duck beneath the hole in the fence and dart to the nearest window. The house appears to have been ransacked. Overturned furniture covers the floor along with heaps of clothing and shoes and bits of ceiling streaked in sludge. In the farthest corner, an office-size photocopier lay on its side, coughing up moldy papers as if it had been bludgeoned. Do smugglers make photocopies? Maybe of contracts—or receipts?

Nearby is a house with a few licks of paint and some long-retired blinds. The truck out front suggests it might be occupied, so I knock. The blinds rustle. A woman's face becomes visible, then disappears. I wait a while before knocking again, louder this time. The door creaks open, and a thin man in a threadbare cap emerges.

"Are you Immigration?" he asks in Spanish, anxiety pinching his face.

I assure him I'm only a writer, but that seems equally bad. Shaking his head, he says that he's sorry, he would like to help me but he can't, it's too dangerous, this isn't the kind of neighborhood where you can walk around writing things, I really should just leave. Yet he makes no motion to leave himself. If anything, he more firmly establishes his presence on the doorstep. We are sizing each other up now. No tattoos, pistol-bulges, or signs of unaccountable wealth: this man looks safe to me. He, in turn, seems to be digesting my college-ruled notebook. I start making small talk, banking on a year's worth of experiences in Mexico that, in the end, the men always open up, whether out of politeness or machismo or a plaintive desire to be heard. Sure enough, after a few exchanges about the weather, this one does too.

On the morning of the stash house raid, he says, he woke up early to get ready for work and saw squad cars and Border Patrol circling his street. He told his wife to turn off the lights and not to answer the door. His family waited quietly in an unlit room, missing work and school, until finally the neighborhood emptied. He later learned that a friend had been arrested in the raid for the crime of living next door to the stash house. For thirty days, he got interrogated in a detention center[1] until deemed innocent. Then he

---

1. While awaiting deportation from the United States, many immigrants are held for weeks if not months in a network of more than 250 detention centers that are often owned and operated by private companies like Halliburton in isolated stretches of the country. Even the "better" centers are equipped with not-enough blankets, inedible food, overhead lighting that wards off sleep, and pneumonia-inducing air conditioning. In the worst, immigrants must also fend off physically and sexually abusive guards—and

was dropped off at the international bridge in Brownsville and forced to retreat into Matamoros.

"He got bronchitis while he was in the detention center and they didn't give him any medicine," the man says, indignant on his friend's behalf. "They took his money and they didn't give it back."

The friend had to hire a coyote to cross the border again—a debt he'll be paying for years to come—but now he's back in the neighborhood. They both work at the same construction site.

I ask if he had known so many immigrants were being held at the stash house, and he admits to having noticed some unusually nice trucks in the neighborhood lately. Having lived here seven years, he sensed something was wrong, but he knew better than to ask any questions.

"The people involved, they are very bad. Whenever we see a new car, we know to stay away because we don't want any problems."

He shows me where the stash house is located, down a distant caliche road. "But don't go down there. They know what's happening in this area. They keep watch."

"They're still here?"

"Of course. They've got two or three more houses just like it, right down the street," he says.

I turn around to look.

"Don't!" he hisses. "They are watching. Get in your car and don't come back. And don't use my name. Or identify my house. Please."

After thanking him profusely, I climb back in the Honda to confer with Greg. Whatever nerve I had to investigate further evaporates when a shiny new Ford Expedition with chrome grilling approaches from the opposite direction. Though Greg will later say it didn't, I am (almost) positive it pauses when it passes us. I try to sneak a glimpse at the driver, but the windows are impenetrably tinted. We watch as the Expedition cruises down to the caliche road, then makes a right.

SOMEHOW SHE SURVIVED THE STASH HOUSE STAY. The coyote might have crammed her in with fifty others and the toilet was clogged and there was no place to shower or even to sleep and she ate only tortillas for four

---

unlike in the criminal justice system, immigration detainees have no guaranteed right to a lawyer. To learn more, watch Maria Hinojosa's *Frontline* exposé "Lost in Detention," which aired on PBS in 2011.

days straight, but Immigration never came, so early one morning she got corralled into a dark-windowed van with some other travelers and glided down the street. At first the signs were in Spanish—Casa De Empeño, Yusma Paleteria, Iglesia Rosa de Saron—but gradually the buildings grew taller and the signs got fancier and started saying things in English, too. Wendy's, KFC, Domino's, Subway, Family Dollar. Then came the restaurants with flashing neon signs, the multileveled stores, the impossibly glamorous shopping malls. *So this is El Otro Lado*, she might have thought. No street vendors selling *helado*, no mothers carrying babies on their backs or groceries in their fists, no pack animals, hardly even anyone on their feet. Just an onslaught of trucks and eighteen-wheelers, plus palm trees in the medians.

Soon enough, she exited the city. Now the landscape consisted of a narrow strip of road ahead and a narrow strip behind with nothing along the sides but brush. Well, sometimes a fruit stand. A vacant restaurant called El Luzero. An abandoned Hop N Shop. Remnants of burst tires and bits of raccoon and deer. The grass grew darker and thicker. She settled into the drive. She knew she should nap, but she felt too anxious. So long her journey had been, but surely it would be ending soon.

Perhaps an hour had passed when the driver slowed and turned down a gravel road. He followed it far from the highway, stopping to open and close gates along the way. He finally parked beneath a mesquite tree and everyone climbed out. *The pinche checkpoint is up ahead*, the coyote might have said. *We have to go around it, just a few miles, no problem.*

No matter how far she walked to avoid the first border crossing, no matter how many blisters she formed or how badly she sunburned or wind-burned or dehydrated or overheated, she needed to do it all over again. Probably no one told her this. But the chokepoint at Falfurrias was notorious for catching immigrants, upward of 10,000 a year. She'd come so very far. The next one couldn't be her.

So she was hiking again. *Just a few miles*, the coyotes said (when in fact it was nearly thirty). She carried, at most, a gallon of water, when what she actually needed was three. She'd packed, at most, a granola bar, when what she really needed was a cache of protein. She wore, at most, a cap, when only a beach-size umbrella and SPF 50 sunscreen would do. She was profoundly unprepared, but she didn't know that yet. Houston, the coyote said, was just a few miles away. But really, it was more like three hundred.

LAVOYGER DURHAM IS STRAIGHT OUT of central casting for an old Western flick. Everything about him is big: his voice, his earlobes, his cowboy hat, his smile, his white Ford Excursion with the Super Duty extended cab. His starched button-down shirt is monogrammed with his initials on the cuffs and topped by a silky black vest. He grew up roping cattle on the King Ranch and has been managing the 13,000-acre El Tule Ranch in Brooks County for twenty-two years. His chief responsibility is entertaining high-end hunters, which have included Bushes Senior (who was his best man at his wedding) and W., as well as Dick Cheney (with whom he lunched the day after Harry Whittington got shot). But Durham also devotes considerable time to dealing with "the situation," as he puts it.

He invites me aboard his boatlike Ford one morning to show me "the little spot where illegals trash me up." I take a seat between a rolled-up *Wall Street Journal*, a pair of silver spurs, some Elvis CDs, and multiple boxes of 9mm Luger 100-round Winchesters and .22 Long Rifles bullets. Not far from El Tule's main gate, we turn onto a dirt trail that leads into a blur of huisache and live oaks. Almost instantly I lose my bearings. In every direction, the scenery is identical, with nothing long or tall enough to gauge distance. That's probably why once or twice a month, Durham hears a thump at his door and opens it to find a hopeful or desperate immigrant on his step.

"I ask where they are going, I find out what is the deal, and then I say, 'I'll give you a ride up to the highway,'" he says. "I send them on a pipeline so it's easy to follow, and then I call the Border Patrol. I just get rid of them and that's it."

We are driving parallel to the highway now, perhaps 250 yards away. A gallon jug of water comes into view, uncapped and on its side, gleaming in the sun. Then another. Then a third. Then a sweatshirt and a shoe. Then a dozen jugs of water and a pile of sweatshirts and shoes. We pull up to a massive live oak tree that has been draped in plastic bags and hoodies as if it were a demented Christmas tree, with baseball caps, squashed energy drinks, backpacks, bottles, and plastic jugs strewn beneath. Footprints crumble the dirt.

"That's about a year's worth," Durham says. "I don't clean it up because I bring people like you out here to see it."

While a somber sight for me, it must be a welcome one for the immigrants, as it means they have successfully evaded the chokepoint. Hanging a hoodie could even be a celebratory act. *I won't be needing this anymore; I'm going to Houston!* From here, they just have to wait until their driver honks, then dash through the brush and into the getaway van. Assuming, of course, a driver does indeed come for them, and that they are still capable of dashing when he does. Durham points out a spot where two bodies were recently discovered.[2] "You only find 25 percent of the bodies before the javelinas and the vultures get hold of them. They start to eat, and then you might find one bone over here and another two hundred feet over there."

Right on cue, a pack of javelinas waddle out from the brush. Pepper-black and prickly, they resemble wild pigs with sizable tusks. They have a reputation for meanness.

Horseshoeing at the live oak, we start heading back to the gate. After a time, a Border Patrol SUV appears in the rearview mirror. Durham pulls over and rolls down the window.

"We got the bodies," an agent announces.

"They were dead?" Durham asks, surprised.

"No, we got the *subjects*," the agent corrects himself. "We got eight, but four or five scattered by the creek."

"Shit, they'll probably be coming by my house next," Durham says. With a sigh, he rolls up the window and taps the accelerator. He wishes the Border Patrol would shut down that Falfurrias checkpoint altogether and beef up security at the border so more immigrants would get caught the first time around. That way, whoever made it through could just hop on 281 and cruise on into Houston, waving at Brooks County through the rearview mirror. Durham thinks immigration is too grave a problem to handle locally. "The piglets have outnumbered the teats on the old sow around here," he says.

THE FIRST HOUR PASSED QUICKLY. She believed the coyotes. Houston was just a few miles away. The sun prickled her skin and the burrs ripped her jeans, but her energy was ample. She clutched her bottle of water, and every now and then she sipped from it.

At some point in the hike, her group probably met up with another coyote and his travelers. She likely felt grateful for the additional company— until someone collapsed. Maybe he was older; maybe she had a bum knee or heart condition. Whatever the case, their coyote probably made a face and said *We're already late* and *Do you think you can manage?* The traveler gasped yes but could barely hobble. The coyote made a show of placing a call on his

---

2. Between 2011 and 2014, Durham found seven dead immigrants on the ranch—so many that, with the help of the South Texas Human Rights Center, he started setting up water stations across the property.

cell phone. *A van is coming for you,* he said, *so stay right here. The rest of you, come with us.*

She exchanged glances with the other travelers. How could they know for certain? It seemed they should wait, to be sure. It wasn't right, abandoning someone in the brush with only half a jug of water.

And yet, the future of their families depended on whether or not they made it to Houston—and Houston was just a few miles away.

When the coyotes turned to walk deeper into the brush, she followed close behind.

THE GUATEMALAN CONSULATE OF MCALLEN, Texas, has no distinguishing features, neither a flag nor a sign, and hardly any windows. Unlike the Mexican Consulate a few blocks over, which is so overpopulated that mothers and children spill into the street, this beige brick box seems vacant. But when I knock upon its mirrored door, a sharp-dressed man whisks me inside to the office of Consul Alba Caceres. In her early thirties, she wears a silky floral blouse and dangly earrings. Smiling warmly, she invites me to sit. When I say that I am researching immigrant deaths in Brooks County, she shakes her head slowly, as if remembering each one by name.

"That's the biggest mortuary in the United States," she says, adding that the remains of forty-seven Guatemalans were recovered there in 2012. That's why they decided to open this consulate in November 2011 in the first place: so many were dying in South Texas, they could hardly keep track of them all from Houston. They processed 1,393 cases of missing persons during their first eleven months of operation through this one office alone. Their biggest obstacle isn't logistics or resources but rather gaining the trust of the families they serve.

"Say someone dies and goes to the mortuary," Caceres says, sliding her hands across the top of her desk as if to simulate a battlefield. "The coyote will still make the family believe he is still alive. The coyote will call and say he needs money for medical attention. We try to fight the situation, we call the family and try to explain it to them, but then the coyote will call and say we are lying. The families need to believe their relative is still alive, and so they do. They believe the coyote."

Consider what happened two months ago. A rancher found the body of a Guatemalan man, and as soon as he was identified, the consulate called the family to deliver the news. Yet two days later, the family wired $3,000 to his coyote, who had convinced them that their father/husband/son wasn't dead but injured and accruing medical expenses that needed payment.

When I ask how anyone could trust a coyote over a consul, Caceres points out that families tend to know the first coyote their relative hires. He is usually not only a community member but also one "with status," meaning a nice home and a large truck. Yet this coyote escorts his clients only across the Guatemalan border. From there, they are transferred to someone else to guide them across Mexico and over the U.S. border, to a third to sidestep the checkpoint in Falfurrias and continue on to Houston, and to a fourth to transport them to their final destination. With so many people in multiple nations, it is easy for the original coyote to shrug off responsibility when something goes wrong.

When it comes to finances, however, the coyote is more fastidious. The full transaction for Guatemalans costs $5,000 a head, plus a 9 percent interest rate every month, Caceres says. Many take out loans against their property to raise the funds, meaning their families could go homeless if they don't make it to the United States. And coyotes generally grant travelers only two chances. With stakes that high, you'd think only the very reckless or the very desperate would try it, yet through this single consulate, some 12,000 Guatemalans were apprehended, processed, and sent back home last year.

"The problem is, they know someone from their same town who came to the U.S. for one year, and they made enough to buy a house and a car all in one year. They know they would need to work twelve years in Guatemala to have those same things. So Houston is like Israel. It is the promised land," Caceres says, her large brown eyes growing moist.

She can relate to this sentiment because she was once an undocumented worker herself, in Spain. Her boss there was so lecherous, she quit—then realized how privileged she was to do so. Her family back home was politically connected and financially solvent; no one needed her income for survival. She started working for the consulate with hopes of helping those less fortunate. Yet the tragedies she witnesses here daily—the frantic cell phone calls fielded all hours of the day and night, the corpses to process, the mothers to console—eventually become so devastating, she will resign from her post in 2014.

As I exit the beige brick building, I notice the Guatemalan Consulate has a distinguishing feature after all. The vacant office next door retains the imprint of a sign removed long ago. WORKFORCE, it says in ghostly script.

AT SOME POINT IN THE HIKE—after a few whiffs of white powder, perhaps—the coyotes might have separated the men from the women and the women from each other. Undoubtedly the men protested as their wives and girlfriends and sisters and daughters were led into another section of the woods, but the coyotes reasoned that men walk faster and could make better time without them. Yet the coyotes grinned when they said this, and when the wives/girlfriends/sisters/daughters soon began screaming, they laughed. This mortified the men, but what could they do? Each coyote carried a Glock in his pocket. They controlled the GPS system. They alone knew where they were, where they were going, and how to move between the two.

The women, meanwhile, tried to dissuade them. They appealed to the coyotes' lapsed Catholicism, their buried-but-beating belief in La Virgen de Guadalupe. They told them they were menstruating. They told them they had a rash down there—warts, a disease, anything. If they were remotely young or pretty, these tactics probably did not work. Especially not for her. Her body was so small, her hair so long.

She must have known this was a possibility. She must have prepared as much as a woman could—sliding on tights beneath her jeans, swallowing tiny pills. She took these precautions because she heard it might happen, and a few miles into her hike to Houston, it possibly did.

WHITE VIGILANTES HAVE BEEN TORMENTING ethnic Mexicans since the borderline was first drawn. Well into the twentieth century, lynch mobs hung Mexicans[3] from trees for crimes ranging from cattle theft to suspected murder, often with the approval of local law enforcement. Vigilantes also helped U.S. military and the Texas Rangers persecute suspected sympathizers of a 1915 uprising called the Plan de San Diego. So many Mexican corpses[4] were found

3. In their book, *Forgotten Dead*, historians William D. Carrigan and Clive Webb document 547 cases of mobs lynching Mexicans from 1848 to 1928, not only in the Southwest but also in states like Nebraska and Wyoming. Many became public spectacles with crowds of thousands watching.

4. Named after the Texas town in which it was supposedly conceived, the Plan de San Diego manifesto was written by Mexican rebels and advocated the killing of white males over sixteen and the overthrow of U.S. rule in the Southwest. While 21 whites are believed to have died in the raids it incited, historians estimate that between 300 and 5,000 people of Mexican descent got killed in retaliation. Subsequent racial tension induced a Jim Crow–style segregation that restricted the voting rights and educational opportunities of Tejanos, despite their U.S. citizenship. It also inspired the founding of groups like the League of United Latin American Citizens and, decades later, the Chicano Civil Rights Movement.

rotting in Texas fields—some burned, some decapitated—scholars have since deemed it some of the worst state-sanctioned racial violence in U.S. history.[5]

So it was disconcerting when, in April 2005, headlines announced a new breed of vigilante. Cofounded by a Vietnam veteran and a former kindergarten teacher, the Minuteman Project urged citizens to take out their shotguns and stage watch posts to "do the job our government refuses to do" along the border. Likening themselves to white Martin Luther Kings with a new civil rights agenda, they claimed to have recruited more than 1,300 volunteers nationwide (including, according to an early website, "17 American Mexicans, 5 American Armenians . . . 4 wheelchair-bound paraplegics, and 6 amputees"). The bulk of participants observed by the media, however, were white men over fifty. Then-president George W. Bush denounced their tactics, but they found support in right-wing Republicans like Representative Tom Tancredo and CNN anchor Lou Dobbs after (dubiously) claiming to have helped the Border Patrol thwart "thousands" of illegal crossings.

These days, the Minuteman Project is mainly a publicity machine for its founders, but one offshoot still runs operations: the Texas Border Volunteers. Its spokesman, Mike Vickers, might be the best-known immigration critic in South Texas—or at least the one who garners the most newsprint. After a year of playing phone tag, I land an interview with him in Falfurrias, the same day I witness the recovery of the woman in the woods. When I arrive at his workplace, Las Palmas Veterinarian Hospital, his secretary says he's still in surgery.

"You could check out our fancy city," she chirps, brushing away a wisp of bright blonde hair with a manicured fingernail. "You could get a frappé at McDonald's, a mini-Blizzard at Dairy Queen, or a Red Velvet Bluebell Ice Cream at H-E-B."

I plop on the sofa instead. The end table features a stuffed and coiled rattlesnake baring its fangs and wearing a sign that says PROTECT YOUR DOG WITH RATTLESNAKE VACCINE. As if to prove it, a dog in a distant room howls so mournfully, it echoes off the Saltillo tiling.

---

5. Professors John Morán González, Trinidad Gonzales, Sonia Hernández, Benjamin Johnson, and Monica Muñoz Martinez commemorated the centennial of this little-known history by launching a multifaceted project called "Refusing to Forget" that included an exhibit at the Bullock Texas State History Museum, just a few blocks from the capitol, in the spring of 2016. The media called it the state's first official acknowledgment of this troubled past. Learn more at www.refusingtoforget.org.

An hour later, Vickers emerges. In his early sixties with Mark Twain hair, he wears knee-high work boots over dark blue jeans and a ball cap that says TEXAS DEER ASSOCIATION. I follow him into his office, where my eyes fall upon a poster of a cartoon cowboy kicking a caricature of President Obama square in the butt, alongside the slogan DON'T MESS WITH TEXAS. Fourteen sets of antlers festoon the walls, along with photos of a blonde-haired, blue-eyed girl beaming her way through puberty.

"Well I was out hunting nilgai—which is really fine meat—on Saturday morning when I found this guy at 7:15 A.M., dead on the road," he says, whipping out his digital camera and clicking through the images. He leans over to reveal a man stretched out on a county road. "His buddies left a marker on the fence. He was Salvadoran, number thirty-four this year."

Number thirty-four, or the one directly preceding the woman discovered earlier that afternoon. Could they have been part of the same group? Did this mean she was Salvadoran too?

No time to ponder: Vickers is already launching into the history of the Border Volunteers. He got riled up listening to Minuteman Chris Simcox on the Bill O'Reilly show one evening, and when some frustrated folks in Goliad reached out to him, he decided to host a border watch on his property (1,000 acres in Falfurrias and 3,000 acres south of Hebbronville). Nearly 200 people showed up with their motor homes and pup tents. Initially a branch of the Minuteman Project, they seceded when the group's "standard operating procedure" of no fewer than three monitors to a stationary post proved unsuitable for Texas's feral terrain. Plus, they wanted to align themselves with local law enforcement.

"It took a while for the Border Patrol to respect and trust us, but now, it is really good. We're not going to get shot at when we call," Vickers says, still flipping through his digital images and pausing now and then to show me the gory ones. "We report a lot of traffic they don't see."

Here's how it works. Once a month or so, Vickers reaches out to his membership, currently 300 strong. They don Gen 3 night vision equipment and camouflage hunting gear, drive out to one of fifty participating ranches, spread out over the most heavily trafficked trails, and then hunker down and wait for someone to emerge from the mesquite.

"Isn't that dangerous?" I ask. "I thought coyotes were armed."

"We've had gun encounters, but there has never been a shot fired," he says. "We present ourselves in large numbers."

Those numbers typically come from gun shows, where Vickers does the bulk of his recruiting, along with presentations at local chapters of the Rotary Club, Republican Party, and Tea Party. He says that every member undergoes a background check and vetting session with a retired naval officer to ensure no one has "a chip on their shoulder." Members hail from as far away as Wisconsin and Florida, and he claims that a good 10 percent are Hispanic.

"They see it in the same light as we do," he explains. "A lot of them are first generation American citizens, and their parents came in the legal way. It angers them that these people are just stealing through."

Whenever the Volunteers spy a group "stealing" across the brush, they ring up the authorities to arrest them.

"We have reported hundreds over the years," he says. "Thousands!"

I ask how many tend to be women.

"We find a lot of dead women," he says. "We suspect foul play. These people don't accidentally get lost. The coyote just dupes people of their money. They tell them they'll be in the brush for thirty minutes, and twelve hours later they are all cramped up and can't walk anymore. During the last op, we rescued a woman in labor, and that night she had a baby. A lot of the women we encounter are pregnant."

It hadn't occurred to me that the woman in the woods might have been pregnant. I had noticed the extraordinary girth of her belly but assumed it was from intestinal bloating. Maybe that was her motivation for crossing. She wanted her child to be a U.S. citizen. According to Vickers, such is often the case. He once found a Guatemalan woman right outside his office door, utterly lost and heavily pregnant.

"She was running a 108 temperature," he says. "I brought her inside here, put her in a cold bath, and ran a cold IV."

Then he called the police. When I ask how he could do that, after all she had suffered through, he says, "I feel sorry for them, but you have got to draw the line. This issue has overwhelmed our country. It has broke our own county, our hospitals."

From his perspective, the Texas Border Volunteers are not derailing immigrants' hard-chased dreams of a better life; they are saving them from a miserable death. "We'll probably have a hundred dead this summer," he says.

At the moment, this comment feels flippant, as if he's overselling his point. Yet of all the people I interview in the summer of 2012, Vickers's death toll prediction is the one that is vindicated.

AT SOME POINT IN THE HIKE, calamity struck. If not an injury, a rape. If not a rape, a raid. Men in jalapeño green materialized out of the wilderness. The travelers saw their headlights and heard their Jeeps and the coyotes yelled and everyone scattered.

She managed to follow the coyote for a few hundred yards but then lost him in the brush. Still, she kept on, darting this way and that, beneath prickly pear and thorny mesquite and across rivers of huisache until her heart nearly burst. When she finally stopped, there was no one behind her. This must have seemed impossibly lucky—until she realized how quiet the day had grown. All around her, all she could see was mesquite and huisache, huisache and mesquite.

Which way to Houston just a few miles away?

She probably took out her cell phone at that point. Read the numbers; pressed its many buttons. Of course there was no signal. There probably was no battery. That LG cell phone, the same one she'd used to call her mother and her lover, the one she'd used to coordinate this journey in the first place, was as useless as those twenty-eight dollars in her pocket. Even if she could call someone, what would she say? She had no idea where she was besides Houston a few miles away.

ONCE A BODY IS RECOVERED from Brooks County, it is typically dispatched eighty miles south to a town called Mission, where a family-owned funeral home called Elizondo Mortuary and Cremation Services processes it. In January 2013, half a year after witnessing the retrieval of the woman in the woods, I give the Elizondos a call. The daughter, Dina, agrees to meet with me.

One of the larger cities in the Rio Grande Valley, Mission is also one of the quietest. Its downtown consists of an art pueblo–style cinema called The Border and a long strip of brightly painted *fruterías*, *tortillerías*, taquerias, and auto shops with clay tile roofing. Beyond the Best Little Warehouse in Texas, the Mission Boot Shop, the Snow Hut, and restaurants advertising BBQ, MASA, and PAN DULCE is a stretch of housing projects. Between a water tower and a glitzy First Cash Pawn Shop stands a building bedecked with a hearse, a dove, and my mother's maiden name in floral script.

Inside, I am greeted by the patriarch, Raul Elizondo. A sweet elder, he has a debilitating stutter. "I knew someone who was a mortician, and I thought, well, if I work with dead people, I don't have to talk to them. They won't know I stutter."

He escorts me to his daughter's office, which has coffins pushed against the walls and a glass case full of urns shaped like angels and teardrops. Dina rises from the desk and extends her hand. Her cinnamon hair is streaked blonde, and she wears rhinestone-studded jeans and necklaces festooned with heavy silver crosses. A dozen red roses are arranged atop her desk, along with a vase of peacock feathers. Two lines on her office phone are ringing, and when she pauses to answer, her cell phone rings, too.

"Amiga, I am always busy, but I always have time for you," she coos to one caller. "I'll be at Chili's at seven if you want to go."

Four calls later, she flashes an apology. The funeral business is unrelenting, she says. Not one call can be missed, twenty-four hours a day, seven days a week, lest a potential client skip down to the next funeral home on the list. She was literally born into this work. Her father used to pick her up from school in their limousine (or hearse). All of her life, there has been a dead person in the next room and a family openly grieving. Only at this funeral home, the family tends to be thousands of miles away.

"The wife lives over there and the husband lives over here, and they die crossing back," she summarizes the profile of her typical client. "The desert is cruel. It has no mercy on anyone's soul."

About 80 percent of her clients are undocumented immigrants, she says, so their stories are often distressing. A couple months ago, they received the remains of a ten-year-old Honduran boy and had to coordinate plans with a mother and father living three countries apart. "How could a mother let her son leave like that?" she asks, shaking her head. "She put her child with a stranger to cross all the way to Reynosa, to cross the water, to cross a field, to cross the desert. Her thing was, 'Well, he wanted to see his dad.' But he couldn't defend himself at ten!"

Then there's the elderly lady who calls every single day, looking for her brother. "She'll say, 'I am so sorry to bother you,' and we'll say, 'No, you are not bothering us,' and she'll say, 'I just wanted to know if you've heard anything,' and we'll say no, and she'll say, 'Hablo mañana.' She has done this every day for three years."

I ask how the Elizondos developed their relationship with Brooks County, and she says that bodies used to be dispatched north to Corpus Christi, where they underwent autopsies before being sent back to Falfurrias for burial. "We once looked at one of the bodies, and we found some ID on their belt that they had missed, and were able to send them home to their family."

She convinced Brooks officials to send the bodies to her in Mission instead, both as a cost-saving measure for the county and—she says—to improve the chances of identifying the bodies (albeit not their cause of death). The Elizondos have since become a sort of clearinghouse for missing immigrants. Not only do consulates send in reports of lost citizens, but families call or e-mail as well. Dina lifts up her desk calendar to show me a stack of Post-it notes beneath, each scribbled with someone's last known details.[6]

"The family will call and say, oh, they have a tattoo here and a birthmark there, and freckles, but I'm like, no. They don't understand that the bodies have decomposed. I need clothes, I need shoe size, I need to know what kind of belt," she says, counting each item off on her fingers. "You'll remember details, too, like the body was wearing a certain kind of sweater, and then when you get a call from a family member saying their loved one was wearing a sweater, you'll connect the two."

In addition to matching up clothing, the Elizondos also photograph teeth and send them to consulates to check against dental records, she says. Once a body has been identified, a family member based in the United States sometimes shows up and asks to see the remains.

"We say, 'No, don't see him,' and they say, 'You don't understand,' and I say, 'No, *you* don't understand. It's better to remember the way he was, because if you see him like this, it will stay with you forever.' But they are insistent, and afterward they usually say, 'I shouldn't have seen him.' It is hard. It is still hard for us. It haunts me. It is overwhelming. But it is life. What isn't fair is death, and we all go through it."

I ask what it's like to receive the bodies from Brooks County, how she manages to unzip those black bags.

"Every day you see something different," she acknowledges, the epitome of diplomacy. "I don't do it very much because the smell penetrates your clothes, and I am needed here in the office to visit with the families.

---

6. Though I wasn't aware of it at the time of this reporting, civil rights groups in South Texas were already pressuring Brooks County to send the bodies to the University of North Texas Center for Human Identification instead, as it conducts DNA testing free for law enforcement, plus has a computerized database system (as opposed to Post-it notes). Autopsies and DNA samples for unidentified persons are actually required by state law, but Brooks County hadn't been obtaining either due to its lack of resources. It is unclear whether the Elizondos were aware of this law when they started processing bodies for the county.

But when I do, I just think, what were you thinking out there? What were your last words? Did you ask for forgiveness? I also ask why. Why, why, why."

These are questions she especially asked in the summer of 2012, when they received upward of four bodies a day—so many, they had to buy a new cooler in October.

"A new cooler," I repeat.

"Oh yes," she says, standing up from her chair.

We walk around to the warehouse out back. A massive steel construction has a sign taped to it: PLEASE REMEMBER TO PUT A TOE TAG ON THE BODIES. This newer cooler can hold up to forty-five bodies, she says, whereas the old one barely fit twelve. Some bodies stay here for months (at a rate of $50 a day) while plans are firmed with families back home. The first decision is the worst: casket or cremation. The former is prohibitively expensive. To transport bodies from Brooks County to Mission, fill out and file the paperwork, dress them in a suit if they are full-bodied (or hot-seal them in a bag if they are not), lay them in a casket, and board them on a one-way flight from McAllen to Dallas to Miami to their final Latin American destination costs about $3,600—a considerable percentage of what it cost to cross the border in the first place. Dina tries to convince families to cremate instead, but it's a hard sell.

"Mexicans don't believe in cremation. Salvadorans, Hondurans, they don't want it," she says. "I know how they feel; I would want all of them home, too. But we have to tell them, he's not a full body. It's so much cheaper, and we can send ashes much faster too."

When we return to her office, I ask Dina about the fate of the woman found July 3, 2012. She consults her records, but no woman is listed from that day. Brooks County had no information about her either when I checked the day before; she remained unidentified, according to their records. This deeply unsettles me. If I cannot, with all of my resources and privileges, track her down, what are the chances of her family doing so?

Sensing my upset, Dina offers in a low voice that she doesn't see immigrants just at the endpoint of their journeys. She sometimes sees them midway, too.

"Where I live is real secluded, and sometimes I'll be driving and a truck will stop right in front of me, and people will run out from the bushes and into the truck. When I see them wearing an orange shirt and white socks, I pray to God that I won't see them again here, and know that I saw them alive just a few days before. I try not to look when I see them in the street, because I don't want to remember."

THERE WAS SUN AND MORE sun and all sun and only sun and slowly the sun began to cook her. Her organs roasted inside her. Intestines. Liver. Kidneys. Heart.

What did she think when she collapsed to the ground, when she rolled on her back in surrender?

Who will take care of my family now?
Will someone find me before the animals do?
Where is this Houston a few miles away?

SACRED HEART BURIAL PARK is on the outskirts of Falfurrias. Take Travis Street west until it becomes Cemetery Road and keep going until a burnt-orange brick gate appears beneath the mesquite. Even from a distance, you can tell that Tejanos are buried here. It is awash in color, with far more flamboyant floral displays than you ever see in gringo graveyards. It also has fresher mounds.

After visiting Elizondo Mortuary, I drive an hour and a half north to this graveyard, then slowly tour through it. Gradually the marble tombstones give way to granite markers, handmade wooden crosses, and then plastic flowers sprouting from the dirt. I park the car and step out. Here, on a parched strip of land, is where unidentified immigrants get buried, beneath tiny markers that seem to have been fashioned out of tin cans. Rather than names, they list numbers: Unknown Female, 436663. Male Unknown, 417654. Male 90709 Sep 7 09 Poco Grande Ranch. They form haphazard rows, just inches from each other, with a fake daisy for adornment tied with a purple ribbon.

Chances are, this is where the woman in the woods got buried, her LG cell phone and twenty-eight dollars sealed in a Ziploc bag beside her. Undocumented when she was found, she has plenty of papers now. A death certificate. An Electronic Death Registration number. All buried in a particleboard coffin, six feet down.

That's the best-case scenario, anyway. In just a few months, visiting forensic anthropologists from Baylor University and the University of Indianapolis will discover body upon body crammed inside these barely marked graves of Sacred Heart Burial Park—up to five deep. Some corpses won't even have rated coffins but will have been rolled instead in blankets or stuffed in body bags, burlap bags, kitchen trash bags, or even shopping bags. Many of the remains will not have been identified or their DNA samples obtained, despite state laws requiring otherwise. The anthropologists— headed by Dr. Lori Baker of Baylor University in Waco, Texas—will quickly act to change that.[7] Beginning in May 2013, bodies will cease being sent to Elizondo Mortuary for processing and will instead be transported to Webb County Medical Office for DNA analysis before moving on to Baker's lab to await identification.[8]

In 2014, a widely publicized investigation by the Texas Rangers of the Texas Department of Public Safety will ensue, and all parties involved—from law enforcement to funeral home directors (including the Elizondos)—will plead a lack of funding, personnel, and resources as their defense. No criminal charges will be filed. In 2015, the *Texas Observer* will publish an in-depth critique of that investigation citing "rampant violations" of the law by all of the parties cleared by the Rangers. In addition to failures in securing autopsies[9] or DNA samples and egregious burial practices, reporter John Carlos Frey will discover that Funeraria del Angel Howard-Williams, the funeral home that recovers the bodies from the ranches, was charging Brooks County $145 per body bag—despite the fact that body bags generally run about $30 apiece and that many of the remains were buried in bags that cost a few dollars if not a few pennies each.

On this brisk afternoon in January 2013, however, there are no Texas Rangers or forensic anthropologists or other reporters in sight. There's only me, walking among the graves in hopes of finding one with the same death date as the woman in the woods. There are no maps for this cemetery, no records whatsoever of who is buried where. I spend an hour bending over the flimsy markers, reading the many labels, searching for a trace of her. Yet I find only ribbons wrapped around fake flowers, blowing in the wind.

7. Since the fall of 2012, Dr. Lori Baker and her students have recovered 168 bodies from Sacred Heart Burial Park and local funeral homes and transported them back to Baylor University. There, the team submits DNA samples to a national database called Codis, sends biological profiles to the National Missing and Unidentified Persons System, cleans each set of remains by hand, preserves everything in meticulously labeled boxes, and then stores the boxes on a shelf to wait for identification. "It looks like a mass disaster in here, with body bags everywhere," Baker says when I reach her by phone at her lab. "I am Catholic, as are most of the people who cross over, so I've had Catholic priests come in to bless the lab and the bodies and the students, so that at least we can tell the families something respectful is being done for their loved ones."

8. As of September 2015, two bodies have been conclusively identified and sent back to their families, and a third one seems imminent, thanks to Baker's efforts.

9. Of the seventy-two autopsies ordered by Brooks County between 2007 and 2013, the *Texas Observer* obtained fifty-eight reports under the Texas Public Information Act. Frey describes the reports as "scattershot at best," often lacking critical data such as bone measurements, specificity about distinguishing teeth features such as cavities, and photographs, all of which are part of standard forensic procedure.

10

The Healing

STORIES HAVE A WEIGHT UNTO THEMSELVES. IMMERSING YOURSELF in the heavier ones can feel like drowning. Some writers I know drink because of this, as a way of relieving vicarious suffering. I tend to harbor too much guilt to allow such indulgence—*it didn't happen to me; I have no right to grieve*—but what is the appropriate reaction to witnessing the pain of others? Writing about it only shares the tragedy. Yet it is my instinctive response.

Another is ceremony. One night in Corpus, a friend builds a fire in her backyard and invites everyone over to burn what they must release. We toss old letters into the flames, a stressful bank statement, a medical diagnosis, the shirt of an ex-lover, and—for me—difficult pages from a notebook. A story is told with every toss. Another night, someone suggests gathering at the beach. Huddled on the sand, we each share something that the waves carry away—a song, a poem, a sadness. I have found few forces as redemptive as ritual, and because of that, I try to be open to the practices of others. Who knows where they might lead you?

Like now. It's another day, another dinner party, another gathering at Santa Barraza's ranch. As Greg and I enter her kitchen, warm and fragrant with the smell of roasting chicken, I am delighted to see Homero Vera seated at the table. A self-taught historian, he directs the Kenedy Ranch Museum in Sarita and is my favorite source of local lore.

Before Santa has even sliced the chicken, the tales are flying. First up is Homero. His wife, Letty, recently attended a spiritual meeting sponsored by a group called America Needs Fatima. After screening a disturbing film about Nazi Germany ("to make them feel bad," Homero conjectures), the speaker hauled out a four-foot statue of the Virgin Mary and asked for donations. Finding the experience rather distasteful, Letty left before the hostess even served the cake. When she opened her cell phone to check her messages, she found La Virgen de Guadalupe there, glittering across the screen.

"La Virgen de Guadalupe?" I interrupt.

"Yes, La Virgen," he says. "So she called me up and said, 'You're not going to believe this, but La Virgen de Guadalupe is on my phone.'"

"*La Virgen*?" I ask again, glancing over at her portrait on Santa's wall.

"Yes, La Virgen."

Letty sped home to show him. They decided to return to the gathering in case the America Needs Fatima rep had something to do with it. He casually examined the phone and said, "So, she is with you, too."

"Just like that!" Homero says. "He didn't think nothing of it."

Homero and Letty climbed back in their truck and started driving home. Homero wanted to consult their priest, but Letty said no, it was getting late, they should wait for morning. No sooner did they resolve this than their priest came cruising down the highway. They followed him home and showed him the phone.

"He said, 'You're blessed. That's how she presents herself.'"

"La Virgen de Guadalupe," I say softly.

"Yes, La Virgen."

"Is she still there?"

"Yes. Only now, you have to open the phone real quick to see her. Then she fades away. Usually she's on the right-hand side, but she has also appeared on the left, as a double."

"She moves around?"

"Yes," he says, spearing a piece of chicken.

I ask to see her, *pero* no. Letty is in Mexico City, visiting her ailing mother, and took the cell phone with her.

Sensing my disappointment, Santa says, if you really want to see La Virgencita, go to Robstown. She appeared at St. Anthony's Catholic Church years ago, when a maintenance crew pulled up the carpet in the pulpit. Mass starts in an hour. If you hurry with that chicken, you'll make it.

"A LITTLE LATE, WEREN'T YOU?"

An elderly deacon stands by the chapel doors, hands on hips, blocking our exit. It's true: Greg and I didn't arrive until the parishioners had already lined up for communion. We barely caught ten minutes of Mass.

"We drove all the way from Kingsville," I say in our defense.

"It's not that far," he snaps, then peers over at Greg. "Remove your cap, son."

"We heard that La Virgen de Guadalupe . . . uh . . . is here?"

"Ah," he says, then turns on his heels and pushes through the doors, muttering, "Where is she where is she where is she?" He pauses at the altar near the entrance. "Ah, yes. Here she is."

Beneath the statue of a saint adorned with *milagros*[1] is a large wooden frame the color of honey. Through its glass, I can make out an image on a panel of wood—dark and oblong, with a vaguely feminine shape.

"Here are her shoulders," says the deacon, pointing toward the top of the image, "and there's her veil," he adds, sweeping his hand down and out. "And here are the rays." Balling his fists near the center of the image, he makes jazz hands and moves them outward, as if mimicking emanating light. "We found her when the carpet got pulled beneath the tabernacle."

"And then what happened?"

He looks at me sideways. "We put her in the frame."

"I mean, what happened *of significance*?"

He shrugs. "I've seen this before. Our Blessed Mother appears on grain silos out here."

I try again: "What do you think La Virgen is trying to *tell* us?"

"The same as her last words in Scripture: 'Do everything he tells you.'" With that, the deacon heads back into the vestibule, his white robe rippling behind him.

An elder in a red windbreaker grips a ring of keys, waiting for Greg and me to leave so that he can lock up for the night. I ask if he sees La Virgen inside the frame.

"Not really," he says. "To some people, she is there, but not to me."

I glance over at Greg. He's thinking what I am: *We should have stayed at Santa's.*

Then he continues: "The real Virgen was at my house."

"Excuse me?"

"She was at my house, La Virgen."

"Oh? When was that?"

"*Pues*, it was real late at night, maybe one or two. She was kneeling at my altar in the living room, in the corner."

"Did she say anything?"

"She told me to pray the rosary every day. And I do."

---

1. *Milagros*, or miracles, are tiny votive charms made of silver or tin that represent parts of the body—hands, legs, eyes, lungs, hearts. Next time you or a loved one falls ill, buy a milagro, string it with red ribbon, and proffer it to your favorite saint with a prayer and a kiss. Practiced throughout the Americas, this custom is believed to have originated with the ancient Iberians along the coast of Spain.

"Why do you think Robstown is so ... *blessed* by La Virgen?"

"There are a lot of believers here," he says, his oystery eyes wistful. "One night, I had this dream that I woke up and looked to my ceiling but there was no roof, just the sky, a beautiful blue full of stars, and then I saw the Virgin Mary in the sky, just from the waist up, and then a few seconds later, Jesus appeared, Jesus Christ, and he pushed her down, so that I could see him."

Smiling to himself, he jingles his keys, signaling it's time to leave.

SANTA CALLS AS WE DRIVE BACK TO CORPUS. Did you see her? Did you see La Virgencita?

I can't say that I did—not because she wasn't there, but because I was so busy asking questions, I forgot to really *look*. I don't want to admit this to Santa, though, because La Virgen de Guadalupe is profoundly significant to her. Twenty years ago, while still teaching at Penn State, she once spent a late night at her studio, preparing a painting of La Virgen for an upcoming show. Suddenly, she was overcome by a sadness so consuming, she called her daughter to ensure everything was all right. Unable to regain focus, she went home to try and sleep it off. Santa's sister called early the next morning to say that their mother had died of a heart attack, right about the time Santa had spontaneously started grieving. Santa stopped at her studio to check on the painting en route to the airport and realized that the face she had given La Virgen was her mother's. What's more, she had painted a bleeding heart inside La Virgen's chest.

I am also reluctant to admit my failure to see La Virgen because it feels like an indictment of my identity. As Mexican writer Carlos Fuentes once said, "One may no longer consider himself a Christian, but you cannot truly be considered a Mexican unless you believe in the Virgin of Guadalupe." She has been making public appearances since December 1531, when she surprised a campesino named Juan Diego Cuauhtlatoatzin by springing up beside him on a hilltop near Mexico City. She asked him to convince the local bishop to build her a shrine and—as proof of their encounter—filled his arms with red roses (a miracle, since it was winter). Juan Diego raced down the hill, pounded on the bishop's door, and opened his cloak to show him the roses. The bishop was far more struck by the image of La Virgen emblazoned on his cloak, her skin as brown as theirs.[2]

2. This crucial matter of skin tone is what prompted the Mexican writer Carlos Monsiváis to say of La Virgen, "She is, on the one hand, the pacific moment in the Christianization of the Indian peoples and, on the other, the Mexicanization of faith."

Ever since declaring myself a Chicana in college, I've been plastering La Virgen de Guadalupe on my bedroom wall and magnetizing her to my refrigerator. I light candles to her at my desk whenever I begin a new project. I've even made a pilgrimage to her famous cloak hanging in La Villa basilica in Mexico City. But is honoring her the same as *believing* in her? I want it to be as badly as I don't—and for that sentiment to make any kind of sense, I must defer to our great sage Edward James Olmos, who spoke every Chicanos' truth in the movie *Selena* when he griped about the existential dilemma of having to be "more Mexican than the Mexicans and more American than the Americans, both at the same time!"

Interpreting my silence as a no, Santa has a suggestion. "If you *really* want to learn about La Virgencita," she says, "you must meet Gilbert and Berta. They make their living filming weddings and *quinceañeras*, but what they're *really* doing is creating a documentary about miracles. Here's their number."

IT's JUST BEFORE NOON when Greg and I pull into Robstown. An elder sells grapefruit out of his truck bed. Two women hawk blankets in a vacant lot. A yard sign says CATHOLICS COMING SOON! We pass Mr. J's Drivers Ed and Barrera's Fried Chicken (ONE BITE . . . AND WE GOT YOU!) before parking between a monster truck and a rusty El Camino. Taqueria Jalisco is bustling with parties of six or more. Patrons wear rump-sculpting jeans and bandannas or cowboy hats. With forks and rolled tortillas, they mow trails through heaps of enchiladas, tacos, tamales, rice, and refried beans smothered in neon cheese. Wherever I turn, I see images of Jesus—upon the walls, tattooed along men's forearms, dangling inside ladies' cleavage.

A waitress plunks down a basket of deep-fried tortilla strips and a cup of salsa. We devour three rounds and two bucket-size teas before Berta calls to say they are running *un poco* late. By the time they arrive, the lunch crowd has emptied and the jukebox is blasting Los Tigres. Berta looks straight out of a Botero painting: soft and round with long hair and feathered-back bangs. Gilbert has a moustache and ruddy cheeks and wears two large religious medallions around his neck. Setting down a wooden box secured with cables, they apologize for making us wait, *pero* every time they climbed inside their car, they remembered another miracle to show us and ran back inside to get it.

The first miracle they witnessed was La Virgen-Beneath-the-Carpet at St. Anthony's. Gilbert spent the whole day—"October tenth in the year 2000"— in bed. He had worked in the oil refineries until arthritis disabled him, then underwent two hip replacements in a row. He was preparing for his third and couldn't walk without a cane—two, for a fair distance. Berta had just tuned in to the five o'clock news when someone called to say that La Virgen was down at the church and could they come take pictures? By the time they arrived at St. Anthony's with their camera bag, a crowd had assembled on the sidewalk. The church had already closed for the night, but Father Bob promised to hang La Virgen in the sacristy in the morning. The people were waiting for sunrise. Berta and Gilbert milled about the rosary-chanters until Gilbert started feeling emotional. "Berta, we have to go, I am going to start crying, I don't want nobody to see me crying," he whispered.

They barely made it to the car before his eyes dribbled. "And then he started repeating, 'Rosas, rosas, rosas.' Me and my son just looked at each other, wondering what to do, and finally Gilbert said, 'She is asking me to bring roses.'"

Which La Virgen is wont to do. The heady perfume of roses has accompanied her sightings for five centuries now. But none could be found in Robstown at that hour, so they drove all the way to the H-E-B in Annaville. "By that point, Gilbert was just soaking wet with his tears and I ran inside and came back with pink roses and he said 'Why didn't you get the red ones?' but that's all they had so we said let's go and by the time we got to the church there were fifty or seventy people just walking around the sidewalk and we see Father Bob coming outside and Gilbert went up and said, 'Father, Father, can you please give these to our Blessed Mother?' and he said, 'No Gilbert, you need to do it, I feel a miracle's about to happen.'"

Gilbert, Berta, and their son entered the church with the not-red roses. Approaching the pulpit, Gilbert cast aside his cane and sank to his knees. He cried with so much love, so much fervor, he started bouncing on his knees, this man who could barely walk. He started receiving messages and repeating them in Spanish. "And not in Tex-Mex but in real correct Spanish!" Berta says.[3]

"And I didn't even speak Spanish before," Gilbert says.

"And the priest was running back and forth completely freaking out saying, 'Can he see her? Can he see her?' and Gilbert's words were just

---

3. While living in Mexico, I often heard this saying: "English is the language of business, German is the language of war, and Italian is the language of love, but Spanish is the language of God." Some trace it back to Charles V, who supposedly declared in the sixteenth century, "To God I speak Spanish, to women Italian, to men French, and to my horse—German."

coming out in a blur but I could understand everything and I said, 'You're scaring Father' and he turned and looked at me and they weren't regular tears, they were big big tears, like rain."

Father Bob knelt beside Gilbert and, when Gilbert calmed, murmured a blessing. Then the men rose, Gilbert without his cane, and headed back to the sacristy. "Only I wasn't walking. I was floating. It was an out-of-body experience. It was the Holy Spirit."

When the crowd saw Gilbert walking free of cane, they shouted his name and tugged at his shirtsleeves. Gilbert patiently answered their questions—"She said to pray the rosary every single day"—before granting Channel 3 News an exclusive.

"He told them everything but they didn't use anything except 'I haven't cried like that since I was a little boy,'" Berta says.

"I didn't want people to see me crying and then the whole world saw me crying. After that, people would come up and say, 'Hey, were you that guy crying on TV?'" Gilbert says.

Opening a folder, Berta removes a laminated photograph of the wood panel inscribed with La Virgen. "Once you focus, you will see a baby in her stomach. See? It is like a sonogram," she says, pointing to a blip of darkness in the belly-shaped mound of La Virgen–shaped image.

They say they have processed more than 20,000 copies of this photo. For years, Gilbert drove to the church each morning to parcel them out to passersby. "And I would go to write a check to pay for the photos but my bank account never decreased, it only went down if I used it for my business," Berta says. "Or other times, the workers at the photo shop would say this stack didn't come out right and they would give us the whole stack for free."

"And sometimes the photos would smell like roses," Gilbert adds.

Before, Berta says, they were the kind of people who listened to Ozzy Osbourne. Gilbert didn't even like church. She struggled to rile him out of bed. "And now, he pushes *me* to go. He tells me, hurry up! We used to sit in the third-to-last row at church. Now we sit up in the very front. Before we were into none of this stuff. Now, I do all the driving in case Gilbert receives the Holy Spirit."

I have to ask. "What's it like, receiving the Holy Spirit?"

"You feel full of vibrance, like you're full of glitter," Gilbert says. "It always hits me in my mouth. It's like a gush of wind going right through my mouth."

I ask about the other miracles they've witnessed, and they unearth them one by one—from their pockets, from their wallets, from their wooden box

wrapped in cables. Rosaries. Medallions. Copper lockets. An old stole blessed
by the pope. A sliver of a bone of St. Teresa of Avila and the fringes of a frock
worn by Padre Pio of the Giovanni Rotunda of Italy, fresh off the Internet.
And photos, piles of photos, nearly all of clouds, only they don't see clouds
but crosses and chalices. And maybe this is when I lose focus, where I start
writing "donuts" instead of "doves," where my neck goes slack and my head
swivels back as they keep spinning stories—stories like the one about the old
lady in Sinton who keeps a rock in her yard with La Virgen etched on one side
that grows bigger every year and was the size of a pineapple last they checked;
stories like the one about the church in Laredo where an image of La Virgen
"sprays glitter out of her head" and a little girl sprinkled some on the tongue of
a dog lying dead in the street and he started barking and wagging his tail. And
while something inside me will never allow for such suspension of disbelief—
the journalist?—I can't help but think about the month I once spent at an art
colony near Barcelona, where I befriended a photographer who invited me
to visit the shrine of La Virgen de Montserrat, the patron saint of Catalonia.
We waited in line for more than an hour to see her, during which I prepared
myself for the inevitable *I fought all those crowds to see the Mona Lisa and this
is what I get?* disappointment, but when I entered La Virgen's chamber, I got
swept up in the rush of cool air and the perfume of stargazer lilies and the
glow of lamps and the gleam of the gold altar, and when I leaned in close to
examine La Virgen's face, I was surprised to find a smile upon it. Catholic
virgins usually look so dour, but this one appeared on the verge of laughter.
I smiled back at her, then exited a series of darkened doorways until I was
back in the sunlight where my friend awaited. When I remarked how nice it
was to see a happy virgin, she said, "What do you mean? She was frowning."

We argued about this until we entered the gift shop, where every pen-
dant, bracelet, candle, spoon, coffee mug, snow globe, shower gel, and bottle
of Liquor Crema Catalana depicted La Virgen de Montserrat the exact same
way: serene but severe. "Well," my friend said, tilting her head, "maybe she
smiled at you."

And that is why, when Gilbert and Berta ask—after two and a half hours
of narcotizing us with miracles—if we'd like to attend a healing mass next
Wednesday, I exchange glances with Greg and say we do.

GREG PARKS ON TEX-MEX STREET and we weave through a jumble of trucks
toward St. Anthony's, dodging a thicket of signs reading ABORTION KILLS
BABIES as we do. The door swings open and the merriment of an accordion

jingles out. Parishioners fill the vestibule and nearly every pew, and all eyes are fixed upon the man in the sanctuary. Very tall and very black, he wears a white robe and wields an enormous gold monstrance.[4]

"Where's *he* from?" I ask quietly.

"Africa," an elder whispers.

"Ethiopia, I think," says another.

"Ghana," pipes a third. "Or Kenya. One of those."

Wherever he's from, he towers over the Tejanos beside him. His hair is shorn close, and the cloak around his shoulders is embroidered scarlet and gold. Raising the monstrance high above his head, he speaks in a rumble that evolves into a roar.

> Lord, heal us:
> for the sin of idolatry,
> for the loss of faith in God,
> for sinful addictions,
> for those who use drugs and narcotics and are addicted to
>   pornography,
> for those who are addicted to masturbation,
> to homosexual activity and to lesbianism,
> for those who engage in child abuse,
> in prostitution,
> for those who are addicted to gossip,
> for those who conduct wicked acts,
> who steal,
> who don't respect others,
> for those who have sex before marriage,
> for the sin of divorce,
> for murderers,
> for impure thoughts and impure actions,
> for those who abuse their spouse,
> for those who abuse their children,
> for sexual abuse,
> for emotional abuse,

4. The monstrance is the vessel that holds the large circular wafer that—during Communion—transubstantiates into the body of Christ. As such, they tend toward the extravagant, plated in precious metals, embedded with jewels, and weighing many pounds. Monstrances are also used to hold the relics of saints.

for psychological abuse,
for those who find it hard to forgive,
for those who practice witchcraft,
who practice sorcery,
who have excessive anger, excessive hatred,
who have alcoholic parents or drugs in their family,
for the sin of contraception,
for the sin of abortion,
for those who practice birth control,
for those who are completely burned out in life,
who think themselves unworthy,
who have lost their job,
who have anxiety attacks,
for those who need healing of their whole entire body,
we take this blessed sacrament, Amen.

Greg nudges me. *That's us.*

A hunched-over man in the first pew shuffles up to the crossing. The priest descends a few steps to greet him and lowers the monstrance against his forehead. Seconds later, the man is gone. I no longer see the back of his head. A middle-aged woman in a floral dress is next. She too receives the blessing from the priest—and vanishes. One by one, a row of parishioners disappears.

I steal up the gospel side of the nave, past the confessionals marked *privado* and *cara a cara*, past the Stations of the Cross, past the stained glass windows, past hundreds of parishioners bent in prayer. Up in the transept near the statue of Mary stands Gilbert, wearing multiple rosaries wrapped around his wrists. Filing in behind him, I gaze out into the crossing. Three bodies stretch in dead-man poses upon the floor. They strike me as the kind of people who wouldn't lie on the floor unless the paramedics were on the way, yet there they are, covered with blankets featuring the trinity of South Texas: La Virgen de Guadalupe, the Mexican flag, and the Dallas Cowboys.

The priest is tending to a young woman now. She bows her head as a man in a maroon shirt that says 100% ROSARY PRAYING JESUS LOVING CATHOLIC takes position behind her, his hands above her shoulders. The priest slowly lowers the monstrance, and the instant it graces her forehead, she collapses into the arms behind her. It is an effortless fall. Graceful, even. She doesn't step back or look back; she simply falls back from 90 degrees to 120 degrees, where she is caught and lowered to the floor. Another 100%

ROSARY PRAYING JESUS LOVING CATHOLIC covers her with a blanket, as if she were sleeping. The priest gravitates to the next parishioner, and the next.

Nuns fall the fastest—so fast, you can't help wondering if it's a contest. One plummets before the priest even raises the monstrance. There's barely enough time to catch her. An alarmingly thin nun keels forward instead of backward and lands in child's pose at the priest's feet. He moves on within a beat.

By the time he has worked his way to the gospel side of the crossing, the priest's vestments are slick with sweat. He mops off with a towel and drains an entire bottle of water in a single gulp. His hands tend to quiver, particularly when worshippers don't immediately drop. He takes his shaking hand and clamps it atop their skull, as if squeezing a cantaloupe for ripeness. This generally does the trick, but one or two parishioners hold their stance, including a six-year-old in a purple dress. She bends beneath the weight of the monstrance and further still beneath the priest's grip but doesn't surrender until her mother marches over. Then she topples.

But for the most part, the parishioners fall with ease, even the ones whose bodies swell with diabetes or shrivel with age. They fall with abandon, never once looking back to ensure someone is there. They fall trusting they will not be dropped or stepped on; they fall trusting they will make it safely to the floor. And once they do, they shut their eyes and still their bodies, though sometimes their stomachs quake. When they wake, they seem disoriented. They struggle to their knees. So easy to fall; so hard to rise.

Two hours later, Greg taps me on the shoulder. I follow him outside, where the sidewalk swarms with crickets.

"What do you think?" he asks. "Should we do it?"

As usual, I feel torn in two. The half of me who has spent half her life outside the borderlands looks at everyone strewn across the floor and thinks, This is how Jim Jones[5] came to be. Let us run, while we still can.

The half who was raised here and returned here, however, is impressed by the parishioners' courage. Even if they fall out of unexamined ardor (or worse: a lack of alternatives), they are willing to open themselves up to possibility. This is what I've come to admire most about the Tejanos I've met these last few years, from the activists and artists to the law enforcers, nuns,

---

5. For those too young to remember or who have tried to forget: Jim Jones was the leader of the religious cult Peoples Temple who convinced more than 900 followers to swallow a cyanide-laced drink in Jonestown, Guyana, in 1978. Jones died of a gunshot wound to the head, in an apparent suicide, soon after. Until 9/11, it was the greatest single loss of U.S. civilian life from a deliberate act.

and dealers. When they sense something is lacking, whether in their own lives or in others', they risk everything to fill it, no matter what border they must cross—internal, international, or preternatural.

A cricket is hopping toward Greg's foot. A cricket is hopping toward my foot. We are about to get covered in crickets. Skepticism seems too easy an out. Something profoundly spiritual could be taking place here. Even if I'm not aware enough to fully experience it, shouldn't I at least try?

As soon as we enter the doorway, someone beckons us into the crossing. I am three parishioners away from healing. Weirdly nervous, I lift my palms and recite those desert songs of long ago. *IBelieveInOneGodTheFatherAl-mighty.* Someone falls. *CreatorOfHeavenAndEarth.* Another one goes. *AndInJesusChristHisOnlySonOurLord.* And then the third. I sense someone taking position behind me, but before I can check, the priest appears before me. For a moment, there is only white robe and black skin—and then the monstrance descends upon me, brilliantly gold and shaped like a cross and diving straight toward my head. I follow it with my chin until I am in the throws of a backbend and the man behind me hisses, "Open your heart. Give it up to the Lord."

My right foot steps back.

"Praise be Jesus," the priest stage-whispers above me. "Praise be the Lord Jesus Christ."

"Give it up. Give it up to the Lord."

"Jesus. Praise be Jesus."

My left foot joins my right as I bend even further.

The priest's free hand begins to shake. His long bony fingers reach for my skull. I am being pressured, spiritually pressured, and in the panic that ensues, I transport back to the healing center I once visited in Cuernavaca where I stripped to my bathing suit and crawled inside a *temazcal*[6] that was hot and dark and moist, and the *temazcalero* led us in rounds of Spanish prayer as he doused eucalyptus tea on the volcanic stones so that fragrant smoke spiked the air. Then he demanded I lay face-down in the dirt so he could thrash *aceite* leaves against my body—a sensation that reminded me of driving through the carwash with my childhood friends and clapping with

6. An ancient Mesoamerican sweat lodge, temazcales are womb-shaped constructions of mud or adobe heated by a pit of volcanic stones and firewood. Tradition dictates temazcales burn for four hours prior to use, symbolizing the four cardinal directions and the four earthly elements. Indigenous people throughout Mexico gather inside these chambers for curative ceremonies.

delight as the sudsy strips danced around us—but when the temazcalero flipped me on my back, he announced he would now clean out my heart, and I could scream or kick or cry as needed. Before I could digest this, he thrust his knuckles against my chest and began to twist the skin above my heart. While it wasn't exactly pleasant, it didn't exactly hurt, so I neither screamed nor kicked nor cried because I figured it would only get worse and I should show some reserve and be a brave *gringuita*, and sure enough the temazcalero pulled back his knuckles and gasped for breath and dove back in, more forcefully this time, and reminded me to scream if I needed to, to scream or kick or cry, but the pain still didn't warrant so dramatic a reaction, so he did it a third time, plunged deep inside my chest, and it occurred to me that this could continue indefinitely so I scissor-kicked and groaned a bit, at which point he collapsed on the dirt in a fit of coughing and wheezing and I scooted back to my spot against the wall thinking *I cannot wait to write about this!* But then the temazcalero asked in a gravelly voice how I felt, how I felt when he cleaned out my heart. Truthfully, I felt nothing when he cleaned out my heart save some soreness inside my chest. "Bueno!" I chirped. This was clearly insufficient. He then asked what color I saw, what color I saw when he cleaned out my heart, but color didn't occur to me when he cleaned out my heart, *nothing* occurred to me when he cleaned out my heart except what a great story I now had, but because I had already disappointed the temazcalero enough for one day, I said *rojo*, as it's my favorite color. When he shouted "*¿Rojo?*" I realized I should have said any color but rojo, but of course it was too late to say "*Azul*, I mean!" because he was already raging about how rojo signified anger and hatred and bloodshed and how no one in his history of heart-cleanings had ever said rojo except maybe psychopaths. Again he asked, "*¿Cómo te sientes? ¿Cómo te sientes?*" but *I was not feeling anything* so I said, "Liberated. I feel liberated," as if I had been freed from all that sullied my heart. And of course he knew I was lying. He probably even knew I knew he knew I was lying, but he let it go until the end of the temazcal, when we all crawled out into the sunlight and poured buckets of water over each other's heads. He pulled me aside and said, "Listen, mija. You need to relax. You're too much like a gringa. You just work work work like a stiff little broom when what you really must do is release."

Release. I must release.

So when the priest's hand clamps my skull and his fingers squeeze my temples: I do.

PART II

The New York–Canada Borderlands

Welcome to Akwesasne! While a visitor to our community you will be under the jurisdiction of the following: Canada, the United States, Mohawk Nation, St. Regis Mohawk Tribal Council, Mohawk Council of Akwesasne, Haudenosaunee Confederacy, New York, Ontario, Quebec, Huntington County, Franklin County, St. Lawrence County, New York State Police, Mohawk Police, Quebec Police Force, Ontario Provincial Police, Royal Canadian Mounted Police, Federal Bureau of Investigation, US Border Patrol, Canadian Customs, US Customs and soon—the National Guard! Drive Carefully and Have a Nice Day!

AKWESASNE NOTES, FALL 1989

The Sort of Homecoming

ONE OF THE TRUEST DECLARATIONS IN GLORIA ANZALDÚA'S OPUS, *Borderlands/La Frontera: The New Mestiza,* is this: "I have so internalized the borderland conflict that sometimes I feel like one cancels out the other and we are zero, nothing, no one. A veces no soy nada ni nadie. Pero hasta cuando no lo soy, lo soy. At times I am nothing, no one. But even when I am not, I am." Throughout my South Texas sojourn, I wonder if this psychic wound festers in all border communities or just in my own. How have others internalized their ancestral division? Is nepantla a universal condition? An opportunity to find out arises in the summer of 2012, when I land a job near the other U.S. border, the one we rarely hear about.

Mom helps with the move. Flying out from opposite ends of the country, we meet at midnight in Syracuse, New York, and catch a red-eye bus toward Canada the next morning. As we hand our tickets to the driver, a husky woman with tobacco-stained teeth, she informs us that cell phones are not permitted on board. We climb inside to find the male passengers sporting ZZ Top beards and the female passengers wearing bonnets. I look back at Mom. Is this the right bus?

"Let's go," the driver snaps.

We do. Maneuvering through the aisle, it seems that everyone is in excellent spirits, twisting around in their seats, passing babies back and forth, doffing their straw hats, and chattering away in a guttural language that sounds vaguely German.

"Are they Amish?" Mom asks, as if they cannot hear us.

"Parece," I whisper back in Spanish. Appears so.[1]

---

1. With more than 16,000 members, New York has the fastest growing Amish population in the nation. In the North Country, many belong to the ultraconservative Swartzentruber community, which permits battery-operated flashlights but few other technologies. Though their buggies' lack of mirrors, lights, and warning triangles occasionally causes disgruntlement, they otherwise enjoy a harmonious relationship with

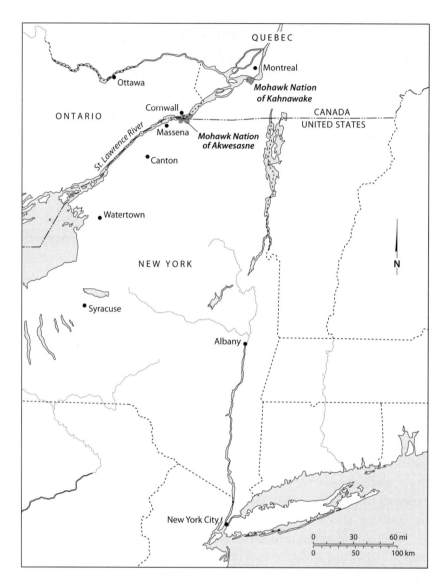

QUEBEC

• Montreal

• Ottawa

*Mohawk Nation
of Kahnawake*

ONTARIO

Cornwall

CANADA
UNITED STATES

St. Lawrence River

• Massena   *Mohawk Nation
of Akwesasne*

• Canton

• Watertown

NEW YORK

N

• Syracuse

Albany •

New York City

0	30	60 mi
0	50	100 km

U.S.-CANADIAN BORDER

—————

their "English" neighbors, exchanging services like hoof-trimming and carpentry for
emergency car rides and telephone calls. In 2014, North Country Amish made international headlines when two sisters got abducted from a roadside vegetable stand. Worlds
collided when police asked their family for photos to issue an alert. They had none to
offer, due to their religious beliefs, but consented to allow a sketch artist to make an illustration of their twelve-year-old (albeit, not their seven-year-old). The sisters resurfaced a
day later, and the suspects were arrested and charged with kidnapping.

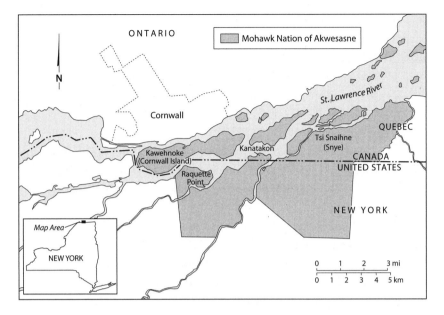

ONTARIO

N

Cornwall

St. Lawrence River

QUEBEC

Mohawk Nation of Akwesasne

Tsi Snaihne
(Snye)

Kanatakon

CANADA

UNITED STATES

Kawehnoke
(Cornwall Island)

Raquette
Point

NEW YORK

Map Area

NEW YORK

0   1   2   3 mi
0 1 2 3 4 5 km

AKWESASNE, AT THE U.S-CANADIAN BORDER

Whoever they are, they occupy the bulk of the bus. The only other passengers are a boozy-looking white couple and a young African American,
seated in the very back. We sit behind an elderly Amish man snoozing over
a vintage hard-shell suitcase that's a polar shade of blue.

Heading north from Syracuse, we pass only trees for more than an
hour—pine and maple, beech and birch—until we exit the interstate near
Watertown. U.S. 11 leads us into the countryside, rolling and green. Farms
with centuries-old houses dot the landscape. Roadside stands offer pints
of blueberries and pyramids of tomatoes; fresh-baked pies and jellies with
handwritten labels; quilts and baskets. Bonneted women in long dark dresses
pull wagons laden with children. There is a remarkable range of roadkill—
squirrels, porcupines, raccoons, deer, foxes—and obscene amounts of
horseshit. I understand the latter when the bus pulls into a gas station where
five horse-drawn buggies line up in a row. A young couple yanks out their
suitcase from the overhead bin and ducks out the door, where a bearded-
and-bonneted family receives them. Soon, the other passengers prepare for
departure. The women remove their bonnets, shake them out, secure them
back with bobby pins, and carefully retie their bows. The men run combs
through their finely oiled and curled hair.

Two hours into our journey, we slow to a stop in the middle of the road. Peering out the window, I see something I thought we'd left behind 2,000 miles ago: the U.S. Border Patrol. Half a dozen agents block the road with cones. One climbs aboard the bus. Unlike our agents back in Texas—brown and compact in jalapeño greens—this one is white and tall and clad in khakis. He stands in front of us, hands on hips, sunglasses shielding his gaze.

I glance around at our fellow passengers. The Amish are still gossiping away in what might be German. The African American is listening to his headphones. The couple is battling their hangover. Only Mom and I seem to have noticed this obstruction in our journey.

The agent scans us over for approximately 2.5 seconds, then gives a little wave. "You have a good morning, now."

Apparently, this is a corner of the United States where nothing says "citizen" like a German speaker wearing a bonnet. As we roll away, I crane my neck to gawk at the roadblock. Who or what are they looking for?

FOR THE NEXT YEAR, I'll be living in Canton, a town of 6,000 in the poorest, remotest, and coldest region of New York State. You could call this "upstate," but to some people (including myself, before I got here) that implies any-where north of the Bronx. No. This is north of the Hudson, north of the Catskills, north of the Adirondacks, even. Locals call this the North Country because the only thing it's south of is Ottawa. I got a taste of its seclusion when I was flown in for a job interview and the ticket cost $1,100 and culminated with a ride on a nine-seat Cessna flown by a pilot questionably old enough to shave. I didn't realize how far I'd be from urbanity, though, until I saw horses pulling buggies down the street.

My title here at St. Lawrence University is "Visiting Professor." To me, this conjures an image of one foot planted in academia while the other kicks freely about. That nicely sums my sentiment: I want a secure income and a fixed residence as badly as I fear that those things will crush the itinerant writer I have worked so hard to be. "Visiting" is not just a title, then, but a metaphor for who I am right now. Half here, half not. Half committed, half not. Just as likely to bolt as to invest in curtains and nest.

And that's not the only border I'll be straddling here. When my students stroll into class on the first day laughing about the "nineties party" they had attended that weekend where they dressed up in Doc Martens and moshed around to Pearl Jam, I see with sobering clarity that I have crossed into the realm of the middle-aged as well. This feels slightly unfair, given that I still have no partner, no child, no pet, no plant; no stocks nor bonds nor 401K; no furniture that didn't have half a dozen owners before me. No matter. My Doc-wearing, Pearl Jam–moshing undergrad days have been rendered into retro kitsch. I am thirty-eight years old now, which for a single woman is a nepantla all its own. Last chance for childbirth. Last chance to find a partner who hasn't already got an ex-wife and three screaming kids. Last chance to attribute your nomadic lifestyle to Bohemianism without seeming like a total flake.

Before arriving here, I didn't think the northern borderland could differ more starkly from the one where I grew up. Temperatures, for starters, tend to be sixty degrees apart. South Texas feels like a large wet dog is sitting on your face. The heat and humidity are that oppressive. The North Country is more like a cat hissing and scratching you. It is that visceral, that persistent, that extreme. And yet the hot-boil of the sun and the raw-freeze of the snow affect me the same way: both make me retreat inward.

And when I step into the car and in twenty minutes reach a bridge that requires a passport to cross and descends into a shockingly different economic strata, I realize I have been here once before.

And when I learn that a nearby community is rallying to deify an ancestor as a saint, and those very same people are also battling poverty, obesity, and industrial waste, I realize I will once again be caught in the suspension of disbelief.

And when I read about people getting arrested for smuggling "aliens" by speedboat and drugs by snowmobile, I realize that I am yet again living on an edge.

And when I finish teaching at 4 P.M. on Thursday and it occurs to me that—unless I stage an intervention—I will not see another human being until 10 A.M. the following Tuesday, I realize I am alone.

In other words, when I stare around this remote new world, I realize that I am home.

12

The Trade

AFTER NEARLY TWO DECADES OF CRASHING ON OTHER PEOPLE'S futons, I finally have a place suitable for hosting. My new job comes with a free and fully furnished Victorian house built in the 1850s. Before the moving van has even arrived, I welcome my first visitors: Uncle John and Tía Marie. They met while he was stationed at a naval base in South Texas fifty years ago and then absconded to the Bronx, where they made a mint in the auto springs business. They maintained their Tejano ties by flying back to Corpus Christi every Easter wearing cowboy boots beneath their New York Yankees jerseys and taking home a year's supply of tortillas from H-E-B. When I ask around for entertainment options in the North Country, someone mentions a casino at the nearby Mohawk Nation of Akwesasne.[1]

My only reference for this community is the 2008 Oscar-nominated film it supposedly inspired, *Frozen River*. The story revolves around a white woman (Melissa Leo) struggling to raise two sons on her Dollar Store salary after her husband takes off with the money they'd been saving for a double-wide. Increasingly desperate, she partners with a Mohawk woman (Misty Upham[2])

---

1. Though many maps, signs, and literatures call it the St. Regis Mohawk Reservation, I will be referring to the nation by its Mohawk name, Akwesasne, which means "the land where the partridge drums."
2. In October 2014, Misty Upham's body was found in a ravine on the Muckleshoot Nation located within the city of Auburn, Washington. She had been missing for nearly two weeks, but the Auburn Police Department had not yet opened an investigation, despite requests from her family. They had to organize her search party themselves and later released a statement that the police "had animosity against Misty due to a previous encounter." A medical examiner determined Upham died of blunt-force injuries to her head and torso and that her blood alcohol level was .33. It remains a mystery whether her death was an accident, a suicide, or a murder. A thirty-two-year-old Blackfoot, Upham was one of Hollywood's top Native American actors, working alongside Meryl Streep

who claims "There is no border here" as they shuttle undocumented immigrants across the frozen St. Lawrence River from Canada to the United States in the trunk of a car. A disaster strikes that has haunted me ever since.

Contrary to its bleak portrayal in the film,[3] Akwesasne feels upbeat as we drive through it. The highway is dotted not with campers and trailers but with standard HUD models and a few stately colonials. Everywhere we look is another tax-free, full-service gas station or smoke shop, and shuffled in between are a library, a museum, a bookstore, tribal government offices, a Chinese Canadian restaurant, a sushi cafe, a Brass Horse Pizzeria, a Subway, a Papa John's, a Jrecks Subs, a Dunkin' Donuts, and its Canadian cousin, Tim Hortons. The casino is located on the far eastern side of the nation, marked by a water fountain and sculptures representing the Mohawks' major clans: bears, turtles, wolves, and snipes. One traffic lane spills into an RV park; the second into a massive lot with cars bearing license plates from Quebec and Ontario; the third to valet. A Comfort Inn hovers above the premises as well as the skeleton of a luxury resort set to open next spring.

A Mohawk built like a linebacker ushers us inside the casino doors. The sensory assault is immediate: an arctic blast of air-conditioning followed by a sound wave of 1,800 ringing, pinging machines. Suddenly, it is nighttime. Suddenly, there is excitement—or at least a manufactured glee. As we moth toward the blinking lights, a herd of ladies amble by with walkers and canes. Their nails are polished, their hair is permed, their blouses are silky or sparkly. Husbands wearing hearing aids trail behind. Canadians, most likely. The North Country crowd is younger and clad in ragged jeans. They grip their beers and furrow their brows as they stake out their spots. Hardly any of the gamblers appear to be Mohawk, but at least half of the employees do, along with the bulk of the security guards. They wear black suit jackets and stern expressions—until they recognize someone in the crowd, whereupon they crack jokes like, "Does your sister know you're here?" The Elvis impersonator seems to be Mohawk, too. Decked in a white pantsuit festooned with

---

and Benicio del Toro. She was also one of more than 1,000 indigenous women missing in North America during the time her family spent looking for her.

3. This isn't the only issue Mohawks have with *Frozen River*. Most upsetting seems to be the portrayal of Upham's character, Lila Littlewolf, who aspires to take back her young child who got swiped away at birth by her mother-in-law for reasons never fully explained. Mohawks say such a scenario is impossible, due to the tribe's powerful matriarchal structure. Even if a mother couldn't care for her child (which Lila presumably could), the responsibility would be passed on to one of her female relatives, not to an in-law.

sequins, beads, and feathers, he croons love songs against a backdrop of ham sandwiches in the food court.

The last time I gambled, slot machines had manual levers and spat out coins with a satisfying clunk into a bucket. Here, financial transactions run through plastic cards that the gamblers fasten to lanyards worn around their wrists. When they stick their card into a slot, the machine takes on the appearance of a life support system, flashing colored light onto the gamblers' faces as it drains them of their money via the lanyard on their wrist. The aesthetic is so unsettling, I follow Uncle John around instead. With his thick Bronx brogue and sailor tattoos, he commands people's respect—especially in joints like this.

After exchanging a bundle of bills for a pile of chips, Uncle John swaggers over to a blackjack table where bets start at twenty-five dollars. The dealer is a white man with fast hands. Seated at first base is a blonde in a zebra-print blouse who signals for hits by scraping a card against the green felt table. Next up is a fiftyish man whose bleary eyes and rumpled clothing suggest a weeklong binge, and a younger man with well-gelled hair who bets obscene numbers of chips. Uncle John waits until the dealer's shoe has emptied before stepping in. As the dealer prepares a new round, a Mohawk woman walks up and taps his shoulder. He bids us well with a nod of the head, and she takes his place as dealer.

"Oh no," says the bleary-eyed man, rising from the table. "I'm not playing with her. No, no, I'm outta here." He grabs his chips and splits.

What this means, I cannot say. If the dealer knows, she does not reveal it. No one reacts to his departure, for the game is under way. After tossing each player a card with a flick of the wrist, the dealer looks at me. Her eyes are startlingly green. Shaking my head, I back away from the table and watch as she deals herself an eight and a queen. Then a jack and a king. Then nine, six, and five. Within minutes, everyone's chips have shrunk considerably. After twenty, Uncle John's are gone.

I feel bad for him, of course, and for the rest of the table, too. I feel bad for everyone here, blowing money they shouldn't. Yet hours later, when we wend through the maze of slot machines toward the exit, past all the other white folks being intravenously bled of their resources, I can also see the perverse appeal of this spectacle, given the disastrous history of Native/white relations in this country. Once I learn how bitterly gambling has divided some Indian communities (particularly this one), this impression will change. This first glimpse, however, feels like witnessing karmic payback, which is inherently gratifying—even when it's vicarious, even when it's ancestral, even when it's mean. Stepping through the cold-fog doors into the blinding sun, I flip through my mental calendar to figure out how fast I can return.

I ASK AROUND ABOUT AKWESASNE, but people know little about it. Despite our distance from other destinations of note (80 miles to Ottawa; 115 to Montreal; 350 to New York City), no one seems to visit. Everyone is apologetic about this. A few even express guilt. But aside from recommending *Frozen River*, no one has much wisdom to impart. Eventually I will meet two St. Lawrence University professors with decades-long ties to Akwesasne who will share invaluable contacts and resources with me: Bob Wells, who founded a master's program there and helped build its public library, and Celia Nyamweru, who teaches a community-based learning course that takes students there once a week for research and volunteer projects. For now, however, I must forge my own connections. And so I set out.

The road to Akwesasne, northeast from Canton, mostly consists of farms and forest until Massena, a working-class town of 13,000 that drops off at the St. Lawrence River. Hang a right on Route 37 and blaze past a hockey arena and a succession of churches. When Border Patrol vehicles start sprouting like mushrooms, Canada is near. Rather than turn north toward the international bridge, however, keep heading east. Smoke shops will signal your arrival: Twinleaf Express, Mohawk Junction, Akwesasne Cigarette Depot, Bear's Den Trading Post, Wild Bill's One Stop, Tree Top Smoke Shop, Smokey's Tobacco Shop, and so on. Some are specialty stores with neon signs blinking in the windows; others are convenience stores that sell cigarettes on the side. The flashier establishments offer drive-thru services, while the humbler ones—like the camper with the hand-painted sign—require walking up and rapping on a window. The way they line up, one after another, reminds me of border towns back home. Entire city blocks consist solely of drugstores where you can buy anything from acne medication to Viagra super-cheap and prescription-free. Another block mostly sells tequila, some bottles *con gusano* (with a worm), some without. A third specializes in hand-embroidered dresses; a fourth, in tiny guitars.

Along the Mexico border, however, you can actually see the clientele milling about the street: busloads of senior citizens loading up on cheap meds, college students flocking to bars, couples haggling for tchotchkes for their in-laws back in Omaha, balding men prowling around for blow jobs. Akwesasne seems deserted by comparison. Granted, its casino draws in 1.3 million visitors a year, but it is also located miles away from the main business strip. I don't see many gamblers as I cruise up and down the highway. I don't see much of anyone, actually. Who buys all these cigarettes?

I pick a shop at random—Smokin' Arrows—and park. A woman is tending a garden outside, but no one is working the counter. One sidewall is lined with essential oils and bundles of incense with names like "Bewitching," "Elemental Enchantment," "Gambler's Fast Luck," and "Cannabis." Dangling from mounted hooks are herbal medicines sealed into cellophane packets along with manually typed instructions. Bay laurel, a card notes, can either be cooked to aid digestion or placed under a pillow to "induce prophetic dreams." Nettles relieve urinary tract infections, while sheep sorrel wards off fever, inflammation, scurvy, boils, cysts, and tumors. The opposite sidewall continues the healing theme, with a shelf full of books about cancer-curing and two rows of vitamins in orange-and-white bottles.

The back wall, meanwhile, is stacked with tax-free cigarette cartons from floor to ceiling. Golden Arrows Reds. Smokin' Arrows Gold. Class A. All Natural Native. Seneca. Each box contains two hundred cigarettes, some for as little as fifteen dollars apiece, significantly cheaper than any of the vitamins. As I consider the implied regimen here—start with the back wall, then return for the sides when problems arise?—the door swings open and a white couple walks in, followed by the gardener I noticed earlier. The man strides over to the back wall and pulls down every carton of Seneca.

"Got any more?" he asks.

The gardener/clerk shakes her head as she rings up the total: $230 for 2,000 cigarettes.

I ask the man where he's from, and he looks at me suspiciously. "Watertown." That's a two-hour drive away. He and his wife trot back to their van with a spring in their step, as if eager to start smoking. Turning to the clerk, I ask for medical advice as a way of initiating conversation. She looks up from her receipt book. In her mid-fifties, she is freckled with moles and wears a watch with a turquoise-studded band. "What's the problem?"

At the *yerberias botanicas* along the southern border, the ladies behind the counter ask all matter of questions—medical, personal, spiritual, financial, sexual—before determining your prescription. Here, I am not halfway through my list of symptoms when the woman walks over to the sidewall and thrusts a bottle of tea tree oil into my hands. "It'll boost your immune system," she mutters as she heads back to the cash register.

"Are you a healer?" I ask as I pull out a twenty-dollar bill.

She looks me up and down. "I'm a cancer survivor," she says, then shares how she spent a year driving back and forth to Long Island for treatments before deciding to tackle her illness traditionally. Elders gathered herbs for her, and healers suggested how to take them. She's been in remission for five years now. The trick, she says, is protecting your autoimmune system and ignoring the government, as none of the "real" cancer-fighting medications have FDA approval. Walking over to the shelf of books, she taps a few spines. This is a lending library, she says, free for any tribal member.

"Isn't it . . . ironic, selling cigarettes alongside cancer prevention books?" I ask.

She glances at the back wall and chuckles. "I didn't get lung cancer," she says, then walks out the door to resume her gardening.

I drive on to another shop plastered with logos of cigarette brands. Like the first store, this one also melds divergent lifestyles. To the right are racks and stacks of clothes for little girls destined to be divas: satin panties with triple-layer ruffling, dresses with hot-pink boas sewn along the neckline, tutus, fairy wings, tiny top hats draped in netting and tied with bows. To the left is tobacco in every conceivable form. A wall's worth of cartons of Tomahawk, Nation's Best, All Natural Native, Signal, and Seneca cigarettes sell for $23 to $28 each. Individual packs swim in a wooden barrel for $1.75 apiece. Dip is sold in tins, rolls, and tubs in flavors ranging from Rum-Cured to Vanilla Cavendish. A glass case displays Zippos fanned out on a swatch of velvet.

I try to picture the customer who would patronize both sides of the shop and decide I'd like to meet her, but the only other person here is standing behind the counter. Nineteen or twenty, she is wearing a black hoodie. I buy a copy of the local weekly, *Indian Time,* and ask permission to read it at the diner-style booth beneath the window. She glances up from her cell phone long enough to nod. Her eyes are stunning—not jade-green, like the dealer at the casino, but the amber-green of autumn.

Three minutes later, a rusted Buick with a tattered American flag fastened to its antenna pulls up. Two blonde women step out. One is obese; the other has eyeglasses the thickness of ashtrays. They wear flip-flops, tank tops, and tight denim shorts. "What kind did Clarence want?" one asks as she heads toward the shelf of dip.

"Idunno," the other mumbles, sorting through the barrel. She stacks a tower of packs, does the math, tosses them back, and settles on a freezer bag of logo-less cigarettes. They buy forty-four dollars' worth of tobacco products before walking out the door. A minute later, one returns.

"Can I have a Band-Aid?" she asks the clerk. "I had my boyfriend pop a blister on my toe yesterday, and now it's bleeding all over."

It's true: her foot is a mess. Upon receiving a bandage, she kicks off her flip-flop, bends over until her tank top reveals her bra, lifts her foot, stumbles, grabs the counter, steadies herself, and tapes her bloody toe. Balling the wrapper, she hands it back to the clerk, who accepts it without expression. As soon as the customer steps out of the store, however, she looks at me and wrinkles her nose. "Thanks for sharing."

We laugh.

"We get *all* kinds here."

"Where do they come from?"

"Troy. Canada. Vermont. What about you?"

When she learns of my own border origins, she nods. "I hear it's pretty bad down there. But we got smuggling here, too. Once a girl came in the store and asked if I knew where she could get a boat. She says, 'I got two guys to transport,' and I could see them in her car. They had luggage and everything. I didn't know what to say, I was so shocked. Finally I says to her, 'My mom works for the police, I can't help you!'"

Before I can probe, a new customer glides in wearing a baseball cap and sunglasses. She marches to a shelf and swipes two freezer bags and four cartons: 1,000 cigarettes for $100. No sooner has she accepted her receipt than a TransAm pulls up and three white guys spill in. One notes aloud that cartons of Braves cost $23 here. Shaking their heads, they retreat.

"It really comes out the same, when you think about all the gas they are wasting, driving around," the clerk observes.

"Is it always this busy?"

"This? This isn't busy. Fridays, we got two people working the same time because we can't keep all the stock on the shelves. Last Saturday, I got shin splints running back and forth. It's so busy, you can't eat lunch. Some people have been coming here for years. They are like family."

At that, an elder strolls in. "Hi, Princess," he greets her. Without being asked, she pulls a carton of Tomahawks off a shelf and hands it over, accepting folded bills in return.

"See ya in a couple-a weeks," he says as he shuffles out the door.

I ask where Tomahawks come from, and she says that—with the exception of Seneca—every cigarette they sell is made right here at Akwesasne.

They used to sell name brands like Marlboro and Winston but stopped last summer because of the cost.

"No one has eighty dollars for a carton of cigarettes out here," she says. "It wasn't fair to charge our customers that. Besides, they would only buy one pack at a time. When we switched to only selling Native products, no one really said anything."[4]

Another customer walks in. As she shifts her attention back to work, I wrestle over what else I can ask. I'm dying to return to the topic of human trafficking, but I can only imagine how many reporters have traipsed through here, notebooks in hand, post–*Frozen River*. I don't want to be yet another writer hounding her about the troubling aspects of her nation, but I am also intensely curious about what else our communities have in common. After a few more customers cycle through, I decide that questions related to tobacco are germane, considering we're surrounded by it.

"So I guess cigarette smuggling is an issue here, too, huh?" I ask after an athletic-looking man tucks two cartons of Nation's Best beneath his armpits as if they were footballs and then charges out the door.

I thought I had phrased this question diplomatically, but that isn't how it is received. Her whole body stiffens as she folds her arms across her chest. "It's not smuggling," she says firmly. "We have a treaty so we can transfer cigarettes from one reservation to the other."

She then delivers a history lesson I will hear dozens of times in the year ahead. About how Mohawks have been living in this river valley since time immemorial, long before white men drew arbitrary lines across it. About how tobacco has played a vital role in nearly every aspect of their culture, from praying to ceremonial rituals to medicinal practices, also since time immemorial. About how the United States and Great Britain signed a treaty two centuries ago granting Indians the right to trade with each other and how that is what Mohawks are doing when they transport tobacco from one Indian nation to another across those arbitrary lines. They are *trading*. Not smuggling.

---

4. This decision was likely also influenced by the fact that, after years of trying but failing to collect taxes from tribes for cigarette sales, New York State finally won a court ruling in 2011 allowing it to demand tax payments from the wholesalers that supply tribes with name-brand cigarettes. In response, tribes sent the Marlboro Man packing and started promoting their own brands in their stores instead. Lobbyists are now pushing the state to tax Indian brands as well, calling tribal manufacturing of the product a form of tax evasion.

This rationale works for me, but the Canadian and U.S. governments would beg to differ. The province of Ontario (where part of Akwesasne is based) has a cigarette allocation system allowing smoke shops on Indian reserves enough tax-free cigarettes to cover the needs of "Status Indians" only. Between 2011 and 2012, those shops apparently sold 29 million tax-free packs, which means either that every Indian in Ontario is lighting up seventy cigarettes a day or that non-Status folks are trickling over to help out. The Royal Canadian Mounted Police reported that the Canadian government lost upward of $2 billion in lost tax revenue in 2008 alone due to such "contraband" and that 90 percent of those "illegal" cigarettes originated here on the U.S. side of Akwesasne before being "smuggled" to Mohawk nations in Canada across the St. Lawrence River. In Canada's eyes, then, this activity is not an ancient cultural rite but a crime. The United States also loses billions in revenue from untaxed cigarettes, yet its policies are a tad more lenient, permitting anyone of legal age to possess up to two cartons of tax-free cigarettes at a time for personal use. Every carton beyond that, though, carries fines— which means I'm witnessing risky behavior from my compatriots.

The door swings open and a Mohawk walks in. He chats up the clerk, asking about her mother and her grandmother and her neighbors down the street before wandering around the store, carefully considering all of the merchandise before selecting a pack from the barrel. Once he leaves, the clerk turns back to me.

"We get a lot of bikers up here. Like, the Hell's Angels and stuff," she says. "Once, they found a duffel bag with a body all chopped up inside."

Violence should never be a contest, but I cannot resist telling her about El Pozolero, the Tijuana "Stew Maker" who disposed of the bodies of his boss's narco-victims by dissolving them in barrels of lye. Her eyes grow bigger and brighter until she shakes her head in horror. It gets crazy here, she says, but not *that* crazy. She turns to straighten a few cartons on a shelf. At first, I think she's stalling for time to think up a story that's even more outrageous. (As a Texan, that is what I would be doing.) But no. When she turns around, it's to tell me about prescription drug addiction instead. That's the worst problem at Akwesasne, she says, at least among her age group. "I have a friend who had a baby in October that weighed only four pounds. She was doing Fentanyl patches at the time, scraping it and snorting it like cocaine."

We commiserate over the havoc drugs have wreaked in our respective communities, then gravitate to other topics. I ask how she likes working here, and she says she feels lucky. Most smoke shops are family-owned and hire only relatives, but this owner knows her mom, so they made an exception. She makes $10 an hour here, or $2.50 more than when she worked at the nearby trading post, the Bear's Den. That company mostly hires non-Natives, she says with disdain. In January she'll start taking classes online so she can apply for a better job in tribal government. That's the only other employment option besides the casino, she says, and she'd rather not work there. It's good money, but you always have to pick up other people's shifts.

I have been sitting in this booth for two hours now, far exceeding whatever rent I might have purchased with the newspaper. I thank her for her hospitality, and she says to come back on a Friday so I can see some "real action." Her invitation rings in my head for the rest of the afternoon, but I wait a couple of weeks to accept it, so as not to seem overeager. When I ask for her, however, the new clerk—an older woman—says she's been out a week already. I must look confused, because she adds, "She's about to pop."

Pregnancy had neither been mentioned nor observed the entire time we spent together that afternoon. I try to determine if this is happy news.

"Is she . . . does she . . . live with the father?"

"No," she says. "He's a total loser. As most of them are."

We stare at each other for an extended moment—she probably awaiting an explanation for my interest, while I hope to extract more information. When none arises, I admit that I am a writer, a profession that tends to be as (un)welcome in Native communities as a government agent, and for a good reason. Even the best-intentioned white writers often perpetuate stereotypes of Indians as being mystical healers, noble sufferers, or drunkards. While I have long been drawn to indigenous issues, guilt-ridden fear has kept me from researching them—fear of disrespecting a people still reeling from centuries of exploitation; fear of participating in the genre deemed "colonial literature" by Spokane/Coeur d'Alene writer Sherman Alexie;[5] fear of spreading injustice while striving for its antithesis. Yet here I am, pen in hand. There are just too many similarities between this particular community and my own

5. In his 2000 *Los Angeles Times* review of Ian Frazier's travelogue *On the Rez*, Sherman Alexie said, "Many Indians, myself among them, believe that the concept of tribal sovereignty should logically extend to culture and religion." In a later interview with *Atlantic Monthly*, he clarified: "Non-Indians should quit writing about us until we've established our voice—a completely voluntary moratorium. If non-Indians stop writing about us they'll have to publish us instead."

to ignore. If anyone understands the existential ramifications of division, it is a people who straddle not only the world's longest international borderline but the chasm between tradition and modernity as well. Story-addiction trumps fear here. As for guilt, perhaps diligence could be its antidote.

The clerk looks out at my red Hyundai parked outside, then at the notebook sticking out of my bag, and finally at the eager way I lean against her counter before proceeding. "She likes to talk a lot," she says of her former colleague, then purses her lips.

And she does not, undoubtedly also for a good reason.

13

The War

BEFORE ENTERING MO' MONEY PAWNSHOP—A CINDER BLOCK
building that stands alongside Lt. Dan's Camo Gear & Accessories on Route
37 in Akwesasne—you must first contend with the sign taped to its door.
BLACKLISTED, it reads in eye-chart *E* font size, followed by a dozen names.
Mine isn't among them, so I push through the door, causing bells to jingle.

Pawnshops in the southern borderlands generally have fluorescent lighting that casts a greenish pallor over cases of wedding rings, rows of flat-screen
TVs, and enough guitars and trumpets to equip a mariachi brigade. The atten-
dants are invariably young Tejanas with slicked-back ponytails who follow
you around, peppering you with questions, while the mustachioed Tejano
behind the counter strong-arms clients into hocking heirlooms to pay off
their electric bill.

Mo' Money feels homey by comparison, with its racks of DVDs and VHS
tapes and a smattering of camping gear, lacrosse sticks, and vacuum cleaners.
The table and chairs in the back of the room suggest democratic negotiations,
while the artwork on the walls attests to cultural pride: dream catchers, beadwork, images of wolves and moons and ravens. The jewelry cases are light on
diamonds but flush with turquoise, some stones the size of my fist.

The manager seems to be in her mid-sixties and has a booming voice and
a regal gait. Golden corncobs swing from her earlobes, and three strands of
beads adorn her neck. Her eyeliner is thick as kohl. At the moment, she is
assisting a middle-aged couple sorting through cocktail rings. The wife tries
on a topaz number, and the manager sugars her up. It's vintage, she purrs,
7.5 carats for just $250 with only 30 percent down. The husband jokes that
they'll have to stop at the casino first.

"Don't do that; I went to the Bingo Palace Friday night and they took all
my money!" the manager says. "So I tells my friend I had no luck, and you
know what he says? Take some antler bone and wrap it up in black silk with

a pinch of tobacco and put it in your bra, on the left side next to your heart. Try that and your luck will turn around."

"Did it work?"

"I don't know, I've never done it."

Why is it that, of the many cities I've lived in—Austin, Seattle, Moscow, Beijing, Brooklyn, Querétaro, Princeton, Iowa City, and Washington, D.C., to name a few—I overhear conversations like this only in the borderlands? When you live a few miles away from an arbitrary line that places you in an entirely different consciousness with its own history and culture and references and rules, your mind must become more receptive to additional imaginative leaps.

The telephone rings and the manager scoops it up. "Mo' Money, this is Vera." After a long pause, she says, "No, no, I have no place to put it," and hangs up. A woman emerges from the back of the store, asking who it was, and Vera says it was so-and-so wanting to know if she could come hock her fridge so she can play bingo tonight.

By this point, I have gravitated toward a case of dangly earrings fashioned out of beads and something I cannot identify. Sensing a sales opportunity, Vera strolls over and pulls out a pair for me to examine. "Porcupine quills," she says, running a fingertip down their tubular length. "I made them myself."

I ask where she found the quills and she says all you have to do is sneak up and throw a blanket on one, and he'll release a few for you.[1] They've got upward of 30,000 quills apiece, and they grow back quick.[2] Doesn't even hurt them. Otherwise, you wait till you find one dead on the side of the road. "Their spirit then protects you."

When I admire her craftsmanship, she says she learned as a child from an elder next door. "She taught me that I needed to do some sort of craft so I would always be able to make something I could sell so I could eat. We would go to near Montreal and sell our crafts. My dad would say, 'You're learning all these backward ways.' But if you live in a world where you don't respect who you are, your spirit is not happy."

1. Months later, I'll relay this explanation to a Mohawk, and she'll laugh and call it a "bullshit performance for white tourists." I will join in the laughter and say I had thought as much, but truthfully, I hadn't.

2. Another factoid about porcupines that seems improbable but isn't: they can climb trees. Because they prefer the tenderest buds on the farthest tips of branches, they can also fall out of trees. Many a North Country camping story includes a porcupine nearly landing on somebody's head.

She opens another glass cabinet and removes a belt of rawhide strung with hundreds of purple and white beads. "This is a wampum. It's what Natives used to write their treaties on while the white man used paper, which could be burned in fire."

I accept the wampum with both hands, impressed by its heft. The purple beads form the backdrop to four white rectangles engulfing a spade-shaped tree. I've seen this design on flags and billboards, bumper stickers and T-shirts, even tattooed around some guy's bicep, but haven't yet learned its meaning. Vera explains that it symbolizes the original five nations of the Haudenosaunee, or People of the Longhouse (also known as the Iroquois Confederacy). "This one represents the Mohawks," she taps a white rectangle, "and this is the Oneida, the Onondaga, the Cayuga, and the Seneca. The Tuscarora didn't join us till later."

The other woman strolls over and announces she is leaving for the island.

"Watch yourself on that bridge," Vera warns, then looks at me. "I hate it when those customs agents ask where I am from. I always say, 'I am Mohawk, I am from here. Where are *you* from?'"

"Do you go to Canada a lot?" I ask.

"No, but I go to our island," she says. "And we gotta drive clear to Cornwall for that."

Before I can clarify, the man by the cocktail rings intervenes: Does she take MasterCard?

"Nope," Vera sings out. "We are cash-only savages."

"Oh, okay," he nods, then continues consulting with his wife.

I can't tell if he caught Vera's joke or not, but I burst into laughter. A grin slides across her face. "So what else can I tell you?" she asks.

After hearing I'm a writer, she offers her assistance. There is much to learn here, she says, about the border, the bridge, the casino, the war.

"The war?"

She looks at me with something like pity. "Oh yeah, every ten years, we buckle down for another little war here. My brother always said that, instead of the barbecue pit, we get out our AK-47s and hunker down for the summer."

I vow to do my research, and she promises to introduce me to her friends. "Just come on a day when there's no bingo, like Monday, Tuesday, or Wednesday," she says. "We used to be razzle-dazzle, but now we're old ladies, so we play bingo."

AFTER A FEW WEEKS AT THE LIBRARY, I see that Vera wasn't kidding. The Mohawks have been a warring tribe throughout recorded history, not only battling other tribes but fighting in the French and Indian War, the American Revolution, and the War of 1812 as well. Anthropologists like William Engelbrecht and Dean Snow depict their penchant for scalping or beheading enemies as a way of capturing their souls and their eating enemies' hearts as a way to absorb victims' courage, displaying these trophies on poles that rose high above the village palisade. Yet according to the Seneca scholar John Mohawk, the Mohawks were also the first tribe to follow the great philosopher known as The Peacemaker. Disheartened by all the feuding between the clans of the northern woodlands, The Peacemaker pointed out that whatever life force had created the world surely didn't intend its inhabitants to abuse one another. He united the Haudenosaunee Confederacy[3] under a constitution called the Great Law of Peace that later influenced many of the world's participatory democracies, including our own.[4]

There was, however, in the late 1980s a brief period when Akwesasne resembled Belfast, complete with street barricades, car chases, firebombs, evacuations in the middle of the night, and—before state troopers finally marched in—bloodshed. While any number of events might have sparked this violence, the rise of high-stakes gambling fully ignited it.

No one knows for certain when Native Americans started playing games of chance, but early travelogues describe tribes throwing stones and bones until they literally lost their breechcloths (after first squandering away their wives and horses). The Apache warrior Geronimo gambled so relentlessly that the Dutch Reform Church expelled him to try to set an example. Mohawks disagree about their own tribe's traditional stance on the issue. Some say that gambling was forbidden by a revered prophet named Handsome Lake 200 years ago, while others find its moral justification in teachings that supposedly date back even further.

North America's first tribally operated gaming venture opened its doors a few days before Christmas in 1979: Hollywood Seminole Bingo, located

---

3. Exactly when this historic event took place is subject to much debate. Scholars who take oral tradition and solar eclipse data into consideration generally say 1142. Those who don't say 1451 or later. Whatever the case, it seems to have predated colonization.

4. The Haudenosaunee take great pride in counting Benjamin Franklin as one of their confederacy's many admirers. Some scholars say that certain features of the U.S. Constitution, with its balance of federal authority and states' rights, were inspired by the Haudenosaunee's governing system.

between Miami and Fort Lauderdale. At the time, the tribe's annual operating budget was not even $2 million; three decades later, it was netting $600 million. In 2006, the Seminoles further stunned the business world by dressing in traditional patchwork and capes, scaling a marquee in New York's Times Square, and announcing they had just acquired Hard Rock International for $965 million, the first tribal purchase of a major international corporation. "Our ancestors sold Manhattan for trinkets," one Seminole declared. "Today, with the acquisition of the Hard Rock Café, we're going to buy Manhattan back one hamburger at a time." Within a single generation, gambling had granted tribal members the right to a free education, free health care, full care for their elders, and fat dividend checks.

At least 240 tribes in twenty-eight states have since followed suit, opening more than 450 gaming establishments that range from a single slot machine in a trailer to the 9-million-square-foot Foxwoods Resort Casino owned by the Mashantucket Pequot Tribal Nation in Connecticut. All told, Indian gaming generates some $28 billion in gross revenue a year—so much, journalists have deemed it the "new buffalo."

The U.S. government didn't start regulating Indian gaming until 1988, or three years after Akwesasne's tribal council licensed its first bingo parlor. Before Albany and the tribal government could hammer out an agreement under the new federal policy, illegal slot machines started cropping up in the back rooms of truck stops and restaurants across Route 37. Then a Mohawk named Tony Laughing—who had amassed a small fortune in the cigarette trade—opened a full-blown casino called Tony's Vegas International, regulations be damned. Canadians arrived by the busload to play his extensive selection of slots and tables, and Laughing boasted that he was grossing a million dollars a week.

Reactions varied wildly. Some Mohawks interpreted Laughing's antics as a defiance of the Great Law of Peace, which champions working together for the collective good. Others applauded his capitalist streak, arguing that gambling could be the path out of poverty the tribe had long been seeking. Meanwhile, more and more gambling joints opened along Route 37: Burns Casino, Lucky Knight, Silver Dollar, Hart's Palace, Onkwe Bingo Jack, Golden Nugget, Billy's Bingo Hall. State troopers and FBI agents began raiding the casinos in the early morning hours and confiscating all the slot machines they could carry, but the owners would replace them by nightfall. During a July 1989 raid, Laughing led his would-be captors on a thirty-minute high-speed chase before his car stalled on the railroad tracks and he darted into the forest. Police found $87,000 in his car, as well as a woman and a thirteen-year-old girl.

This earned Laughing a twenty-seven-month prison sentence, but his fellow casino owners were not deterred. They simply hired (and armed) a strapping bunch of guards called "the Warrior Society."[5] The tribe thus splintered. Gambling opponents argued that casinos not only would bring drug trafficking, prostitution, corruption, and overall lawlessness to their nation but also would weaken their identity by luring so many outsiders into their community. Pro-gamblers countered that the tribe would grow so prosperous from casinos that they could fund cultural institutions like language schools and museums that would help *preserve* their identity, plus wean themselves off of federal aid and become more self-sustaining. Both sides deemed their line of thought "traditional" and the truest way to sovereignty.

Failing to persuade casino owners to close their doors, opponents tried appealing to the gamblers themselves by picketing the casinos, first with signs, then with barricades. Enraged by this threat to their business, the owners—and moreover, the Warriors—responded with shouts and then fists. Clans, neighbors, friends, and families fractured over the issue, as did tribal leadership. When Akwesasne's print media—the weekly *Indian Time* and the lauded national journal *Akwesasne Notes*—sided with gambling opponents, their building burned to the ground.[6] The homes of prominent opponents got torched as well, including those of four subchiefs. Then someone set the Lucky Knight Casino aflame.

Yet the gamblers kept arriving by the busload. By December 1989, Akwesasne's unregulated casinos were grossing $200,000 a day. The following month, a Mohawk who won considerable fame carrying the Olympic torch during the 1980 Winter Games at Lake Placid burst through the doors of Tony's Vegas International with his 12-gauge shotgun, ordered everyone to leave, and opened fire, obliterating video display terminals, the cashier

5. Though I haven't found references to this society prior to the 1980s in (outsider) scholarship, Warriors themselves say they have existed for centuries and were simply "reengaged" during the casino war. Historically, they say, the society advocated for peace unless instructed otherwise by the clan mothers.

6. Most books refer to this incident as a firebombing, yet two *Indian Time* staffers I interviewed—Helen Lazore and Deb Cook—say that their building suffered an electrical fire. "The community was so divided, it was easy to believe it was arson," Cook said. Lazore added that the morning after, "we went there and we all cried. Everything was gone, all the typewriters burned, the desks, everything. *Indian Time* too."

window, the floor, some furniture, and the ceiling. Violence escalated as winter thawed to spring. Jaws broke, windows shattered, barns were incinerated, cars got blasted into rubble. Families began to evacuate. Traditional leaders repeatedly sought intervention from Albany, but Governor Mario Cuomo refused, deeming the problem internal. In mid-April, someone firebombed the North American Indian Traveling College, a twenty-year-old cultural institution. Later that week, the U.S. Postal Service stopped delivery to parts of Akwesasne. Then the elementary school shut down. Nearly half of the population had fled by month's end.

On the night of April 30, 1990, eleven gambling opponents and two Canadian reporters gathered at the home of David George for a showdown. Crouching behind a fieldstone wall, they exchanged thousands of rounds with the Warriors, who used the nearby home of Diane Lazore as their fort. The arsenal included hand grenades; AK-47, AR-15, and M16 assault rifles; 9mm Uzis; two .50-caliber heavy machine guns; a M72 light antitank weapon; and two speedboats named *Pride* and *Joy*. When dawn broke, the bullet-riddled bodies of two Mohawks were discovered: Matthew Pyke (who, at twenty-two, opposed gambling) and Harold Edwards Jr. (a thirty-two-year-old said to have supported it). Hours later, 500 troops descended upon Akwesasne and declared martial law. Doug George-Kanentiio, brother of David and editor of *Akwesasne Notes,* was arrested for the death of Edwards but got acquitted ten days later and moved off the nation soon after. Several Warriors got arrested too, albeit not for murder. To this day, no one has served time for either killing.

The independent casinos folded after the standoff. Nine years later, with Albany's blessing, the tribe opened the Akwesasne Mohawk Casino, which injected some $79 million into the tribal economy between 2003 and 2010 alone. While tribal members do not collect dividend checks from the casino, they do receive stipends for certain expenses like heating fuel during winter. Casino profits also fund community resources like the Akwesasne Boys and Girls Club, the senior center, the volunteer fire department, and the local ambulance.

Yet, given all the hate and ache, it's hard not to wonder: was it worth the battle?

VERA SUGGESTS MEETING FOR LUNCH at the Bear's Den. Matriarch Theresa Bear opened the trading post in 1953 with two gas pumps and a souvenir stand, which her son later expanded to three outlets along an eight-mile stretch of highway. The flagship store still feels midcentury. The instant you drive up, white men in matching shirts dash out to fill your tank and wash your windows, while in the restaurant, a middle-aged woman with a name like Arlene escorts you to a booth, plunks down a laminated menu and a pot of hot coffee, and rattles off the pies of the day. Although the Bear's Den is one of the nicest places to eat at Akwesasne, some Mohawks avoid it because of the owner's politics. Among other things, he was the first to install slot machines in the eighties.

Vera is already seated in a booth, stirring a mug of coffee. Several pounds of silver gleam from her neck, wrists, and fingers, but my eye is drawn to the turtle-shaped brooch hovering above her heart. "This represents my clan," she says, tracing it with a manicured fingernail. She can track her lineage to 1704. Her forefather Silas Rice was playing in a flax field in Westborough, Massachusetts, when a band of Mohawks came barreling through. Having lost so many of their own children to smallpox and war, the tribe needed replacements and so swiped up Silas, his brother, and two of their cousins and brought them to their camp. His cousins eventually ran away, but Silas and his brother lived as Mohawks until the end of their days.[7]

Vera's father fought in World War II and then—like many Mohawk men of his generation—became an ironworker. Every Sunday, he drove 300 miles to a construction site in New York City or Philadelphia and did not return home until late Friday night. Mohawks have helped erect so many national landmarks—the Empire State Building, Rockefeller Center, the Chrysler Building—they've been deemed "skywalkers" for their purported immunity to acrophobia. Yet Vera says that her dad once told a *National Geographic* reporter that he pursued high steel not because of a cultural calling; rather, "If I had a college education, I wouldn't be here."

Vera left Akwesasne twice herself: once to study painting and jewelry making in Santa Fe and another time to marry a German man out in Rochester. "I thought I did valiantly for eleven years, but we divorced," she says, biting into her turkey club sandwich and grimacing. "The culture shock was too much. We were living on Long Island, and their life had no meaning

---

7. According to a 1769 pamphlet called *The Story of the Rice Boys* by the Reverend Ebenezer Parkman, which I found in a library, the Rice brothers "mixd with the Indians; lost their Mother Tongue; had indian Wives, & Children by them and liv'd at Cagnawaga. Their Friends among us had news of them not long since, that they were then alive; So that they may be in all probability there still."

to me. They'd dress up and go sailing on weekends. What life is that? I didn't want to stay in the white world."

She returned to Akwesasne in the early eighties and has lived here ever since, selling crafts, delivering meals, and—for the past two years—running the pawnshop. "I get everyone in there, teachers to hillbillies. There are people who are really down and out. They try to sell to help their existence. There are sad things I see. Women trying to raise a family and the husband leaves them and they need to pawn off their wedding ring. I try to work something out with them. I think women should help other women. But it's a business and your mind has to be quick. You have to read people, and I can read them like a cheap novel."

Like now. Even though I am firing off the questions, Vera seems to be sizing me up too, noting everything from my intonation to where I rest my eyes. And she's not the only one. Often at Akwesasne, I feel myself falling under the same scrutiny I did while living in Moscow in the mid-nineties. Yet Mohawks silently notice things, whereas Russians are very verbal about their observations: "Are you sick or something? You look awful." "Don't you have a hairdresser? Your ends are all split." In Moscow, I attributed Russians' observational prowess to the fact they had just endured seventy years of political terror. Here at Akwesasne, the legacy must have rooted half a millennium ago.

Since people-reading is a logical transition to gambling, I ask what she thinks of it. She approves of the Bingo Palace, not only because she likes to play herself but also because it is considered Class II gaming and thus doesn't fall under the jurisdiction of New York State.[8] By virtue of being Class III, the Akwesasne Mohawk Casino is subject to regulations by both tribe and state (and, as Vera puts it, "Once you let the state in, you never get rid of them"). She participated in tribal discussions before the casino opened in 1999 and remembers one subchief asking the contrarians, "Why are you worried about getting a casino? Everyone will have a Cadillac in their garage. The only thing you will have to worry about is what color you want."

"But we never got a per capita and we never got a Cadillac," Vera says, her wide eyes narrowing. "The chief said we didn't need a per capita, because if we did, we would just sit on our porch and drink it."

---

8. As per the Indian Gaming Regulatory Act of 1988, Class I (social games) falls under jurisdiction of the tribe, Class II (bingo and related games) under the tribe and the National Indian Gaming Commission, and Class III (all other games) under the tribe and the state.

At that, an elderly couple walks past our table. The woman stops at Vera's side and, in a quiet voice, asks if she'd heard that a kid died last night.

"Overdose?" Vera asks.

The woman nods.

"There were two last week," Vera says.

Nodding solemnly, the couple moves on, and Vera resumes our conversation without acknowledging the previous one. Her biggest gripe with the casino, she says, is that it employs too many white people. When I counter that the ethnic breakdown has seemed evenly split during my own visits there, she says that I probably only saw the security guards. The folks who make the real money, the managers and such, are either white people or Indians who used to be gambling opponents.[9] Of course, Vera notes, the casino isn't the only place that hires whites over Natives. "Look around."

I do. Every staff person within eyesight appears to be white, while nearly all of the customers seem to be Mohawk. "The owner doesn't hire Natives, only whites, because if they are Native, you can't treat them the way you can treat these people," she says.

Since my interactions with "these people"—who presumably hail from nearby towns like Massena and Fort Covington—are regrettably limited to service transactions, I don't know how they view their own "treatment." Premature wrinkling suggests they clock in more than their fair share of hours, though.

"The only successful people on this rez are the ones with a white parent and no clan," Vera continues, ticking off some high-profile examples. "When you have white in you, your first thought is to gain control. It's a capitalist European gene."

This conversation is growing increasingly difficult to process. Chances are, Vera is simply sharing her perspective with a reporter. But could she also be speaking to me as one representative of a historically oppressed group to another, as a way of invoking solidarity? Or is she speaking to me as a white person, with an intention of making me feel guilty? Or—if she is as perceptive as she says and knows my biracial origins without me even claiming them—is she explaining a part of me to myself?

---

9. A report published by the tribe—*The Economic Impact of the St. Regis Mohawk Tribe 2008* by Jonathan B. Taylor—confirms that 72 percent of casino employees and 60 percent of bingo employees are non-Indian. According to the tribe's website, www.srmt-nsn. gov, its 1,600 employees make St. Regis one of the largest private employers in the North Country.

Whatever the case, we have been talking for two hours. Mo' Money awaits. Next time, Vera says as I escort her to her minivan, we'll go on a tour with her friend. I wave good-bye as she peels away, but rather than return to my own car, I cross the street to a brick building surrounded by a palatial lot. A quarter century ago, this was the site of Tony's Vegas International, or ground zero of the casino war. To the chagrin of tribal government— which strives to eliminate competition with its own casino—Tony Laughing reopened his business in 2010 under the name Three Feathers Casino.[10] Every time I drive by it, however, it looks closed. In December, I'll pick up a *Watertown Daily Times* and learn that Laughing (along with four others) has been indicted for operating Three Feathers and could face additional charges for allegedly stealing $200,000 worth of electricity to do so. The newspaper will note that this is his third federal sentence, after a 1998 charge for racketeering and money laundering while "smuggling" cigarettes and alcohol into Canada. The story will also mention that Laughing is sixty-five years old.[11]

A red flag featuring a multi-rayed yellow sun flies above the casino. As I step closer, the profile of an Indian's head and shoulders emerges inside the sun. A single feather rises from his braid. The Mohawk artist and writer Louis Karoniaktajeh Hall created this image in the seventies as a call upon all Indian nations to unite under the Great Law of Peace. Decades later, it remains a fixture at Native protests in both the United States and Canada. Here at Akwesasne, the symbol seems to especially resonate with the Warriors, who paste it to their windshields, tattoo it on their biceps, and fly it from their

10. Because New York State did nothing to stop operations at Three Feathers Casino (or another unlicensed casino opened by a Mohawk outside Akwesasne)—despite the tribe's exclusivity rights—the tribal government began withholding tens of millions of dollars in revenue-sharing to the state in 2010, then later used that money as leverage in its decades-long struggle to take back some of its contested land in neighboring counties. In 2015, the Mohawks celebrated their first victory toward expanding their nation by regaining a thirty-nine-acre parcel in the nearby town of Fort Covington. Monitor future reacquisitions at www.resolvetheboundary.com.

11. A year later, in December 2013, three of these defendants were cleared of charges when the jury decided that the controversy over Three Feathers Casino was an intertribal conflict and not a federal one. Laughing received a mistrial for not attending the trial, due to illness. One of the freed Mohawk defendants—a former ironworker named Tommy "Salt" Square—sat in jail for the ten months prior to the trial as a form of protest. "They appointed me a lawyer and I didn't accept because you can't fight as a sovereign people with their lawyer," Salt told me a few months after his release. "I have been a researcher of white man commercial law, so I spent the whole time [in jail] reading."

homes and businesses. I stare at the flag a long while, contemplating its suggested resilience.

AFTER THE BEAR'S DEN, Twinleaf is the most upscale truck stop at Akwesasne. Located on the far west side of the nation, it features a dozen gas pumps operated by men in red shirts, a convenience store selling everything from Haudenosaunee koozies to John Grisham paperbacks, and a restaurant that bakes made-to-order pizzas in a brick oven. I arrive to find Vera seated at another brightly upholstered booth, stirring another cup of coffee and sporting another turtle brooch. We chat until a heavy-set woman in a denim jacket and sunglasses opens the glass doors and lumbers over.

"Here she is, queen of the Snye!" Vera calls out.

The woman grins as she lowers herself into our booth. Vera introduces her as Diane Lazore, and I scan my mental files before realizing with a jolt that she is the Warrior "den mother" I have been reading about. As I reach out to shake her hand, I see that my internal lightbulb has been noted. Her face forms a scowl that is downright scary. An instant later, however, it is gone and she bursts into laughter. "Gotcha," her eyes say.

A waitress appears like a genie, notepad in hand. I offer to buy us lunch, and the orders start flying. Vera picks the soup of the day, an entrée, and a slice of pie, while Diane requests the scrambled egg platter. "That's about the only thing I can eat these days," she explains, her upper lip curled over her gums.

I should state here that I never took a side in the so-called casino war. Warriors just happened to be more willing to talk about the events of 1989–90 than any of the gambling opponents I contacted.[12] I start this interview with the obvious: how did Diane get involved with the Warriors? She arches one brow. "It was like lightning struck."

Lightning is not a bad working metaphor for this woman. Every few minutes, a new emotion grips her face—anger, triumph, grief, sass—and then vanishes. Even her hairstyle is kinetic, alternating black strands with silver and gray, some dyed amber at the tips. It's easy to picture her blasting an assault rifle.

12. Great resources for a gambling opponent's perspective can be found in Doug George-Kanentiio's 2006 book, *Iroquois on Fire: A Voice from the Mohawk Nation*, and in Bruce Johansen's 1993 book, *Life and Death in Mohawk Country*.

"I never set out to be the Warrior Queen, but I tried to impart my under-standing of our teachings to a crew of people who very sparsely knew the language, who had, as my father would say, no discipline or idea of what was right or proper," she says. "I have the historical perspective of cosmology. I was trying to instill reason and a little bit of teaching into the young men at the time."

In an hour of prying, however, Diane never articulates those teachings beyond the basic principles of sovereignty, which many Mohawks support regardless of their stance on gambling: "If we are who we are, we have the right to make determination for our community" and "If we willingly accept the authority of New York State or the United States, we are finished as a people." Although she is extensively cited in books and articles, she insists her role in the skirmish was minimal. Her mother was dying then. Caring for her was Diane's foremost concern, though occasionally she got dispatched from her mother's sickbed to the casino strip to check on her brother, a Warrior nicknamed "Noriega." (He too appears in the history books, including for getting shot at a few days before the final standoff in April 1990.) Diane also permitted the Warriors to use her home as their base camp on the last night of the standoff. The morning after, it burned to the ground.

"Diane's house was estimated at $600,000," says Vera. "When it got blown up, there were irreplaceable things in it, like a buckskin dress with beadwork. She got nothing for it."

"Blown up?" I ask Diane. The books I've read called it a house fire.

She nods. "I know who did it, who blew it up. But they are pawns. I want the king, and I am going to get the king."

Diane contends that much of the fighting in 1989–90 resulted from per-sonal vendettas rather than ideological differences. "There were fifteen agen-das running at once. There were people who said, 'He stuck gum beneath my chair when I was in second grade; I'm going to get him.' People used the war to settle the score."

And those scores unraveled many ties within the nation. Soon after the standoff, Diane's ailing mother asked her and her brother to go pay their respects to a dying uncle on her behalf.

"They were all antis, so it was like walking into a room of vipers. And we put our tails between our legs and we went. They all shriveled when we walked in. Our uncle was sitting there at the table, with his oxygen, and he acknowledged us. He stood up, even though he struggled. That sent a mes-sage to all in the room. We had no choice but to go to the table and shake his hand." Diane pauses to chew a spoonful of eggs. "That is the division this left in our family. We will all show our faces at a funeral, but you will never see us drinking coffee around a table together."

Vera and Diane share a sigh that has probably been collectively resounding within this nation for the past quarter century. Ian Kalman, a doctoral candidate at McGill University who is also researching the border's impact here, has a helpful framework for this: Akwesasne is a community united by divisive issues.

The glass doors open again, and a man breezes by. "What, you don't say hi anymore?" Diane calls out.

Pivoting on his heel, he backtracks. Maybe forty years old, his face is round and cratered. Diane asks how his neck is doing, and he launches into a story about how a state trooper started following him down the highway one day, even though he'd done nothing wrong. Figuring it must be racial profiling, he sped off toward Akwesasne, sparking a high-speed chase that culminated with his car flipping off the road. "I spent seven months in a cast," he concludes, wrapping his thumb and forefinger around his neck to show where. Then he nods to each of us and continues on his way.

Throughout our conversation, Diane has yelled for more napkins and coffee and cutlery while Vera has demanded the music be turned down so she can hear. Now that our plates have been cleared, they shout for the check and grin when the (white) waitress comes running. Time for the tour, Vera says after I sign the credit card slip. We pile into Vera's minivan, which is full of laundry and novels, and pull onto Route 37. Somewhere, Diane procured a broad-rimmed hat with a feather tucked in its band. Plopping it on her head, she instructs Vera to hang a left at Raquette Point. The slender road curves past a string of old-time gas stations and HUD houses that are gradually spaced farther and farther apart. Then come the abandoned houses, the condemned houses, the burned houses. Swap the trees for cactus, and we could be back in the colonias of South Texas. The houses exude the same blend of exhaustion and fortitude, while the yards showcase similar assortments of auto parts, tricycles, furniture, and toys. We turn on a side road and follow it down to a tree-shrouded marina that is just wide enough for a speedboat. The river spills before us.

"This is where you take cigarettes across," Diane says. "A Mohawk died on the river last summer when he got chased by a Border Patrol agent in a speedboat. The waves were so big, he lost control and hit a block of concrete."

A nearby grassy knoll is crested by a house that has been stripped to the bones. Vera says her aunt Shirley used to run a speakeasy there. "I was only twelve years old and was out serving drinks."

We laugh as she thrusts out an arm and pretends to palm a tray. Before there was a weapons trade, people trade, drug trade, or cigarette trade, there was a whiskey trade here at Akwesasne. Al Capone grew rich and famous smuggling cases through the Canada-Michigan border during Prohibition, but Vera claims plenty of bottles passed through here, too.

"My grandmother's husband died transporting whiskey from Canada in a bootlegging accident right here on the St. Lawrence River," Vera says. "He was six-foot-two and got caught by his bootstrap. People still dive in the river today and bring up bottles. There are old barns with whiskey inside the walls, packed with straw."

She backs out of the marina and follows a road that winds along the riverfront. The houses increase in size and value until we reach a veritable mansion behind a tall stone wall. "Why don't they just put up a fluorescent sign with flashing lights that says 'Drugs sold here'?" Vera asks.

Diane informs me that the owner's son just got forty years for masterminding the murder of a drug dealer. His mother is currently under house arrest for money laundering.

"She wears her anklet to Walmart!" Vera says. "She is proud of it."

We continue past a row of colonial homes with Escalades parked in the driveway and boats tied at the dock. Vera and Diane claim to know the story behind each one. This guy trades pharmaceuticals; that one owns a cigarette factory. This family runs their own construction company. I scribble a page full of notes, but when I look up again, we're back among the HUD houses. A modest cemetery comes into view, and then we pass a road sign marking the speed limit in kilometers instead of miles.

"And now we're in Quebec," Diane announces.

Panic grips my chest as I poke my head between the front seats. "Wait, what? I didn't bring my passport!"

Diane lets out a cackle, then turns to face me. Don't worry, she says. There's no checkpoint.

"But . . . isn't this illegal?" I crane my neck to peer through the windshield, half-expecting a Border Patrol SUV to emerge from the trees.

Vera laughs as Diane explains that the U.S.-Canada borderline cuts Akwesasne in two. That means some Mohawks technically live in New York State while others technically live in Quebec, Canada, even though they all inhabit the same contiguous landmass that has always been home to the Mohawks. You can cross the border without even realizing it, as we just did. There is also a third portion of Akwesasne called Cornwall Island located in the section of the St. Lawrence River claimed by Ontario, Canada.

Complicating matters further, Diane adds, is the fact that the portion of Akwesasne located in the United States falls under the jurisdiction of a government known as the St. Regis Mohawk Tribal Council, whereas the part in Canada is governed by the Mohawk Council of Akwesasne. Both are elected by community vote. There is also a traditional form of government called the Mohawk Nation Council of Chiefs, which upholds the teachings of the Haudenosaunee Confederacy and is chosen by the clan mothers. Decisions made by one government are not always supported by the other two—to say nothing of all the external forces Mohawks must also contend with: Albany, Washington, Ottawa, the New York State Police, the U.S. Border Patrol, the Sûreté du Québec, the Ontario Provincial Police, the Royal Canadian Mounted Police, and the Canada Border Services Agency (to name a few).

"And they wonder why we aren't normal!" Vera says after catching my dazed expression in the rearview mirror.

It will take time for this to fully compute. For now, I just try to accept the fact that we are suddenly in Quebec, a part of the world I previously only associated with separatists and brie. Up ahead, the road splits in two, and we veer right toward the village of Kanatakon. We pass a post office, a currency exchange, and a couple of government buildings before some single-story houses appear, each with its own stoop, yard, and stash of cars and ATVs in the driveway. The steeple of a Catholic church appears in the distance, but Vera cuts left and we glide instead by a sign for Big Russ' Chip Stand featuring the silhouette of a portly woman posed in classic mudflap position. We park where the Raquette River flows into the St. Lawrence River—one water dark, the other nearly green.

"There was a story my father would tell me, many moons ago,"[13] Diane says, beckoning me closer. "When scouts arrived here, looking for new land, they camped near Yellow Island. One said, 'I'll fish for supper,' while the other set up camp. As he cut some wood, he tripped over a log and inside it

---

13. According to the Mohawk who said that claiming to gain the spiritual protection of a porcupine by snaring its quills is an identity "performance," the same is true of telling time by the moon. Tejanas, of course, are guilty of this, too. Show us an organic, vegan, gluten-free tortilla, and see how we wax poetic about the hand-rolled, lard-laden, GMO tortillas our abuelitas used to make (while stashing the other kind in our cupboard).

was a fish, a magic fish. The man cooked and ate the fish, and then he got so thirsty that bowls of water would not quench it. So he went down to drink from the river, and his form changed into a sea creature. He told his friend to go back and tell the elders never to name anyone after him again. He also said that if anyone ever needed him, to hit the water seven times with a red willow branch and call his name."

She twists around in the front seat to face me. "That is the legend of the sea creature, and this is where he lives. Every now and then he pulls cars in, and every so often there will be multiple deaths. Kids on snowmobiles go into the water and die."

¡Aye! This is worse than La Llorona, the ghost-woman of Mexican folklore who scours the waterways, searching for the little kids she murdered. Way worse, actually, because no matter where you travel in Akwesasne, water is near. At least in South Texas, you can avoid what is wet. Diane lets out another cackle, and we peel out of Kanatakon, back toward the main strip. Vera points out an abandoned building that used to house slot machines in the eighties.

"We must have had, what, eleven casinos back then? And they only employed Indians, every one," Diane says.

"That was the first time Indians were able to have both a car and a truck and could buy groceries every week," Vera adds. "Now all the whites get the jobs and the Indians get nothing."

Which system would better support the average Mohawk: a bunch of freewheeling independent casinos that hire friends and family, or one mammoth casino that doles out equal benefits for all? It is strange to think of a casino as a socialist enterprise, but that might be the case for the Akwesasne Mohawk Casino. So was the 1989–90 war a rare instance of communalism defeating capitalism? Or did it follow a more typical narrative of a string of mom-and-pop shops getting quashed by a larger, sleeker moneyed operation?

"That was Wild Bill's," Vera says, pointing through her side window. "It used to be a full-blown casino. Now it's just a gas station. That blue building there was Lucky Nights. Gone. Three Feathers used to be jumping. Not any more."

The more bolted planks the women point out, the more I recognize another feature of southern border life: the ghost town.

"You would never believe the money Indians used to have. There were two money exchange places here. At the mall, there was a store in every cubicle," Vera says.

"And now," Diane says, twisting backward in her seat for a final time, "now there is nothing at all."

14

The Saint

RIVULETS OF FOG BURN OFF THE ST. LAWRENCE RIVER AS I DESCEND into the Mohawk reserve of Kahnawake from the lower lip of Montreal, Canada. The sky is slate and moody. At the foot of the bridge, I consider the options.

Continuing south onto Highway 138 will deposit me in the so-called Las Vegas, Atlantic City, and Monaco of the online gambling world. Mohawk Internet Technologies is its name, although people prefer its collegiate acronym, MIT. The web-hosting company runs hundreds of the Internet's biggest poker, casino, and sportsbook sites[1] out of an old mattress factory that's been converted into a high-security fortress off the side of the highway. Non-governmental gambling is illegal in Canada, but Kahnawake Mohawks shrug off such technicalities by asserting their sovereign authority granted by their First Nation status. They issue their own passports (the Haudenosaunee), employ their own police force (the Peacekeepers), and otherwise "do all they can to live a political life robustly, with dignity as Nationals," according to Mohawk scholar Audra Simpson. Their highway defiantly yields a string of (in Canada's eyes, illegal) poker houses that deal Texas Hold 'Em, Omaha, Seven Card Stud, Lowball, and Draw High twenty-four hours a day, plus scores of tax-free smoke shops: Brad's Butts, Best Butts, McSmokes, Diabo's Discount, Mohawk Discount, and Another Dam Cigarette Store, to name a few.

All the fun is south of here, in other words, but today I'm feeling pious. Turning west, I follow the river toward an old fishing village dotted with fieldstone houses. Streets have no names in Kahnawake. The official town map lists only landmarks: "behind Mohawk Market," "near Eileen's Bakery," "behind Pit Stop Convenience," "Blind Lady's Hill." But my destination is

---

1. According to a 2015 *New York Times* special report, one of MIT's sites—Bovada— received 190 million visits from computers during a twelve-month period; 97 percent of that traffic purportedly came from the United States.

easy to find. I simply follow the traffic to an eighteenth-century Catholic church with a weathercock atop its steeple. Television crews swarm the entrance while beefy Peacekeepers lean against their squad cars. I follow a mother herding her young sons through the double doors but get halted at the vestibule. The church is packed to the apse.

Peeking over shoulders, I catch a few glimpses. A gold-robed bishop wielding a staff like a shepherd. A pew full of women wearing long navy capes that, when flicked over the shoulder, reveal a scarlet lining beneath. Baskets of dried corn tied with ribbons. An elder in a buckskin vest and a traditional feathered headdress called a *kastowa*. Intricately beaded bands wrapped around wrists. A dark-robed monk fingering prayer beads. And the focus of everyone's attention: a white marble tomb laden with lilies.

Mass is half an hour away, but the pews are so packed, the aisles are filling too. The ushers don't like this one bit. Each is wearing a traditional calico shirt with brightly colored ribbons streaming from his shoulders. One gravitates toward the stragglers in my vicinity. There is a spillover room at the school, he says. Live-stream footage, straight from the Vatican.

No one acknowledges him. History is happening upon that altar, inside that tomb—history three centuries in the making. Some of us crossed multiple time zones to be at the Mission of Saint Francis Xavier today. No way we're leaving.

The first usher walks away scowling and a larger one returns. We try to look busy, the stragglers. We scramble for the church bulletins. We dunk our fingers into holy water and flick it all over ourselves.

"You must leave," he says. "All of you."

We continue maneuvering around the vestibule with purpose, as if a new pew will materialize from the woodwork any minute. The usher takes a middle-aged Filipina by the elbow. "If you don't leave now, you'll be arrested."

"This is a church," she yells. "It is open to the people."

For an instant, there is energy. Ushers vs. Stragglers, center vestibule. But then the doors swing open and uniformed Peacekeepers march in. The Filipina seems up for the fight, but the rest of our collective will vanishes at the sight of armed officers. We hustle toward the door.

"You force us away," the Filipina accuses the men with ribbons dangling from their chests. "May God have mercy on your soul!"

With that, we are back in the street with the camera crews. I spot the lone newspaper reporter and walk over. He greets me with a cheery, "This is the most action this place has seen since Oka!"

Which is saying a lot. Soon after Akwesasne's casino war quelled in 1990, tempers started flaring here in Kahnawake over the proposed expansion of a golf course onto ancestral land in nearby Oka, Quebec. One band of Mohawks (including Warriors from Akwesasne) descended upon the town and staged an armed standoff that lasted seventy-eight days; another barricaded the bridge connecting Montreal to the South Shore for a month. In the protests that ensued, a Sûreté du Québec police officer was killed, hundreds were injured, and Mohawk symbols were burned in effigy. A quarter century later, Oka remains the three-letter reason why Ottawa strives to avoid conflict with Kahnawake.

The reporter adds that he has interviewed people who drove twelve hours to be here this morning, people who don't even have a place to sleep. They're all in that gym now, he says, nodding toward the elementary school across the street. Praying and waiting.

I depart to do the same, inside the schoolhouse that bears her name.

THE OUTSIDE WORLD has called her many things. Katharine, which her tribe pronounced as Kateri. Lily of the Mohawks, because the delicate flowers purportedly sprung from her grave. The Mohawk Maiden. The New Star of the New World. The Fairest Flower That Ever Bloomed among Red Men. The Venerable. The Beatified. Today—October 21, 2012—she will acquire her grandest name yet: Saint Kateri, Native America's first Catholic saint. Earlier this week, hundreds of Mohawks chartered flights to Rome to celebrate her canonization at the Vatican. I have joined the hundreds who converged at her tomb.

While Mohawks claim Kateri as their own, her mother was actually a Catholic Algonquin who studied with French missionaries before getting kidnapped by a Mohawk war party. Forcibly adopted into their tribe, she married a chief and bore him a son as well as Kateri in 1656. Four years later, smallpox nearly obliterated the family. Little Kateri lost her father, mother, and brother as well as some of her eyesight. Forever after, she'd wear a shroud to shield her damaged eyes from the sun. The disease also ravaged her face (though she later expressed gratitude for this, as it helped repel suitors). An aunt and uncle absorbed Kateri into their own family at a longhouse[2] tucked in the present-day Mohawk Valley of upstate New York.

2. These traditional wooden dwellings tended to be a couple hundred feet long and about twenty feet wide and housed dozens of families in small compartments. A dearth of doorways made the structure efficient for heating and defending. Around the mid-eighteenth century, families began building smaller log cabins of their own but retained longhouses

Jesuit missionaries were widely recruiting Indian souls at that time. Having a spiritual culture of their own, the Mohawks initially rejected Catholicism, turning the priests into slaves and occasionally drinking their blood.[3] But after losing a few key battles to the French, they conceded to admitting Jesuits into their villages. Kateri encountered Catholicism around age eleven and took to it with fervor, abandoning her Longhouse duties to devote herself to prayer. This angered her elders, particularly her aunts, who wanted to marry her off. By the time the Jesuits baptized Kateri at twenty-one, she had become the scorn of her tribe, accused of everything from laziness to sorcery. When an opportunity arose to join the Mission of Saint Francis Xavier on the bank of the St. Lawrence River, she snatched it.

At Kahnawake, Kateri caught the attention of Fathers Pierre Cholenec and Claude Chauchetière, whose writings immortalize her today. Watching her take the body and blood of Christ for the first time, Cholenec noted, "She approached or rather surrendered herself to this furnace of sacred love that burns on our altars, and she came out of it so glowing with its divine fire that only Our Lord knew what passed between Himself and His dear spouse during her First Communion."

Thus betrothed, Kateri commenced a life of extreme asceticism. She gave away her beads and her dresses, her moccasins and her necklaces, and wore only a plain blue frock. She sprinkled ashes in her food to deny her palate pleasure. In the frost of winter, she would arrive at the chapel door long before it opened and linger well after it closed. She befriended an Oneida woman who shared her zeal, and the two took turns beating each other with tree branches—1,000 slashes per session—as blood rippled down their shoulders. (Among her confessed sins: loving her body more than she should.) Although Cholenec noticed "mysterious light" engulfing Kateri as she flagellated, he encouraged her to use less punishing weapons: a whip, a sackcloth, a hair shirt, an iron girdle bristling with spikes. Instead, Kateri moved on to branding crosses into her legs. To plucking coals from the fire and placing them between her toes. To gathering armloads of thorns, scattering them across her bed mat, and pressing them into her flesh as she slept.

---

as gathering places to uphold their traditional ceremonial practices (aptly known as the Longhouse).

3. Father Isaac Jogues, the so-called Apostle of the Mohawks, met an especially gruesome fate. His first captors chewed off his fingers and kept him as a slave, while his last hacked off his head and tossed him into the Mohawk River. He was canonized as a North American martyr along with seven other Jesuits in 1930.

"And although in my heart I admired her, I pretended to be displeased," Cholenec wrote.

Reading her biography today, you'd be forgiven for drawing the worrisome conclusion that Kateri was a masochist whose suicidal tendencies were encouraged by kinky priests. Yet historian Allan Greer argues otherwise in his book *Mohawk Saint.* For starters, he says, seventeenth-century Haudenosaunee were master torturers—not only of their enemies but also of themselves. Shamans reached into fire and grabbed hot coals during ceremonies; warriors lacerated themselves as a way of mentally preparing for battle. Greer suggests that the self-torture of Kateri and others might have been a sort of hardening exercise to elevate their courage in their quest to achieve spiritual power. After enduring so many years of sickness, war, and dislocation, they aspired "not only to invest their suffering with meaning but also to cross the threshold of the divine," he writes.

Kateri's body ultimately lacked the resilience of her spirit. She grew wretchedly ill not long after her arrival. Rather than seek medical attention for their prodigy, the priests argued over her purity, as incest was rumored in her home village. Kateri spent her final weeks alone on her mat, vomiting and praying before gasping, "Never give up mortification" and "I will love you in heaven, I will pray for you, I will assist you." Then she coughed and said no more, dead at twenty-four. Cholenec later remembered, "[Her] face, so marked and swarthy, suddenly changed about a quarter of an hour after her death, and became in a moment so beautiful and so white that I observed it immediately (for I was praying beside her) and cried out, so great was my astonishment. . . . I admit openly that the first thought that came to me was that Katharine at that moment might have entered into heaven, reflecting in her chaste body a small ray of the glory of which her soul had taken possession."

Six days after her death, a priest glimpsed Kateri in the rising sun. Friends heard her calling their name in the night. Prophecies came to pass, of the destruction of a chapel and the torching of an Indian at a stake. Mourners began to fill tiny bags with earth from her grave and wear them as amulets around their necks. They steeped the ashes of her clothing and drank it like tea. Women cried out to Kateri as they suffered through labor—not only Mohawks but French Canadians as well. In Montreal, they sought her intercession for everything from resisting vice to harvesting crops. The cult of Kateri grew over the centuries. Churches from Santa Fe to Manitoba erected shrines in her honor. Schools and summer camps adopted her name. Devotees invested in her reliquary. People in need of a miracle asked for one, no matter how extraordinary. Today, Pope Benedict XVI will canonize Kateri for stopping a flesh-eating bacteria from killing a Lummi boy in Washington in 2006—after a whole team of doctors could not.

Maybe this is what draws so many people to Kahnawake today: the prospect of impossibility.

I, however, have come because of a nostalgia that started percolating last Sunday, when I attended Mass at St. Regis Catholic Church back at Akwesasne. During the homily, the Reverend John Downs[4] commented on how Native Americans had long struggled with the fact that foreign missionaries introduced them to Christ but now had a sense that "once we have a saint, we will truly be part of this church, because one of us will be declared holy. We will have better self-esteem and a better image of ourselves as First Nations people because of it."

Afterward, I met up with Bernice Lazore, the seventy-year-old founder of the Kateri Prayer Circle. She was introduced to Christianity by her grandfather and became enamored with Kateri when an aunt told her, "Whenever you are down or need something, pray to her." And Bernice did, throughout her childhood. Eventually, though, her grandfather left the church for the more traditionally Mohawk Longhouse and took most of their family with him. Bernice wanted to join them but couldn't bear the thought of abandoning Kateri. (The fact that Christian Mohawks routinely derided Longhouse members as "pagans" didn't help matters, either.) Her grandfather finally suggested a compromise: come to the Longhouse to receive an Indian name and learn a Mohawk song, then continue on with Catholicism. Bernice has pursued two spiritual practices ever since, upholding certain ceremonies of the Longhouse as well as making regular pilgrimages to Kahnawake to pray at Kateri's tomb; traveling to Fonda, New York, for retreats at Kateri's temple; and flying to the Vatican to celebrate Kateri's advancements toward sainthood.

This story of straddling divergent worlds sounded familiar, of course, as did the blending of belief systems that could be considered a form of spiritual

---

4. According to the Reverend John Downs, only one Mohawk has led this congregation in its 260-year history: Father Jacobs, sometime between the 1940s and the 1970s. The rest of the priests have been white, he said, and some quite disapproving of incorporating Mohawk culture into the church. In recent years, however, the parish has been led by a Filipino named Jerome Pastores who encourages the melding of traditions, including singing hymns in Mohawk, praying to the four winds, hanging up wreaths of sweetgrass, and installing altars to Kateri.

mestizaje. Yet déjà vu didn't fully strike until Bernice mentioned the time her cousin was making chicken and dumplings, got called out on an errand, returned home to clean up the mess, and then made a surprising discovery.

"She called me and said, 'You wouldn't believe what happened. Kateri is on my flour board.'"

"*Flour board?*" I asked.

Oh yes. Bernice ran over with her camera, and sure enough, there was Kateri, emblazoned across the flour. "You had to imagine it to see it, but I could see the outline of her face. While we were talking, all of these people were coming in to look at it. Then my cousin was pouring coffee and she spilled it right in the middle of the board, but it was okay, the coffee faded and didn't even stain. To this day, she has the flour board on her altar with photos and candles."

That's when I realized why Kateri seemed so familiar. Though it's disrespectful to compare such complicated belief systems, I couldn't help seeing flashes of the icons of the southern borderlands—Mother Julia, La Virgen de Guadalupe, and La Malinche—in this northern saint.

BACK AT KAHNAWAKE, the spillover room is spilling over too. Some 300 Haudenosaunee men in ribbon shirts, First Nations women in floral skirts, Anglophones, Francophones, and nuns in puffy coats gather around a projection screen in the middle of a gym, kneeling, sitting, standing, and shaking hands as Mass dictates. I watch a while, then wander over to the cafeteria, which is decorated with children's artwork. One poster depicts Kateri as a barefoot maiden draped in a blanket and dragging a hulking cross. Another says KATERI IDOL in huge block letters and lists the top contestants: Arlene Goodleaf ("Leader of the Pack"), Winter Aaliyah ("Call Me Maybe"), and Hayley Deer ("Eye of the Tiger").

Seated around the lunch tables are the pilgrims who found no room at the gym. The Filipina from the vestibule is telling whoever will listen how she drove all the way from Ottawa only to get shut out in the cold. She's boycotting Mass altogether now. When I ask her about the Filipino connection to Kateri, she explains that one of their own[5] is being canonized today, too.

---

5. Saint Pedro Calungsod braved typhoons and jungles in his mission to catechize the Chamorros of Guam during the mid-seventeenth century. Suspected of poisoning babies with his vial of holy water, he got martyred at age seventeen with a spear to the chest and a machete to the head.

Those who couldn't fly all the way to Rome traveled to Kahnawake instead. I can't decide if this makes perfect sense or no sense whatsoever, visiting a stranger's tomb in a faraway place because she is being recognized on the same day for the same achievement as another stranger buried even farther away—but it probably makes about as much sense as being here at all.

A First Nations woman appears then like sudden snow: white shoes, white pants, white coat, white scarf, white hair cascading past her elbows. Gripping her walker, she maneuvers toward some bags of groceries and attempts to lift one up. I offer assistance in English and she accepts in French. We head out to her minivan, speaking a hybrid of the two. Her name is Marie-Louise, and once she shares key biographical facts—she's Algonquin, the daughter of a fur trapper, and an alumna of the Amos Indian Residential School—a possible story line takes shape.

Her father's profession hints of a childhood spent in the bush. From her elders, she learned the plants that nourished and the plants that healed. She watched the men hunt and fish and helped the women gut, skin, and cure the meat. She bathed in the river. She danced in the woods. She plaited her hair in two. At night she burrowed between the crook of a brother's back and the hump of a sister's shoulder, absorbing their warmth. (As the second oldest of nineteen, she would have had many nooks to choose from.) She spoke Algonquin, prayed in Algonquin, dreamed in Algonquin—until the day a truck pulled up to their cabin in the bush and white men in black robes stepped out.

Nuns probably separated Marie-Louise from her brothers as soon as they arrived at the school. Genders mixed only on feast days. They lobbed off her braids and scrubbed her scalp with anti-lice shampoo. When she reached for her clothes, she was handed a uniform instead. Mass must have followed, along with a succession of classes taught in French, a language she hardly knew, and chores of all sorts: peeling potatoes, scouring pans, mopping floors, scrubbing toilets. After a bowl of gruel and a round of indecipherable prayers, she crawled into her first European-style cot in a dormitory lined with a hundred more. So many bodies, but none near enough for warmth.

"It was like the army," Marie-Louise says, doubling the creases on her forehead. "'Don't go there, don't touch, don't speak your language, you must speak French.'"

Besides whispering with her sisters, Marie-Louise likely heard her mother tongue only at recess, when the nuns blasted Christian prayers in Algonquin, Atikamekw, and Cree through the loudspeakers in hopes that the children would later recite them to their parents. Occasionally she might have been asked to "play Indian" by donning a headdress and welcoming a chorus of singing missionaries for the school play. Beyond that, she probably reunited with her culture only during her brief visits home each summer. Over the years, her Algonquinness evaporated like a rare, essential oil.

"But we must go there," she says. "We have no choice. They say we go to the fire, to the demon."

Residential schools for First Nations and Inuit children began opening in Canada in the 1830s and became compulsory in the 1920s.[6] The last didn't close until 1996. While their mission evolved over the years from "civilizing" Aboriginal children to helping them better "integrate," their tactics were invariably cruel. For speaking their native languages, children were beaten with clappers, rulers, whips, and cords. For other violations, they were locked in closets or forced to spend the night kneeling by their beds, their hands clasped in prayer. For simply being Indian, some were sterilized in Alberta and British Columbia. And for being isolated from their parents and separated from their siblings and bereft of any protection whatsoever, many were molested or raped. At least 4,100 children died at residential schools, often from diseases like tuberculosis, and thousands more ran away or committed suicide.[7]

Meeting an alumna, then, is like meeting a survivor[8] of a concentration camp. You can't help but stare with awe and horror, contemplating all

6. Sir Hector Langevin, Secretary of State for the Provinces, told Canada's Parliament in 1883, "In order to educate the children properly we must separate them from their families. Some people may say this is hard, but if we want to civilize them we must do that." Richard Henry Pratt, the founder of the flagship Carlisle Indian Industrial School in the United States, explained his own pedagogy as "Kill the Indian in him, and save the man." According to one source, of the 10,000 indigenous children who attended Carlisle from 1879 to 1918, only 158 graduated.

7. Post-traumatic stress disorder, alcoholism, addiction, and domestic abuse are among the legacies of these residential schools, along with the near-destruction of indigenous culture. Some alumni do, however, credit the schools for teaching them discipline. Scholar Marie-Pierre Bousquet suggests this is why a number who graduated through the system later became key First Nations leaders.

8. After a flurry of residential school survivor lawsuits in the 1990s, Canada appointed a Truth and Reconciliation Commission to address their grievances. In December 2015, just-elected prime minister Justin Trudeau vowed to implement all ninety-four recommendations of a scathing 3,231-page report about the treatment of Aboriginal people throughout Canada's history. Trudeau also inducted two indigenous leaders into his cabinet of prime ministers (half of whom are women).

she endured. Marie-Louise manages a few more sentences in English, then removes her glasses and wipes her eyes as I finish stacking the bags into her van.

"It's a big, long walk with us, Catholicism," she says quietly. "I reject it."

Then why, I ask, is she here?

"My grandmother. She was a believer. She was Catholic and she pray very much. I am here for the respect of my grandmother."

And so, in a sense, am I.

KATERI'S INNER WORLD called her many things, too.

In the beginning: Tekakwitha, which has been translated as everything from "She Who Gathers Things Together" to "She Who Bumps into Things." Once she started devoting all her time to the Jesuits, however, the names grew less affectionate. Lazy. Insolent. Traitor. Witch. Whore. Other Mohawks thought the young woman was blessed, however. They called her Kateri as the Jesuits did, enunciating each syllable with respect.

Three and a half centuries later, this division persists. I have met Mohawks who roll their eyes at Kateri, who dismiss her as a slutty opportunist. Who believe her canonization is a cynical gesture by the Catholic church to beg forgiveness for 500 years of transgressions—and to recruit more members while it's at it. Who think Kateri is the very embodiment of colonization, and what self-respecting Indian would celebrate that?

Yet just as many Mohawks seem to think of Kateri as the reincarnation of Sky Woman on Earth, a prophet who is finally being recognized for her gifts. They don't deny how badly their ancestors suffered under Christianity, but they believe they emerged from the experience more spiritually powerful than before. They see Kateri's canonization as the Vatican legitimizing half a millennium of their faith.

To better understand this ideological split, I invite Darren Bonaparte to lunch in Akwesasne. A historian who runs the popular site Wampum-Chronicles.com, he recently published a book about Kateri called *A Lily among Thorns*. Author photos usually show him in traditional regalia, but he walks through the doors of Twinleaf wearing a dark leather jacket, jeans, and sunglasses (that is, modern regalia). In his early forties, he still has a boyish face, dimpled and smooth, with a cautious grin.

His interest in history dates back to the casino war. His mother, Rosemary, was tribal chief at the time, the first woman to ever hold the position, but got voted out because of her anti-gambling stance. His best friend, meanwhile, got shot and killed during the final standoff. "It was a really confusing time, sitting up all night listening to gunfire. My boring little town was turned into Beirut. It was a wake-up call: You're Indian; this means something. My first kid came along then, too. I had a baby; I couldn't walk around with hate in my heart. I let that fuel my desire to learn."

His studies gave him a special appreciation for the spiritual world his ancestors envisioned. Like their creation story, which opens with the Sky People, a matriarchal society that dwelled in the farthest stretches of blue. After bickering with her husband, a pregnant woman fell from a hole in the sky and landed on the back of a turtle. Clenched in her fists were seeds from the sky tree she had grabbed moments before tumbling. Sky dirt was embedded in her fingernails. She spread these artifacts as she walked about the new world, breathing Earth into being, plant by plant. Sky Woman was the first human inhabitant; her baby girl, the second. Not only did these stories give rise to a society where women are highly valued, they also led to elaborate ceremonies celebrating the individual contributions of all living things, from fish and berries to thunder and streams.

"Then the Europeans came with their guns and diseases, and that rich culture went into the Dark Ages. But there was a watershed moment when the French were out there burning their villages and the Mohawks said, 'Hey, let's stop fighting these guys.' And then in the ritualized life, the Mohawks realized, 'Hey, these people might be funny-looking, but they are bringing back this sophisticated life we used to have.'"

The Jesuits, meanwhile, marveled at the similarities between Native spirituality and their own. After learning enough Mohawk to decipher their creation story, they decided that Immaculate Conception and transubstantiation fit right in. "Christianity was just added to an existing culture," Darren says. "It's not like they emptied out a bucket and filled it with something else. The bucket was already full. They just stuck a crucifix in it. Kateri just followed what was already programmed in her mind."

"Like beating herself to a pulp?"

"Could be," he muses, flipping open a menu. "The Mohawks learned that Christ suffered without crying out, and that was what our warriors traditionally did when they got captured. We would taunt our tormentors: 'Is that the best you can do?' So when Christian Indians found out about flagellation, it became a fad. They would be like, 'What do you think would hurt more, fire or ice?'"

The Jesuits didn't encourage mortification among their young Indian converts, Darren stresses. They only wanted to baptize them, preferably before they died of smallpox. They never imagined an Indian could attain true holiness—until they met Kateri. She challenged their entire understanding of Native people. When they caught her pummeling herself to unconsciousness, they could only stare.

"At the end of the day, something profoundly supernatural took place, and they were very honest in how they wrote about it. It wasn't a propaganda piece; they considered themselves to be witness to something. It was like a sequel to the Bible. They were seeing the bride of Jesus," Darren says. "Yet that is what killed Kateri. They were not keeping close enough watch."

I ask about his personal relationship with Catholicism. He smirks. "Catholicism was how my mom tortured us."

Forced to rise for Mass every Sunday of his childhood, he rebelled in his teenage years. A class on the Old Testament turned him into a "flaky Jesus freak" in college, however, and he eventually returned to the church. Kateri was merely an image on his mother's wall until he moved away from Akwesasne in his twenties and realized she was "a Native thing." His interest deepened when his mother attended a healing mass featuring a relic of Kateri. "She was blessed with it, and her whole body lit up like a Christmas tree."

That's when he started pouring over translations of seventeenth-century texts about Kateri. "What really endears people to her is when they find out how much time she spent alone, in isolation, because everyone feels alone, deep down. Kateri never had children and she died young, so she is always a daughter, always an eternal child."

Some 300 books have already been written about Kateri over the centuries, but Darren decided to add one more to offer a modern Mohawk perspective.

"There's been a lot of idiotic coverage of Kateri, with headlines that say, 'She Traded Her Totem Pole for a Crucifix.' Some say she is a symbol of colonization, but no: she is a symbol of the failure of colonization. It killed her, but she ended up with the last word because she still has a positive effect on people today. She overcame and conquered death. Colonization, as bad as it was, we survived it."

Our food arrives: a burger for Darren, a wrap for me. As we eat, he expresses amazement that Kateri's day has finally come.

"I didn't think she'd ever be canonized. I thought it would open up a can of worms for the Catholic church; we'd have to read about the French burning our villages, about smallpox. But it turns out, they did want to open the worms."

He chews thoughtfully for a minute before uttering what's fast becoming a refrain.

"I'm just glad my mom could see it in her lifetime. That's really why I wrote the book, as a way of acknowledging her."

MASS HAS ENDED IN KAHNAWAKE. As the pilgrims from the gym spill into the cafeteria, I hurry down the road back to the Mission of Saint Francis Xavier, where pilgrims fill the courtyard and camera crews swarm the periphery. Men in feathered kastowa are especially targeted for interviews. "What does it mean?" they are asked, microphones in their faces. "How does it feel?"

Swerving through the crowd, I enter the vestibule. Someone hands me a prayer card featuring Kateri's most vaunted image: the 1690 oil painting by Father Chauchetière. Kateri stands on the banks of the St. Lawrence River shrouded in a blanket, pointy shoes on her feet. One hand clutches her heart; the other, a crucifix. Her expression is pained yet peaceful.

A crush of pilgrims line up to visit her crypt: Mohawks, Filipinos, Taiwanese, Nigerians, Francophones, Anglophones, monks, nuns, Peacekeepers. I slip in behind a tall woman who turns to smile at me. In her early forties, she has long black hair and indigo eyes. I ask where she's from and she says Hamburg. "As in Germany?" I ask. She nods. Growing up, she says, her mother always told her she looked like Kateri. When she got older, she met someone who worked at an Indian center who confirmed it. "I've been praying to Kateri ever since."

By all historical accounts, Kateri was a pitiful sight. In addition to the scarring from smallpox, brandings, and switches, she barely stood four and a half feet tall. She hobbled when she walked, partly from injury, partly from half-blindness. This woman, on the other hand, has a ballerina build and flawless, porcelain skin. But perhaps, in her mind, resembling a Mohawk saint denotes an earthy exoticism. Or an angelic aura. Or a set of enviable cheekbones.

The crypt is ten feet away now, its marble so white it gleams. A wooden statue of Kateri towers above it wearing a headdress of beads. Rivers of calla lilies and snapdragons pool at her feet. As pilgrims approach the crypt, they hand an object over to a man wading in the floral arrangements. Bibles, rosaries, scarves, crucifixes, scapulars. He accepts them one by one, presses them against the tomb for an extended moment, then passes them back as newly minted fifth-degree relics. I scavenge through my bag for something to bless. Notebook, tissues, wallet, a tampon. The lady from Hamburg removes a cross from around her neck and hands it over with reverence. Water bottle, cough drops, camera, another tampon. The man looks at me expectantly. I glance around for ideas and see a Filipino clutching the prayer card distributed at the vestibule. I hand mine over too. Accepting it with a nod, the man thwacks it over the tomb like a quick game of slapjack while I try to imagine what I imagine everyone else is imagining, that the bones inside the crypt have been informed of their elevated status and are doing a celebratory jig, that whatever vessel contains them has acquired a celestial glow, that the crypt itself is now as consecrated as the host and can therefore transform Bibles and rosaries and scarves and crucifixes and scapulars and prayer cards into reliquaries the same way water turns to wine turns to blood and bread turns to body turns to Christ. The man hands back my prayer card and I wish to think *It's warmer!* the same way I wish to have chatted with the miracle tree back in Concepcion and collapsed in rapture back in Robstown, because wouldn't that make everything immeasurably more reassuring, constantly finding affirmations of a realm beyond your own?

But maybe warmth isn't the point here. Maybe the point is simply to honor something vaster than the self, to express humility through devotion, to acknowledge there is something more than *this*, and it potentially could be *that*, so let us try and see what that brings. Following the pilgrims' procession toward an altar of burning candles, I bow my head and pray.

AT SOME POINT IN THE BLUR of junior high, my mother enrolled me in a preparatory course to receive one of Catholicism's seven sacraments: confirmation. She wasn't religious but she was Tejana and therefore saw catechism as a parental duty on par with orthodontia. Every week for two years, I sat amidst a passel of teenagers and listened as the monsignor harangued us about the vileness of sin as we whispered, napped, passed notes, and sneaked outside to smoke. Then I would slip into Mom's Buick, where Sade crooned from the tape deck, and try to make sense of what I'd heard. Mom would listen to my confusion about one doctrine or another, then suggest I stop overthinking things. "Just let it go," she'd advise.

How can you overthink something whose implications are so huge? I continued worrying until the course ended and a Mass was arranged to confirm us. Before the bishop could anoint us with chrism—the blessed oil that would forever seal our bonds to the church—the monsignor said we must first go to confession to absolve ourselves of sin. Mom waited in the Buick one afternoon while I ran inside to do so. Sinking to my knees before the darkened screen, I rattled off every sin since my last confession, then paused.

"Anything else?" the priest asked.

Stopoverthinking, stopoverthinking, stopoverthinking. Too late: I was already launching into my litany of doubt. Before I'd even finished, the priest delved into one of his own. These thoughts of mine were dangerous, he said. Wasn't I concerned about the state of my soul? Had I not contemplated the pains of hell?

I ran out of the confessional crying and dove inside a pew. After calming myself down—surely hell was a long way off?—I stared up at the stained glass windows, the fourteen Stations of the Cross, the candles flickering yellow and blue. Then I heard a noise behind me. Four rows back knelt a girl from my class. Pressing her hands into her forehead in prayer, she looked so holy, so pure, so not overthinking. Rising from the pew, I genuflected before the altar and made the first adult decision of my life.

Back in the Buick, I told Mom I couldn't be confirmed. "That would be," I somberly said, "unethical."

It was the first time I had ever questioned Mom's judgment about anything. She was our family's breadwinner, the one who marched off to IBM each morning wearing a power suit with shoulder pads and who interrogated every suitor my sister or I brought home. I never protested when she signed me up for ballet or gymnastics or modeling or piano lessons despite my disinterest because I trusted she knew best—even when it meant enduring a humiliating season of catching fly balls with my face in Southside Little Miss Kickball.

But when I told Mom my decision, her voice grew uncharacteristically soft. She felt obligated, she said, to baptize her daughters and guide them through their first communion and confirmation. She didn't explain why then, but it occurs to me now that Catholicism might have been one of the few cultural attributes she could actually pass on. After a lifetime of linguistic discrimination, she had refrained from teaching me Spanish. She hated to cook, so I hadn't inherited any recipes for rice or beans. My jazz drummer dad controlled our household's soundtrack, so I grew up hearing Frank Sinatra instead of Pedro Infante. We carved pumpkins for Halloween rather than decorated sugar skulls for Dia de los Muertos. I had never even been spanked with a *chancla*.

Do this for me, Mom pleaded.

Sitting there in that Buick, I made the second adult decision of my life. I agreed to be confirmed—for the same reason Bernice Lazore has juggled two conflicting spiritual practices for over half a century; that Darren Bonaparte locked himself into his office for a year, reading a mountain of manuscripts before composing one of his own; that Mary-Louise drove to the Mission of Saint Francis Xavier this morning despite a childhood of trauma at a Catholic Indian Residential School. It might even be for the same reason Kateri Tekakwitha beat herself with an ardor that finally killed her. Maybe she wasn't searching for Jesus at all but for the memory of her Catholic mother's caress—that reassuring stroke across her shoulder, that tickling kiss on her forehead.

Which is why, however much I empathize with their wrath for the church that Christianized them by force, I can't help but wince whenever Mohawks bash Kateri. She reminds me too much of Mother Julia, who has also united a marginalized people eager to see one of their own deemed holy and who grants them miracles in their time of need. Kateri reminds me of La Virgen de Guadalupe, whose skin is as brown as many of her followers and who has been making public appearances for five centuries and counting.

Above all, Kateri reminds me of La Malinche, the Nahua woman who served as translator and mistress to Hernán Cortés during the conquest of Mexico. She too suffered throughout her life, sold into concubinage at fourteen and handed over to the Spanish a few years later. Though essentially a slave, she grew so vital to the mission of Cortés, he was sometimes called "Lord Malinche." She bore him a son, one of Mexico's first mestizos, but Cortés eventually took him away. To this day in Jaltipan, where she is supposedly buried in an unmarked grave, locals hear her crying as she wanders around the river, searching for the lost son who gave rise to an entirely new identity.

Despite Malinche's hardship, despite all of the sacrifices she made as she tried to survive, she is often derided as a traitor by her progeny—not unlike Kateri. Yet to hate these women is to hate our grandmothers, to hate our mothers, to hate ourselves. Haven't we done enough of that already?

This is ultimately why I have traveled to Kahnawake today. Now that I have lost much of our language and tradition, now that I have abandoned our homeland, now that I have bypassed the chance to pass on our seed, Catholicism is one of my last remaining ties to my heritage. This is why I will keep my tomb-blessed Kateri card, despite no perceivable warmth, and why I will add it to the shrine of devotional items atop my writing desk. This is why I will remain Catholic, no matter how it morally or intellectually devastates me: because I am ancestrally so.

15

The Activist and the Obelisk

I'M BACK IN THE SLICE OF AKWESASNE THAT MOHAWKS CALL SNYE,[1] Canadians consider Quebec, and New Yorkers assume is still the Empire State, this time with a passport, a colleague, and three young Chinese women in tow. They are students from St. Lawrence University, but when we step off a dock and into a speedboat and start zipping across the St. Lawrence River, it occurs to us that—if we are stopped by the U.S. or Canadian customs agents who patrol these waters—they will likely be perceived as something else: human cargo. This stretch of river is, after all, the region's most notorious smuggling corridor, and Chinese are among the most heavily trafficked citizens. Scenes from *Frozen River* flicker in my mind until my colleague—the unflappable Celia Nyamweru—makes an executive decision to stop thinking about it.

Piloting the boat is a Cree elder named Bob. We met a few weeks ago at Akwesasne's annual powwow, where he stood out even among the dancers in full regalia. Imposing with his wrestler's build and long silver hair, he also wears a bear-claw necklace. Each claw extends a full four inches before curling in toward his chest. Something about it commands the awe of a bandolier—maybe even more, as claws imply a power that can never be spent. A medicine man gave him the necklace forty-eight years ago, he says, and he has worn it every day since. Also hanging from his neck is a beaded pouch made of moose hide. It holds his cell phone.

Clouds darken the river as the Adirondacks climb blue in the distance. We pass another island every few minutes and a boat every five. Either duck hunters or smugglers, Bob guesses. Whoever they are, they rough up the waters so that it feels like we're getting spanked. Eventually Thompson Island comes into view, and we pull up to its dock. Bob steps out and extends a hand to each of us. A retired fur trapper, his grip is herculean.

1. And Snye, in turn, has a few nicknames of its own. Mohawks who live on the other side of the nation joke that it's "Snyberia," because it's so far away. Those who live there prefer "Snyami."

Thompson Island is lushly forested with just enough land cleared for a bungalow, a volleyball net, a ring of canvas tents, some Adirondack chairs, an outhouse, and a teepee. We enter the bungalow, which smells of wood and soup. Bob's wife and brother-in-law are preparing lunch in the kitchen. A hunk of cured salt pork tops the counter along with turnips, carrots, onions, and cans of kidney beans. They greet us as they knead circles of dough that will soon be fried into bread.

We shuffle into the main room, where a wood-burning stove crackles and pops. Dried corn decks the walls, tobacco leaves line a basket, feathers fill a jar. "Before I came to get you, I saw an eagle steal a duck from a hunter," Bob says. "Maybe we can find her, eh?" Grabbing a tall, gnarled stick, he heads out the back door and we follow close behind. Soon we are immersed in a forest that my urban mind registers as a scenic workout venue. Bob sees something else entirely.

"Stinging nettles," he says, pausing at a plant whose leaves are cut as delicately as snowflakes. "If you grab it, you get stung. But if you pick it right and cook it, it's very strong, like spinach. Warm it up with butter and it tastes real good."

A few steps more and he stops again, this time before ruby berries growing in clusters. Sumac, he says. Boil the berries, let them sit, then strain off the floaters. Medicine people give the juice to women when they are menstruating. Those dark purple berries? Those are elderberries, good for the blood. You can boil them into jam or bake them in a pie. Medicine people use the stems to treat rheumatism.

"And this we call Indian Band-Aid," he says, plucking a bright green leaf with a long skinny stem and wrapping it around his wrist. "Boil it, cook it, and add a little olive oil and beeswax to make a salve."

For every ailment, there is a plant that offers a remedy. You just have to know where to look, he says.

We continue on, past mushrooms the size of dinner plates and grapes a tangy blue. Bob points out black ash trees, white oak trees, walnut trees, cottonwood trees, wild garlic plants, and wild onion. You can find anything out here, he says, even marijuana. Ten years ago, while hiking about, he came upon a stash of seven-foot cannabis plants growing in pots. He reported it to the Mohawk police, who in turn contacted the Royal Canadian Mounted Police, which estimated a $130,000 street value before hauling the pots away. They never caught the growers, but Bob thinks they were Quebecois.

The forest thickens. We are hiking single-file now, holding back limbs so no one gets whacked in the face. I gradually notice an ethereal noise emanating from above, like a fairy humming.

"It's the trees," Bob says. "See how they rub together?"

Another thing the southern and northern borderlands have in common: vocal trees. Their song amplifies the farther we hike into the forest, each cluster contributing a different octave as their trunks nuzzle in the wind. Some groan the feral melody. Others shriek it. The sound is haunting but beautiful.

The trail, meanwhile, has turned as springy as a tumbling mat. I look down to find it carpeted in moss an electric shade of green.

"There she goes!" Bob calls out, and I glimpse the expansive wing of a bald eagle as she alights high up in a cottonwood tree. The students and I applaud, but she deigns to reveal only the white of her crown. Our trail, meanwhile, has vanished beneath a jumble of vines. Gripping his stick, Bob bushwhacks a new trail to the riverbank. White-crested waves lap against the shore as golden leaves swirl in the tide.

"You must catch some serious fish out here," I say to Bob.

"Oh no," he says. "No, no. The Natives stopped fishing here twenty, thirty years ago. There is a warning not to eat fish more than once a week, and pregnant women are not supposed to eat them at all. With a warning like that, I don't either."

He explains how, just two generations ago, this river ran thick with sturgeon, bass, walleye, eel, and pike—plenty to feed your family and sell extras on the side. Wild game roamed the region too: deer, elk, rabbit. Beavers kept the fur trappers busy, while black ash trees offered up splints to basket weavers. Well into the twentieth century, Mohawks could subsist off the land as they had since Sky Woman fell onto the back of a turtle.

Then in the 1950s, Canada and the United States started building the St. Lawrence Seaway, a system of canals, locks, and channels that enabled ships to launch in the Great Lakes and sail clear to the Atlantic Ocean. One of its many regional side projects entailed a massive hydroelectric dam that straddled the international borderline. Its construction drowned six villages and virtually all of the area's beaver hutches, displacing some 6,500 people[2]—many of whom were Mohawk—and decimating the trapping industry.

2. Families were offered market value compensation for their homes but at the depressed rate incurred by the seaway. Here is how Edmund Wilson describes a bulldozed house at Akwesasne in his 1959 book *Apologies to the Iroquois*: "It remains in my mind as a symbol of the fate of the individual at the mercy of modern construction: the house had been scrunched like a cockroach, a flattened-out mass of muddied boards."

The dam also brought new businesses into the area, including General Motors, Reynolds Metals, and the Aluminum Company of America (ALCOA), all three of which opened factories on the outskirts of Akwesasne, near the town of Massena. Mohawks initially welcomed the job prospects but got hired only for manual labor (if that). And they soon started noticing rank smells emanating from their neighbors. Yellow-gray smoke slithered from the smelter stacks and drifted toward their homes and farms. One by one, their cattle went lame, the swelling in their legs so severe they had to lie down to graze and crawl to forage. Then the bees vanished. Many of the partridges from which Akwesasne derives its name did, too. Mohawks contracted bronchitis, then asthma. Midwives reported an increase in babies born with abnormalities. School nurses documented children's teeth turning gray. Medicine people tried to cure the rashes, but no plant could heal them.

In the early seventies, institutions like Cornell and the University of Montana started finding evidence of fluoride poisoning at Akwesasne. Reynolds cut down on its hourly fluoride emissions in 1980, yet the health problems persisted. Finally, in the mid-eighties, GM admitted in a report to the EPA that it had been dumping polychlorinated biphenyls (PCBs), trichloroethylene, formaldehyde, and other cancer-causing toxic wastes in and around Akwesasne since its opening. Reynolds and ALCOA made similar confessions, inciting a flurry of investigations, lawsuits, and fines. For one study, the New York State Department of Conservation captured a female snapping turtle whose fat contained 835 parts per million of PCBs. (The federal standard for edible fish: 2 parts per million.) Given the sacred role turtles play in their cosmology and clan system, Mohawks were distraught by this. When the government issued warnings against eating more than half a pound of fish a week, many refused it altogether, putting a hundred commercial fishermen out of work. As news leaked out about the contaminants, families abandoned their gardens, too. Canned meat and commodity cheese replaced sturgeon and greens as the staples of a Mohawk diet. In his book *Life and Death in Mohawk Country*, Bruce Johansen estimates half of all Akwesasne residents over forty were diabetic by 1990. A quarter century later, a diabetes prevention worker I interviewed put the tribe's obesity rate at about 75 percent.[3] The only place where I have seen unhealthier-looking

3. Regarding her nation's obesity epidemic, Sweets Jacobs of the Mohawk Council of Akwesasne told me, "Our generation grew up on commodity foods. We no longer have gardens because of the environmental contamination. We no longer fish because of the EPA guidelines. Our recreation is gone, our food is gone, you can't hunt any

people is my hometown, which *Men's Health* renamed "Corpulent Christi" in its "America's 10 Fattest (and Leanest) Cities" report in 2010.

Thompson Island is one of many tribal initiatives to combat these threats. Year-round, Mohawks travel here for vision quests, spending days and nights alone in the woods with neither food nor water to better hear the Creator. In the summer months, it becomes an environmental camp where indigenous youth study basketry, trapping, canoeing, woodworking, and plants. Elders travel to the island to harvest medicines. Tourists travel here on holiday. As the director of these endeavors, Bob worries about the long-term effects of lingering toxics. The old GM plant is so poisonous, it has made the Superfund National Priorities List,[4] while Reynolds and ALCOA have both been declared state Superfund sites. Remediation is under way at all three facilities, but no one knows when it will be safe to fish or garden again, which is the equivalent of saying no one knows when Mohawks can live as traditional Mohawks again.

Bob raises his walking stick to the sky, where menacing clouds are fast approaching, and cracks a joke about our not making it home tonight. "Don't worry, though, you won't starve," he says, turning away from the river and tramping back into the forest. "We've got lots of mushrooms and berries, eh?"

IT LOOMS ABOVE THE DINERS and donut shops of Route 37 like a lotus: Koi Express, Akwesasne's only sushi café. I try to eat sushi every few weeks because my intestinal tract always feels like it's had a hot shower afterward, but this particular café strikes me a bit suspect, given what I've learned about the surrounding waters. Nevertheless, I try it one evening with a colleague and a student. Though it is dinnertime, we are the only customers. A noodle bowl sounds tempting, but I can't help asking the waitress about the origins of the fish. She looks up from her notepad. The back of a delivery truck, obviously. Not wanting to be obnoxious, I order the bowl. Its brown chunks of fish are tougher than mutton and bereft of flavor. I eat only noodles and bypass dessert (fried ice cream or fried dough).

---

more because there is no more land left, and everybody is on four-wheelers so no one walks any more."

4. The GM site finally shuttered in 2009, abandoning an 800,000-square-foot building and depriving 500 people of employment. Beginning in the fall of 2012, EPA crews oversaw the removal of its PCB-laden concrete and soil. They initially expected to clear out 77,000 tons of waste, but as of February 2014, they had removed more than four times that amount.

Our next stop is the Akwesasne senior center, a spacious facility decorated with autumn foliage, gourds, dried corn, and a bingo flashboard. A suit-and-tie EPA administrator asks us to sign in and—if we'd like—take a number. Tonight the agency will be fielding public commentary on remediation plans for the Grasse River, the nearby tributary of the St. Lawrence River where ALCOA dumped PCB-laden wastewater for twenty years. Since ordering its cleanup in 1989 and supervising some waste removal in 1995, the EPA has been determining how best to complete the project. The ten possible courses of action range from doing nothing to investing $1.3 billion into dredging and capping the river. The majority of Mohawks want the river returned to its pristine state, no matter the cost, but many citizens of nearby Massena (who held a similar hearing yesterday) are willing to settle for far less. ALCOA employs more than a thousand people there and is currently considering expanding its operations. Massena wants to seem as accommodating as possible.[5]

Among the first arrivals, we take a table near the front and watch everyone else file in: retired steelworkers, clan mothers, elders, chiefs, and a handful of people under forty. Nearly everyone wears either a hoodie or a black leather jacket along with totems signifying their clan: wolf, bear, turtle, snipe. Some of the older women have shorn their hair ear-length while most of the younger women and nearly all of the men wear ponytails. They mingle among their friends, laughing and joking, before ambling over to the tables.

A slide projector beams an image of an indigenous couple silhouetted against a full moon inside a dream catcher. THE WORDS THAT COME BEFORE ALL ELSE, the caption reads. After a time, a subchief stands in front of the room and begins to recite something in Mohawk that quiets everyone immediately. He is a soft-spoken man, middle-aged and shy-seeming, yet his words are melodic and continue on for some time. Every so often, he scrunches his face, thrusts his hands into his pockets, and backtracks until he finds the rhythm again, whereupon he smiles as more words surge forth. After certain passages he becomes completely silent, during which moments the crowd verbalizes the affirmation "Tho."

My colleague leans over to explain that this is the Ohen:ton Karihwatehkwen, or the Haudenosaunee's traditional Thanksgiving Address.

---

5. Poor Massena. Despite its many concessions and sacrifices, ALCOA decided in November 2015 to "idle the potlines" there anyway and laid off 500 workers, devastating the town's economy.

No two people say it alike, but they follow a similar trajectory of individually acknowledging and thanking every life force in the universe: the people, Earth Mother, the fish, the plants, the herbs, the animals, the trees, the birds, the four winds, the thunders, the sun, Grandmother Moon, the stars, Enlightened Teachers, and finally the Creator. All six tribes of the Haudenosaunee Confederacy express this communal gratitude before every gathering of minds, from ceremonies to social functions to meetings. Some schools even open and conclude each day this way. The complete address can take up to three days to deliver. This version has been whittled down to five minutes. By the time the subchief returns to his seat, the energy of the room has shifted. People are focused now and ready to rouse. An EPA administrator starts calling out numbers, and one by one, a Mohawk stands to address the room.

"I might look like you, but I am not like you," a middle-aged woman clad in black tells the table of EPA personnel. "I try to live my life as our original instructions gave us. We live off the land here. We eat fish and deer. But now, do I know where the deer has drank his water from? Where the fish has swam? What if I have a grandchild born with two heads or no legs? Would you like your grandchild born like that?"

Then an elder in a tracksuit: "I worked for GM twelve years. Every day I had a bloody nose and a migraine headache. I probably would have died from that place. I don't know you guys; I don't trust you guys. No matter what plan you choose, we are still looking at thirty years before we can start to eat fish again. Maybe my great-great-great-grandchildren can eat fish; maybe not. That's all I got to say."

Next, a woman wrapped in a fringed shawl: "People on the front lines, we knew something was wrong here long before the scientists told us. There were tumors in our fish; there was a change in the meat, in its color, in its texture. I saw the anger, I saw the hurt, when fishermen realized they might be poisoning their community. We were denied the ability to provide for our families. It goes deeper than eating the fish. It is our relationship to our land. The techniques, the respect, the language that goes along with these practices will soon be lost."

Then a man adorned with multiple piercings and tattoos: "I have three sisters, and they had twenty miscarriages between them. You could take the teeth out of all of their mouths and still not have enough for a pair of dentures. Just about every single one of us has diabetes. So many of us have thyroid problems. That comes from our 'advancement' in civilization. Once we put up all the steel, guess what? They laid us off. You could count on one hand all the Indians working at that plant, and not one of them is alive today."

I attended dozens of public hearings back when I was a newspaper reporter. Maybe one in seven speakers said something quotable. Here, practically everyone is an orator, speaking without notes but with narrative precision. Some weep as they do so. Others quake with rage. Two hours into the evening, six women try to allay the mounting tension in the room by pulling out drums and rattles and breaking into song. "My grandmother said the water was nice a long time ago," one says. "When you were thirsty you could take the water right out of the river and drink it."

Toward the end of the hearing, a woman in jeans and a hoodie walks to the front of the room. Her dark hair is cropped close to her head; reading glasses perch on the tip of her nose. Nothing about her seems extraordinary—until she opens her mouth. She doesn't just say her lines, she fillets them, leaving them hemorrhaging on the floor. "I want to know who the ALCOA people are." A table full of white men in business suits meekly raise their hands. She glares at each one, then asks the EPA representatives to raise their hands. "I have no faith in you's whatsoever. EPA, you allowed them,"—she stares daggers at the ALCOA executives again—"to pollute and destroy our land, the minds of our children, the bodies of our women, the bodies of our men. You stood by the corporations more than you stood by the people. You did one study after another. You make it sound like you did a wonderful job, but you have dumps hidden behind all of our trees!"

She thunders on, ticking off sixty years of corporate and federal transgressions while the Mohawks whoop and the executives stare ahead with no expression whatsoever. Though I know the Mohawks' preferred $1.3 billion remediation plan would never be selected, I can't help but wish that the power of their discourse could make it so. I join in their cheering when the woman finishes, then settle back in my seat for the next speaker, a hulking man wearing bear clan insignias. "I am not here to make a comment," he informs the executives. "I want to speak with your attorney."

A thin man with a balding head walks to the front of the room, a cashmere sweater over his pink button-down shirt. The Mohawk stands half a foot taller and a hundred pounds heavier. The attorney must tilt his head back to make eye contact as the Mohawk presents him with a wampum made of rawhide and beads. "This is from our nation to yours. You tell the people you represent this message that I give you." He then reads from a typed edict outlining the ways in which natural law supersedes corporate law. "You have ten days to respond. If you don't, we take it you agree with everything that is in there."

The microphone is then seized by a man whose head has been shaved completely bald save for a thick raised mound running from his crown to his nape.[6] He looks ripped beneath his black leather jacket. His face and fists are riddled with scars. Clenching the microphone, he walks toward the ALCOA table, leans in close, and sneers: "This is one of the faces you will see as one of your worst nightmares." He then proceeds to stare at them without blinking.

And this, more than anything, seems to explain the Mohawks' participation in these proceedings. They too know that the EPA will ultimately choose a tepid remediation plan[7] that will require many more studies and several more decades and millions more dollars before there will even be a chance that they can fish and hunt and garden and otherwise live as their ancestors once did. Many likely see these proceedings as yet another federal dog-and-pony show and thus respond with a performance of their own. This is not to suggest cynicism or complicity on the part of the Mohawks but rather tenacity. Being here tonight gives them the rare opportunity to stare into the eyes of ALCOA executives and tell them exactly what they think of them, to brand their faces right into their consciousness. It might not make a speck of difference, no. But it's the verbal equivalent of taking a bullet in the chest instead of in the back.

BEFORE LEAVING THE EPA HEARING, I ask the word-slayer, Dana Leigh Thompson, for her phone number. Her husband is Kanietakeron, the man who proffered the wampum to the attorney. They invite me over one cold December morning with instructions to turn off Route 37 at the 2,000-foot driveway. I assume I've misheard, but no: it really is that long and leads through

---

6. Traditionally, Mohawk men individually plucked each hair until only a small square remained at the back of their head, which they then braided. The spiky "Mohawk" hairstyle favored by punk rockers worldwide can actually be traced to the Pawnee.

7. The $243 million plan ultimately chosen by the EPA calls for the removal of 109,000 cubic yards of contaminated sediment near the shore along a 7.2-mile stretch of the Grasse River. In addition, several hundred acres of sediment will receive some form of capping to isolate contamination. During the May 6, 2013, meeting where this plan was unveiled at Akwesasne, Mohawks quickly noticed that the bulk of the capping would occur in the stretch of river closest to Massena. "*That* is where the poor people live," Chief Ron LaFrance protested, pointing at the cap-less swath of map of his nation. Dana Leigh Thompson, meanwhile, accused the EPA of "being part of the genocidal process."

the woods and a thicket of NO TRESPASSING signs to a sprawling estate on the river. German shepherds trot over as I park between a wooden gazebo and a three-car garage with a speedboat inside. In addition to running Onkwe Bingo Jack in the eighties, the Thompsons made a princely sum in the cigarette trade. This particular property is owned by their son, who breeds show horses.

No need to knock; the dogs announce my arrival. Dana Leigh and Kanietakeron greet me on their porch. She's wearing pink fleece over jeans and reading glasses; his steel-and-silver hair hangs loosely around his shoulders. I open with small talk. Can you believe it's December already? How are you spending the holidays?

"We don't celebrate the holidays," Dana Leigh says flatly.

Of course not. They are Longhouse, not Christian, meaning my question was as tactless as asking whether they cooked a turkey for Thanksgiving. While I stumble over an apology, Dana Leigh asks Kanietakeron to get us breakfast. He heads over to his Ford F-150. She then tells me to get in my car, as we'll be meeting in her library this morning. I follow her through the woods to a second estate on the river, park by a two-story building, and marvel when its door opens to reveal row upon row of ceiling-to-floor bookshelves lined with thousands of volumes. Dana Leigh leads the way up a flight of stairs to an office featuring a ziggurat of lateral filing cabinets, computers, and photocopiers; a conference table that seats nine; and piles of paper stacked as high as my chest. I once worked at a nonprofit that staffed ten people with only half this much equipment.

"Are you . . . a lawyer?" I ask.

"Nah, I had to learn all this on my own," she says, pouring water into a kettle and nodding at a nearby law book. "To try to understand how their system works, you have to read all of this shit. I call it investigative journalism for survival."

Her files represent decades' worth of research into topics ranging from tribal law and sovereignty to the health effects of PCBs. These findings have not only fueled the couple's activism but also enabled them to defend themselves in their many quarrels with the law, including one that sent Kanietakeron to federal prison for eighteen months in 2000 for manufacturing cigarettes without a certain license. Dana Leigh also serves as pro bono counsel for a young Mohawk woman who launched a human rights tribunal against the Canada Border Services Agency for harassment.

We are settling down to tea when Kanietakeron arrives with a box of Dunkin' Donuts and sausage-and-egg English muffins. "Now we will break bread," he says with a pleasant formality. His face is creviced and pitted, but he has the prettiest eyes, so pale a green they are almost translucent. Although he is the one who has been featured in media around the world, Dana Leigh does most of their talking. He'll start a story with an amicable air, but she'll steal it to give exact stats and facts.

They met in 1979, when Dana Leigh traveled from her home in Kahnawake to Akwesasne to monitor the political situation at Raquette Point, where Kanietakeron's family homestead is located. Weeks before, the St. Regis Mohawk Tribal Council had decided to build a fence around its territory and needed to clear trees to do so. Apparently without permission, it sent a work crew that started cutting a trail right across the Thompsons' property. This so incensed Kanietakeron's older brother, Loran, he confiscated the chainsaws, which in turn angered the council. It dispatched the tribal police to arrest him, but by the time they arrived, hundreds of Mohawks had barricaded the property with sandbags and were crouched inside a trench, rifles at the ready.[8] The ensuing standoff lasted thirteen months and involved not only New York State Police and Governor Mario Cuomo (who threatened to invade the nation) but also white sympathizers like Peter Matthiessen (who chronicled the ordeal in his book *Indian Country*).

United by the standoff, Dana Leigh and Kanietakeron fell in love. Together, they set about building a family on Raquette Point. Dana Leigh especially relished the summer months there, when she could slip off her sandals and sink her toes in the soil. She spent the whole season tending a garden that not only fed their family but healed their ailments, too. Yet just beyond their fence loomed the massive aluminum engine–casting plant owned by GM. It began attracting attention of its own, soon after the standoff.

"Now come the scientists, the universities knocking at the door, asking for permission to go out and catch frogs and pick grass and, oh, can we test this, can we test that? There were people all over the world that came. We didn't know what was happening. We said this is crazy, so I educated myself," Dana Leigh says.

---

8. Trees, of course, were merely the timber of this skirmish. Though sources vary about the true igniter (everything from land claims to corruption in the local police force), the standoff is likely traceable to a long-standing conflict between the St. Regis Mohawk Tribal Council and the Mohawk Nation Council of Chiefs. The former is the "legal" tribal government, or the one elected by popular ballot and recognized by New York State and Washington. The Council of Chiefs, meanwhile, is the tribe's traditional government elected by clan mothers and sanctioned by the Haudenosaunee Confederacy.

She started by reading Rachel Carson's *Silent Spring*, which offered a crash course in toxics as well as corporate cover-up. Even before GM admitted to its longtime use of PCBS, the Thompsons had their suspicions.

"GM had a huge dump right by our house," Kanietakeron remembers. "When I was a kid, we would find barrels out there and use them to collect rainwater. There was a stream connecting our properties, and when we got hot, we would drink right from it. There were two or three ponds full of pure PCBS that made a nice ice-skating rink. Once, a kid fell in up to his waist."

He points at the many scars blemishing his face. "They call this chloracne. I've always had these breakouts on my hands and ears that were the size of a dime and filled with maybe a hundred individual blisters, itchy as hell. I started getting them at age eight or nine, and they lasted all the way to high school. I used to wear a bandanna around my forehead just to cover it."

His father worked for ALCOA back then, he says, and grew so asthmatic he could hardly breathe. Diabetes cost him a toe and then a leg before killing him at sixty-nine. Kanietakeron's mother died of a heart attack at forty-three, as did a brother at thirty-nine. He and another brother have both undergone open-heart surgery, and one of their sisters endured sixteen miscarriages and only one successful birth. She now has kidney cancer.

One morning, Dana Leigh awoke to burning feet. Kicking off the covers, she discovered them peppered with the same blisters Kanietakeron had as a kid. Cortisone shots and creams proved useless. Convinced they were being poisoned, she told Kanietakeron they must leave. She met the same kind of resistance Suzie Canales did at Dona Park: *What? This is our homestead. My parents lived here. My brothers and sisters still do. It is the site of our family story.* Yet Dana Leigh was firm, and her husband finally consented to transferring to their current plot, which is about as far away from GM, Reynolds, and ALCOA as you can get at Akwesasne. "I go to Raquette Point now and see all these people with gardens, and I will say to them it's not good, but you can tell by their face they don't want to hear it," she says with a sigh.

In 2010, GM's bankruptcy estate pledged $773 million to clean up eighty-nine of its old industrial facilities around the country. The Superfund site near Akwesasne received the biggest cut—$120.8 million—but that didn't feel sufficient to the Thompsons, considering the company's stature.[9] They also resented the lack of urgency suggested by the cleanup's timeline. "I went to

9. According to *Forbes*, GM is the world's sixty-fourth biggest public company. In May 2015, the magazine estimated its market cap at $59 billion.

the clinic one morning, and my sister was there with her kidney cancer, and my buddy was there looking grayish in color, and I said, 'When is this going to stop?'" says Kanietakeron. "So I went to a [St. Regis Mohawk] tribal council meeting, and people who signed that agreement with GM were there, and I said whoever signed that should be shot. Once the leaders sign something, they lock everyone in; there is no more recourse."

Not officially, anyway. So Kanietakeron and Dana Leigh devised a recourse of their own. On August 12, 2011, before a circle of supporters and camera crews, Kanietakeron chained himself to the steering wheel of his backhoe, drove onto the property of the old GM site, excavated a hunk of landfill, transported it over to some railroad cars, and unloaded it as a way of showing—as he puts it—"Now what's so hard about that?" On his return trip to the landfill, a truck rumbled over, blowing its horn. The New York State Police had arrived as well as the site's new owner, RACER Trust. An enormous payloader proceeded to corner Kanietakeron's backhoe between a chain-link fence and some pipes.

"I thought they were going to use that machine to stop me and Taser me and then all the Indians would come to my rescue. The only way to get out was through the fence, which they had locked, so I just went right through it and was back on the reservation."

Dana Leigh opens her MacBook to show me the YouTube video. A camera zooms in on Kanietakeron riding high in his backhoe as it bursts through the fence. Afterward, he informs police, "You're going to have to carry me to the car." While they discuss this—"Are you going to resist if we carry you out, or can we just carry you out?"—the camera pans across the landfill where Kanietakeron says he played as a child. With its 25- by 25-foot crater, it looks like it has just been bombed.

Kanietakeron spent four days in jail before getting slapped with a felony count of criminal mischief, misdemeanor charges of reckless endangerment and resisting arrest, and a $70,000 fine from RACER Trust for upsetting its landfill and ruining its fence. He showed up to court wearing traditional regalia and announced that he did not recognize New York State law but rather "natural law." His trial gets under way in a couple of weeks.[10]

Media mostly portrayed Kanietakeron's story as a heroic act of civil disobedience, but Mohawks' reactions were more nuanced. The St. Regis

10. Ultimately, these charges will be dropped against Kanietakeron, including the $70,000 fine. He will, however, be banned from entering the GM Superfund site again.

Mohawk Tribal Council publicly criticized him for driving the contaminated backhoe around the community. How, council members asked, could someone so concerned about PCBs so carelessly spread toxics like that? (Only after repeated requests did Kanietakeron consent to having his backhoe cleaned.) Others grumbled about the couple's flagrant abuse of the law for thirty years running. Yet the Thompsons are accustomed to clashes. That's why they revoked their tribal membership in the mid-nineties. They hated being bound to the chiefs' decisions, Kanietakeron says, "because it meant we were subjects of the queen."[11]

He believes the only legitimate authority figures of Akwesasne are the clan mothers. In fact, he invokes their name so often and with such reverence, I start to envision an assembly of oracles convening by candlelight, deciding the fate of their nation. A romantic image, yes—until you remember that even this traditional system split in two a quarter century ago, with gambling opponents constituting the majority of one longhouse and Warriors another, each with its own set of clan mothers to guide it. The Thompsons then further ceded from the tribe by destroying their official tribal cards and passports and issuing documents of their own. When I ask to see one, Kanietakeron opens his wallet and produces a laminated card that is purple on one side, pink on the other. *ID of the Onkwehonwe of Americus Empire (AKA) Turtle Island*, it reads.

"How many people use this?"

"The clan mothers told us not to tell," Kanietakeron says.

"That is the original ID of the land," Dana Leigh adds. "We use it to cross the border."

Most Mohawks use their tribal cards for this purpose, which exempts them from paying international bridge tolls. Kanietakeron, however, says he insists that customs agents honor this ID. "I tell them, you are on my territory and that is the ID we use. It is superior to yours."

"What do they say?"

He chuckles before rattling off examples of being detained for hours (and hours) while agents tried to clear his name. Of singing Indian songs instead of signing papers. Of lying on the ground so he could be handcuffed. Of enduring a three-day hunger strike at an immigration detention center while puzzled inmates from Iran, Russia, and Eritrea looked on.

---

11. Both the St. Regis Mohawk Tribal Council and the Mohawk Council of Akwesasne were imposed as governing bodies of the tribe in the late 1800s by the United States and Canada, respectively.

"The border is not meant for us, but for Europeans," he explains. "When you say, 'Oh, I am in Canada now,' in the long run, you give it recognition, and that can do a lot of damage."

Which is why, in November 2009, he climbed in his backhoe and drove around Akwesasne, unearthing three granite obelisks that marked the international borderline. He deposited each one in front of the Warrior longhouse and, before cheering supporters, flicked on his jackhammer and smashed them to bits. The tribal police drove up to inform Kanietakeron that the obelisks were the property of the federal government. They threatened either a jail sentence or a fine, but nothing came of either. Six months later, however, the Thompsons received a visit from the very same outfit that once knocked on the door of their Tejana counterpart, Suzie Canales: the FBI.

"We offered him a peace pipe and asked, 'Do you come in peace?' Then we had a three-hour meeting and explained everything to him. He said, 'Can we have the markers back?' So we showed him the video so he could see they got jackhammered. Then he asked why we did it."

At this, Kanietakeron pauses theatrically.

"And you said . . . ?"

"On commandment of the clan mothers!"

Not even the FBI could argue with that. The agent left soon after, and they haven't heard from him since.

When Dana Leigh's cell phone rings for the umpteenth time, I realize I've sapped four and a half hours of their day. After thanking them profusely, I make a final faux pas, asking if my next destination is on the U.S. or the Canadian side of the border.

"We say north of the river or south of the river," Dana Leigh says.

Kanietakeron leans in close, as if to reveal a secret. "When you acknowledge the border," he says, his eyes widening, "you make it real."

16

The Movement

WINTER SETTLES OVER THE NORTH COUNTRY, SLICKING THE ROADS and icing the trees. I glance down at my hands while pumping gas one afternoon and discover they have desiccated into lobster claws, red and crinkled. Worried I could lose a finger in the time it takes to fill a gas tank, I retreat to the Victorian, crank up the thermostat, and refuse to leave except to teach. When temperatures plunge into the negative twenties and I must not only shovel a path to the garage each morning but also chip away the ice that sealed its door shut the night before, I abscond to Texas.

Bad timing. While I'm gone, one of the biggest indigenous rights movements in Canada's history erupts. Called "Idle No More," it is triggered by legislation intent on eliminating key protections for water, fish, Aboriginal land, and Native sovereignty. Four Saskatchewan women hold a teach-in widely touted in social media, and flash mobs soon begin descending upon shopping malls and performing round dances before bewildered Christmas shoppers. Other protesters block major railways, highways, and ferry lines. Attawapiskat chief Theresa Spence erects a teepee on Victoria Island by Parliament Hill and launches a hunger strike[1] to persuade Prime Minister Stephen Harper and the governor general to meet with her and other indigenous leaders. The following day, an Attawapiskat elder swears off food as well.[2] The movement spreads, with solidarity demonstrations in Stockholm, London,

---

1. For forty-four days, Chief Spence subsisted on a diet of lemon water, medicinal tea, and fish broth. Prime Minister Harper ultimately conceded to the meeting, but Chief Spence did not attend, partly because of her faltering health post-strike and partly because the meeting wasn't held under the terms she specified.
2. Raymond Robinson continued his fast until Chief Spence ended hers. In his statement to the media afterward, he identified himself as a survivor of three different Indian Residential Schools. "Can I have the same opportunities that you guys enjoy, instead of trying to shove me in a corner, or bury me alive, with these genocidal bills that have been

Berlin, Auckland, Cairo, and a number of U.S. cities, as well as at the Mall of America[3] in Minneapolis. I watch these developments with excitement and longing from my MacBook in Corpus Christi. The hardest day to miss is January 5, when thousands of Indians shut down border crossings throughout Canada. At Akwesasne, Mohawks occupy the bridge connecting the portion of their nation called Cornwall Island with mainland Canada for three hours as they round-dance, drum, chant, and sing.

As soon as I return to the North Country, I call Bob, the elder who showed me around Thompson Island. Not only am I eager to discuss Idle No More, I also want to learn more about him. During our hike through the forest that afternoon, we discovered we have mixed parentage in common. While I relate much more strongly with one heritage over the other, however, hybridity is his identity. He calls himself "Métis" with a pride seldom heard from mestizos.

Bob lives with his wife, Marie (a Mohawk), on the far eastern tip of Cornwall Island. From the bridge, you pass a Peace Pipe Tobacco and Convenience Store, a string of self-built houses, a snowman, young men joyriding an ATV, and an arena shaped like a turtle before turning on the last road before the gravel falls into the St. Lawrence River. Marie's homestead spreads across five acres of fields. Bob envelops me in a hug, his bear claw necklace tickling my face, and invites me inside. Every room contains a conversation piece—artwork, hanging textiles, a box of dried corn, a bowl of tobacco leaves, dozens of old photographs—but he is most eager to show off a hand-woven sash festooned with fringe. Back in the nineteenth century, French Canadian men tied sashes around the waists of their coats to keep out the cold. The style has since been adopted by the Métis.

"I was talked down to by the whites for being Indian, and by the Indians for being white. 'Half-breed' is usually considered derogatory, but the Métis are proud of it," Bob says as he drapes it over my outstretched palms. Cherry-red, it is patterned with arrowheads colored yellow, green, and blue. Then he shows me the Métis flag, which features the sign for infinity: a horizontal number eight. It represents the two cultures coming together forever—"nine months after the first Europeans arrived!" he jokes.

---

created by the government?" he asked. "What can I do to tell you that I'm as human as you are?"

3. On New Year's Eve 2012, nearly a thousand Indians and their supporters flooded the rotunda near Sears and danced, chanted, and drummed in a circle. One year later, two Idle No More organizers got arrested for attempting a small-scale reenactment.

That's pretty much how it happened, though. European men (particularly fur trappers) quickly realized that Native women were essential to their survival in the punishing new climate. Not only did they provide food and pleasure, but they assisted with translations and culture clashes as well. The trappers invited women to live with them in the villages surrounding the trading posts where they sold their pelts, and together they had children who eventually became employees of the trading companies too.

While European men mostly benefited from this arrangement, it was a grave risk for the women. Until 1985, under Canada's Indian Act, Aboriginal women were considered "disenfranchised" when they married non-Native men. Not only did they (and their children) lose their status as Indians, but they were also prohibited from living on their reserve, inheriting family property, receiving treaty benefits, and being buried in their ancestral cemetery.[4] Aboriginal men who married non-Native women, meanwhile, could keep all their rights plus gain Indian status for their wives (despite the fact that many tribes are matrilineal). This, Bob says, is partially why Métis rights organizations were formed. "A Native woman would marry a white man and he would abuse her and leave her, and she'd be left on the outskirts of a reserve with her children trying to fend for herself, because her tribe would not take her back," he said. "Our organizations sprang from there, to get those women housing, to give them some support."

Gradually, the offspring of these mixed couples developed a culture of their own with a distinct music, dance, dress, and language (a fusion of Cree and French called Michif). Although Bob says their population is well over a million, the government estimates less than half that amount. One reason for the discrepancy is confusion over who can claim to be Métis. The Supreme Court devised the following test in 2003: self-identifying as such, having an ancestral connection to a Métis community, and being accepted by that community as a member. That method is hotly debated in Aboriginal communities, along with whether or not Métis should have treaty rights, yet as someone long afflicted with an inferiority complex over her hybridity, I am actually impressed that they receive group recognition[5]

4. From a feminist perspective, the reversal of this code might seem like a victory. However, in her 2014 book *Mohawk Interruptus*, the Mohawk scholar Audra Simpson points out that the law actually helped protect indigenous communities from being taken over by non-Indian (read: white) men.
5. Simpson also makes an important point about "recognition" in *Mohawk Interruptus*, calling the term offensive as it gives so much authority to outsider gaze. She argues on

at all. I once interviewed fifty biracial people for a book project about mixed identity. Every single one of us struggled over existential isolation but were so guilt-ridden that we could hardly admit it. I eventually abandoned the project for the same reason.

"My mother was Cree and my father was like Daniel Boone, a crazy Irish fur trapper," Bob says as we sink into the couch with glasses of iced tea. "He was nineteen and she was sixteen when she got pregnant, and a priest got the authorities to throw him in jail for six months. But when he got out, he went back to her and proved he would be with her, and they stuck it out."

The couple reared five children in a region so remote, the nearest full-fledged hospital was a three-hour flight away. This distance proved disastrous when she contracted tuberculosis after giving birth to Bob. When it was clear she would not recover,[6] the father brought their baby home alone. The government soon took away Bob's four older siblings and sent them off to Indian Residential School (or "Catholic concentration camp," as he calls it) while Bob got placed with his maternal great-grandmother. Having lost his entire family, his father headed south.

Out in the bush, Bob was raised as a traditional Cree. His grandfather and uncles taught him how to trap animals with fine pelts—muskrat, beaver, otter, squirrel, weasel—and brought him along when they tracked down caribou and moose. His great-grandmother taught him how to harvest sweet flag and hold a sliver beneath his tongue to alleviate ache. He spoke Michif at home and studied English at school.

When Bob was ten, his father paid him a visit. He had married another Cree and started another family (for an ultimate headcount of fourteen children with three different women). He invited Bob to join them. Devoted to his great-grandmother, Bob said no, yet she contracted cancer soon after and checked into a hospital. All of thirteen, Bob found himself alone in the house and then—when she died two years later—in the world. He worked

---

behalf of the political and ethical stance of "refusal," which I interpret as: stop playing the game that dismisses you, and start calling your own shots.

6. Bob's mother languished in the hospital for nine years before dying. He shows me a sepia-toned photo of her standing against a fence post, wearing a suit jacket over a pleated skirt. Her hair is short and stylish, and she is laughing. When I comment on her pretty clothes, he says, "They were not all wearing buckskins and loin cloths, eh?" I then ask if they ever visited her. "How? It was seventy years ago, not like today when you can travel. Back then you were lucky if you could get on a steamboat. I never really met her."

odd jobs to save some cash, then set about finding the siblings who had scattered across the country post–residential school.

"[At school] my brother used to wet the bed a lot. Those nuns, they threw him out in the snow bank to punish him," he says. "When he was fifteen, he beat up a priest who was mean to him. He ran away from the school, and the authorities chased him down and threw him into boarding school where runaway kids go, like a jail. He got out, ran away, stole a car, which got him four years of jail, then he got out and did the same thing, stole a car and got four years. Then he did it again. Three times, twelve years of jail."

He found his three sisters in Edmonton, Calgary, and British Columbia. "One of them lost an eye at the school. She got hit with a slingshot, and no one ever fixed it. She suffered for it all her life until she was fifty and then got it done herself," he says with a wince. "The kids were not looked after at those schools, eh? They just forced them to go to church and pray. They punished them for speaking Cree. They bullied them to work day and night. They fed them poorly. My brother never recovered."

"Where is he now?"

"Dead."

His family dispersed, Bob decided to make a new one. He married a Czech woman in Vancouver, landed a good job at Housing Authority, and started having children (for an ultimate headcount of eight, with three different women). None of these joys salved his binary ache, though. Despite his traditional upbringing, he received a cool reception from the urban Native community. He, in turn, distrusted most white people. Whiskey became his confidant. He got charged with drunk driving five times in five years. As his addiction intensified, he took to Skid Road, a Vancouver strip famous for its single-room occupancy hotels, bars, drunks, derelicts, and prostitutes.

"Native people, we had nothing in our own community, so we would go to the city to find even less, so we would go to Skid Road because we couldn't handle it," he says.

A Native Friendship Center helped him sober up in the late sixties. He started dancing in powwows and combing the shelves of libraries. Riding the fervor of the era, he politicized, too. For many years, he advocated for the rights of Native fur trappers, dressing in buckskin and setting up tee-pees whenever Greenpeace and animal rights groups staged a protest. Then he became involved with the Métis, serving as president of the Northwest Territories chapter and assisting with negotiations to include them as a constitutionally recognized Aboriginal group along with the Inuit and the First

Nations in 1982. Since moving to Akwesasne with Marie in the late eighties, however, he has curtailed his involvement.

"There is a divide-and-conquer mentality among the Canadians," he says. "Mining companies and nuclear companies use the Métis to say they have Native involvement when the First Nations don't want to get involved. Métis jump in like a dirty shirt. No wonder First Nations don't like us. The Métis are starting to work against other Aboriginal people."

Which brings us to the Idle No More movement. Bob has been urging Métis leaders to get involved but with scant success. "They fear losing funding from the government, even though the government just gives them an office and salary, nothing terribly significant."

After telling me about the great local actions I've missed, Bob assures me the best is just ahead. In early January, six young Crees left their remote village of Whapmagoostui, Quebec, on the shores of Hudson Bay and started snowshoeing across Canada in the name of peace. Hundreds have since joined them for what has been pegged "The Journey of Nishiyuu," or the Journey of the People. They'll be arriving in Ottawa at the end of March to petition Parliament for better conditions for all Aboriginal people. Indians will be driving in from all over to greet them at the end of their thousand-mile trek, Bob says. We vow to do so, too.

WINTER INTENSIFIES. In the mornings, I trudge past snowdrifts taller than me, past icicles shaped like daggers. The sun sinks before class is over, and I walk home in darkness between snow banks glowing with moonlight. Some days it snows and some days it ices and some days it sleets and one day it spits tiny ice-balls that bounce. Some days I awake to sunlight and excitedly plan a hike, but by the anointed hour the sky has grayed all over again. One thing the North Country teaches you is to seize the sun, because you never know when it will return.

In the worst of it, I build a fire, pull the blankets close, and click on the website of the Nishiyuu. Even when temperatures plummet to fifty degrees below zero, they keep walking. They wear white hooded ponchos over layers of furs and wool and snowshoes made of rawhide and wood. They drag their provisions on sleds. The youngest is a sixteen-year-old named Stanley. He walks with a staff whose colors represent the grandmothers. The other five "originals" range in age from seventeen to twenty-one, and a forty-six-year-old Cree serves as their guide. They call him the White Wizard because he always knows the way, no matter how blinding the snow. He leads them along the

Cree's traditional trading routes, and when they camp each night, members of other tribes join them. Inuits. Algonquins. Attikameks. Ojibwas. Mi'kmaqs.[7]

In March, the North Country becomes a mud pit. Lawns melt into ankle-deep slush in the afternoon, freeze throughout the night, then melt into shin-deep slush the following morning. Icicles dangling from rooftops drip, drip, drip, then fall. I dart in and out of buildings, fearful of being impaled, and wade across town in Muck Boots.

But then one morning, I awake not to snow-muffled silence but to birdsong. One morning, a squirrel climbs down from a tree and sniffs. An Adirondack chair tentatively appears on somebody's front porch, and by evening three more have joined it. One morning I awake to find all the maple trees wearing buckets. One morning, the thermometer hits thirty-nine degrees and students come to class wearing flip-flops. One morning, the Amish return to town in their horse-drawn buggies and set out their pickles and jellies. And one morning, Bob calls to say the Nishiyuu walkers are about to reach Ottawa.

We head over in Bob's 1999 Cadillac Deville. I leaf through his CDs and pop in one of Métis music, anticipating drumming and chanting, but a merry burst of fiddling spills forth instead. Bob starts jigging in the driver's seat, slapping his hands against the steering wheel and snapping his fingers as we jet past the farmhouses and grain silos, wineries and orchards of Ontario. Caught in traffic on the outskirts of Ottawa, he points out the many rearview mirrors adorned with dream catchers.

We park at the Canadian War Museum, which proves it's not an oxymoron by displaying a tank on its lawn. Bob pops the trunk of his white-stretch Caddie and searches for regalia. First up is his Métis sash, which he wraps around his waist so it dangles down his leg. He exchanges his tennis shoes for snow boots and his baseball cap for a furry, ear-flapped number that

---

7. The Nishiyuu can be viewed as upholding a long tradition of athletic feats for Native rights. One of the most famous occurred in February 1978, when 2,000 activists set off from Alcatraz Island in San Francisco and headed toward Washington, D.C., in protest of anti-Native legislation. Twenty-six completed the entire 3,000-mile trek, arriving at the capital that July and holding a series of rallies that helped dissuade Congress from passing some of the bills. Known as the "Longest Walk," it memorialized other grueling marches that Native Americans have endured, such as the Trail of Tears, and was reenacted thirty years later with an 8,000-mile hike promoting environmental sustainability. The Cherokee Nation, meanwhile, hosts an annual 950-mile "Remember the Removal" bicycle ride that retraces the tribe's forced eviction from its ancestral land to territories out west in 1838.

resembles a Russian *ushanka*. "I got it at a muskrat store, ever been to one of those?" He tries to slip on a fringed buckskin jacket, but it doesn't fit. "I'm too fat!" he sighs, then tosses it back in the pile. Next come a staff, gnarled and polished, and a puppet with a floppy tongue. "Husky?" I ask. "Wolf!" he says indignantly. He hands them both to me before pulling out his final accessory: a stretch of rope. He loops it around his neck like a tie and tightens it like a noose. "This is what Harper is doing to us," he explains, then snaps the trunk shut. "Off like a herd of turtles."

Up ahead, a woman with long black braids walks along a snow bank, her crimson robe rippling behind her. We follow her to Victoria Island, where Indians waving banners and journalists wielding cameras line the bridge. Burning sage perfumes the air. Bob greets almost everyone, barking at children with his wolf puppet and telling elders in wheelchairs, "I'll carry you." At one point, he jumps in front of a stalled car and mimics cranking its wheel. People laugh and take his picture. "Don't!" he says. "I'll send you one when I was good-looking."

Bob isn't the only one who primped for this event. First Nations women wear long patterned skirts over jeans and feathers in their hair. Inuits sport knee-high sealskin boots and fur-trimmed cloaks. Supporters have dressed up too, either in Guatemalan huipiles or anarchist shirts emblazoned with slogans like "Harper's[8] Killing Canada."

Three rivers converge at Victoria Island, which made it a sacred space for Algonquins for thousands of years before the British deemed it a prime piece of real estate. Eventually the land was returned to the tribe, and it has since become a "summer village" for tourists as well as the symbolic headquarters of Idle No More. Down by the old stone millhouse, Algonquin elders in full regalia tend a fire on the snow bank. As I draw near, the hypnotic drumbeats begin to pulse inside my chest. I huddle into the folds of the crowd and absorb the sonorous warmth.

Suddenly, everyone rushes toward the Portage Bridge, shaking their signs and cheering. The Nishiyuu have arrived. The crowd forms a receiving line from the bridge to the fire and applauds as the walkers stride past, a reported 270 in all. The white hooded ponchos depicted on their website have since become canvases for Sharpie autographs, embroidery, and beadwork.

---

8. Much is made of the fact that, rather than greet the Nishiyuu at the end of their heroic march, Prime Minister Harper chose to fly to Toronto to welcome the arrival of two giant pandas on loan from China instead.

A few walkers wield staffs, but most carry nothing whatsoever. No backpacks or CamelBaks or fanny packs. No water bottles or globs of energy Gu. No specialized hiking boots with micro-adjustability. The walkers wear Converse and sunglasses and that's about it. They are young and they are virile and some puff on cigarettes as if to prove it. No one seems especially exhausted, although a number are limping. The original six walkers are easy to spot, and not just because of the traditional snowshoes strapped to their backs. The windburn and the sleet and the blisters and the cold have weathered their young faces into a placidity normally found only upon statues of bodhisattvas.

As they gather around the fire for the welcoming ceremony, the crowd backs away to give them space. They bow their heads beneath the drumming and the chanting and the blessings. After a time, some peel away to greet the family they haven't seen in days or weeks or months. One young walker stands by me. She wears an orange and green skirt beneath her poncho and a sash that says NISHIYUU JOURNEY 2013. She self-identifies as a James Bay Cree, one of the last nations that manages to sustain itself hunting and fishing despite losing much of its forest to forty years of hydroelectric projects.

"How far did you walk?"

She pauses to consider. "Four hundred kilometers? Five?"

"Why did you do it?"

"It was somebody's dying wish," she manages before her wind-burned face crumples. "She passed while I was walking."

An older man walks over and hugs her from behind, but she continues: "She was . . . she was like my mother. I talked to her about the walk but found out she was sick. She told me to go ahead and do it, and to finish. So . . . I did." She turns around to embrace her supporter and sob.

Several thousand people have gathered on the island now, some by the fire, some by the fry bread line, but most along the snowbanks. I meet another James Bay Cree. When I admire his tribe's commitment to traditional living, he says the most devoted practitioners can be found in the village of the original Nishiyuu. "They live in the part of Canada where you must fly in. If they built a road to it, it would be 300 kilometers long. It is wide-open barren land, like you're in outer space. They have the strongest culture there, the strongest language. Everything is related to the land over there."

Once all of the walkers have been blessed and the fry bread depleted, the march to Parliament begins. Wellington has been closed to traffic for the occasion, so we file into the street. "I-dle" someone shouts. "No More," we respond. Banners unfurl, one of which features a wampum belt that reads HONOR YOUR WORD. Drummers pound a cadence and people dance-step in time. A man with red ribbons woven in his braids does the Fancy Dance, striking a different pose after each round of beats. We make our way up Parliament Hill, past the Library and Archives of Canada, the Supreme Court of Canada, and the House of Commons to the steps of the Peace Tower, 300 feet of gargoyles topped by a four-faced clock.

"Brothers and sisters, there is no word to describe the pride we feel for our people today," the emcee says before passing the mike to a Cree elder. He launches into a melancholic song. Midway through it, everyone points at the sky. I look up to see a bald eagle soaring directly above. A collective cheer rises to greet her.

The original six Nishiyuu are called to the mike. Visibly dazed, they address the crowd in a decibel above a whisper. The emcee must repeat their remarks so we can hear them. "I truly didn't think I'd complete this journey," says eighteen-year-old Raymond Kawapit. "I took this walk to find strength in my life after I lost my brother on February sixth. I went to see my grandmother, and she says when people walk across the land, that is where they will find healing. I thought I was alone in this grief until I started meeting other people along the journey and seeing they are grieving too. Now I start to find the healing."

Other walkers are called over, too. One is a twenty-something woman whose dark spiky hair has been streaked blonde. When the members of the crowd train their eyes on her, she turns away. "She's kinda shy, so please put your head down and don't look at her," the emcee says.

A long pause later, she accepts the mike with shaking hands. "The reason I walked is that so many committed suicide," she manages. "There's no one to help them when they are in need. I myself struggled five years ago when I went to school in Ottawa. I wanted to take my life. I don't want that for anybody. I started walking, and I made it all the way to Ottawa. Don't hide your emotions. Let it out."

At that, she begins to cry into the microphone. Her sobs reverberate across the snow. There is something about her sadness, her candidness, that opens the fissures in us all. I am crying, Bob is crying, the man in front of us is crying, the girl beside us is crying, the woman behind us is crying. For these are nations who have lost their land and their trees, their rights and their treaties, their language and their tradition, and now they are losing their sons and their daughters too, at a shattering pace.[9] Their youth kill themselves because of poverty. They kill themselves because of domestic violence, sexual assault, and addiction. They kill themselves because their friends kill themselves, because their neighbors and their cousins kill themselves. They kill themselves because they inherited an intergenerational trauma that rivals the stress disorders of veterans returning from war.

All of this agony, all of this grief, the Nishiyuu walkers have suffered, too. Yet they somehow developed the inner strength to make the collective decision to live. And that is what fuels our spontaneous cry-in. We cry not only for the dead and the dying, however sorely we mourn their loss. We cry for the miracle of the living.

9. In April 2016, the Northern Ontario First Nation of Attawapiskat declared a state of emergency when 11 members attempted suicide in a single day, in a community of 2,000. Suicide rates among Canada's First Nations youth are staggering: twenty-one times higher than the national rate for females and ten times for males. In the United States, the rate is at least three times the national average overall and up to ten times within some nations. According to the *Washington Post*, Native youth also suffer twice the rate of abuse and neglect as any other race and are twice as likely to die before the age of twenty-four.

17

The Mother Tongue

A LONG WHITE SCHOOLHOUSE STANDS AT THE FAR END OF A WOODSY road. Parking in its gravel lot, I follow the trail of painted rocks to the door. Several dozen students are seated on benches lining the hallway, yet they do not make a sound. They peer up at me, wordlessly. Many of the boys have shaved their heads in the traditional fashion. Realizing I have interrupted something, I apologize and duck inside the nearest room. It turns out to be the administrative office. A woman wearing a St. Lawrence University shirt stands to greet me. Her name is Okiokwinon. Though she is—at age twenty-two—essentially the principal, her title is "office manager" to emphasize the fact that parents collectively run their school. With a Dunkin' Donuts iced mocha in one hand and a cell phone in the other, she joins me beneath a poster that says LET'S NOT LOSE IT: LET'S SPEAK MOHAWK. Her glossy brown hair hangs in a ponytail; multiple rings dangle from her lobes. Her energy is ebullient.

As we talk, parents bearing tribal tattoos drop in, their children peeking behind them. Several of the fathers wear the same hairstyle as their sons. Okiokwinon addresses the children in Mohawk and the parents in English because, while the children are fluent in both, most parents speak only the latter. That's why they've enrolled their kids here: to keep the mother tongue alive.

The Akwesasne Freedom School is the phoenix that flourished from the ashes of the 1979 standoff at the Thompson homestead on Raquette Point. During that armed confrontation, traditionally minded parents decided they could no longer send their kids to local public schools. (The latest indignity: a school pageant in which Mohawk children were dressed up like Christopher Columbus and George Washington and instructed to dance about, celebrating America's discovery.) They devised a holistic educational system that promoted indigenous ways of being and built a schoolhouse shaped like a traditional longhouse. The total Mohawk immersion program now serves pre-kindergarten through eighth grade.

Every day, the Freedom School opens and closes with the Ohen:ton Karihwatehkwen, with students taking turns expressing gratitude to the life forces that construct the universe. (This was the ritual I interrupted with my arrival.) They then move through courses in science, social studies, history, reading, art, and math interpreted through a traditional Mohawk lens. In social studies, they learn about the clan mothers instead of the Founding Fathers and the Haudenosaunee Confederacy instead of Congress. In science, they study the growth cycles of medicines and how and when to harvest. They walk down to the river to try out ancestral methods of fishing, to the forest to tap maple trees, to the community garden to tend vegetables, to the orchards to press cider. They descend upon the longhouse to usher in each new season with ceremony. Every activity is intended to empower them to be the best possible leaders seven generations into the future. Only in their final two years do teachers incorporate English into their curriculum, to prepare their transition into public high school.

"We have given others ideas on how to turn their culture into curriculum too," Okiokwinon says, stirring the last of her mocha. "Cherokees took our idea. The Maori came here and hung out for a month. Now they have two schools like ours."

After the schoolhouse empties, Okiokwinon offers a tour. Fifty-three students have registered for classes this year, she says, and the hall's walls showcase their artwork and murals. Seedlings grow by the windows. Tobacco dries in the sills. The brightly painted classrooms display educational posters that, upon closer inspection, show signs of alteration.

"Whatever teachers buy at Office Max, they cover up the English and add in the Mohawk," she says. "Any book we have must be translated, too. We have an adult language program, and their final project is to translate an entire book so we can use it."

The last room is an industrial-size kitchen where parents take turns cooking stews and porridges each day. Meals eat up the bulk of student tuition, which is $500 plus a quilt each year. I actually caught the final bidding war of the school's annual quilt auction a few months ago. The last quilt was extraordinary: a swirl of turquoise stars shooting out of golden arrows alongside bursts of drifting feathers. As I debated whether or not I could part with, say, $350, the woman behind me opened with a bid of $1,000. Someone countered with $1,250, and in less than a minute the bid reached $5,000.

Then a girl who couldn't have been over eighteen hollered the figure no one could beat: $6,500. What had originally sounded as quaint as a bake sale raked in almost $40,000 in under an hour. Yet despite the generosity of parents and supporters, the Freedom School struggles financially, as it refuses federal and state aid. Teachers earn just $18,000 a year here, Okiokwinon says.

She shows me the outside garden that yields sunflowers and tomatoes each summer. Farther away are a performance stage and a playground. As we stroll about the wooded area, I ask about her own tenure here. She enrolled in 1994, when she was four. Tension over gambling still lingered. "Some teachers wouldn't talk to each other. Parents, too. It was hostile to be in school," she says. "But it wasn't until I started asking questions when I was in sixth grade that I started to understand why. I wanted to go to someone's house for a birthday party and my mom said I wasn't allowed because it was at Snye. My parents were antis, they were traditionalists, and you could see a lot of Warrior flags hanging out of my friend's house."

Her older siblings eventually dropped out of Freedom School, but Okiokwinon continued on through eighth grade. She is now the only fluent Mohawk speaker in her family, as well as the most knowledgeable about tradition. Adjusting to English-only high school in nearby Fort Covington proved more annoying than challenging. "I walked into my first class and was like, what the fuck? I hadn't had any white friends before then. But it was pretty easy to make friends because I played on a lot of different sports teams."

After graduating from eighth grade in a class of six, she was unaccustomed to the number of students at the high school, but at least Mohawks constituted the bulk of the body. When she enrolled at SLU four years later, she had to contend with being one of only thirteen Native students on the entire campus.

"The second week of class, this [white] girl asked me how I got out. She was like, 'Isn't there a wall at the reservation?' I told her I dug a hole for two weeks before I escaped, and it was really hard because I had to wake up at 1 A.M. and dig a hole underground and all I had was a spoon. She was so shocked. Finally, I said, 'I drove out, just like you did.'"

Even worse was the night some club threw a "Cowboy and Indian"–themed party and drunken students milled about wearing war paint and feathered headdresses. Yet Okiokwinon managed to devote herself to studying and graduated last year. Law school is next on her list, as she hopes to practice treaty law someday. Until then, she plans to work where she found her Native consciousness.

"I always had it in mind that I would come back here as a teacher," she says, picking up a maple leaf and twirling it in her palm. "This is my home; I grew up in these classrooms. I figured out who I was as a Mohawk woman."

ALTHOUGH 187 NATIVE LANGUAGES are currently spoken in the United States and Canada, scholars estimate that children are learning only about 20 percent of them. Without serious intervention, many will go extinct within the next few decades. At Akwesasne, only about 1,000 people fluidly converse in Mohawk, along with 2,000 more in Kahnawake and beyond. The majority are elderly.

Multiple forces propelled Mohawk's decline. First was the century of compulsory enrollment at Indian Residential Schools, where staff literally beat the language out of children with whips and clappers, food deprivation and chores, and other humiliations. Many survivors opted not to pass on the tongue that caused them misery. The opening of the St. Lawrence Seaway and the influx of companies like GM to the region in the 1950s further prioritized English. Parents taught their children accordingly. Public school and Hollywood, CNN and MTV, Grand Theft Auto and reality TV have provided the latest fusillade of distraction.

Any new language is difficult to learn post-childhood, but Mohawk is notoriously intricate. Carole Ross, one of Akwesasne's most reputed teachers, told me, "You must reconfigure your mind to speak Mohawk." It has only 11 letters—*A, E, H, I, K, N, O, R, S, T, W*—but they emit 400 distinct sounds. (English, by comparison, has only 44, despite containing twice as many letters.) Moreover, Mohawk words tend to be phrases that are at least 15 letters long[1] and are peppered with diacritic apostrophes, colons, and accent marks, making it daunting to pronounce. And there isn't just one Mohawk language but three: one for everyday life, one for formal occasions, and a sacred one for ceremonies.

Yet its rewards are immense. For starters, the language is fantastically descriptive. Rather than assign a single noun to an object, Mohawk conjures an image of it. Refrigerator is "that which makes things cold," while rabbit is "that with two ears side by side." The names of the months predict what will happen within them: April is "when the leaves start growing," June is "that time when berries start to ripen," and December is "when the cold sets in."

---

1. The word "dog," for instance, is *ehrhahrhokon:'a.* "Black stove polish," meanwhile, is the remarkable *teienonhsa'tariha'tahkhwahtsherahon'tsistahstarathe'táhkhwa.*

It is also a precise language, with ninety different words to pinpoint familial relationships and twenty-six for baskets. Mohawks contend that their language is much funnier than English. Stories seem fuller somehow, more vivid and true. Language is also the touchstone of their culture, the primer on ways of being. Its very structure implies respect for the winds and for the rains. Matrilineal heritage is emphasized, as is agricultural tradition. And because so many words place objects in relation to the self—chair, for instance, is "the place where you put your thighs on"—Mohawk reinforces a sense of interconnectedness.

The Akwesasne Freedom School is one of several tribal initiatives to preserve their language, and the most rigorous for children. For adults, the tribal governments on both sides of the river sponsor free language classes for public employees. Kahnawake is even more aggressive about reviving Mohawk: in 2006, its council hired Rosetta Stone to develop software for the language and then invested in thousands of CD-ROMs for community members. Classes have been compulsory for public employees there ever since.

One afternoon, I visit the adult school on Cornwall Island. The instructor is Dorothy Lazore, a lovely woman in her mid-sixties wearing a snakeskin-patterned jacket and a long floral skirt. Over lunch, she tells me that her grandmother attended an Indian Residential School but never disclosed it to her children. Dorothy only recently found out when she turned the page of a book she was reading about the school system and saw a photo of her grandmother there. Fortunately, that was not the end of their linguistic lineage. Dorothy grew up speaking Mohawk and upholding all of its traditions except the Longhouse. "That was considered taboo when I was younger," she explains, adding that the Catholic church in St. Regis used to warn parishioners that Longhouse ceremonies were a form of devil worship. Only later in life did Dorothy begin exploring traditional spirituality.

Dorothy started teaching Mohawk when she was twenty-four years old. There were no educational aids back then. For her first job, she had to write her own textbook. "I didn't even know how to write Mohawk; my mom had to teach me. I searched for books and found a Mohawk dictionary and then I got a French language book and followed the pattern."

She has since developed a curriculum that she's taught at Akwesasne and Kahnawake and presented at conferences around the world. She's also helped Native Hawaiians develop their own pedagogy. "Our Native people have always had to own up to other people's standards," she says, spooning a bite of spaghetti. "We had to live up to Catholic standards. We had to live up to someone else's education system, someone else's health system, even someone else's government system. Even the language isn't our own standard. We are not living our natural life through our own language. It's a wonder that we survived as a people."

Back at the school, I join Dorothy at a table that is shaped like a horseshoe and surrounded by white boards, language charts, and a flat-screen TV. Five energized older women file in, along with a younger woman who seems shy. They launch into a discussion that sounds serious with its mile-long words and ethereal inflections. After a while, Dorothy leans over to whisper-translate: "They are talking about last night. This woman says she made a pot roast with carrots, and that one said she watched the *Big Bang Theory* until she fell asleep."

When the lesson begins, she hands me a workbook so I can follow along. I thumb through pages of sentences like "The bear is over there at the back of an airplane" and "I see two yellow birds flying and I see four white canoes." Accompanying illustrations include a decapitated moose (*ska'nionhsa*, or "he that has a big nose") alongside a slab of steak and a bloodied knife.

Class concludes with the women taking turns reading aloud the essays they wrote the night before. The youngest one wrestles with every word. At one point, she grows so frustrated, her entire face flushes. The older woman seated beside her lays a hand on her shoulder. "It will come back to you," she promises. "Just keep on going."

The other women nod in agreement. I glance over at Dorothy. She smiles in return, as if acknowledging that yes—there will, in fact, come a point when her students find their ancestral rhythms and it will be like they've known Mohawk all along. Because, in a way, they have.

I WOULD LIKE TO THINK Spanish is buried inside me too, but I've had a hell of a time extracting it, despite twenty years of trying. Like many Mohawks, I can also pinpoint where it died in my lineage: the South Texas public education system of the 1950s. One story I have been telling audiences for years is how my mom got pulled out of her chair one day and marched to the front of her elementary school classroom. Her crime: speaking Spanish. Her punishment: a bar of soap, which the teacher shoved into her mouth.

I couldn't visualize this more clearly if I'd witnessed it myself. I can practically smell the lye in the soap. Yet I just recently asked Mom for more details, and she has no recollection of it ever happening to her. I insist that she told me once, but she does not remember that, either. How, then, did I acquire so much rage about it? Is it a case of memory repression, memory inheritance, or memory invention? I do not know. Yet every time I have shared this story with Tejanos, at least one elder has nodded and said her mouth was publicly washed out, too.

And that wasn't the only humiliation they endured. In the town of Driscoll in 1956, a second grader who spoke only English got placed in a Spanish-speaking class because their skin tone matched her own. When her parents complained, they were shunted aside. Although the Supreme Court had outlawed segregation, Texas schools still found ways to divide the races. The 2013 documentary *Stolen Education* depicts how Tejanos were forced to repeat first grade three times[2] because administrators did not want the "retardation of Latin children" to hinder the education of white children. Many Tejanos didn't graduate until well into their twenties (if at all). And so, the girl's parents rallied families together and—with the help of the American G.I. Forum—filed a class-action lawsuit against the school district. During the federal proceedings, eight children testified against their teachers at the witness stand. Incredibly, they won the battle.

I can't say they won the war, though, because three decades later I too wound up in a predominantly Spanish-speaking class in South Texas, despite knowing hardly a word. I've written reams about this before, but here are the pertinent details. One morning, our teacher announced that our class was too large and needed to be split in two. All the brown kids got sent to one side of the room while all the white kids went to the other. When asked if I was Hispanic or white, I froze. Mom was Mexican; Dad was white. What did that make me? Since most of my friends were in the brown group, I ran to their side. That felt right until the new teacher asked us to read aloud. Hearing my classmates stumble with their English was worrisome. *If I stay with them, I will fall behind.* Afterward, I begged the teacher to put me in the white class. She agreed.

That was the first time I crossed my inner borderline. It changed the way I moved in the world. Prior to that experience, all my friends had long silky hair and melodic names and invited me to homes brimming with brothers and cousins and parakeets and mothers stirring *habichuelas* on the stove. After that experience, my friends' houses smelled like Lemon Pledge and their mothers zapped everything we ate in the microwave—hot dog, bun,

2. The first year was called "beginner's first grade," the second "low first grade," and the third "high first grade."

and all. For years, no Mexican ever asked why I acted white, and no one white ever questioned if I was Mexican. My senior year of high school, however, a guidance counselor urged me to claim a Hispanic "H" on my transcripts to better position myself for scholarships. Though this felt dishonest—I'd been checking the "W" box for White for years—I did as she suggested and was shocked by the results: a college education, free of charge. I enrolled at the University of Texas at Austin in a state of elation—until I started meeting other scholarship recipients. Some were the children of farmworkers. Some had been involved in a gang or barely escaped its violence. Many sent portions of their scholarship checks to families back home.

Once I realized I had only profited from being an "H" without enduring any of its hardships, I descended into a guilt-laden identity crisis that didn't subside until I moved to Mexico when I turned thirty. That journey has been recorded elsewhere, but its gist is this: the last time I crossed my inner borderline, I stayed there.

GIVEN MY PREOCCUPATION WITH CHICANIDAD, I am curious about what constitutes Mohawkness. Membership in the St. Regis Mohawk Tribe is determined on a case-by-case basis but generally mandates a 25 percent blood quantum and a verification of ancestry. An even more complex potion must congeal before someone actually *feels* Mohawk, however. To better understand when identity angst first strikes, I visit the Akwesasne Boys and Girls Club, which works with more than 300 Mohawks between the ages of six and eighteen a year. It is located in a former bingo hall surrounded by a chain-link fence off the main highway. My host is program manager Ryan King. With his coppery skin engraved with Haudenosaunee tattoos, he seems to epitomize Mohawkness. He has even shaved his hair to create a raised mound across his head.

As we stroll down hallways plastered with student photographs and statements like "I'm awesome because _____," he talks about his organization's struggle to balance the New York State educational system with traditional Mohawk values. Students must spend their first forty-five minutes here doing homework, but afterward they can play lacrosse or volleyball, log on to a computer, or participate in arts and culture programming that is specifically oriented toward identity formation.

"Not knowing your culture is a sore spot here," Ryan says. "They all know specific Mohawk words, phrases, and commands, but only one or two are actually fluent. We push them to speak more. And if you don't know ceremony, or if you don't know a song or dance at a social, it is a self-esteem thing for them."

Appearance is another concern, particularly for girls. "If they are fairer, they get picked on more because they don't look Mohawk. 'You look white' is the worst thing you can say here. When a baby is born, we always ask, 'Are they dark?' We like darker features; that is considered much more positive here."

At thirty-two, Ryan is the son of a longtime chief of the Mohawk Council of Akwesasne. His family contains Longhouse members as well as Catholics, which makes him conversant in both spiritualities. Yet certain aspects of Mohawkness evade him, too, such as language. "When I was three or four I was raised by my grandma and she was fluent, but when I enrolled in the public school system, it left," he says.

He left too for twelve years, to study public communications at Buffalo State College and work in the field. He never questioned whether to return, though. "Go out and get an education, but always make sure you come back; don't ever forget home. That is ingrained in us at a very early age," he says. "If I hadn't left the rez, I would probably not be doing too much now."

These are the ideals he promotes at the Boys and Girls Club, and I imagine he's persuasive. In addition to his traditional creds, he drives a new car and wields the latest iPhone. Diamond studs line his ears. Yet college can be a hard sell at Akwesasne, given the lure of the river. "The drug trade is a lot of easy money. These kids are looking at that, working for an hour or two, and then not having to work for the next month. They will say, 'I will make more money in an hour than you will in a week,'" he says with a cringe. "A lot of them just don't look at the dangerous part. I have friends who've been held up at gunpoint. I have friends who've been robbed. I have friends who've had to go into hiding."

His voice trails off as his eyes grow distant. Then, as if remembering the pen in my hand, he shifts topic. "We get a lot of press for drugs, but nobody ever focuses on the good stuff. We have the best lacrosse program here. Some of our kids play for Albany University[3] and for Syracuse. Our girls are the best volleyball players, and they play for colleges too. One of our summer employees

---

3. ESPN called the University of Albany's "Thompson Trio"—brothers Miles and Lyle and cousin Ty—the best lacrosse attack liners in collegiate history. They hail from the Mohawk and Onondaga Nations, claim to have never taken a sip of alcohol, and pledge to return to their communities as soon as they can.

is valedictorian at Massena High School. We don't ever hear about that, about how talented our kids are, about how much pride we have in our kids."

With that, he shakes my hand. Dozens of those kids will be arriving within the hour, and he wants to be ready to receive them.

AS SOON AS BRENDA STEPS out of her Ford Trailblazer and strides toward Canton's Blackbird Cafe, I see we have something in common. Her dark hair and cashew-colored skin could pass for anything from Brazilian to Lebanese. Only when we sit down for lunch do I notice her indigenous bone structure and arms bereft of hair. She also has pale green eyes. Though our conversation feels formal at first, it escalates in intensity until we are in tears within an hour of meeting.

Brenda comes from a tight-knit family whose roots at Akwesasne run deep. Six of her mother's nine siblings still live on the same street where they were born. Growing up, her father worked in the high steel industry, which kept him away for weeks at a time, while her mother stayed home with their six children. As the oldest, Brenda assumed a lot of responsibility at a young age, especially since one of her brothers had muscular dystrophy. "Basically, I was the other adult in the house," she says, biting into a panini.

Education was the only viable path out of poverty, so Brenda immersed herself into her studies. Her grades were unfalteringly stellar. Yet her teachers never seemed to push her as much as they did the non-Native students. No one urged her to take advanced classes or nominated her for leadership programs. If she wanted to succeed, it seemed she must create opportunities for herself. And so, in eighth grade, she signed up for a college preparatory program that required spending the next five summers in Canton, an hour away. Then she applied and got accepted to SLU and found a financial need program to pay for it. Opening so many doors through sheer persistence was thrilling, but she worried it was also isolating her from her nation. No one in her family had attended college before. Brenda would be the first.

"There is a fear that once you leave, you come back different, and you never truly belong again," she says. "And there is also this sense, if I do go away and come back, what can it offer me?"

Her apprehension heightened when she attended a summer preparatory session at SLU. "The first thing people often said to me was, 'You're not white, but what are you?' When I said I was Native, they would ask if I spoke the language, and I had to say no. That is when the guilt and shame felt the strongest. But everybody is a product of their immediate family and how they grew up. My parents don't speak Mohawk, so I don't either. I was also brought up in the Catholic church, which—in retrospect—felt like an automatic hindrance to my identity as a Native American because I was not exploring the traditions associated with Native American people. If your grandparents aren't Longhouse, you don't take that route, and it made me feel less Native in a way, plus having fair skin."

Casting her eyes down to her hands, she adds, "If you see me alone, people often mistake me for Puerto Rican. Yet if you see me with my family you will see I am Native."

Once classes began, she confronted another barrier. SLU's tuition was about three times the average per capita income at Akwesasne. She couldn't relate much to classmates who wore designer labels and went skiing on the weekends. Some of her high school friends attended the local community college, so she spent most of the next four years there.

"I realized early on what I wanted to do, to help Native youth realize their potential. College should be an expectation for all of us.[4] I really wanted to give back."

Brenda not only received her bachelor's at SLU but has completed two master's degrees as well. For nearly a decade now she has been working there, too, fostering her alma mater's ties to her nation by implementing community-based learning opportunities there for SLU students and doing what she can to increase Mohawk enrollment. While she has achieved much more professionally than anyone seemed to think possible, Brenda worries about the toll it has taken on her identity.

"College changed me, so that I feel more white than Native. I am a completely different person when I go back to the rez than I am here. It's like I have to flip a switch," she says.

Forty-five miles separate her workplace from her nation. She needs every minute driving between the two to make that mental shift. Sometimes she transitions back to her Native mind on her own. Sometimes the Border Patrol triggers it for her.

---

4. According to the National Indian Education Association, the high school graduation rate for Native Americans enrolled in public school is 67 percent, compared with 81 percent for all other students. Among those enrolled in a Bureau of Indian Education school, the rate drops to 53 percent. The stats for higher ed is even more sobering: just 39 percent of Indians enrolled in a four-year postsecondary institution in 2004 earned a bachelor's degree by 2010. At tribal colleges, the rate dips down to 20 percent, according to the *Atlantic*.

"One time [at a roadside checkpoint], the car ahead had out-of-state tags, and they handed over their paperwork right away and I could tell they were nervous. Then I was up, and they could see my feathers hanging from the rearview mirror, and right away they asked me to pull over. And I said, 'Why are you making me pull over, when that other car had out-of-state tags?' And he searched through my stuff, even went through my dirty laundry bag. You know they are profiling you because they think you have drugs in your car," she says, her entire body stiffening. "I used to have the Haudenosaunee flag on my car, but I had to take it off because there were so many problems."

She has moved back to Akwesasne several times to help out her family, including living with her grandmother for the first three years after her grandfather died. Even when Brenda spent her entire day advocating for Native youth at SLU and her entire night at Akwesasne, she still felt misplaced somehow. Binaries aren't just a matter of blood.

"Even though I am as full Native as I can be, I still feel white. It is hard because you want to be able to respect your parents. They have lived their entire life on the rez, but I haven't. It is hard to bounce between these two worlds."

Brenda currently lives off-nation. The rest of her siblings either remain on the homestead where they all grew up or close by. Though she visits once or twice a week, the distance is palpable—and not just because of her professional life. Her tendency to date non-Natives has also caused upset, she says, "because my parents belong to a race they feel is dying." When she introduced her first black boyfriend to her family, her dad said, "What's wrong with you? Don't you know who you are, where you come from, what your culture is?" (The white women her brothers have brought home have been more readily accepted.)

Brenda has also been trying to have a baby, "but it is not working," she says. Sadness thickens her throat as she shreds her napkin in two. "My cousins started having their children early, while I prioritized my education because I thought I needed to have this aspect of my life in place first."

She sets down her mangled napkin and looks into my eyes. "I just feel like I am an outlier. I still feel proud to be Native, but it is a constant struggle because I just don't look it. So do I just keep quiet, or do I speak out?"

I glance down at my own napkin and find it shredded, too. These are the same questions I have long tried to resolve within myself. The only force stronger than my allegiance to my Mexican American identity is my insecurity that I am not really Mexican at all—that I am still benefiting from something others have suffered for, that the identity upon which I have built my entire personhood is a sham.

Looking back at Brenda, whose face is as ethnically indeterminate as my own, I decide that this is what it means to live in nepantla. To always question, to always doubt, and to always, always ache.

18

The Bridge

THEY EMERGE FROM THE LONGHOUSE, A DOZEN AT LEAST, ELEGANT as only chiefs can be, wearing buckskin vests, hair braids, hawk- and eagle-feathered kastowa crested with deer antlers, and—the fiercest accessory of all—sunglasses. A hundred people follow, waving Haudenosaunee flags. They turn onto Route 37, where the rest of us file in: young mothers pushing strollers, workers who've taken the day off, elders wearing clan symbols, children scrambling to keep up. Many wear dress shirts embroidered at the wrist, hem, and necklines with brightly colored ribbons streaming from the shoulders. Few talk. The quiet is punctuated by the thump of a drum.

Our destination is approximately five miles away. To get there, we must first leave Akwesasne and then New York's Franklin County before cutting through a corner of St. Lawrence County and entering the otherworld that is U.S. Customs and Border Patrol. There, we'll cross one bridge that will briefly return us to Akwesasne—Cornwall Island, which Canada also claims—and then a second bridge that will deposit us into the otherworld that is the Canada Border Services Agency (CBSA). From there, we'll finally step into our destination, the city of Cornwall in Ontario, Canada.

So while this march will be only five miles in length, we must pass through seven governing spheres to complete it. And that's not counting all the Mohawks who drove in from the portions of Akwesasne that are technically in Quebec. It's also not counting all the Indians who drove in from the other nations of the Haudenosaunee Confederacy: the Onondaga, Oneida, Seneca, Cayuga, and Tuscarora.

That makes a total of twelve different jurisdictions that wield some degree of power over roughly 13,000 Mohawks—four counties, one state, two provinces, two countries, and three different tribal governments—every one of which is monitoring today's proceedings. Should calamity strike, any of the following law enforcement agencies could be summoned to deal with it: the Akwesasne Mohawk Police, the St. Regis Mohawk Tribal Police, the New York State Police, the FBI, the U.S. Border Patrol, the Sûreté du Québec, the Ontario Provincial Police, the Royal Canadian Mounted Police, and/or the CBSA.

And that's why everyone is marching in the first place. As the elder I trot behind puts it: "The situation is driving us nuts."

This is also what it means to live in nepantla, suspended between peripheries. Your ancestors might have tended this soil for centuries, but your citizenship can still be questioned and your identity tested on back roads so remote, no one will hear you when you scream. What I deeply admire about Mohawks: they keep screaming anyway.

WE ARE APPROACHING U.S. CUSTOMS NOW. A couple dozen Border Patrol agents and New York State troopers are waiting for us, their arms crossed over their chests. One officer gives a little wave as we walk by; Mohawks shake their flags in response. As we stream through the customs stations, giddiness sweeps through the crowd.

First of all, it is a spectacular morning. Fleece is necessary all but six weeks a year here, if not a full-length, Michelin Man–style puffy coat. But the sun burns bright this May morning, crystallizing the mountains in the blue distance and, closer in, the gray plumes of ALCOA East. Second: it is Victoria Day, a public holiday celebrating the birth not only of Queen Victoria but of Canadian sovereignty as well. Of all the calendar days to reaffirm Mohawk autonomy, this one seems particularly auspicious.

So spirits are high as we march past the Duty Free Americas shop touting "2 for $28 Stars and Stripes Vodka." Here comes the first bridge, a classic suspension number dotted with cables and solemn-looking piers. That's the extent of my architecture observational ability, but I am marching among the world's experts. As the legend goes, when the Dominion Bridge Company started building a cantilever railroad bridge across the St. Lawrence River in 1886, supervisors had to contend with swarms of curious Mohawks. Years later, an official remarked in a letter to *New Yorker* writer Joseph Mitchell, "These Indians were as agile as goats. They would walk a narrow beam high up in the air with nothing below them but the river, which is rough there and ugly to look down on, and it wouldn't mean any more to them than walking on the solid ground . . . and it turned out that putting riveting tools in their hands was like putting ham with eggs."

Disaster struck in 1907, when an unfinished span of the Quebec Bridge collapsed and killed ninety-six workers, a third of them Mohawk. Yet they've pursued the trade for much of the past century, crisscrossing the nation to erect such iconic ironworks as the World Trade Center and the San Francisco Bay Bridge. Ironwork has even been deemed a modern form of hunting in that it requires a Mohawk to leave his family for weeks at a time for a job demanding nerve and skill, then return home as a hero laden with paychecks and presents.

But for every bridge Mohawks have helped build, they seem to have closed another in protest. The most notorious instance was the 1990 "Oka crisis" over the proposed expansion of a golf course onto ancestral turf that prompted Kahnawake Mohawks to barricade the Mercier Bridge connecting their nation with southern Montreal for a month, enraging 70,000 would-be-commuters a day. A concurrent armed standoff lasted even longer than the Sioux's famed 1973 standoff at Wounded Knee.

Today's plan is to block traffic across the Three Nations Crossing bridge for several hours, right at the start of the holiday weekend—and not just because they want to inconvenience a few Canadians (though some undoubtedly do). No: to a Mohawk, a bridge closing is a historical act. It is a political act. And it is a symbolic act. It is a wordless way of saying *Hey. We built this bridge connecting your nation to ours to theirs, over land and water that our ancestors have always roamed. We can shut it whenever we like.*

WE ARE DESCENDING ONTO Cornwall Island now. A couple hundred Mohawks await us there, also clad in ribbon shirts and waving Haudenosaunee flags. Some hand out bottles of water; others offer apples and oranges. Everyone mills about as the chiefs discuss the next move.

When Mohawks refer to "the situation" today, they mean this spot right here, where Canada used to operate its border post. Until 2009, Mohawks had their own lane and simply had to flash their tribal cards before driving wherever they pleased, either to a destination on their island or continuing on to the next international bridge and nation. Granted, they were subject to periodic searches. Granted, they occasionally fielded questions they considered insulting, like "Where are you from?" Granted, a few Mohawks felt so mistreated by the CBSA, they filed complaints that launched human rights tribunals. But for the majority of Indians, border crossing was hassle-free until May 1, 2009, when Canada announced that its Border Service officers would be permitted to carry 9mm Beretta pistols there starting the first of June.

Even among Akwesasne's "touchy" subjects—gambling, the tobacco trade, drug and human trafficking—firearms are volatile. Guns first became an issue here in 1989, when a university shooting in Montreal left fifteen dead[1] and prompted Parliament to pass sweeping gun control laws.[2] A black market for weaponry soon flourished. The Ontario Provincial Police estimate that 60 percent of the guns used in local crimes are smuggled across the U.S. border, "often" through Akwesasne, with price markups of 2,000 percent or more.

Most Mohawks I've met hold libertarian views about firearms and keep their homestead stocked with mini-arsenals, but hardly anyone wanted Canadian border agents wielding arms on their island. Not only was this considered an affront to Mohawk sovereignty, but residential neighborhoods were just a few hundred feet away from the checkpoint as well, along with a bus stop and recreational fields. Soon after the CBSA announcement, Mohawks descended upon the facility in protest. Some brought drums and started pounding. Others quoted treaties signed centuries before. Many camped out, and—in the morning—supporters brought them corn mush. Demonstrators built a wooden shelter across from the checkpoint for round-the-clock occupation and christened it the "People's Fire."

Tension mounted as June 1 drew near. By the eve of May 31, several hundred Mohawks had gathered, some wearing bandannas around their faces, Zapatista-style. They lit six bonfires, one for each nation of the Haudenosaunee Confederacy, and waited for the midnight showdown. Ten minutes to twelve, however, the Canadian agents abandoned post. The demonstrators rejoiced. Strike one up for sovereignty! They raised purple Haudenosaunee flags where crimson maples once waved, and cheered.

In the six weeks that followed, the bridges were mostly blocked—only by Cornwall City and New York State Police rather than by Mohawks. Considering those bridges average 2.3 million passenger transits a year, this was no small inconvenience, particularly for the islanders. Community leaders swung into action. One was Brian David, a subchief of the Mohawk Council of Akwesasne, whom I met for lunch one afternoon.

1. The twenty-five-year-old killer burst into a classroom full of engineering students at École Polytechnique de Montréal, ordered the men to leave, and shouted, "You're all a bunch of feminists, and I hate feminists!" before killing as many women as he could (and ultimately himself). Canada has since marked December 6 as the National Day of Remembrance and Action on Violence against Women.
2. That's right. It took only one mass shooting before the Canadian Parliament enacted gun control.

"I started ferrying people across the river," Chief David said, stroking his moustache at the memory. "I could carry five safely in my boat, and there were nurses to take across, doctors, people having emergencies. When my boat got too small, I got a larger one and turned into a ferry captain for six weeks. I transported 500 people a day: lacrosse teams, soccer teams, kids taking their final exams, people traveling to a funeral."

After forty-two days of negotiations, the CBSA finally reopened its checkpoint, albeit on the northern side of the bridge, in the city of Cornwall, Ontario. Mohawk triumph fizzled when they realized that, from that point forward, anyone wishing to visit the northern half of their nation from the south now must drive over both bridges, check in at the CBSA in Cornwall city, and then turn right around to recross the second bridge and return to the island—a journey that can take anywhere from twenty-five minutes to two hours, depending on traffic. Islanders, meanwhile, must check in with the CBSA every single time they leave home base.

And that's not all. Every vehicle's license plate is photographed upon exiting the United States or Canada. If, upon entering the next country, the license plate shows up out of traffic sequence on an agent's computer screen, it will serve as proof the driver made a pit stop, for something either as innocuous as a bathroom break or as scandalous as a contraband pickup. The law clearly states you must report "forthwith" to the CBSA. Failure to do so will cost you $1,000 for the first offense and $1,000 more per subsequent offense until the fourth, when your car will be impounded. If you can't hand over a credit card then and there, you'll also be charged $60 a day by the towing company until you do.[3]

Canada has impounded at least 230 cars under this policy, according to Chief David. One is a 1994 Cadillac owned by Dana Leigh and Kanietakeron Thompson. Tribal government has a standing offer to cover the first offense of any member, but that doesn't help the Thompsons, since they withdrew from the rolls long ago. The CBSA seized their Caddie three years ago, and they refuse to pay the fines out of principle.

"The queen has it now," Dana Leigh said when I asked her about it, ashing a cigarette and frowning.

---

3. Bridge crossing has become such a hassle at Akwesasne, many Mohawks with the means to do so have invested in a second car. They use one car for traveling from the island to New York and the other for running errands in Canada. The former is known as the "getaway car."

The federal bridge closure of 2009 didn't sit well with the Thompsons, especially when a friend died on the island and they wanted to attend the funeral. A YouTube video shows Kanietakeron striding up to the police barricade at U.S. Customs, scattering ashes in the shape of a serpent, taking out a beaded wampum belt, and informing the officers that they are violating divine law. If they disrupt his passage, he warns, they will be disrespecting the clan mothers, and "natural law will befall you." With a nod to his cameraman, he then turns around, sidesteps the barricade, and heads toward the bridge.

A CRITICAL MASS HAS GATHERED NOW: 400 Mohawks and a smattering of camera crews. It is time to ascend the northern bridge into mainland Canada. Someone lights a fistful of sage. Musky sweetness spices the air.

Architecture usually doesn't intimidate me, but whenever I see this bridge, dread pools in my belly. Driving over it, you can only envision a nineteenth-century insane asylum at the end. The bridge is overly tall and curves so sharply, you cannot see the car in front of you until you're about to smash right into it. Midway through, a chain-link fence rises above the railing, reinforcing the sense of imprisonment. The road, meanwhile, is riddled with potholes.

"This bridge has destroyed every car I have ever owned," Darren Bonaparte, the historian who wrote a book about Saint Kateri, says as I fall in step beside him. "But this is the fastest I've gotten over this bridge in a long time. By foot."

Mohawks have shut down this bridge a fair amount too, most famously in December 1968 when Canadian customs officials charged one $4.70 in duties on a truckload of groceries that he claimed he was bringing "for hungry Indians in Alberta." As any Mohawk will tell you, such a fee clearly violates the 1794 Treaty of Amity, Commerce, and Navigation, between His Britannic Majesty and the United States of America (commonly known as the Jay Treaty), which grants Indians the right "freely to pass and repass, by land or inland navigation," between the two countries and to "freely carry on trade and commerce with each other."

This particular Mohawk had a hidden agenda: his grocery mission was actually a ploy for a film he was narrating called *You Are on Indian Land*, produced by the National Film Board of Canada. So cameras were rolling when scores of Mohawks parked their station wagons across the slender strip of highway connecting the international bridges, obstructing traffic for five hours. Forty-seven were arrested that day, dragged away by officers through the snow.

Ahead of me, a young father is pushing a stroller up the bridge's steep incline. He proudly tells his friend that this is the second time his daughter has helped block this bridge. I quicken my pace to peek in the carriage. Bundled in blankets, she appears to be eight months old. That means her first take-over was the Idle No More flash-mob closure back in January. Temperatures dipped into the teens that day as protesters occupied the bridge for four hours. In Mohawk Country, little girls earn their activist creds early.

WE ARE APPROACHING THE CBSA station now. All three lanes contain a windowed booth staffed by an agent wearing sunglasses. The drumbeats quicken as we ford into Canada without showing any ID.

Up ahead, a lone man in uniform stands in the middle of a vacated avenue: Steve MacNaughton, the CBSA's regional director. He grins with all of his teeth as the chiefs surround him, and the rest of us follow suit. One chief lights up a long wooden pipe and starts puffing. I keep thinking he'll pass it over to MacNaughton, but no. He just stands there in his gloriously feathered and antlered kastowa, blowing smoke rings at the sky. Another chief begins to speak in a Haudenosaunee language, gesturing in a way that seems to incorporate the sun, the sky, the river, the trees, and the earth, along with every one of us. Minutes pass before a third chief begins to translate so softly that I catch only phrases:

"We have come here to remind you that you are in our land."

". . . the things we agreed to many years ago . . ."

". . . that line does not belong to us."

For a moment, it feels like witnessing a ritual steeped in history. Then somebody's cell phone rings with the opening riffs of "Bad to the Bone," and my focus disperses. No matter: the current function of the crowd seems to be that of a hype man in hip-hop, here to back up the chiefs with drumbeats.

MacNaughton accepts a missive from the chiefs outlining their concerns about "the situation" and then gallantly steps to the side. One of the chiefs turns to face the crowd. In his late fifties with a graying moustache, he is wearing a purple ribbon shirt topped by a bear claw necklace. Ever so slightly, he cocks his head. With that, we march on toward the city.

CORNWALL GETS A LOT OF GRIEF from its countrymen. *MoneySense* magazine recently ranked it the 167th best place to live in Canada—out of 190 options. Among its attractions is "Big Ben," a toxic dump that becomes a ski hill each winter. But there's also a winding riverfront with a bike trail, a teahouse that serves warm scones and clotted cream on vintage English saucers, and surprisingly good Thai food. I, for one, would visit more often if it weren't such a pain to get here.

Standing on a grassy knoll beneath a flagpole is the mayor of Cornwall, Bob Kilger. Conditioned, perhaps, by his previous stint as referee of the National Hockey League, he seems undaunted as 400 members of the Haudenosaunee Confederacy surround him. Quite a lot of media have gathered by this point, too. I must elbow a few cameramen to get near the action. Again, the chiefs orate and translate.

"We need you to know we are not going anywhere," they say. "We need to be respected in the same manner as everyone else."

Kilger listens carefully before responding, adopting the chief's use of first person plural:

"We are glad you are here."

"We are friends and neighbors."

"We hope you feel at home in our home."

The chief in the bear claw necklace turns to the crowd. With a cinematic gaze, he takes in the young mothers cradling babies, the elders wearing clan symbols, the reporters tweeting on their Androids. Then he retreats toward the bridge.

"Should we clap?" someone whispers.

No one does. When the chiefs walk away, 400 follow.

ON THE RETURN TRIP over the dreadful bridge, I remember how crossing into Mexico used to unnerve me, too, though for non-architectural reasons. As a child, I was distraught by the sight of barefoot kids my age hawking Chiclets along the bridge—especially after Tío Valentin told me about the time my great-grandmother lacked the funds to cross the bridge herself. Her husband had just been struck and killed by a runaway mining cart in Nuevo Leon, leaving her with five young sons. She packed them each a change of clothes and headed for the border, only to find the bridge toll too expensive. Late at night, she convinced a man with a canoe to paddle her family toward their new life in Texas at half the price. Certain that Chiclets would have been my fate, too, had she not been so persuasive, I would run from seller to seller, dispersing my allowance. Then I would steel myself for the radical differences between the world where the bridge deposited me and the one where I started, moments before.

Like now. Downtown Cornwall feels long ago as I fall in step with a chief wearing a kastowa of especially handsome plumage. Sienna-skinned and oval-faced, he has combed his hair into braids that dangle past his ribs. His presence is so commanding, I am unsurprised to learn he is the Tadodaho of the Haudenosaunee, elected for life to run the meetings of the Confederacy. Slung over his left arm is a beaded replica of the Two Row Wampum, which represents an agreement between Dutch explorers and Haudenosaunee chiefs dating back to 1613.

"This is the river of life," the Tadodaho explains, pointing to the yellowing quahog shells that form the belt's backdrop. Then he glides his forefinger along the two purple lines running parallel across it. "And this is your people traveling in a ship and our people traveling in a canoe. We travel together in peace and in friendship, but our paths do not cross."

Although some scholars are skeptical of this treaty, the Netherlands has fostered a special relationship with the Haudenosaunee because of it ever since. It is one of the few nations that accepts their confederacy passports rather than insisting upon U.S. or Canadian passports at the border. (In 2010, Great Britain rejected the sovereign passports of the Haudenosaunee lacrosse team, inciting the team to withdraw their participation in the world championship there, despite having invented the sport.)

Up ahead is a chief of the Onondaga Nation, Jake Edwards. The Tadodaho introduces us. Nodding at my notebook, Chief Edwards mentions that, in July, the Haudenosaunee will commemorate four centuries of peaceful coexistence by canoeing down the Hudson River from Rensselaer, New York, to Pier 96 in Manhattan. The thirteen-day journey will culminate in a march to the United Nations.

"The Two Row shows we live side by side, as long as the grass is green, as long as the waters flow downhill, as long as the sun rises in the east and sets in the west. The Europeans agreed with that. They wrote it down, but they lost it. We still have it here," Chief Edwards says, pointing to the wampum on the Tadodaho's wrist. "We will do this journey to remind them of their promise."

WE ARE BACK ON CORNWALL ISLAND NOW. Women have prepared a feast at the People's Fire, across from the abandoned checkpoint. I join the line snaking out of the building and am promptly handed a plastic baggie containing a bologna sandwich, fruit cup, granola bar, and spork. Waiting inside are cauldrons of traditional dishes like meat pie, corn bread, corn mush, and—my favorite—corn soup (cured salt pork, turnips, kidney beans, and carrots, plus corn kernels cleaned with ashes and boiled until they burst into juicy white pearls). I serve myself a steaming bowl, then sit among the families gathered around the park benches.

In January 2014, the Federal Bridge Corporation will replace the dreadful bridge with a $75 million low-level structure. Though it will significantly decrease crossing time, Mohawks will still be required to "check in" with Canada whenever visiting part of their own nation.[4] Hundreds will sign a petition requesting the station move from Cornwall city to the New York side. Even if Canada ultimately agrees to do this, Chief David says it would take at least a decade to implement. Until then, "the situation" will likely remain the Situation.

So often, the word "bridge" is deployed as a metaphor for connectivity. Politicians speak endlessly of "building bridges" between troubled communities—just as they promote "fences" as either neighborly gestures or terrorist-detractors. Why, then, in borderlands north and south, have lawmakers erected so much architecture that does the opposite?

I think back to the story that Vera, the manager of Mo' Money Pawnshop, told during our tour that day: "So many people have dreamt of that [dreadful] bridge collapsing, of the water tearing it down. Native seers came here this winter, and they said we are headed for a year of darkness because this area would be flooded. I take it with a grain of salt . . . but thoughts create reality. Maybe if enough people dream it, it will happen."

Of course it is morbid to imagine the bridge collapsing into the St. Lawrence River, hurtling cars and trucks and people into its icy current. Yet there is something deliciously anarchic about the vision as well. For if all the borderlands' walls and bridges crumbled, wouldn't the borders too?

4. Of course, non-Indian drivers must also check in with the CBSA when visiting the island (plus pay a $6.50 round-trip bridge toll). It's worth noting, however, that 70 percent of all Three Nations Crossing bridge users are from Akwesasne. At other points along the St. Lawrence River, such as the ritzy Thousand Islands region, boaters simply make a phone call to report their border-crossing activity or check in at one of the videophone stations at the docks.

19

The River

AFTER NEARLY A YEAR OF VISITING AKWESASNE ONCE OR TWICE A week, I finally find what has thus far eluded me: not a "contact" or a "source" but a friend. For reasons that will become apparent, I have changed her name and altered certain details. The following, however, are true: she's single, pushing forty, and writing a book. Given the existentially isolating nature of each of these endeavors, we instantly bond when we discover having all three in common. Though I originally reached out to her for a formal interview about other matters, we wind up gabbing about our personal lives the entire time. Admittedly, this feels unprofessional, yet, for better or worse, I am not a journalist or scholar bound to prescribed codes of conduct. I am a writer struggling to make art out of the messiness of life. Forging friendships with my "characters" is one of the many ethical minefields I negotiate.

So when "Keetah" invites me to her home a few days later, I accept with my usual cautious excitement. She lives on a rural road lined with HUD houses and trailers not far from the river. Her front door opens to blue walls and piles of laundry, with lacrosse sticks and juice pouches scattered about. A makeshift writing office has been carved into the kitchen area, complete with a printer topped by a Crock-Pot. We have just settled onto the couch when a kid-whirl swoops in, fresh off the school bus. Three are Keetah's and the rest belong to her sister Kai. The living room erupts in chaos, but they soon break for the backyard, where a sprinkler awaits. It is seventy-eight degrees. For a Tejana, this necessitates a long-sleeve shirt and a scarf in your purse. For a Mohawk child, it means stripping to your *chonies* before you melt.

"Don't forget to water the puppy!" Keetah calls after them. His name is Thunder.

With kid-shrieking as our soundtrack, I ask Keetah what sense they make of the border. "I show them a map and tell them our government was here first. But then people came from the East and they were from different countries and they decided to draw a line right through Akwesasne," she says. "I tell them, you are not U.S. citizens and you are not Canadians. You are Haudenosaunee. You don't belong to this government or that government. You belong to the earth. That's where you come from, and that's where you will go."

The front door swings open and her sister Kai walks in, eyes affixed to cell phone. A text session with a new beau is under way. She pays us no mind as we discuss the bridge situation—until Keetah mentions its impact on contraband.

"The bad thing about smuggling is it made our people lazy," Kai announces.

"Lazy?" I ask. Of the many adjectives smugglers bring to my mind— reckless, opportunistic, ethically compromised, desperate—lazy isn't among them.

But Keetah concurs. "They are so used to fast money, to making thousands a week. They aren't up for doing what we do, making $400 a week at $10 an hour. People in their thirties have it rough, because for fifteen years they could make fast, easy money, and now they can't."

This was supposed to be a social visit, but there is no stifling my inner reporter. "Do you know anyone who does it?"

"My ex," Kai says, running her fingers through her hair. "We built our house with the money."

"What was his product?"

"Cigarettes and other things, but I didn't know about the other things. He left me for a woman with a riverfront property who did it too. He wasn't happy with my $400 contribution. I never went on runs. I never packed a car."

"Nuh-uh," Keetah laughs. "Our mom used to pack a car with us in it!"

The sisters crack up at the memory.

"Wait, what?" I ask. "Your *mom*?"

Oh yes. After divorcing their father, she used to stuff cartons of cigarettes beneath the back seat of their station wagon, plunk all the kids on top, and drive to Kahnawake whenever she needed extra cash. I must seem shocked because Keetah turns serious. "It is our right to trade tobacco. Those are our traditional trade routes."

Which is why, twenty years later, she and another sister started trading, too. At $36,000 a load, Keetah profited enough to finance her college education in just four months. Her sister bought a new car. "Ontario shouldn't regulate my trade with my cousins in Kahnawake. No. I am an indigenous woman and I'm taking it to another indigenous person in a First Nations community," she says, twisting the drawstring of her Old Navy hoodie.

Then came the 2009 fiasco. Of all the industries affected when Canada moved its border post from Akwesasne to its mainland, tobacco was hardest hit. Back when the checkpoint was still located between the international bridges, Mohawks simply had to transport their product across the river by boat or snowmobile, discreetly pack it into a truck waiting at an island dock, and then drive it into Canada via the northern bridge. Nowadays, however, there is no avoiding the Canada Border Services Agency. That's a big reason why Keetah quit the trade that year. Another is that her sister got caught. Although the penalty was minimal—$2,000 in fines, plus a year of house arrest—it remains on her record, which prevents her from ever working for an official tribal enterprise, including the casino. That, of course, leaves her little choice but to continue working in contraband.

"I would say there is a one-degree separation from it, for everybody on the rez," Keetah says.

"*I* never did it," Kai clarifies. "But it's what I bought groceries with."

Dripping children appear at the back door. Two options, Keetah says: Campbell's soup or bologna sandwiches. They opt for the latter, which Keetah cuts into triangles. As they race back out to the sprinklers, the front door swings open again. This time it's an old family friend—middle-aged, pockmarked, effusive—and she's on a mission.

"Gotta check in!" she sings, making a beeline for the computer.

We gather around as she logs onto a dating website. She clicks on a message that is so bold, I blush. The other ladies cheer. As Kai narrates a colorful response, Keetah walks me out to my car, as I have another meeting lined up. What a shame: I'm debating trying online dating myself, and there is clearly much to be learned here. Keetah is juggling multiple suitors as well, and she has a few pointers.

"Men always tell me, you're so strong. But I keep my heart right here." She thumps her fist against her chest. "I keep it for myself."

BORDERLANDS HAVE LONG BEEN (reductively) synonymous with smuggling, but it is hard to decipher the volume at Akwesasne. According to a 2013 report by the conservative think tank the MacDonald-Laurier Institute, Cornwall is the "contraband capital of Canada," with guns, cocaine, and heroin funneling north while people, ecstasy, and weed travel south. Although the report cites U.S. statistics of $1 billion worth of illegal drugs getting exported through Akwesasne/Cornwall, the authors claim to have found "little evidence of extensive smuggling" within the Mohawk nation in recent years.

Considering that neither the United States nor Canada even has a proper population count of Akwesasne (as so many Mohawks refuse to participate in census surveys), I regard such reports with skepticism, but few better resources present themselves. There is *Indian Time*, which seems to feature another bust every couple of issues (albeit a modest one, by Texas standards). And there are people's stories, which tend toward the outrageous. My favorite comes the morning I chat up the man whom St. Lawrence University dispatched to the Victorian to wage war on its centipedes. As he squirts poison in a corner, he says he can hardly wait to go fishing this weekend.

"Isn't that kind of risky?" I ask, thinking about PCB contamination.

"Oh yeah," he says, "I seen a lot of things."

Once, he was having lunch at a dock when a thirty-foot boat pulled up, manned by "a big guy built like a Viking in a Speedo" and his girlfriend, wearing a bikini. She stepped off the boat, walked over to a van idling by, opened its door, and crouched on the ground.

"I thought to myself, she's going to pee, but she pulled a plastic bag out instead."

"A bag?"

"Yeah, yeah, she pulled it right out of her," he says, shaking his head in disgust. She handed it through the van's window and got a thick envelope in return. Then she climbed aboard the boat and the couple sped off to Canada.

Granted, this reeks of urban legend. No matter: I am inspired to spend the rest of the morning calling the region's Border Patrol stations for their take on smuggling. Though I've been granted interviews and even ride-arounds in South Texas with just a day or two of advance notice, the North Country stations balk at my requests. Weeks of e-mails and phone calls go nowhere, until a sympathetic colleague mentions that one of her neighbors is an agent. We persuade him to join me for a beer. Hearing I'm from Texas, he says he worked in Laredo for four years before moving up here.

"Oh?" I say, squeezing a lime into my Corona. "How was that?"

"A hellhole," he says, taking a swig of Canadian Pilsner. "Being white and six-foot-one, they know what you do, and they don't like you. They know you are either a Border Patrol agent or a truck driver, and I didn't look like a truck driver. They keep their distance."

I ask about the biggest difference between patrolling borders north and south.

"Here, it's not nearly as busy, but it's just as dangerous. Maybe even more dangerous, because you don't know who you are dealing with. There, it's mostly Latino. Here, it could be anyone: Irish, Russian, Sri Lankan, anyone," he says.

"Down there, we'd apprehend a hundred people a day. Here, we might not apprehend one person a month. Down there, the people you chase in the brush are just people trying to find work. Here, the people you chase are smugglers doing something illegal. Sure, down there in the brush, someone may have a pocketknife on them, but most don't even have two nickels. Out here, anything can happen. Down there, you go to work and you apprehend someone. It's just a given, and it's gratifying. Out here, you go out and you work and work and work, and you don't have anything to show for it."

"What about Akwesasne?" I ask.

He stares down his beer. "That's the weak point of the border. Nine times out of ten, the people we deal with come from there—either they are from there, or they are working with people there."

He doesn't care to elaborate beyond that, however.

Next, I try outfits like the New York State Department of Taxation and Finance, which has been trying to impose taxes on Akwesasne's tobacco for decades. No one will talk to me there, either. Finally, I call Brian David, the Mohawk chief who spent the summer of 2009 shuttling community members across the river after the New York State Police barricaded the bridge. Not only does he agree to a meeting, but he also invites me aboard his walleye boat one afternoon to conduct it. A retired ironworker, Chief David has a thick gray moustache, a slender ponytail, a big laugh, and the mettle to answer whatever you ask. Settling down between a fishing pole and a coil of rope, I start with how smuggling got to be so sensitive around here.

"Well, 9/11, of course," he says, steering us into the indigo.

As they searched for answers in the immediate aftermath, some local media outlets speculated that the terrorists entered the United States through Akwesasne. It took years to correct that misperception, he says. Mohawks did in fact play a crucial role that day, but not at the border. "Our steelworkers climbed right off the buildings and down into the rubble. They pulled bodies out that day, and they wore no masks for protection."

Human trafficking hit its zenith at Akwesasne in the late 1990s, when a crime ring sneaked some 3,600 Chinese across the river over a two-year period for an estimated $170 million. The St. Regis Mohawk Tribal Police assisted the Immigration and Naturalization Service and the Royal Canadian Mounted Police with the arrests. News reports indicate that the volume lowered from there, until the U.S. State Department announced that Akwesasne was no longer a major point of entry in 2012. Chief David concurs with this. "There was an incident here four or five years ago where a boat overturned and two [undocumented] people drowned. They didn't have life jackets, and it was cold. That is where our people put their foot down. There is a hierarchy of taboos here, and people who smuggle people are on top."

Drug smugglers are several rungs lower, since a number of community members empathize with—and even respect—their reasons for doing it. What with the destruction of traditional economies like hunting, fishing, trapping, and farming and the waning of high steel,[1] there simply aren't many employment options for Mohawks in their nation. The better jobs in tribal government usually require either a college degree or the right connection (and often both). Many young people just have the casino, gas stations, or smoke shops to choose from.

"People are into smuggling because they don't have jobs," Chief David says. "If they have survived, it is because they have good management skills. They are constantly making master plans and contingency plans that they must change at a moment's notice. It would be a waste to condemn that portion of the population. You can say they are bad, or you can say they are resourceful. Their job is risky and very high stress. I don't know if I could do it."

Whether tobacco traders rate a rung on the hierarchy of taboo is debatable. Few Mohawks consider the practice illegal, but it does have critics. Doug George-Kanentiio, the former editor of *Akwesasne Notes* who moved away from the nation after the casino war, speaks and writes eloquently about the detriment of basing a community's economic well-being not just on a single product but on "one that kills." He has also noted that working conditions at Native tobacco factories tend to be poor, with minimal health and safety precautions and no labor protections.[2] Yet because they refuse to

---

1. A venerated tradition for more than a century, ironwork has greatly declined among Mohawks in recent years. In addition to their reticence to put so much of their paychecks toward increasingly exorbitant motel or apartment fees in New York City, where high steel thrives, there is stiff competition for the limited slots at the apprentice training schools where workers learn their trade. Hopeful applicants must pass entrance exams that favor formal education over vocational training, giving graduates an advantage over legacies. The bulk of the last remaining Mohawk ironworkers—believed to number only one hundred or so—are now in their fifties.

2. Though I never visited a tobacco factory myself, I did meet a (non-Native) woman who spent six years rolling cigarettes at Akwesasne. She said she was paid $9 per case, or about $54 an hour for handling 60,000 cigarettes. Every week, she received a little yellow envelope filled with upward of $2,000 in cash. "It was great," she enthused. "You could

acknowledge the borderline, the majority of Mohawks I've asked view this form of trading as a perfectly legitimate business.

"It has been done for hundreds of years. If we are not trading sugar, we are trading gasoline. These days the product is cigarettes," Chief David says. "And the bulk of the tobacco manufactured here is sold to the domestic market. Why do they go after the traffickers who are just trying to make a living and feed their families? Why not go after the biker gangs in Ottawa, or the Oriental gangs in Toronto?"

He has cut the engine by this point. As we drift about, our conversation does too. This is the swath of river where he spends his happiest moments, he says, fishing for muskie, walleye, and the occasional sturgeon. He likes to go late at night when the only light is the moon. That's when the water is fast, he says, when it has its own spirit. When there is an uncertainty about what is in front of you.

"But isn't fishing risky?" I ask, thinking again of PCBs.

"I have caught fish that have partial gills," he says. "I have caught fish that are deformed. When I do, I take them to be inspected."

"But you eat the ones that seem okay?"

He nods. "That is a risk I am willing to take now. There was a twenty-year period where I didn't eat it, but now, I could eat fish every day and by the time it catches up to me, I'll already be gone. But I would not feed it to my grandchildren."

A U.S. Coast Guard boat materializes in the distance. Chief David scoots over to the engine and fires it up.

"It's okay, I've got my passport," I shout above the roar.

"I don't," he laughs. "I don't have my boater permit either."

We zip across the glassy water. "We're going to check out the Canadian fish now!" he calls out.

Once we've crossed the aqua-border, he cuts the engine again. We are floating in blue: water and sky and faraway mountain.

"You are at a place that is not like any other in the world. New York, Quebec, and Ontario all meet here. I want to put a barge right here and hold a Mohawk court in it," he says, folding his arms across his chest with a grin. "Then we could say, 'What jurisdiction are you in now?'"

---

smoke all day if you wanted to, and talk. There was always the threat of getting raided, but we never did. Sometimes the factory would close down for a while, or it would keep weird hours, but nobody cared because the pay was so good, it would tide you over."

KEETAH'S FRIEND IS THROWING a pool party, and I can tag along if I want. "It will be interesting," she promises.

Everything is interesting to me, so I forget this remark until I enter her friend's two-story colonial and behold its sumptuous leather furniture, its gargantuan flat-screen TVs, its array of electronic equipment, and the region's rarest luxury: central air-conditioning. Interesting, indeed. Knowing no one besides Keetah—who promptly disappears—I try to make myself useful by cutting up the watermelons and pineapples atop the granite counter and arranging them in a bowl. By the time I'm done, the house has emptied. The kids have jumped in the pool, which is decked with a spiral slide and crammed with inflatable toys. I watch them splash about, then wander off in search of the adults. Adjacent to the backyard is a warehouse. I peek through its door and ogle at its contents. A sports car that looks like it could levitate. An impossibly ornate Harley Davidson. A pair of snowmobiles and a pair of Jet Skis. Slot machines. An ATV and a speedboat. A bar with a crowded liquor cabinet, a mountain of Budweiser beer, and a sound system that could blast us clear to Cornwall.

Keetah is sitting with the other moms at a picnic table nearby. As I slip in beside her, she laughs at my expression. "You should talk to him," she says, nodding in the direction of her friend's husband, who is flipping burgers at the six-burner gas grill. A stripe of hair, from his forehead to his nape, ends in a long, thin braid. He is covered in tattoos.

Swilling a Bud for courage, I walk over. He doesn't look up. I stutter about the weather. He grunts in return. I marvel about the party. He plops a raw patty on the grill. Grasping at topics, I notice a flag hanging behind the bar—the one with the Indian wearing a single-feathered headdress inside a sun.

"So! What's the story behind that flag?" I ask. "Louis Hall designed it, right?"

He squints at it. "The yellow? That's the sun. And the red, that's . . . Well. You know."

I glance back at Keetah. She nods encouragingly. I've told her how embarrassing it's been, failing to find a compelling drug runner in Texas. Here she is, nice enough to bring me to one's pool party. The least I can do is ask him a damn question.

"So! That's quite a collection you've got in there, huh? I mean, that Harley, wow. How'd you get it?"

He (finally) looks at me. Takes in my (over-) eagerness, my (blatant) whiteness, my (total) outsiderness. Then he stabs a burger with a grilling fork and flips it over. It sizzles, along with my nerve.

"Great talking with you!" I chirp, then hurry back to the picnic table. If Charles Bowden[3] were here, he'd be barbecuing with the man—drinking, smoking, telling dirty jokes, maybe even going for a ride on the Harley. Because Bowden knew that the best stories aren't obtained by asking questions but by building trust. And trust takes time. Lots of time. Yet I'll be moving cross-country in two weeks—meaning that, once again, the dealer's point of view will escape me. Feeling inept, I eat a plate of potato salad and wash it down with Bud, consoling myself with the notion that, if it was ethically compromising to write about people's penchant for smuggling down in South Texas, it is probably even worse reporting about the alternative economies here at Akwesasne.

An hour later, though, I am sunning by the pool when the dealer's wife sits beside me. Maybe thirty years old, she has Cleopatra eyes and thick, glossy hair. I initiate conversation by inquiring about her kids, mention I'm a writer, and, as casually as possible, ask: "So . . . what do you do?"

A family business, you could say. She seals high-grade marijuana into bricks, and he transports them across the river. Often, the whole family joins him for the ride, to ward off suspicion. Sometimes even his mother tags along. Of course she knows what he does: she got him into the business in the first place, when he was still in high school. Their family has been shuttling contraband for four generations: alcohol back in the day, and now marijuana and cigarettes. They avoid hard stuff like coke and pills, she says, because the penalties are much stiffer.

Remembering Walter White's dilemma on *Breaking Bad*, I ask where she keeps the money. "Do you have an offshore bank, or do you launder it somewhere?"

"Yeah, I launder it. In the laundry basket!" She laughs and sips her beer.

I laugh too, because I assume she's joking. But no. Lots of dealers hide their money in their laundry, Keetah later tells me, and when word spreads of a raid, they throw it down the chute. Either that, or they bury it in their backyard.

---

3. Author of necessary reads like *Down by the River*, Charles Bowden is one of the greatest border-chroniclers the United States has ever produced: unrelenting, compassionate, poetic, yet deeply haunted. One of his last stories for *Harper's* detailed his friendship with a *sicario* who used to boil people alive in a kettle while extracting information for a Juarez cartel. Despite enraging murderous men throughout his long career, Bowden managed to die in his sleep in August 2014, at age sixty-nine. For a memorable last interview, read Scott Carrier's "Charles Bowden's Fury" in *High Country News*.

I ask how many other people are in the business. She turns around in her chair and starts pointing at nearby houses. "This one does coke. That one does weed."

"So . . . it's kind of, like, a neighborhood business?"

She gives me a sharp look. "It's a shitty business. One day you're loaded, the next day you got nothing. Or you're making money but losing your freedom because you get so into it."

She ticks off the pitfalls of the profession: the backstabbing, the lying, the family forever dropping by to "borrow" $35,000. It has only worsened since the bridge situation. Before 2009, she and her husband owned seven trucks, two cars, and a van. Now, money has gotten so tight, they are trying to sell off their warehouse collection. Problem is, the only people making offers are doing so with contraband instead of cash.

"How do you know who to trust?"

"You don't. And it sucks."

At that, her youngest son runs up, swinging a pair of goggles. He's a shrunken replica of his father, down to the hairstyle. She gently tightens his goggles so they fit his small face. As he shuffles off, I ask what she'd do if he ever expressed interest in the business.

"He already did. He asks my mom, he says, 'How come you don't have a car?' and he says, 'I'm going to have a car and a truck.' She says, 'Are you going to work?' and he says yeah, and she says, 'What are you going to do?' and he says 'Cigarettes!'"

She guffaws. "He was like four years old when his father would have him push cigarette cases out of the truck. In his mind, he was like, 'I'm helping my parents work.' But I says to my husband, you need to stop letting him watch. It's not okay. He should have a job. *We* should have a job."

She stares off into the pool, where her daughter is turning handstands in the shallow end and her sons are chasing each other with water guns. "I want my kids to go to school, to college, to get out of this area."

"Do you think you'll ever quit?"

"I want out now. It's getting too hard. My sister's boyfriend just got caught. It's not worth it anymore."

Her hope, she says, is to become a nurse someday, which admittedly sounds far-fetched—until I remember what Chief David said. She can obviously handle high-stakes situations with a level head. Monitoring all that money has undoubtedly honed her math. Confronting so much danger on a regular basis must have rendered her fearless. Who knows what could happen if she channeled those skills elsewhere?

Keetah strolls over. It's time to drop off her girls at their dad's house. Before we part, I reiterate the likelihood of my writing about this some day and ask her friend how I should refer to her. She spells out her Mohawk name for me.

"No, no, I should change it, right? You know . . . to protect you?"

She thinks a second. "All right. Call me Denise."

"Denise?" I ask. Given the option, people usually pick something more daring.

"Yeah, Denise," she says, then laughs. "I hate that bitch!"

THAT EVENING AT KEETAH'S, I hound her with so many follow-up questions about "Denise," she finally suggests interviewing someone else.

"But I don't know anyone," I whine.

Whipping out her iPhone, she thumbs through her contacts. "Pot or coke?" she asks, and once we've settled that: "Does he have to be dealing still, or is probation okay?"

A mad texting session later, the first one arrives, worrisomely skinny and clutching a bottle of Minute Maid apple juice. He is wearing a Nike shirt, shorts that extend to his knees, and multiple tattoos and piercings. His nose is broken and his veins are prominent. He flounces on the couch beside me.

"Well, I'm kind of retired now," he says when I ask about the business. "The feds put an end to me pretty quick. I'm kicked out of Canada for life."

Currently twenty-seven years old, he started smoking weed at fourteen. He liked it so much, he eventually dropped out of school, got a hold of some seeds, and began growing with a friend. ("Where did you learn how?" "That shit they teach you from first to sixth grade—the bean plant and all that shit.") Their first goal was 300 plants, which they turned into a $6,000 profit in three months. Then they bought five pounds of product and profited even more, so they upgraded to ten pounds next. Within a few years, people were bringing sixty pounds of pot to his house at once.

"Before I was raided, I shit you not, I would wake up at 9 or 10 A.M., smoke a joint, and just sit there. I never left the house. I would just smoke all day and make $1,000 by 1 P.M.," he says.

That business model imploded the same way his front door exploded: before dawn one morning, with a BOOM.

"I had my two-year-old daughter and my girlfriend with me, and I was like, what the fuck? I looked out the bedroom window, and there was tribal police and ICE. They came off the river, they came from the woods, they came in two helicopters. They shut the whole fucking road down. They came after me like I'm some terrorist, and I'm still in my boxer shorts," he says, taking a swig from an apple juice bottle that smells like anything but.

The police confiscated ten pounds of Kush, fifty pounds of pot, and thirteen guns that day: "a AK-47, a AR-15, a couple older guns like World War II, and then I had my boomstick—it spits out six-foot fire at night, fucking amazing!—an old-school Mauser like Nazi Germany, a 30 aught 6, and a 90-millimeter." He spent a week in jail before getting released on a $40,000 bond and is currently serving probation while awaiting his appeals. That doesn't sound so bad to me, but he calls it "hell on wheels" since everything he worked for is gone: his cars, his house, his savings, his guns. He has managed to secure a minimum wage job but has only $40 left after paying his bills—and another baby is on the way.

"If I could repeat, I probably would have stayed the fuck in school. I could be in college now. I could still be smoking pot. I wanted to go to the military, but my parents talked me out of it. Who knows where I'd be now? I could be dead, but that could have been good, too," he says. With that, he caps his bottle of faux-juice and bids us ladies good night.

The second dealer pulls up on a motorcycle a few hours later. With his stout build and cinnamon skin, he could pass for one of my *primos*. When I tell him so, he laughs and says maybe that's why he hung out with all the "Spanish guys" in prison. His childhood dream was to be a police officer, but then he stole a handgun from a friend's father and pulled it on someone, which landed him in a home for wayward youth. His career plan ruined, he started working in contraband when his first child came along at age seventeen. Cigarettes brought him upward of $1,500 a night, but he wound up snorting most of the profit.

"Coke gives you a sense you can't be touched, like you're invisible out there on the river. You do it and you think they can't see you," he explains.

Snowmobiles are his preferred method of transportation, he says, as police don't have many in stock and seem reticent to do high-speed chases with the few they've got. "It's like an interstate out there, in the winter," he says of the river. It is stressful, though, as you never know when the ice will break. He invested $600 in a "survival suit" to hold his neck above water and maintain his body temperature for twenty minutes in case of falling through, but he's never needed it. He has seen a lot of accidents, though, enough to try to sober up. In the late nineties, he made a career change to ironwork, which he calls "an honor job." His first site was thirty stories of structural steel. The thought of scaling it scared him until his coworkers assured him, "You'll adjust. It's in your blood." He lasted four years there, he says. Then his brother started moving marijuana across the river. In 2003, he decided to help out.

"The biker gangs would hire us. It's our corridor, so they have to go through us. I was really sketched out at first, but they were respectable gentlemen. Hard-working men, just like me. They sat us down and said we would make a lot of money," he says.

They were right. He earned $50 for every pound he shuttled across the river for them and moved at least fifty pounds at once. Eventually he made enough connections with suppliers to work for himself. "There was the Mafia—the Italians, the Chinese, and the Russians. They dressed real high-class. You could tell they were wealthy. They drove Maseratis. The Russians would throw big parties in a bar or a strip joint. We'd drink all night. They gained our trust, and we gained theirs."

At his peak, he was profiting anywhere from $25,000 to $50,000 a week, which he stuffed into PVC pipes in his backyard. Addiction inserted its tenterhooks, though—Vicodin and Demerol—and he got caught for possession and was imprisoned for a year. He says he's "been out" for two years now but constantly fields invitations to return. Just last week, some dealers asked him to be their escort, which would have entailed driving twenty minutes ahead of their load to warn them of any checkpoints. Not a bad way to earn $2,500, he says, "but I'd rather have the honor of earning my paycheck. Being an escort, it's too easy. I get scared of going back into my addiction. I have thrown partying out of my life for seven months now. I look toward my daughters now."

These stories are entertaining, of course—especially considering how long I've been raring to hear one. Yet, by night's end, I can't help feeling the same way I did in the summer of 1994, when I moved to Seattle to write about its music scene. Though psyched to interview so many "rock stars," I kept thinking, "That's it?" after each one ended. Their narratives were just so predictable. Ditto with dealers, it seems. For all the films and news stories and policy reports they generate at either border, they turn out to be the least interesting people I have met there. Far more illuminating are those who resist the obvious path and chart one of their own.

THE LAST OF THE NIGHT'S VISITORS is the old family friend. Someone dropped her off a while ago to check the latest on her dating website. Now she needs a ride home. (She has a van but says she "murdered" it after forgetting to change its oil.) Keetah has mentioned that, for many years, this woman battled a crack addiction that so consumed her, she lost custody of her kids. She has since cleaned up considerably, gotten a job at a truck stop, and rented a new apartment that she cannot wait to show us. Walking in, we are dazzled by the sight of hundreds of rhinestones glued to every surface and inspirational quotations stenciled to every wall. The living room is Asian-themed, the guest room is zebra-patterned, and the master bedroom is modeled after Paris, complete with an Eiffel Tower comforter and pillows. Every time I admire something, she says, "I got it at the Dollar Store!" and beams.

Having morally supported her friend throughout her ordeal, Keetah is thrilled by this marker of progress—so much so that she pretends to faint from happiness atop the bed. Laughing uproariously, her friend flings herself up beside her. This sends the bed's wooden footboard crashing to the ground with such force, the friend is bounced off the mattress and lands smack on top of the splintered wood. Keetah and I stare down at her in horror. Is she paralyzed? Dead? What?!

The woman opens her mouth as if to wail, but instead emits the single greatest peal of laughter I have ever heard. Keetah and I join in—so hard, we fall on the ground, too. The more we laugh, the funnier it becomes, until the three of us are positively howling. Because no matter how hard you try in life, shit still falls apart—but if you can find the humor in that, you will somehow be all right. And so we laugh and we laugh and we laugh until we cry, and then we look at each other and start laughing all over again.

20

The Words That Come Before All Else

THE DOWNSIDE TO ITINERANCY? THE TENDENCY TO FORM YOUR fiercest friendships right when the adventure draws to a close. Always knowing that the farewell is imminent makes you wince a bit when you meet good people—or, in the case of Betsy, wince a lot. She and her husband, Tom, are fixtures among the North Country's back-to-the-land community dedicated to blasting their carbon footprints into pixie dust. They live on a solar-paneled, wood-heated estate they built amidst maples and pines, grow most of their own food, chill leftovers in a bathtub sunken beneath their kitchen, and compost their outhouse with peat moss. They think nothing of biking thirty miles for coffee or camping when it's forty below zero.

It's been ages since I have called up a girlfriend an hour before meeting to ask what she's wearing, but I quickly reestablish that habit with Betsy. Only, with her, it's not fashion that's at stake but survival. Fleece-lined pants or corduroys over long underwear? Are snow boots sufficient, or should I bring Yaktrax, too? Can I borrow your deerskin mittens again? For Betsy is the kind of woman who will teach you how to snowshoe one day and cross-country ski the next. How to fell a dying tree, split its wood with a maul and a wedge, pyramid it into a fireplace, and then fan the flames with its bark. We once spent an entire afternoon boring holes into maple trees with an auger, inserting taps, and rejoicing at the sweet water trickling into our awaiting tin buckets with a melodic ping-ping. The buckets then got emptied into a massive sugar pan hovering over some bricks stacked above a fire burning in the snow. After days of boiling and stirring, forty cups of hard-won tree-water yielded but a single cup of syrup—a ratio that seems like it can't possibly be worth it until you down a shot while it's still hot. It dizzies you, like candied brandy.

After the ice-sludge of spring dry-crumbles into summer, Betsy announces our next adventure: biking across Quebec. That sounds ambitious, but it's seventy degrees outside, so why not? We set off into the hallucinatory green. Seventy miles into the auto part of our journey, we reach the border town of Churubusco, New York. Betsy pulls into Dick's, a general store specializing in the four Gs: gas, groceries, guns, and guitars. Browsing its aisles, I wonder if this is what distinguishes a U.S. borderland: the ability to buy an Uzi off one shelf and a banjo off another, with some nice Amish baskets in between.

I'd been assuming we'd wait until Canada to start biking, but after parking in the empty lot of the Immaculate Heart of Mary, Betsy reaches for her helmet.

"Wait. We're going to *bike* across the border?" I ask.

Every land-crossing I have made into or out of the United States has been a traffic-clogged, migraine-inducing mess—particularly along the northern border. Once, while I was taking a Greyhound from Seattle to Vancouver, an agent picked me out of the queue, confiscated my box of tampons, and pulled each one apart as he interrogated certain stamps in my passport. Cycling up to a checkpoint seems absurdly suspicious, but Betsy is already smoothing out the map she ripped from her atlas. Tall, lean, and dirty-blonde, she alights her bike the European way by standing on one side and pushing off with her inner foot while the external works the pedal. I mount mine like a horse. There are no cars in sight, so we ride side-by-side. New York's northernmost roads are hedged with abandoned farmhouses, dilapidated barns, and occupied double-wides and trailers. The few standing houses are wrapped in shredded insulation, their overgrown yards dotted with oil drums.

"We are Mexico out here, compared to Canada," Betsy says. "We are the poor, impoverished community. We are the bedraggled farmers."

These are certainly some of the toughest living conditions I have seen in the rural United States. They might even be harsher than the colonias of South Texas, given the brutality of winter up here. We pass by campers with holes in their doors. Mobile homes with drooping ceilings. Rotting cars and rusting ATVs. Copious amounts of hoarding. Nothing has seen a lick of paint in a quarter century, but every other pole bears a NO TRESPASSING sign in prime condition.

Eventually, we reach a placard reading CANADA UNITED STATES BOUNDARY 1,000 FEET. Betsy says that U.S. border posts used to be housed in "rinky-dink shacks" out here but got upgraded to multimillion-dollar complexes after 9/11. Sure enough, the checkpoint ahead seems fortified for battle. One vehicle is before us and none are behind us. With barely a glance, the Border Patrol agent waves us through. A minute's ride away, Canada's post consists of a mobile home with an awning. Beneath it stands a smiling Canada Border Services agent wearing a bulletproof vest lined with ballpoint pens. After shuffling through our passports, he wishes us a pleasant stay in a lilting French accent.

Cycling forth into Quebec, I experience the same shock of inequality I always do when crossing the bridge from the United States into Mexico—only in reverse. In place of signs warning VIOLATORS WILL BE PROSECUTED, there are now fleurs-de-lis. People mill about, calling out, "Bonjour, hello!" as we ride past. Their houses are hewn of stone. Their yards are immaculately landscaped. Their general stores specialize in cheese. We pass by apple orchards and strawberry fields. Dairy farms and maple sugar groves. Blueberries growing along meandering brooks. Because it has no interior provinces, some scholars argue that Canada is wholly borderland, with the 49th parallel[1] serving as its identity shield. Yet if it's true that "borderlands exist when shared characteristics within the region set it apart from the country that contains it," as Lauren McKinsey and Victor Konrad have posited, the term doesn't seem very applicable to this juncture between New York and Quebec. The only obvious influences cast in either direction are the menus offering poutine.[2]

A couple of hours into our tour, we notice a billboard for a vineyard and ride its seductive path to a country home with a bar out back. The young attendant runs for her mother, who speaks only French and so runs for her son. His English is impeccable, but he keeps apologizing for it as he pours us generous tastings of four white wines and a late-harvest ice wine. He urges us to enjoy their property afterward, and so, in a tipsy glow, we eat cheese sandwiches from the porch swing beneath the shade tree overlooking the vineyard. A herd of goats amble by, the kids jumping over the lawn chairs.

1. Boundary disputes wrought by the War of 1812 established the 49th parallel as the official borderline between British North America and the United States in 1818. Although portions of present-day Canada are technically south of the 49th parallel and bits of Alaska north of it, "the 49th parallel" has since become not only a catchall phrase for the entire 5,525-mile border but a cultural buffer/mindset/metaphor as well.
2. One of Quebec's major culinary exports, poutine is a heap of french fries and cheese curds drenched in gravy. Quebecois seem genetically immune to its caloric impact, but I can attest that the rest of us are not.

Eventually we make our way back toward the signs reading FRONTIERE U.S.A. This next border-crossing point caused a mild uproar in 2011 when the United States decided to give its post a $6.8 million renovation, even though Canada closed its sister facility that same year, citing the lack of traffic. It is now one of an increasing number of stations along the northern border where you can only exit Canada but not re-enter. As we approach on our bicycles, two U.S. Border Patrol agents step out of the station. One is thin and tattooed; the other appears to be in training. Flipping through my passport, the first agent starts the litany: Why did I fly all the way to Singapore for two days? What was I doing for a month in Mozambique, and why do I visit Mexico so often? He hands my passport over to the second agent, who asks the hardest question: Where do I live? As I fumble an answer—"Uh, here, but only for another week, and then I move to North Carolina, but originally I'm from Texas"—they step back into their station and click around on the computer. Time stretches in that special you-know-you're-innocent-but-could-totally-be-perceived-otherwise kind of way before they relinquish my passport and wave us through. Total crossing time: eight minutes. Total traffic pileup: one.

Back in Betsy's Subaru, we decide to take Route 37 toward Canton. As we approach Akwesasne, Betsy remembers hearing about a bar in the area that straddles the international borderline. If so, it wouldn't be the only such establishment: Akwesasne's media outlets—the radio station CKON and *Indian Time*—inhabit a building that is located in all three nations at once.[3] Near the Fort Covington, New York / Dundee, Quebec, crossing, we park and stride up to the nearest agent to ask if he's heard of the bar. A thickset man with a shaved head, he has a jovial demeanor.

"You mean, the Halfway House?" he asks. "When I was a kid, I used to go drink there. They had a line right down the middle of the bar, and if you were eighteen, you could drink if you stayed on the Canadian side. Wild place. But it closed down years ago."

3. The reasons behind this placement are both financial (better access to "local" advertisers and funders) and philosophical in nature. Deb Cook, who has worked for *Indian Time* since its inception in the early eighties, told me, "We did that on purpose to show we are our own nation and it doesn't matter if the building is in one place or the other. We can't be dictated by an outside government." She jokingly conceded, however, that they needed to cut out a path for their non-Mohawk editor so that she could remain in New York all day while she worked and not worry about checking in at the border post whenever she needed to use their photocopier (located across the hall in Quebec).

He points out its former locale. We walk along the river toward the abandoned three-story building adjacent to the U.S. border post. The words CANADA US are engraved along the concrete siding, with WAS BUILT IN 1820 scrawled beneath it in black spray paint. As I pull out my camera, a mustachioed man steps off the last porch in the United States and hurries over. At first I think he's addressing me in French, but no: he's swallowing every other syllable. Naked but for his denim shorts, he has red eyes, chipped teeth, and a second-trimester beer gut.

"The Canadian Customs, they are bad news," he slurs. "They took me down. They slammed me on the floor. They took my car. My left side's all numb. I can't even hold my arms behind my back anymore. Why did they do this to me? I told them I live right next door. Why don't they let me go home?"

While he rages on about the injustice of being arrested for driving while obliterated, I make photos of the otherwise tranquil neighborhood bisected by borderlines. After a time, two young men pull up in an Explorer, ready to cross.

"Are you Mohawk?" the man shouts at the passenger, then hurries over to his window. "You need to watch out for Customs. They will fuck you up. You tell everybody that. We been here one hundred years."

Trying my best to channel Audre Lorde—*there is no hierarchy of oppression, there is no hierarchy of oppression, there is no hierarchy . . .*—I await the Mohawks' response. A complete verbal dismantling would be justified in my book, but they choose to refrain, allowing the man to finish his tirade before continuing on their way. Betsy and I follow suit. As we cut through Akwesasne en route to Canton, she asks my opinion about *Frozen River*. My (lengthy) assessment revolves around the fact that every Mohawk I've asked dismisses the film outright.

"Because of the smuggling?"

"That, and it went too far in its depiction of strife. Most Mohawks are doing much better than the movie implied. Like their casino," I say, tapping the window as we drive by it. "The one in the movie is a dump, but look how chichi it is."

I could go on, but it occurs to me that Betsy's family has lived in the North Country for several generations, too. What did she think of the film's representation of *her* neighbors, as portrayed by the actor Melissa Leo?

"It didn't go far enough," she says. "The double-wides were too nice. They didn't show all the add-ons, or the ceilings caving in, or the junk piled in the yards. It made us seem like we are in better shape than is true."

We drive on in silence past HUD houses that are indeed nicer than most of the other U.S. residences we have seen today. Several Mohawks I've met this year have described the tension they feel from nearby white working-class communities. One woman said that when she shows her tax-exempt card in cities like Syracuse, all of the businesses honor it, but in neighboring Massena, "they just wrinkle their nose, so I just leave my groceries or whatever I was going to buy right there on the counter." This especially bothered her considering that 25 percent of the casino's profits funnel straight into the coffers of the state, which evenly splits the money between the adjacent counties of St. Lawrence and Franklin (two of the state's poorest).

I ask Betsy what she learned about the Mohawks as a child growing up in the area.

She pauses to reflect. "I think I thought that Indians only lived out west."

She doesn't remember any of her teachers mentioning Akwesasne—and if they did, they probably called it "Hogansburg," which is the name of a nearby hamlet. Neither Betsy nor her sons ever took a field trip there in school or benefited from any Mohawk speakers visiting their classrooms. Although her father later taught English at Akwesasne via his professorship at St. Lawrence University, she personally didn't realize the nation's existence until it made international headlines during the 1979 standoff at Raquette Point. These days, she says, whenever she hears about Akwesasne, it is generally in reference to the casino or the abundance of cheap gas and cigarettes.

"We do a really poor job of cultural and historical awareness in our schools and homes up here," she says with a sigh.

Ditto down in South Texas. Though our schools are getting better at promoting Tejano heritage now,[4] the only thing I remember learning about my mother's homeland in school was that its army slayed Davy Crockett at the Alamo. Until the drug war, our border towns were mostly regarded for prurient sex shows and cheap tequila and pharmaceuticals. But while it

---

4. Or so it seemed until May 2016, when the Texas State Board of Education proposed including a new textbook called *Mexican-American Heritage* in the state's public school curriculum. Scholars and activists had been petitioning the board to diversify its materials for years, but not with a text like this, which claims Chicanos "adopted a revolutionary narrative that opposed Western civilization and wanted to destroy this society." A Christian activist who has criticized public education as "a subtly deceptive tool of perversion" is apparently the owner of the textbook's publishing house. Past State Board of Education–approved textbooks have referred to African slaves as "workers" and implied that Moses influenced the U.S. Constitution.

is indeed noteworthy that communities on both borders have managed to exploit the economic system that nearly decimated our ancestors through even more exploitation, it hurts that we are known for little else.

DAYS BEFORE MY DEPARTURE from the North Country, Keetah calls. The first berries of the season have ripened. On Sunday, her Longhouse will celebrate this sign of summer with a ceremony. Want to come?

Few invitations have moved me like this. Of course I want to accept. Yet, of course, there are ethics to consider. For nearly three-quarters of a century, Canada and the United States outlawed many Native ceremonies. The traditions that survived did so because they were conducted in secret by practitioners willing to risk imprisonment. After the bans were finally lifted in the 1950s and traditions were slowly restored, some tribes started getting inundated by spiritual seekers hoping to try out their sweat lodges, vision quests, pipe ceremonies, and dances. Believing themselves thus enlightened, a few proceeded to call themselves "shamans" afterward and charge other non-Indians hefty fees for participating in distorted versions of rituals and healings. The National Congress of American Indians responded with a "declaration of war" against "non-Indian 'wannabes'" in 1993, accusing New Agers of cultural robbery. A decade later, Arvol Looking Horse, a spiritual leader of the Lakota, Dakota, and Nakota people, issued a proclamation banning non-Indians from ceremonies like the Sundance to protect "the survival of our future generations."

Once you've learned such terrible history, it's hard to justify participating in it—out of fear not only of saying or doing something wrong but also of literally *being* wrong. So. Should I take what my guilt-laden inner liberal perceives to be the higher moral ground and say no? Stay true to my writerly pathos and proceed into the ethical minefield ahead? Or embrace the humanity my friend has extended by stopping this mental flagellation and simply saying yes, thank you, I would love to?

"Are you sure it's okay?"

Yes, Keetah says. No one will be wearing a False Face mask.[5] No medicine society will be making an appearance. The Strawberry Ceremony

---

5. Carved out of living trees, False Face masks are said to acquire the power of whatever spirit they represent. As such, they demand a fair amount of placating, including regular massages with sunflower oil and tobacco leaves. When the New York State Museum burst into flames in 1911, elders said it was because the collection's masks were protesting their entrapment. The Tadodaho has since called for the return of all masks to their nations,

is as outsider-friendly as Longhouse ceremonies get. Some Mohawks, like the Kanatsiohareke near Fonda, New York, have even turned it into a festival open to the general public. Keetah already asked the elders, and they welcome my attendance on Sunday, provided I take no photos or (gulp) notes.

This isn't the first time I've been asked to leave behind my notebook. To secure permission to work as an editor for a state-run newspaper in China in the late 1990s, I had to pledge to refrain from writing there, too. In retrospect, that was like a heroin addict signing up to volunteer at a methadone clinic. I spent much of that year locked in the bathroom, frantically transcribing what I had just witnessed. Notes are how I process the world. Abstaining felt almost self-annihilating. Yet when I wrote a book about that experience years later, I wound up cutting the best "material." I had formed close ties with my Chinese colleagues and didn't want to betray their trust.

Compromising is rarely a good artistic decision. When documenting worlds not your own, however, it might be the only conscionable one. At the very least, it helps you avoid the sort of troubles Edmund Wilson brewed in the late 1950s, when he visited the Haudenosaunee nations to research the attacks on their sovereignty by the St. Lawrence Seaway, Niagara Power Authority, and other capitalist ventures. While there, the ethnologist William Fenton invited him along to several Longhouse ceremonies that did feature False Face masks and medicine societies. Wilson then detailed these sacred rituals so explicitly for the *New Yorker*, he unleashed what scholar Dean Snow has called "a storm of indignation, not all of it from the Iroquois." Wilson's subsequent book was aptly titled *Apologies to the Iroquois*, but as Snow wryly noted, "His apologies apparently did not extend to any regret at having published what both Fenton and the Iroquois thought was a confidence."

After much internal debate, I resolve that Saturday to bring along a notebook but keep it inside my car. Then I settle into my final drive toward Route 37. Unlike the vast openness of South Texas byways, North Country roads are so woodsy-labyrinthine, you cannot see where you're going or where you've been—only where you are in the moment. And this moment reveals Adirondack chairs lounging on a deck. Muddy boots by the front step. A meadow smeared golden with dandelions. A poplar releasing puffs of white

---

plus banned future sales to the public. Traditionalists believe they should be restricted from outsiders' view altogether and brought out only for certain Longhouse ceremonies and healing rituals.

fluff. A murder of crows overhead. And finally: an Amish woman selling strawberries from a horse-drawn buggy. I pull over to buy a few baskets. Harvested only hours ago, their skins are still warm from the sun. Their meat is powerfully sweet.

I arrive to find Keetah at her kitchen counter, opening a bag of Maseca. Dropping the baskets beside her, I announce that corn flour is the key ingredient of Mexican cuisine, too. We could make tortillas, I say. Tamales, atoles, empanadas, gorditas!

Keetah smiles. "I had a gordita once. At Taco Bell."

But tonight we'll be making corn bread, she says. Into a giant blue bowl she sifts the corn flour, eyeballs in some Quick Oats, then mixes them together with the back of her hand. Into a vat of boiling water, she squirts a quarter bottle of Great Value Pancake Syrup, imbuing the kitchen with a delicious warmth. The strawberries are hulled and tumbled into another bowl, where they get mashed into compote, drizzled with syrup, and then folded into the blue bowl. Pushing the mixture to one side, Keetah pours in boiling water from a kettle and forms a hot dough ball that she rolls into a patty. The trick, she says, is to wet it just enough so there are no cracks. Otherwise, the corn bread will break when you boil it.

Dipping my hands into the flour bowl, I think of the other women who have taught me dough-making over the years. First were my tías Benita and Mary Lou, who showed me the formidable ratio of lard to masa as we made tamales around the table one Christmas. Next came my Russian friend Elena, who demonstrated how to bake the perfect potato pierogi at her dacha near Nizhni Novgorod, and my Chinese friends Liu and Yuer, who taught me ten different ways to seal a *jiaozi* dumpling in my Beijing apartment. One of my best memories from grad school was the afternoon my friend Maggie held a bread-baking lesson in her Iowa City kitchen while her daughter, T-Bone, played underfoot. There is something inherently joyful about dough-foods. How the recipes get passed down through the generations; how they are best prepared communally, with each woman assigned her own task. The way your hands wind up sticky and your floor gets good and gritty. The pleasure of transforming something raw into nourishment.

Keetah says there is a special song for corn bread–making, as it is one of the Mohawk's most revered foods. She sings a few rounds as we roll out the patties. The melody undulates, as if mimicking kneading hands in motion, and caresses, like a lullaby. One by one, we drop the patties into the vat of fragrantly boiling water and wait for them to surface.

IT'S NOT EASY CAJOLING KEETAH'S little girls out of bed the next morning. However exciting a Longhouse ceremony might be for me, to them it is an impediment to sleeping in and watching cartoons (in other words, church). Keetah dresses them in ribbon shirts and then packs a basket of bowls and spoons. I grab the pot of corn bread as we dash out the door and into her truck. Keetah's eldest slides in a CD. Adele blasts forth, crooning "Someone Like You." This awakens the girls considerably. We sing along at the top of our lungs as we charge down Route 37 toward the Longhouse. The ceremony started at 9, but we don't arrive until nearly 9:30. Indian time, Keetah jokes. If so, we're not the only ones keeping it. There are barely a dozen cars in the lot.

Gender dictates that we enter the Longhouse through the western door while males walk around the rectangular cabin to enter via the eastern door. Inside is a single sweeping room constructed entirely of wood, from the polished floors to the bleachers along the walls to the high ceiling dotted with fans. Rattles made of turtle shells dangle beside a triangular window. Hanging pedestals are topped with feathered-and-antlered kastowa. There are two wood-burning stoves, one at each end. Beyond that, the Longhouse feels almost Quaker in its sparse aesthetic. The Bear Clan sits on the southern side of the Longhouse, while Wolves and Turtles occupy the northern. With their kastowa and ribbon shirts, many of the men are dressed traditionally from the waist up, and—with their cell phones clipped to their cargo shorts and their name-brand puffy sneakers—millennially from the hips down. The women wear skirts or jeans beneath their ribbon shirts and fan themselves with turkey feathers. Tattoos are prominently displayed: feathers, dream catchers, Haudenosaunee flags, clan insignias.

All eyes are trained on a middle-aged man speaking in Mohawk in the center of the room. As we hustle into the bleachers, Keetah whispers that he is reciting the Ohen:ton Karihwatehkwen, or the Words That Come Before All Else (aka the Thanksgiving Address). It continues on for some time, mostly because there is so much gratitude to impart, but also because of the orator's halting command of Mohawk. An elderly clan mother wearing oversized glasses and moccasins makes corrections as needed from her perch on the bleachers.

Toward the end of the address, Loran Thompson strolls in, looking debonair in his kastowa and embroidered shirt. Like his brother Kanietakeron, he is a controversial figure at Akwesasne,[6] but people here seem relieved to

---

6. In addition to igniting the Raquette Point standoff by confiscating the power tools of tribal employees, Loran Thompson played a significant role in the casino war by siding with the pro-gamblers. He is said to have made a fortune through contraband as well.

see him. One of only a handful of truly fluent speakers at this Longhouse, he has an extensive knowledge of ritual as well. Each of the traditional ceremonies—including Midwinter, Maple, Green Bean, Strawberry, Green Corn, and Harvest—occurs only once a year, and some last for several days. It is challenging keeping track of which stories, songs, dances, peach bowl games, prayers, and rituals go when. There is no Haudenosaunee equivalent of seminary school. You learn to lead ceremonies by attending them and soliciting help from the elders—until that daunting day you realize the eldest is *you*.

Now that the forces that construct the universe have been acknowledged, the Strawberry Ceremony begins. I hopefully disclose no confidences with this: there is singing and there is dancing and there is chanting, and often all three at once. Two men keep the rhythm with rattles made of turtle shells while the rest of us dance in a long procession around the room. At first, I try to follow the footwork of the woman in front of me but gradually realize that people are moving to their own internal beat. I do as well, relishing in the freedom. At one point, someone grabs my hand. I look down to find a girl who can't be more than four staring up at me with unblinking eyes. She is wearing a little white sundress embroidered with strawberries. Her silky black hair is parted into pigtails. She seems to want me to lead her, and so I do, clasping her small hand in my own. Together we travel round and round the Longhouse, along with thirty, then forty, then sixty others. Someone makes a sound like "Yee-oh!" The rest of us respond in turn.

An hour into the ceremony, Keetah exits the Longhouse and I trail behind. Next door is an industrial-size kitchen where women are preparing the day's feast, pulping piles of strawberries and sliding them into a bucket of water. Keetah stations me with her Ista (mother), who is making corn mush at the stove. She shows me how to whisk the corn flour and water together until they take on a Cream of Wheat sheen, then how to add in strawberries and maple syrup.

"Has Keetah told you about Sky Woman?" Ista asks, peering at me through her owl-rimmed glasses.

Eventually he got charged with money laundering and served two years in prison. When I interviewed him about all of this, he said, "I've never done anything illegal in my life. I might have broken Canadian law. I might have broken U.S. law. But I have never broken my own set of laws." Nowadays, Loran runs an Internet service provider and presides over the Longhouse frequented by the Warriors.

I recite the stories I've heard, about how Sky Woman fell from the sky one day, landed on the back of a turtle, and walked about sprinkling sky dirt that became earth dirt beneath her feet. Ista nods approvingly, then adds another legend to my library. Sky Woman's husband often tried to test her resolve. Once, he asked her to make corn mush without wearing any clothes.

"See how it's bubbling?" Ista asks.

I glance down to discover that the mush pot has become a lava pit. A giant bubble bursts, singeing my hand with splatter. I yelp and lower the flame.

Ista laughs. "That's what Sky Woman's husband wanted to know. If she could endure the pain."

No Sky Man for me, in other words, but that's okay. Around this time next year, I'll fall in love with a Sky Woman of my own, who heals instead of hurts. But that border-crossing story is better saved for another day.

Back in the Longhouse, a girl is selected from each clan to distribute strawberry juice. I accept a cup and wait to see if a toast will follow. Sure enough, Loran rises to announce that the strawberry is a leader among fruits. When Sky Woman fell, this was the first fruit she found. Likewise, it is the first berry to reveal itself each spring, paving the way for all the other berries to come. Therefore we must honor this brave berry, giving it thanks for ripening yet again for our health and well-being.

With that, Loran tips back his cup. The rest of us do, too. The liquid is tangy but sweet, with just enough pulp to munch. As generations of Mohawks have undoubtedly done before me, I register this in my mental tally of the perks of attending a Longhouse ceremony over a Catholic Mass. Strawberry juice versus communion wine? No contest. Dancing versus scripture? Ditto. As I wrestle over Saint Kateri versus La Virgen de Guadalupe, Loran speaks again.

"But there is a contradiction here," he says sternly. "We are drinking this healthy, nourishing juice out of plastic cups, which are essentially poison. They will have to be thrown away into a landfill, which will pollute Mother Earth and eventually our children. We all should have brought our own cups from home!"

Ah, guilt. Not even the animists are spared of it.

The sermon is fleeting, however, for the time has come to name the baby girls. Three sets of parents climb down the bleachers, holding their infants close. Keetah leans over to explain that no two living Mohawks share the same name. Only when someone passes can their name be released. The elderly clan mother walks up to each family, peeks inside their blankets, and exchanges a prayer with the parents. Then she turns to the crowd to announce each new name. "You have to enunciate the whole name because that is how the universe will know her," the clan mother says. "We raise up each girl's name so it is easier for her to use her power to connect to the universe."

Lunchtime. The women from the kitchen pull a long table out into the middle of the room and set it with every strawberry configuration imaginable: jam, shortcake, compote, muffins, mush, and juice, along with stacks of fry bread and several kinds of corn bread, including one speckled with kidney beans. Elders are invited to line up first, followed by guests, women and children, and then men. I carry a steaming bowl of mush back to the bleachers. Ista joins me.

"What else do strawberries signify?" I ask, blowing on a spoonful.

Holding up her cup of juice, she says, "You see its color? That represents the blood of the woman." Pointing at my mush, she adds, "When you cut a strawberry in half, it also represents the woman. It grows the closest to the ground, so it is the closest to the earth, which is the mother. That makes it feminine, too. The strawberry is medicine for the woman."

Years ago, I helped my friend Rachél organize a "menstruation celebration" for teenage girls in Corpus Christi. We delighted over her idea to serve strawberry shortcake with red fruit punch, but when I shared this menu with others, they thought it kinky. So it's gratifying to learn that Rachél's instinct was right, that strawberries really do symbolize the feminine and have been celebrated as such by Haudenosaunee since time immemorial.

After lunch, we dance again. As the turtle-rattles pound a rhythm into my brain, I feel increasingly elated. Men emit their "Yee-ohs!" Footwork gets fancier. Sweat trickles down our faces. Someone whoops; someone hollers. Not for a god. Not for a prophet. For a berry. Something that leaves behind sustenance instead of commandments. Something that offers a single interpretation: plant and water and harvest me, and I will return. Poison me, and I won't.

One song ends and another begins. More rattles, different rhythms. Round and round the Longhouse we go. Drinking the symbolic blood of women. Eating the gifts of Sky Woman. Another whoop, another holler. Euphoria swirls through the procession.

The chanting stops and starts again. New song. New rhythm. Same motivation. The valiant strawberry. To say you "almost tasted strawberries" is to say you narrowly avoided death. The skyway above is lined with the fruit. You can pluck as many as you want from the patches.

Hours pass. Days, even. Then all too soon, the music ends. A final whoop, a last "Yee-oh!," and we all clamber back onto the bleachers. Loran removes the wampum hanging on a nearby stand and holds it to his heart. Again, we are treated to the Ohen:ton Karihwatehkwen, the Words That Come Before All Else. We thank the Earth Mother and the waters, the fish and the plants, the animals and the trees. We thank the four winds and the thunders, the sun and Grandmother Moon, the stars and the Enlightened Teachers. We thank the people. We thank the Creator. Ehtho niiohtonha'k ne onkwa'nikon:ra. And now our minds are one.

As we exit the bleachers for the last time, Keetah is stopped by a cousin. They talk a moment, then turn to me for introductions. When I mention being from the other border, he rubs his chin.

"You heard of the Minutemen?" he asks. "They tried to come here five or six years ago."

"Really?" I ask. "What happened?"

"The Border Patrol told them they'd get their asses kicked, and they left."

He and Keetah exchange a knowing laugh. Of the many things I admire about Akwesasne Mohawks, this is chief. They own their own power. And as Edmund Wilson concluded in *Apologies to the Iroquois,* "By defending their rights as Indians, they remind us of our rights as citizens."

Glancing at my phone, I am startled to see it is 2 P.M. We have been here for nearly five hours. My movers arrive in the morning. I grab a broom and start sweeping around the women packing food, the men moving tables, the children eating Popsicles. Gradually the crowd thins until only Keetah, her daughters, and I remain. I return the broom to its corner. Keetah flicks off the lights. Together we pull the wooden door closed. When I search for a way to lock it, Keetah says there's no need.

"Are you sure?" I ask, thinking of all the kastowa and turtle rattles inside.

She nods. "This is a sacred space. Our community respects that. We keep our doors open."

We drive back to Keetah's in the rain. No Adele this time. We want to preserve the resounding rhythms in our brains. There's my car, sitting in Keetah's driveway, my notebook inside the trunk. I step out and embrace the girls, one by one. By the time I reach Keetah, I have grown so emotional, I don't know what to say. She has given me time, story, knowledge, friendship. She has shown me not only her self but my own self. I still feel fractured somehow, but if I've learned anything at Akwesasne, it is that you can still be united while divided.

These are the words that come before all else: *Gratitude, gratitude, gratitude.* They are all I can say and everything I can say.

And so I do.

EPILOGUE

The United States of In-between

TELL PEOPLE YOU'RE RESEARCHING THE U.S. BORDERLANDS, AND ONE question is sure to follow: Isn't it *dangerous* over there? They've skimmed the headlines; they've seen *Frozen River* and *Sicario*; they've absorbed the single story. Particularly near the Mexico border, they rarely venture there themselves, for fear of being shot.

Yet the lives most endangered in the U.S. borderlands are those whose ancestors preceded the imaginary lines by centuries. Who understand that violence takes forms besides bullets. Like the vaqueros who lost their traditional lifestyle because of corporate buyouts of ranches. Like the Mohawks who can no longer support their families hunting, trapping, or fishing due to the opening of the St. Lawrence Seaway. Many of us do not speak Spanish because our elders had it humiliated out of them in public school; ditto with Mohawks during their century of Indian Residential Schools. Our fence-line communities are likely being sickened from the toxics released by Citgo, Valero, and Flint Hills; theirs, by General Motors, ALCOA, and Reynolds. Too many of our youth are imprisoned for smuggling; theirs, for trading. In borders north and south, we must contend with the trafficking of firearms right through our neighborhoods. We die in frightening numbers from diabetes caused by obesity wrought by poverty. We grieve the loss of our land, the loss of our culture, the loss of our dignity. The violations of deeds and treaties. The creation of checkpoints. The abundance of chokepoints. The Predator drones that so often target our own.

If an unusually high percentage of border denizens deal in shady economies, it's easy to understand why. They haven't exactly been left a plethora of alternatives. Is it even reasonable to expect someone to respect an arbitrary line that has caused their family such grief? There are existential ramifications when an ancestral land is cut in two. It doesn't matter that the treaties were signed a couple hundred years ago. Their impact is felt every time a Tejano or Mohawk confronts a wall or a bridge and an agent peers over his sunglasses to ask, "Where are you from?" Scientific evidence is emerging that intergenerational trauma could very well be true—that horrors like colonialism are today manifested as post-traumatic stress disorder and depression. Some researchers have even posited that Native Americans have their ancestors' sufferings woven into their DNA.

Considering what these communities have been through, the headlines we really should be reading are how these cultures survived at all. Our languages might have been scrubbed out of our mouths with soap, yet they are somehow still spoken today. South Texas is incorporating more dual language programming into some of its schools, while the Akwesasne Freedom School is working toward expanding its immersion program through twelfth grade. Cultural practices are also making a comeback. While cities like San Antonio realized that promoting Tejano culture could be not only healing but also profitable long ago, this is occurring to towns closer to the border, too. In 2008, two artists in Corpus Christi threw a block party for Dia de los Muertos that has since evolved into a vibrant street festival that draws upward of 35,000 attendees a year—many dressed as skeletons. Minutes from Mexico in tiny San Benito, the Narcisco Martinez Cultural Arts Center has been hosting an annual conjunto music festival for a quarter century.

Elder Mohawks I have interviewed also attest to a resurgence in cultural pride. Not only are community members making Native aesthetic choices in their hairstyles, piercings, and tattoos, they are signing up for classes in traditional arts like basketry[1] at the Akwesasne Cultural Center as well. The tribe recently won an unprecedented $8.4 million settlement from ALCOA to help revive four cultural practices that suffered as a result of the company's

---

1. As baskets rated a mention in their creation story as the receptacle holding the food the Sky Chief sent to express his desire to meet Sky Woman, basketry is the Mohawks' most revered art form. Exchanged at weddings and other key life events, baskets have traditionally been one of women's primary income sources as well. Yet this sacred art is endangered now because of an invasive beetle from Asia called the emerald ash borer that infests the trees Mohawks strip into splints to make their prized baskets. Without serious intervention, scientists believe the beetle will kill off the bulk of North America's seven billion ash trees within the next few decades. Already the insect has been spotted in nearby Cornwall. In response, Mohawks have hung beetle traps around their nation and stored several hundred thousand ash tree seeds in a deep freezer in Fort Collins, Colorado.

contamination: hunting, trapping, and fishing; basketry; medicines; and hor-ticulture.[2] After decades of being derided as devil worship, the Longhouse is thriving at Akwesasne, too—so much so that there is even a concerted effort to reunite the houses after their contentious split many years ago. At a recent meeting, Keetah stood up and told her elders, "If it doesn't happen in your generation, then it will be my burden, but I will take it on and work on it." Then she sat down and watched as, one by one, the other young people concurred.

THE UPSIDE TO NOMADISM? The opportunity to lead many different lives—and, if you're a writer, to then share them. For nearly twenty years I lived on the go, constantly switching locations. Writing became a privileged form of migrant work, following inspiration instead of crops, stories instead of seasons. But while itinerancy remains my instinctive mode of being, I have concluded that it isn't the most sustainable of lifestyles long-term, not only because of practical matters like finances and health but also because of the whims of the human heart. Intimately observing so many communities for so many years eventually got me pining to build one of my own. And so, two years into the making of this project, I started playing academic roulette, first with grad school and then with the job market. Since the fall of 2013, I have been happily nesting in Chapel Hill, North Carolina. The only problem: it is located 800 miles from the northern borderlands and 1,500 miles from the southern. Not only am I nomadic no more, but I have also departed the land of in-between—at least, in the physical sense.

Psychically, the borderlands have left an indelible imprint, and for that I am exceedingly grateful. After a long stretch of insecurity that being only half Mexican made me a "Chicana falsa,"[3] I've come to see the beauty of hybridity. When you occupy a hyphenated space, you realize that nothing is stone-set.

---

2. According to Barbara Tarbell, the tribe's program manager of natural resource damage assessment, Akwesasne envisions a five-year program in which young Mohawks will apprentice with master practitioners to gain threatened skills through mentorship. "At the end, they'll have the knowledge, pride, and spiritual strength to pass it on," she told me. "This is what it means to be Mohawk."

3. I conclude these footnotes as they commenced, with a nod to my friend Michele Serros, who coined this term in her first book, *Chicana Falsa*. A role model until the very end, she kept her thousands of Facebook fans posted as she battled both Chipotle and cancer with her inimitable humor. She parted for the otherworld at age forty-eight on January 4, 2015, leaving this one a little less luminous, yet ever the better for her influence.

At a time when the world's radicals have grown so uncompromising in their platforms, so unyielding in their beliefs, the ability to dwell in ambiguity has become an increasingly vital trait.

Borderlands don't constitute just the edge of a nation but also its frontier. They might be lawless, yes (or worse: militarized), but they are also remarkably innovative. It's time to stop sending more "boots on the ground" to the periphery and start listening to those who are actually rooted there. Border denizens not only elucidate the world's colonial pasts but prophesy futures as well.

No reflection of the borderlands is complete without a meditation on the actual lines themselves. They don't just delineate countries, of course. As we've seen time and again in the United States, political parties are highly adept at redrawing the lines of congressional districts with a legal magic that—at the ballot box—brings about "miracles" on par with La Virgen de Guadalupe appearing on a tortilla (only nowhere near as hopeful). In a word, a borderline is an injustice. It is a time-held method of partitioning the planet for the benefit of the elite. Fortunately, we have legions of activists, artists, and faith keepers out there, petitioning on humanity's behalf, but they need serious reinforcement. For the greatest lesson in nepantla is that many borderlines needn't exist at all. We operate daily within the confines of myriad lines—class, creed, sexuality, gender—that mainly serve to suppress our quality of life. Spend enough time straddling one, and you can't help but wonder what bliss might follow if we all just embraced the spaces in between.

ACKNOWLEDGMENTS

TO ALL THE BEAUTIFUL PEOPLE WHO SHARED THEIR STORIES WITH me: I thank you to infinity.

John McPhee suggested I write this book a decade ago, and mile by mile Greg Rubio made the first half possible, so the second round of gratitude goes to them. Profound thanks are due to everyone in South Texas who deepened my understanding of the region, especially Santa Barraza and Homero Vera, and to everyone at Akwesasne who welcomed me as a guest in their nation, particularly "Keetah" and my fellow Métis/Mestizo, Bob Stevenson. Niawen'kó:wa.

At the University of Iowa, I am indebted to Professors Patricia Foster, Robin Hemley, and Claire Fox for their insight as I commenced this project. Thanks also go to the wise counsel of Professors Bonnie Sunstein, David Hamilton, John D'Agata, Honor Moore, Allan Gurganus, Jeff Porter, and Steve Kuusisto and to the Graduate College for granting the Dean's Graduate Fellowship that enabled my study. *Mil besos a la gente* who made three long winters bearable: Sarah Wells, Santiago Vaquera-Vásquez, Amy Schleunes, Felicia Rose Chavez, Idris Goodwin, Jen Zoble, and Catina Bacote.

At St. Lawrence University, I give gratitude to the English department for bringing me to the North Country in the first place. My colleagues there—particularly Jill Talbot and Sarah Barber—were marvelously hospitable, as were my dear pals Betsy Kepes and Tom Van de Water. I am especially appreciative of Celia Nyamweru, who introduced me to many people at Akwesasne who became friends (as did Celia).

I am crazy-lucky to have landed at the University of North Carolina at Chapel Hill's Creative Writing Program. Many thanks are due to Daniel Wallace and Beverly Taylor for extending the invitation and to the Institute for the Arts and Humanities for the Faculty Fellowship that enabled this book's completion. Thanks also go to my wonderful colleagues—especially Gaby Calvocoressi and Marianne Gingher—and to my brilliant creative nonfiction students, who inspire me daily. Other entities that made this project possible are Lebh Shomea of Sarita, Texas; the Ragdale Foundation of Lake Forest, Illinois; and especially the Sangam House of Nrityagram, India, which granted me time and space to think and create.

Saludos to the friends and family who lift my spirits: Daphne Sorensen, Michael Robertson, Irene Lin, Amy Schapiro, Sonya Tsuchigane, Joy Baker, Tyra Robertson, Sherry Shokouhi, Irene Carranza, Rachél DayStar Payne, Amaya Moro-Martin, Jeff Golden, Kavitha Rao, David Farley, Wendy Call, Sheryl Oring, Laura Halperin, Julia Haslett, Susan Harbage Page, Chuck Whitney, all the Elizondos/Silvas/Quintanillas in South Texas, the Griests in Kansas, and my new Curtis/Biggers/Sauls/Holm clan in Carolina. Gratitude also goes to everyone at the University of North Carolina Press for guiding this book into being and to my insightful readers Daisy Hernández, Celia Nyamweru, and Chief Brian David.

A mighty fist bump goes to all the journalists and scholars who strive to bring justice to the borderlands via the written word, including Gloria Anzaldúa, Alma Guillermoprieto, Cecilia Ballí, Melissa del Bosque, Charles Bowden, Alfredo Corchado, Michelle García, Luís Alberto Urrea, Rubén Martínez, Maria Hinojosa, Maria Sacchetti, Jazmine Ulloa, Dianne Solis, Sonia Nazario, Franc Contreras, John Gibler, Judith Torrea, Mariana Martínez Estens, Julia Preston, Ioan Grillo, Todd Miller, Tom Miller, Cindy Casares, Walter Mignolo, Desirée Martín, John Carlos Frey, Dudley Althaus, Ginger Thompson, Patrick Radden Keefe, John Morán González, Trinidad Gonzales, Sonia Hernández, Benjamin Johnson, Monica Muñoz Martinez, Charlie Ericksen, David Sommerstein, Audra Simpson, John Mohawk, Darren Bonaparte, Doug George-Kanentiio, Bruce Johansen, Ian Kalman, Louellyn White, and the tenacious staffs of the *Texas Observer, Corpus Christi Caller-Times, Indian Time,* the (sadly defunct) *Akwesasne Notes,* and the best radio station I know, North Country Public Radio. My heartfelt respects go to the (painfully) many Mexican journalists who have been slain because of their truth-telling.

The final round of gratitude goes to my ancestors, for rooting me in the borderlands, and to my parents, Irene and Dick Griest; my sister, Barbara, and her husband, Alex; and my niece and nephew, Analina and Jordan, for six reasons to always return.

NOTES

INTRODUCTION: THE DESCENDANTS

(Footnote 2) **Some scholars trace** Dean R. Snow, *The Iroquois* (Cambridge: Blackwell, 1994).

PROLOGUE: NEPANTLA

"America's fattest city" Jaclyn Colletti and Maria Masters, "America's 10 Fattest (and Leanest) Cities," *Men's Health*, April 2010.

Dumbest Craig Wilson, "Looking for Signs of Intelligent Life in Fort Wayne," *USA Today*, January 19, 2005.

Least literate "America's Most Literate Cities," Central Connecticut State University's Center for Public Policy and Social Research, available at http://web.ccsu.edu/ americasmostliteratecities/default.asp.

Worst credit scores "State of Credit," published annually by Experian at www .experian.com. From 2011 to 2013, Corpus ranked in the top ten worst scores nationwide.

(Footnote 2) **the seventh "happiest" city** Edward L. Glaeser, Joshua D. Gottlieb, and Oren Ziv, "Unhappy Cities," National Bureau of Economic Research Working Paper No. 20291, July 2014, available at http://www.nber.org/papers/w20291.

writer Gloria Anzaldúa Gloria Anzaldúa, *Interviews: Entrevistas* (New York: Routledge, 2000).

CHAPTER 1. THE MIRACLE TREE

(Footnote 4) **"spiritual mestizaje"** Theresa Delgadillo, *Spiritual Mestizaje: Religion, Gender, Race, and Nation in Contemporary Chicana Narrative* (Durham: Duke University Press, 2011).

In 1966, *Time* wrote "Botany: The Crying Tree," *Time*, September 16, 1966.

A matriarch named Leonisia Garcia Macarena Hernandez, "Hundreds Flock to Holy 'Weeping Tree' Oddity," *Dallas Morning News*, September 19, 2007.

CHAPTER 2. THE REBEL

when developers foisted off Jo Rios and Pamela S. Meyer, "What Do Toilets Have to Do with It? Health, the Environment, and the Working Poor in Rural South Texas Colonias," *Online Journal of Rural Research and Policy* 4, no. 2 (2009), available at http:// newprairiepress.org/ojrrp/vol4/iss2/2/.

after more than 600 area residents Ann Zimmerman, "Chemical Warrior," *Dallas Observer*, September 10, 1998.

release up to 150,000 gallons According to TCEQ spokesman Terry Clawson, with whom I exchanged e-mails in March 2010, LCS Correction Services was issued the permit (TPDES Permit No. WQ0014802001) on October 31, 2008, to discharge wastes under provisions of Section 402 of the Clean Water Act and Chapter 26 of the Texas Water Code.

At Lionel's urging Geologist Rick Hay of Texas A&M University–Corpus Christi verified these levels during phone call and e-mail exchanges in the spring of 2010.

CHAPTER 3. THE VENERABLE

Growing up the only daughter Quotations and biographical information have been culled from Mother Julia's autobiography, *My Journey: Remembrances of My Life*, which was translated to English by Sister Armida Fabela and revised by Janet Niedosik. No other publication information is included inside the copy I obtained from Sister Maximina Cruz.

one-room house in Kingsville Sister Kathleen McDonagh, "Missionary Daughters of the Most Pure Virgin Mary in the Diocese of Corpus Christi," *South Texas Catholic*, November 1, 2012.

opening forty-five congregations Staff, "Sainthood Close for Mother Navarrete," *Daily Sun News* (Sunnyside, Wash.), June 23, 2004.

However dizzying this collection David Farley, *An Irreverent Curiosity: In Search of the Church's Strangest Relic in Italy's Oddest Town* (New York: Gotham Books, 2009).

It can take decades Staff, "How Does Someone Become a Saint?," BBC.com, April 27, 2014, available at http://www.bbc.com/news/world-europe-27140646.

The first was for her gardener Eric Chapa, "Mother Julia's Solemn Place of Prayer Becoming a Reality in Kingsville," *South Texas Catholic*, August 15, 2008.

CHAPTER 4. THE ACTIVIST AND THE ORDINANCE

race-zoning ordinances Steve Lerner, *Sacrifice Zones: The Front Lines of Toxic Chemical Exposure in the United States* (Cambridge: MIT Press, 2010).

home to six oil refineries Earthjustice, "Community Impact Report Addendum A: The Toll of Refineries on Fenceline Communities," October 28, 2014, available at http://earthjustice.org/sites/default/files/files/10.28.14%20EPA%20Refinery%20Risk%20Review%2003_Addendum%20A%20-%20Community%20Impact%20Report.pdf.

funding for a pilot study "Corpus Christi: Refinery Neighbor Study Shows High Levels of Benzene," Global Community Monitor, September 8, 2008, available at http://www.gcmonitor.org/corpus-christi-refinery-neighbor-study-shows-high-levels-of-benzene/.

A toxicologist hired by Denise Malan, "Environmentalists Make Latest Move in Benzene Study Dispute," *Corpus Christi Caller-Times*, July 13, 2009.

After months of getting bombarded "Bombarded" is how Dr. Donnelly described his treatment in an e-mail to Suzie Canales on December 9, 2008, according to the report "Risk Assessment or Risk Acceptance: Why the EPA's Attempts to Achieve Environmental Justice Have Failed and What They Can Do About It" by Suzie Canales, October 2010, available at http://cla.tamucc.edu/english/techwrit/EJ%20report-2%202010.pdf.

A 2011 federal study Rick Spruill, "Neighborhood Blood Studies Conflict," *Corpus Christi Caller-Times*, January 6, 2011.

Citgo alone has a $345 million annual impact Citgo News Release, April 16, 2015, available at http://media.citgo.com/CITGO-Corpus-Christi-Refinery-Celebrates-80-Years-of-Fueling-Good-in-the-State-of-Texas.

Flint Hills, meanwhile, is owned by Ashley Alman, "Koch Brothers Net Worth Soars Past $100 Billion," *Huffington Post,* April 16, 2014.

Koch Industries contributed hundreds of thousands Andy Kroll, "Will Perry Return Koch Campaign Cash?," *Mother Jones,* October 10, 2011.

Perry in turn repeatedly challenged John M. Broder and Kate Galbraith, "E.P.A. Is Longtime Favorite Target for Perry," *New York Times,* September 29, 2011.

climate change skeptic Andy Kroll, "Who Did Rick Perry Pick as His Top Environmental Cop?," *Mother Jones,* September 22, 2011.

In 2007, Citgo became the first Priscilla Mosqueda, "Victims Disappointed by Small Penalty in Citgo Criminal Case," *Texas Observer,* February 6, 2014.

refines upward of 165,000 barrels Citgo News Release, http://media.citgo.com.

The front page Nancy Martinez, "Activist No Terror Threat, FBI Says," *Corpus Christi Caller-Times,* May 17, 2006.

Soon after, Suzie generated yet another John McArdle and Gabriel Nelson, "Environmental Justice Activist Urges EPA Chief 'To Roll Up Your Sleeves' at Tense W. H. Forum," *New York Times,* December 16, 2010.

When the company finally filed Chapter 11 bankruptcy Mara Kardas-Nelson, Lin Nelson, and Anne Fischel, "Bankruptcy as Corporate Makeover," *Dollars & Sense,* May/June 2010.

A U.S. bankruptcy court and the TCEQ Rick Spruill, "Encycle Plant Set for Demolition," *Corpus Christi Caller-Times,* January 22, 2011.

The EPA has documented asbestos Report available at http://www.tceq.texas.gov/ assets/public/remediation/variousremediationsites/encycle/swr3003.pdf.

and the whistleblower report Report available at https://stateimpact.npr .org/texas/2011/11/25/a-whistle-blowers-report-on-hazardous-waste-in-corpus-christi/.

former mining boomtown of Pincher, Oklahoma Dan Shepherd, "Last Residents of Pincher, Oklahoma Won't Give Up the Ghost (Town)," NBCNews.com, April 28, 2014, available at http://www.nbcnews.com/news/investigations/ last-residents-picher-oklahoma-wont-give-ghost-town-n89611.

By challenging the companies' permits Bart Bedsole, "Anonymous $2M Donation Will Buy Out Dona Park Families," KRISTV.com, February 20, 2015, available at http://www.kristv.com/story/28164064/ anonymous-2m-donation-will-buy-out-dona-park-families.

CHAPTER 5. THE BONDER AND THE DEALER

(Footnote 3) **Sophie wasn't the first** Jeff Winkler, "Amor Prohibido," *Texas Monthly,* September 2015.

One balmy night in September 2006 See Ed Vulliamy, *Amexica: War along the Borderline* (New York: Picador, 2011).

In August 2010, a cartel executed Associated Press, "Mexican Police Helped Cartel Massacre 193 Migrants, Documents Show," December 22, 2014, available at http://www.npr.org/2014/12/22/372579429/mexican-police-helped-cartel-massacre-193-migrants-documents-show.

forty-three college students in Guerrero Alma Guillermoprieto, "Mexico: The Murder of the Young," *New York Review of Books,* January 8, 2015.

At least 60,000 people have died "Mexico's Disappeared: The Enduring Cost of a Crisis Ignored," Human Rights Watch, February 20, 2013, available at http://www.hrw.org/reports/2013/02/20/mexicos-disappeared.

mayor from Michoacan who got stoned Mariano Castillo, "Increasingly, Mayors Become Targets in Mexico," CNN.com, October 29, 2010, available at http://www.cnn.com/2010/WORLD/americas/10/26/mexico.mayors.killed/.

one gets assaulted every twenty-six hours Alfredo Corchado, "Mexico Bureau Chief Defends Freedom of Press at Subcommittee Hearing," *Dallas Morning News* blog, July 29, 2015, available at http://thescoopblog.dallasnews.com/2015/07/mexico-bureau-chief-defends-freedom-of-press-at-subcommittee-hearing.html/.

In his authoritative book *El Narco* Ioan Grillo, *El Narco: Inside Mexico's Criminal Insurgency* (New York: Bloomsbury Press, 2012).

$100 billion a year on cocaine "What America's Users Spend on Illegal Drugs: 2000–2010," prepared for the White House Office of National Drug Control Policy by the RAND Corporation, February 2014, available at https://www.whitehouse.gov/sites/default/files/ondcp/policy-and research/wausid_results_report.pdf.

Analysts say as much as 40 percent Patrick Radden Keefe, "Cocaine Incorporated," *New York Times Magazine,* June 15, 2012.

Even the most famous capos Grillo, *El Narco.*

With nearly half of all Mexicans dwelling in poverty Christopher Wilson and Gerardo Silva, "Mexico's Latest Poverty Stats, 2013," Woodrow Wilson International Center for Scholars: Mexico Institute, available at http://www.wilsoncenter.org/sites/default/files/ Poverty_Statistics_Mexico_2013.pdf.

"ni-nis," short for *ni estudian, ni trabajan* Alfredo Corchado, *Midnight in Mexico: A Reporter's Journey through a Country's Descent into Darkness* (New York: Penguin, 2014).

(Footnote 10) **Santa Muerte is revered** Desirée Martín, *Borderlands Saints: Secular Sanctity in Chicano/a and Mexican Culture* (New Brunswick: Rutgers University Press, 2014).

(Footnote 12) **Corruption, of course, doesn't halt at the borderline** John Burnett and Marisa Peñaloza, "With Corruption Rampant, Good Cops Go Bad in Texas' Rio Grande Valley," National Public Radio, July 6, 2015.

Mexico watchers generally recognize six major drug cartels Mexico Report, InSight Crime, available at http://www.insightcrime.org/mexico-organized-crime-news/mexico.

(Footnote 13) **rebranded the cartel the Knights Templar** Ioan Grillo, *Gangster Warlords: Drug Dollars, Killing Fields, and the New Politics of Latin America* (New York: Bloomsbury Press, 2016).

forty-three ways to kill a man Corchado, *Midnight in Mexico.*

According to the DEA Camilo Smith, "DEA Releases Which Cartels Rule Texas Towns," *San Antonio Express-News,* August 26, 2015.

Juarez, a city that tallied more than 3,000 murders Nick Valencia, "Juarez Counts 3,000th Homicide of 2010," CNN.com, December 15, 2010, available at http://www.cnn .com/2010/WORLD/americas/12/15/mexico.juarez.homicides/index.html.

El Paso, which registered 5 homicides Staff, "2010 Murder Rate Not Seen since 1965," ABC/KVIA–El Paso, July 15, 2012, available at http://www.kvia.com/ news/2010-murder-rate-not-seen-since-1965/53331335.

The writer Chimamanda Ngozi Adichie Hear Adichie's excellent TED Talk, "The Danger of a Single Story," https://www.ted.com/talks/chimamanda_adichie_ the_danger_of_a_single_story#t-114246.

Just a month ago, a sixty-six-year-old man Katherine Rosenberg, "Robstown Man Faces Felony Drug Charges," *Corpus Christi Caller-Times*, July 20, 2010.

pled guilty to drug possession Steven Alford, "Cocaine-Dealing Robstown Taco Stand Owner Pleads Guilty," *Corpus Christi Caller-Times*, January 21, 2011.

CHAPTER 6. THE AGENTS

(Footnote 1) Approximately 250,000 guns Charles D. Thompson Jr., *Border Odyssey: Travels along the U.S./Mexico Divide* (Austin: University of Texas Press, 2015).

being upholstered into the backseat of a van To see the photo, visit "Bizarre Busts" at the *Telegraph*, http://www.telegraph.co.uk/news/picturegalleries/ worldnews/7817733/Bizarre-busts-US-Border-Patrol-pictures-of-the-most-bizarre-attempts-at-smuggling-people-and-drugs.html.

an agent's starting salary Dani Arbuckle, "Salary of a Law Enforcement Border Patrol Person," *Houston Chronicle*, available at http://work.chron.com/salary-law-enforcement-border-patrol-person-3148.html.

sterling silver Border Patrol badges Available at https://www.borderpatrolmuseum .com/giftshop/.

countrywide youth "Explorer" programs Todd Miller, *Border Patrol Nation* (San Francisco: City Lights Books, 2014).

a nearly $13 billion budget "Budget-in-Brief Fiscal Year 2015," U.S. Department of Homeland Security, available at http://www.dhs.gov/sites/default/files/publications/ MGMT/FY%202014%20BIB%20-%20FINAL%20–508%20Formatted%20%284%29.pdf.

more than every other federal law enforcement agency Sarah Stillman, "Where Are the Children?," *New Yorker*, April 27, 2015.

swollen ranks to more than 21,000 "Border Patrol Overview," U.S. Customs and Border Protection, available at http://www.cbp.gov/border-security/along-us-borders/ overview.

up from 8,500 agents in 2001 Miller, *Border Patrol Nation*.

a book was written about his platoon See Martha Raddatz, *The Long Road Home* (New York: Putnam, 2007).

Notions of being "diseased" Rachel Pearson, "Disease Threat from Immigrant Children Wildly Overstated," *Texas Observer*, July 10, 2014.

Dr. Marc Siegel will deem it Michelle Leung, "Conservative Media Stoke Fears about Humanitarian Crisis Causing Children to Enter U.S.," Media Matters for America, June 24, 2014.

16 percent of whom are uninsured Texas Medical Association, available at http://www.texmed.org/uninsured_in_texas/.

According to a 2011 *Frontline* documentary Maria Hinojosa, "Lost in Detention," *Frontline*, PBS, October 18, 2011, available at http://www.pbs.org/wgbh/frontline/film/lost-in-detention/.

If suicide rates are any indication Paul J. Weber, "Increase in Suicides among Border Patrol Agents Causes Alarm," *Washington Post*, August 19, 2010.

(Footnote 4) **Known as "Tent City"** Daniel Blue Tyx, "Goodbye to Tent City," *Texas Observer*, March 26, 2015.

CHAPTER 7. THE WALL

(Footnote 2) **Other U.S. presidents who condemned the world's walls** Roosevelt gave this quote during his State of the Union, "The Four Freedoms," on January 6, 1941; Nixon during an exchange with reporters at the Great Wall of China on February 24, 1972; and Trump during a speech at the Trump Tower in New York City on June 16, 2015.

Here in Brownsville Jazmine Ulloa, "Border Fence Construction Nears Completion in Hope Park," *Brownsville (Tex.) Herald*, December 26, 2010.

Yet when they aired these concerns Melissa del Bosque, "All Walled Up," *Texas Observer*, January 21, 2010.

The following ramifications Facts culled from short essays by Charles Bowden, Miguel Diaz-Barriga, Margaret Dorsey, Denise Gilman, Scott Nicol, and James Tyron in the photography book by Maurice Sherif, *The American Wall* (Austin: University of Texas Press, 2012).

It has inspired an offshore drilling rig designer "Border Fence News," University of Texas at Brownsville, available at http://www.utb.edu/newsinfo/archives/Pages/BorderFence/BorderFence.aspx.

The west side of the Berlin Wall Staff, "Keith Haring Paints Mural on Berlin Wall," *New York Times*, October 24, 1986.

Over in the West Bank William Parry, *Against the Wall: The Art of Resistance in Palestine* (Chicago: Lawrence Hill Books, 2011).

The park was founded in 1971 "Timeline and Slideshows," Friendship Park, available at http://www.friendshippark.org/#!history/c20x9; Joseph Nivens, "Pat Nixon at the U.S.-Mexico Border," *La Prensa San Diego*, August 29, 2008.

In 2004, Arizona artist Alfred Quiroz Quiroz's work can be viewed via YouTube, "Parade of Humanity: Border Wall Project," October 5, 2009, available at https://www.youtube.com/watch?v=5MdoA8bAzis#t=37.

And since 2012, Arizona artists Cindy Carcamo, "Artists Brighten Up U.S.-Mexico Border Fence," *Los Angeles Times*, December 23, 2012.

On April Fool's Day in 2011 Billy Jam, "Guerrilla Street Artist Ron English Takes Risk with Daring US/Mexico Border Art Prank," Amoeblog, April 7, 2011, available at http://www.amoeba.com/blog/2011/04/jamoeblog/guerrilla-street-artist-ron-english-takes-risk-with-daring-us-mexico-border-art-prank.html.

The 18-foot wall that soars above Richard Marosi, "$57.7-Million Fence Added to an Already Grueling Illegal Immigration Route," *Los Angeles Times*, February 15, 2010.

while the 9-foot wall at the Tecate Sherif, *American Wall.*

(Footnote 7) **More than 68,000 unaccompanied children** Haeyoun Park, "Q&A: Children at the Border," *New York Times,* October 21, 2014.

CHAPTER 8. THE CHOKEPOINT

when migration across the U.S. border is at a historic low Jeffrey S. Passel, D'Vera Cohn, and Ana Gonzalez-Barrera, "Net Migration from Mexico Falls to Zero—and Perhaps Less," Pew Research Center, April 23, 2012, available at http://www.pewhispanic.org/2012/04/23/net-migration-from-mexico-falls-to-zero-and-perhaps-less/.

In 2012, the entire state of Arizona "Border Deaths" database, *Arizona Daily Star,* available at http://azstarnet.com/online/databases/border-deaths-database/html_c104ad38-3877-11df-aa1a-001cc4c002e0.html (accessed June 18, 2013).

Although taxpayers spent upward of $90 billion Martha Mendoza, "US Border Security—Expensive with Mixed Results," *Associated Press,* June 26, 2011, available at http://www.nbcnews.com/id/43539092/ns/us_news-security/t/us-border-security-expensive-mixed-results/#.V-7-JrTotSU.

nearly 40 percent live below the poverty line Statistics found at City-Data, http://www.city-data.com/city/Falfurrias-Texas.html#b.

the wife of the justice of the peace Staff, "Judge's Wife Arrested Transporting Illegal Immigrants," KIITV News/Corpus Christi, July 3, 2012.

CHAPTER 9. THE WOMAN IN THE WOODS

About a thousand people are caught Brad Plumer, "Who's Crossing the Mexico Border? A New Survey Tries to Find Out," *Washington Post,* June 2, 2013.

law enforcement busted 237 stash houses Rene Peña, "Trends in Texas Gang Activity," *Prosecutor,* March–April 2014 issue, available at http://www.tdcaa.com/journal/trends-texas-gang-activity.

grisly discovery occurred in Edinburg Jared Taylor, "2 Indicted in Edinburg 'Hell' Stash-House Case," *The Monitor* (McAllen, Tex.), May 16, 2012.

Yet the tragedies she witnesses here daily Melissa del Bosque, "A Cemetery for Our People," *Texas Observer,* August 20, 2014.

(Footnote 3) **In their book,** *Forgotten Dead* William D. Carrigan and Clive Webb, *Forgotten Dead: Mob Violence against Mexicans in the United States, 1848–1928* (Oxford: Oxford University Press, 2013).

Cofounded by a Vietnam veteran David Holthouse, "Minutemen, Other Anti-Immigrant Militia Groups Stake Out Arizona Border," Southern Poverty Law Center Intelligence Report, June 27, 2005, available at https://www.splcenter.org/fighting-hate/intelligence-report/2005/minutemen-other-anti-immigrant-militia-groups-stake-out-arizona-border.

according to an early website Visit the site at http://unitedstates.fm/Minuteman.htm.

In 2015, the *Texas Observer* John Carlos Frey, "Graves of Shame," *Texas Observer,* July 6, 2015.

CHAPTER 10. THE HEALING

As Mexican writer Carlos Fuentes Quoted in Franciscan Friars of the Immaculate, *A Handbook on Guadalupe* (San Francisco: Ignatius Press, 2009).

(Footnote 2) **This crucial matter of skin tone** Carlos Monsivais, *Mexican Postcards* (New York: Verso, 1997).

CHAPTER 11. THE SORT OF HOMECOMING

(Footnote 1) **With more than 16,000 members** Kirk Semple, "Abduction Case Tests Limits of Amish Ties to Modern World," *New York Times*, August 21, 2014.

CHAPTER 12. THE TRADE

(Footnote 2) **In October 2014** Kristen Millares Young, "Misty Upham: The Tragic Death and Unscripted Life of Hollywood's Rising Star," *Guardian*, June 30, 2015, available at https://www.theguardian.com/global/2015/jun/30/misty-upham-native-american-actress-tragic-death-inspiring-life.

(Footnote 4) **This decision was likely also influenced** Thomas Kaplan, "In Tax Fight, Tribes Make, and Sell, Cigarettes," *New York Times*, February 22, 2012.

Ontario . . . has a cigarette allocation system Gregory Thomas and Scott Hennig, "Blowing Smoke on the Reserves," *Toronto Sun*, January 9, 2013.

The Royal Canadian Mounted Police reported "Akwesasne Cigarette Plant Legalizes Operations," *CBS News Ottawa*, April 14, 2010, available at http://www.cbc.ca/news/canada/ottawa/akwesasne-cigarette-plant-legalizes-operations-1.898838; Tom Blackwell, "The New Big Tobacco," *National Post*, September 20, 2010, available at http://news.nationalpost.com/news/canada/post-preview-inside-canadas-underground-tobacco-industry-a-five-part-series.

The United States also loses billions Jon Campbell, "Smuggled, Untaxed Cigarettes Are Everywhere in New York City," *Village Voice*, April 7, 2015.

(Footnote 5) **In his 2000 *Los Angeles Times* review** Sherman Alexie, "Some of My Best Friends," *Los Angeles Times*, January 23, 2000; Jessica Chapel, "Atlantic Unbound: Interviews: Sherman Alexie," June 1, 2000, available at http://www.theatlantic.com/past/docs/unbound/interviews/ba2000–06–01.htm.

CHAPTER 13. THE WAR

penchant for scalping or beheading enemies William Engelbrecht, *Iroquoia: The Development of a Native World* (Syracuse, N.Y.: Syracuse University Press, 2003).

eating enemies' hearts as a way to absorb victims' courage Dean R. Snow, *The Iroquois* (Cambridge: Blackwell, 1994).

Yet according to the Seneca scholar Jose Barreiro, ed., *Thinking in Indian: A John Mohawk Reader* (Golden, Colo.: Fulcrum, 2010).

(Footnote 3) **Exactly when this historic event** Louellyn White, "Free to Be *Kanien'kehaka*: A Case Study of Educational Self-Determination at the Akwesasne Freedom School" (diss. submitted to Graduate Interdisciplinary Program in American Indian Studies, University of Arizona, 2009).

No one knows for certain when Native Americans Ian Frazier, *On the Rez* (New York: Picador, 2000).

North America's first tribally operated gaming venture Jessica Cattelino, *High Stakes: Florida Seminole Gaming and Sovereignty* (Durham: Duke University Press, 2008).

At least 240 tribes in twenty-eight states have since followed suit That, at least, is the number of tribes regulated by the National Indian Gaming Commission, which is an independent agency within the U.S. Department of the Interior. Visit its website at www.nigc.gov.

Reactions varied wildly The facts and figures featured in the remainder of this section about the civil skirmish over gambling at Akwesasne have been culled from Doug George-Kanentiio, *Iroquois on Fire: A Voice from the Mohawk Nation* (Westport, Conn.: Praeger, 2006); Rick Hornung, *One Nation under the Gun: Inside the Mohawk Civil War* (Toronto: Stoddart, 1991); Bruce Johansen, *Life and Death in Mohawk Country* (Golden, Colo.: North American Press, 1993); Harry Swain, *OKA: A Political Crisis and Its Legacy* (Vancouver: Douglas and McIntyre, 2010); and Peter Wilkinson, "Renegade Nation," *Men's Journal*, December 1994, reprinted in *Akwesasne Notes*, Spring 1995.

(Footnote 10) **Because New York State** James M. Odato, "Cuomo Reaches Deal with Mohawks," *Times Union* (Albany, N.Y.), May 21, 2013; James M. Odato, "Mohawks Move Toward Resolving Land Claims," *Times Union* (Albany, N.Y.), May 28, 2014.

In December, I'll pick up a *Watertown Daily Times* Roger Dupuis, "St. Regis Casino Operators Indicted on Illegal-Gambling Charges," *Watertown (N.Y.) Daily Times*, December 19, 2012.

(Footnote 11) **A year later, in December 2013** James M. Odato, "Tribal Ways Trumped U.S. Law at Trial," *Times Union* (Albany, N.Y.), December 26, 2013.

CHAPTER 14. THE SAINT

so-called Las Vegas, Atlantic City W5 Staff, "How a Pig Farmer Made Billions in Online Gambling," CTV News/Ontario, March 13, 2010, available at http://www .ctvnews.ca/how-a-pig-farmer-made-billions-in-online-gambling-1.491399.

(Footnote 1) **According to a 2015 *New York Times*** Walt Bogdanich, James Glanz, and Agustin Armendariz, "Cash Drops and Keystrokes: The Dark Reality of Sports Betting and Daily Fantasy Games," *New York Times*, October 15, 2015.

and otherwise "do all they can . . ." Audra Simpson, *Mohawk Interruptus* (Durham: Duke University Press, 2014).

Soon after Akwesasne's casino war Harry Swain, *Oka: A Political Crisis and Its Legacy* (Vancouver: Douglas and McIntyre, 2010).

The outside world has called Biographical information about Saint Kateri was culled from Darren Bonaparte, *A Lily among Thorns: The Mohawk Repatriation of Kateri Tekahkwi:tha* (Ahkwesahsne Mohawk Territory: Wampum Chronicles, 2009); and Allan Greer, *Mohawk Saint* (Oxford: Oxford University Press, 2005).

Her father's profession hints Marie-Pierre Bousquet, "A Generation in Politics: The Alumni of the Saint-Marc-de-Figuery Residential School" (Winnipeg: University of Manitoba, 2006), available at http://www.academia.edu/1270629/A_Generation_in_ Politics_The_Alumni_of_the_Saint-Marc-de-Figuery_Residential_School.

Residential schools for First Nations "Residential Schools Timeline," National Centre for Truth and Reconciliation, available at http://nctr.ca/exhibitions.php.

(Footnote 6) **Sir Hector Langevin** J. Charles Boyce, ed., *Official Reports of the Debates of the House of Commons of the Dominion of Canada*, vol. 14 (Ottawa: Maclean, Roger, 1883).

Richard Henry Pratt, the founder Darek Hunt, "BIA's Impact on Indian Education Is an Education in Bad Education," *Indian Country*, January 30, 2012.

At least 4,100 children died Connie Walker, "New Documents May Shed Light on Residential School Deaths," CBC News/Canada, January 7, 2014, available at http://www.cbc.ca/news/indigenous/new-documents-may-shed-light-on-residential-school-deaths-1.2487015.

(Footnote 8) **just-elected prime minister Justin Trudeau** Susana Mas, "Trudeau Lays Out Plan for New Relationship with Indigenous People," CBC News/Canada, December 8, 2015, available at http://www.cbc.ca/news/politics/justin-trudeau-afn-indigenous-aboriginal-people-1.3354747.

Kateri reminds me of La Malinche Anna Lanyon, *Malinche's Conquest* (St. Leonards, Australia: Allen and Unwin, 1999).

CHAPTER 15. THE ACTIVIST AND THE OBELISK

One by one, their cattle went lame Janet Raloff, "The St. Regis Syndrome," *Science News*, July 19, 1980, available at http://fluoridealert.org/news/the-st-regis-syndrome/.

institutions like Cornell Mary Esch, "The Faces of Pollution: In N.Y., Toxic Waste, Contaminated Animals Threaten Mohawk Culture's Survival," *Los Angeles Times*, January 24, 1998.

For one study, the New York State Bruce Johansen, *Life and Death in Mohawk Country* (Golden, Colo.: North American Press, 1993).

the only place where I have seen unhealthier-looking people Jaclyn Colletti and Maria Masters, "America's 10 Fattest (and Leanest) Cities," *Men's Health*, April 2010.

(Footnote 4) **The GM site finally shuttered** Associated Press, "EPA Removes 335,000 Tons of Contaminated Soil from Former GM Site in Massena," *Post-Standard* (Syracuse, N.Y.), February 21, 2014.

Since ordering its cleanup in 1989 EPA Report, "Case Summary: Alcoa, Inc. to Conduct $243 Million Cleanup at Grasse River Superfund Site in New York," available at http://www.epa.gov/enforcement/case-summary-alcoa-inc-conduct-243-million-cleanup-grasse-river-superfund-site-new-york.

(Footnote 5) **Poor Massena** Brian Mann, "Alcoa Slashes Nearly 500 Jobs in Massena, Move Called 'Devastating' for St. Lawrence County," North Country Public Radio, November 3, 2015.

No two people say it alike John Stokes and Kanawahienton/David Benedict, *Thanksgiving Address: Greetings to the Natural World* (Corrales, N.M.: Six Nations Indian Museum and the Tracking Project, 1993).

In 2010, GM's bankruptcy estate Nick Bunkley, "G.M. Estate to Provide Millions for Cleanup of Old Sites," *New York Times*, October 20, 2010.

Tribal Council publicly criticized him Brian Hayden, "St. Regis Mohawk Tribe Distances Itself from Larry Thompson," *Watertown (N.Y.) Daily Times*, August 23, 2011.

Only after repeated requests St. Regis Mohawk Tribal Council and the Tribal Environment Division, "Tribe Clarifies General Motors Issue," *Indian Time*, August 25, 2011.

CHAPTER 16. THE MOVEMENT

(Footnote 1) **For forty-four days, Chief Spence** Staff, "Chief Spence Out of Hospital after Ending 6-week Hunger Strike," CTV News/Canada, January 24, 2013, available at http://www.ctvnews.ca/canada/chief-spence-out-of-hospital-after-ending-6-week-hunger-strike-1.1127449.

(Footnote 2) **Raymond Robinson continued his fast** Aaron Wherry, "The Testimony of Raymond Robinson," *Maclean's*, January 24, 2013.

(Footnote 3) **One year later, two Idle No More** Staff, "Idle No More Round Dance Attempt Ends in Arrests at Mall of America," KBJR News 1, December 31, 2013.

the government estimates less than half that amount Government of Canada, National Household Survey, 2011, "Aboriginal Peoples in Canada," Analytical Document 99–011-X, available at http://www12.statcan.gc.ca/nhs-enm/2011/as-sa/99–011-x/99–011-x2011001-eng.pdf.

The Supreme Court devised Rick Ouellet and Erin Hanson, "The Métis," First Nations Studies Program, University of British Columbia, http://indigenousfoundations.arts.ubc.ca.

The youngest is a sixteen-year-old Biographies of the original six Nishiyuu walkers and their guide can be found on their website, www.nishiyuujourney.ca.

(Footnote 7) **The Nishiyuu can be viewed** Staff, "Native Americans Walk from San Francisco to Washington, D.C. for U.S. Civil Rights, 1978," Global Nonviolent Action Database, Swarthmore College, available at http://nvdatabase.swarthmore.edu/content/native-americans-walk-san-francisco-washington-dc-us-civil-rights-1978.

The crowd forms a receiving line Staff, "Nishiyuu Walkers Complete 1,600 Kilometer Trek to Ottawa," CTV News/Canada, March 25, 2013, available at http://www.ctvnews.ca/canada/nishiyuu-walkers-complete-1-600-km-trek-to-ottawa-1.1209929.

Their youth kill themselves because Sari Horwitz, "The Hard Lives and High Suicide Rates of Native American Children," *Washington Post*, March 9, 2014.

(Footnote 9) **the Northern Ontario First Nation** Laurence Mathieu-Leger and Ashifa Kassam, "First Nations Community Grappling with Suicide Crisis: 'We're Crying Out for Help,'" *Guardian*, April 16, 2016.

CHAPTER 17. THE MOTHER TONGUE

Yet despite the generosity of parents and supporters Louellyn White, "Free to Be *Kanien'kehaka*: A Case Study of Educational Self-Determination at the Akwesasne Freedom School" (diss. submitted to Graduate Interdisciplinary Program in American Indian Studies, University of Arizona, 2009).

Although 187 Native languages Daniel Nettle and Suzanne Romaine, *Vanishing Voices: The Extinction of the World's Languages* (Oxford: Oxford University Press, 2002).

Language is also the touchstone Kate Freeman, Arlene Stairs, Evelyn Corbière, and Dorothy Lazore, "Ojibway, Mohawk, and Inuktitut Alive and Well? Issues of Identity, Ownership, and Change," *Bilingual Research Journal*, Winter 1995.

Kahnawake is even more aggressive Marion Bittinger, "Software Helps Revitalize Use of Mohawk Language," *MultiLingual*, September 2006.

The 2013 documentary *Stolen Education* This powerful film by Enrique Alemán and Rudy Luna can be ordered at http://www.videoproject.com/stoleneducation.html.

(Footnote 3) **the University of Albany's "Thompson Trio"** Rachel Siegal, "'Thompson Trio' Lacrosse Stars Showcased in #SCFeatured Debuting Sunday," ESPN Front Row, May 2014, available at http://www.espnfrontrow.com/2014/05/thompson-trio/.

(Footnote 4) **According to the National Indian Education Association** Statistics on high school and college graduation rates were obtained from the National Indian Education Association, at http://www.niea.org. Tribal college stats came from Sarah Butrymowicz, "The Failure of Tribal Schools," *Atlantic*, November 2014.

CHAPTER 18. THE BRIDGE

when the Dominion Bridge Company Joseph Mitchell, "The Mohawks in High Steel," *New Yorker*, September 17, 1949.

But for the majority of Indians, border crossing Lisa Monchalin and Olga Marques, "Canada under Attack from Within: Problematizing 'the Natives,' Governing Borders, and the Social Injustice of the Akwesasne Dispute," *American Indian Culture and Research Journal* 38, no. 4 (2014).

(Footnote 1) **The twenty-five-year-old killer** Julie Bindel, "The Montreal Massacre: Canada's Feminists Remember," *Guardian*, December 3, 2012.

The Ontario Provincial Police estimate Jordan Press, "Increasing Number of Firearms on Ottawa Streets Due to Influx of Illegal Guns from the US, Police Say," *National Post*, December 30, 2014.

Tension mounted as June 1 drew near Shannon Burns, "Six Weeks Later, Bridge Reopens," *Indian Time*, July 16, 2009.

Considering those bridges average Bridge statistics can be found on the website of the Cornwall North Channel Bridge Replacement, http://www.pontcornwallbridge.ca.

Mohawks have shut down this bridge *You Are on Indian Land* can be viewed on the website of Canada's National Film Board at https://www.nfb.ca/film/you_are_on_indian_land.

such a fee clearly violates Carrie Garrow, "The Freedom to Pass and Repass," in *Indigenous Rights in the Age of the UN Declaration*, ed. Elvira Pulitano (Cambridge: Cambridge University Press, 2012).

***MoneySense* magazine recently ranked it** Staff, "*MoneySense* Names Ottawa Best Place to Live," CBC News/Canada, March 20, 2012.

In January 2014, the Federal Bridge Corporation David Sommerstein, "Border Agent Standoff Lingers on Cornwall Island," North Country Public Radio, August 12, 2010.

CHAPTER 19. THE RIVER

Cornwall is the "contraband capital of Canada" Jean Daudelin with Stephanie Soiffer and Jeff Willows, "Border Integrity, Illicit Tobacco, and Canada's Security," Macdonald-Laurier Institute, 2013, available at http://www.macdonaldlaurier.ca/files/pdf/MLIBorder-Integrity-Illicit-Tobacco-Canadas-Security.pdf.

Human trafficking hit its zenith   Staff, "Chinese Smuggling Ring Said to Have Used Indian Reservation," CNN.com, December 14, 1998, available at http://www.cnn.com/US/9812/10/smuggling.ring.02/.

(Footnote 1) **A venerated tradition**   Henry Glass, "Why the Mohawks Are No Longer Walking the High Steel," *Globe and Mail* (Toronto, Canada), August 23, 2013.

Doug George-Kanentiio, the former editor   Tom Blackwell, "The New Big Tobacco," *National Post*, September 20, 2010.

(Footnote 3) **Author of necessary reads**   Scott Carrier, "Charles Bowden's Fury," *High Country News*, October 13, 2014, available at http://www.hcn.org/issues/46.17/charles-bowdens-fury.

CHAPTER 20. THE WORDS THAT COME BEFORE ALL ELSE

Because it has no interior provinces   Lauren McKinsey and Victor Konrad, "Borderlands Reflections: The United States and Canada," *Borderlands Monograph Series* (Orono: University of Maine's Borderlands Project, Canadian-American Center, 1989).

(Footnote 1) **Boundary disputes wrought**   Janice Cheryl Beaver, "U.S. International Borders: Brief Facts," CRS Report for Congress, November 9, 2006, available at https://www.fas.org/sgp/crs/misc/RS21729.pdf.

This next border-crossing point   Dan Heath, "Churubusco Border Work to Resume," *Press-Republican* (Plattsburgh, N.Y.), April 28, 2011.

25 percent of the casino's profits   Susan Mende, "St. Lawrence County, Towns of Brasher and Massena Win Greater Control over Tribal-State Compact Funds," *Watertown (N.Y.) Daily Times*, April 16, 2015.

(Footnote 4) **Or so it seemed**   Cindy Casares, "A Textbook on Mexican Americans That Gets Their History Wrong? Oh, Texas," *Guardian*, May 31, 2016.

The National Congress of American Indians   David Johnston, "Spiritual Seekers Borrow Indians' Ways," *New York Times*, December 27, 1993.

A decade later, Arvol Looking Horse   Arvol Looking Horse, "Looking Horse Proclamation on the Protection of Ceremonies," *Indian Country Today*, April 25, 2003.

(Footnote 5) **Carved out of living trees**   William Engelbrecht, *Iroquoia: The Development of a Native World* (Syracuse, N.Y.: Syracuse University Press, 2003).

Wilson then detailed   Dean R. Snow, *The Iroquois* (Cambridge: Blackwell, 1994).

(Footnote 6) **he got charged with money laundering**   Staff, "4 Admit Guilt in Laundering of Illicit Funds," *New York Times*, November 5, 1998.

And as Edmund Wilson concluded   Edmund Wilson, *Apologies to the Iroquois* (Syracuse: Syracuse University Press, 1959).

EPILOGUE: THE UNITED STATES OF IN-BETWEEN

Some researchers have even   Mary Annette Pember, "Trauma May Be Woven into DNA of Native Americans," *Indian Country Today*, May 28, 2015.

The tribe recently won   Staff, "Saint Regis to Receive Approximately $8.4 Million in Alcoa Settlement," *Indian Country*, March 29, 2013.

(Footnote 1) **Without serious intervention**   Tina Casagrand, "Millions of Ash Trees Are Dying, Creating Huge Headaches for Cities," *National Geographic*, December 4, 2014.

ABOUT THE AUTHOR

Stephanie Elizondo Griest is a globe-trotting author from South Texas. Her books include the award-winning memoirs *Around the Bloc: My Life in Moscow, Beijing, and Havana* (Villard/Random House, 2004) and *Mexican Enough: My Life Between the Borderlines* (Washington Square Press/Simon & Schuster, 2008); and the best-selling guidebook *100 Places Every Woman Should Go* (Travelers' Tales, 2007). She has also written for the *New York Times*, the *Washington Post*, *The Believer*, the *Virginia Quarterly Review*, and the *Oxford American*, and she edited the anthology *Best Women's Travel Writing 2010*. Her coverage of the Texas-Mexico border won a Margolis Award for Social Justice Reporting. A renowned public speaker, she is assistant professor of creative nonfiction at the University of North Carolina–Chapel Hill. Visit her website at www.StephanieElizondoGriest.com or follow her on Twitter and Instagram @SElizondoGriest.

Author photo by Alexander Devora.